THE
AMERICAN
SEASONS

BOOKS BY EDWIN WAY TEALE

A Harvest of Chapters from Edwin Way Teale's
Four Journeys Through the Four American Seasons:

NORTH WITH THE SPRING
JOURNEY INTO SUMMER
AUTUMN ACROSS AMERICA
WANDERING THROUGH WINTER

*Published in One Volume With an Intro-
duction and Photographs by the Author*

THE AMERI

EDWIN WAY TEALE

CAN SEASONS

DODD, MEAD & COMPANY
NEW YORK · 1976

Library of Congress Cataloging in Publication Data

Teale, Edwin Way, date
    The American seasons.

    "A harvest of chapters from . . . [the author's] four jour-
neys through the four American seasons: North with the
spring, Journey into summer, Autumn across America, and
Wandering through winter."
    Includes index.
    1. Natural history—United States—Addresses, essays,
lectures. 2. Natural history—Outdoor books—Addresses,
essays, lectures. 3. Seasons—Addresses, essays, lectures.
I. Title.
QH104.T355 500.9'73 76-11794
ISBN 0-396-07353-0

DEDICATED TO

DAVID

WHO TRAVELED WITH US

IN OUR HEARTS

THE STORY OF THE SEASONS

SOMETIME in the month of November, in the year 1940, I was sent by a magazine editor to Philadelphia. There, under a grant from the Carnegie Corporation, amateur scientists had been mobilized to gather data in various areas of natural history. At the time I was writing articles on everything from super-searchlights to advances in brain surgery to personal-experience stories on riding with a test pilot, accompanying a tug docking an ocean liner, going down in a submarine to spending a night with the New York police radio patrol. This particular assignment seemed to me a prize, for it lay in the field of my own special interest. It concerned nature.

I remember among those I interviewed was Dr. John M. Fogg, Jr., University of Pennsylvania botanist. Under his direction, 200 observers, stationed along a path sixty miles wide, had reported the first blooming dates in spring of thirty different species of wildflowers. Using the yardstick of the dates when the same species of plants first bloom at different positions on the map, Dr. Fogg told me, scientists have determined that spring moves north at an average rate of about fifteen miles a day.

Riding home on the train, on a dull November day, I beguiled myself by imagining what it would be like to drift north with the spring, keeping pace with its long advance. In the following days and years, my wife, Nellie, and I returned to that dream. I began collecting material and poring over maps, making plans for some indefinite future. The Second World War passed and 1947 came before we could start south to begin what proved to be the first of our four long trips through the four American seasons. The end of the trail that began with my visit to Dr. Fogg in 1940 was not reached until 1965, a quarter of a century later.

Our travels *North With the Spring* took place in 1947 and the first edition of the book was published by Dodd, Mead & Company four years later, on November 5, 1951. We journeyed with *Autumn Across America* in the year 1952 and again four years went by before the book appeared from the press on October 15, 1956. Our *Journey Into Summer* occurred in 1957 with publication of the book taking place on October 17, 1960. Our fourth and final trip *Wandering Through Winter* extended from the end of fall in 1961 to the beginning of spring in 1962. When the book appeared, on September 27, 1965, it completed the long project to which we had devoted so many years. Two of the books were written while we lived on Long Island, and two at Trail Wood, our home in the country near the village of Hampton, in northeastern Connecticut.

In his *London Journal*, James Boswell tells of an evening spent with his young friend, Erskine, planning a future in writing. "It was very agreeable," he records, "to look forward and imagine that we shall probably write much, get much fame and much gold." One additional thing Boswell failed to foresee that evening. This is "much labor." At least this has been an important ingredient in each of the four books on the seasons.

From every trip—ranging from 17,000 to 20,000 miles in length—I returned home with hundreds of thousands of words of typed field notes. Set down at the end of the day, often in times of great fatigue, they formed the harvest of our travels and the foundation of the books. Today they stand side by side, eleven large volumes bound in red buckram, on a bookshelf beside my desk. Henry Thoreau, in his inimitable way, stressed the value of such undelayed note making. "The writer who postpones the recording of his thoughts," he observed, "uses an iron which has cooled to burn a hole with."

In our preparations for the trips, and in checking facts and rounding out our understanding of what we had seen after we returned, I read through innumerable books and articles and scientific monographs. The unpublished bibliography of each of the four volumes contains upwards of 1,000 titles. My goal was to achieve a book that would be accurate as well as interesting, that would make the things that we had experienced come alive for the readers, that would, in its way, preserve the transient from oblivion. And always the concrete instead of the general was my aim. In those writing days, I remembered a hundred times a sentence in a letter to Turgenev from Flaubert. Where another might have written a general statement such as: "When I read *Don Quixote* I long to live in the Age of Chivalry," Flaubert put it: "Whenever I read Don Quixote I long to ride my horse down a white and dusty road and to eat olives and raw onions in the shadow of a rock." So as each book took shape, the struggle for accuracy, for vividness, for concreteness continued through the space of several years.

Yet even while I was working the hardest, even in the last months before the final deadline, in days when there never seemed time enough and I was beginning work at five o'clock in the morning, I felt elated. I was reliving intensely the events of our long wandering with a season. With each revision, I was bringing into sharper focus those days we would "gladly live again." But as I completed each finished draft and laid the chapter away there was about the act a sobering finality. It seemed a last good-bye to a part of our lives, a wonderful part now gone forever except in the pages I had written.

I remember a strange interlude of vague dissatisfaction and discontent that came as I approached the last chapters of the last of the four books. I seemed in a kind of psychological whirlpool. Nothing I did, for a time, appeared satisfactory. I think Nellie put her finger on the trouble. I wanted to finish the book. I had to finish the book. Yet at the same time I did not want to finish the book. Unconsciously I desired to hold back the final period that would mean the great adventure of our lives was completely over.

When Rachel Carson, in her last illness after years of work on *Silent Spring*, held a copy of the published book in her hand, she said: "Now it has a life of its own." It was thus, one after the other, with the American Seasons books. Nellie and I seemed watching its fate as intensely interested spectators. We seemed participating in the varied events that befell it. We saw *North With the Spring* run through twenty editions, *Autumn Across America* remain on the best-seller lists for sixteen weeks, *Wandering Through Winter* receive the Pulitzer Prize, and the total sale of the four books reach and pass the half-million mark.

Each of the four books was transcribed into Braille and each recorded as Talking Books for the blind by the Library of Congress. The American Booksellers Association presented a set of the books to the White House Library. Foreign editions appeared. In one, sponsored by the State Department, the quartet of books was translated into Chinese for distribution on the mainland of China. In connection with foreign editions, I recall one amusing letter I received from the professor in Vienna who translated the spring book into German under the title *Mit Dem Fruhling Nortwarts*. He was understandably bewildered by certain local names mentioned in the book. What, he wanted to know, were "hush puppies" and "fishfuddle trees"? His careful work, I was delighted to learn later, was rewarded when the book received a prize as the best translation of the year in its category.

In looking back over the lives of the four books, varied small, vivid memories return in connection with their publication. There was the time I spent a weekend in a rambling old hotel on the New Jersey coast with Raymond T. Bond, of Dodd, Mead. Mornings we worked on the manuscript; afternoons we wandered over the great Tuckerton sea meadows watching shorebirds. There was the time I flew to Chicago with Phelps Platt to address a convention of booksellers and librarians at the time of the winter book's appearance. It was hinted afterwards that perhaps the next time I had better not make my book seem quite so interesting. After the talk someone had rushed down and stolen all the copies from the Dodd, Mead booth.

But the majority of these memories are linked with the one who had most to do with the series, Edward H. Dodd, Jr. There were days in autumn, when all the Vermont hills were aflame with color, when we would work for hours on a manuscript and then walk along the back roads around his farm on Windmill Hill, near Putney. There were other days when we went over manuscripts or plans for the books at Trail Wood, our sanctuary-farm among other hills in the far northeastern corner of Connecticut. Once, I remember, in the crisp autumn dawn, we stacked fireplace wood in the shed before we began the bookwork of the day—an instance of publisher-author relationship at its best! Then there was the blistering ninety-degree day in New York when we finished plans for the uniform edition of the four books, even down to the color of the cloth that would be used in binding the volumes. The books had been redesigned. And behind that fact lay a special story.

When my first nature book, *Grassroot Jungles*, was published by Dodd, Mead in 1937, the member of the staff who planned the book was Avery Fisher. He laid out the attractive design—a design that contributed considerably to the success of the book and that was selected by the American Institute of Graphic Arts as one of the Fifty Books of the Year. At the time I used to see on his desk volumes on music and the mechanics of musical production. This was the area of his deepest concern. It was in that same year, 1937, that he established a company of his own and produced the first of the advanced Fisher radios and record players that were to become a symbol of the highest quality. The former Philharmonic Hall, at Lincoln Center in New York City, has since been named in his honor Avery Fisher Hall. In the mid-fifties, as a diversion from his business responsibilities, he designed the uniform edition of the seasons series. And now, once more, almost forty years after *Grassroot Jungles*, Avery Fisher has designed another book of mine, the present volume, *The American Seasons*.

An author can never become wholly conceited, as Justice Oliver Wendell Holmes once pointed out, because with each new book he subjects himself to public ridicule. So far as the four seasons books are concerned, reviewers, on the whole, treated them seriously and with gratifying enthusiasm. Each book received the leading review in the *Atlantic Monthly*. Other reviews appeared on the front pages of the *New York Times Book Review*, the *New York Herald Tribune Book Review*, the *Chicago Sunday Tribune Magazine of Books*, and *John O'London's Weekly*, in England. Local pride, now and then, produced a mild complaint. One review of *Autumn Across America* in a small paper in North Carolina ended: "This is a fine book but it is not as good as *North With the Spring* because this time the author did not come to North Carolina." Another review of the same book in a paper in the Ozarks took the form of a letter to the author. It began: "Dear Mr. Teale. You are more to be pitied than scorned. You traveled all the way across the country through autumn and missed the most beautiful part of all, the Ozarks."

When *North With the Spring* first made its appearance, the *Saturday Review* ran on its cover a picture of me at work on the book with our pet cat, Silver, curled up asleep under the desk lamp beside me. When the magazine reached the rural mailbox of neighbors who had moved away to another state, the small boy who got the mail came running back to the house shouting: "Guess who's on the cover of the *Saturday Review—Silver!*"

One of those curious, apparently meaningless coincidences that arrest our attention from time to time occurred when the winter book appeared. Among the nearly thirty volumes I have had published, only two were issued on the twenty-seventh of the month—*Grassroot Jungles*, on October 27, 1937, and *Wandering Through Winter*, on September 27, 1965. And of them all, only two—these two—received the front-page review in the *New York Times Book Review*.

In the case of the winter book, twenty-five days of suspense preceded the publication of the review. The front page was all in type, a magnificent review of the book by Roger Tory Peterson, when a strike shut down the paper completely. For three weeks and more, negotiations dragged on. Our prospects went up; our prospects went down. Over and over the strike seemed about to be settled. Then it bogged down again. On the book's publication day, September 27, at a luncheon Dodd, Mead gave me at the Player's Club in New York, Phelps Platt, the president, presented me with a framed copy of the review that might never be published. It had been set in type with the date of issue left blank. Whether a date would ever be inserted in the blank space remained to be seen. Thus, day after day, we dangled over the cliff edge.

At seven o'clock in the evening on October the eleventh, I turned on the radio and heard the strike was over. But for several days afterward, nobody, not even at the *Times*, knew whether the winter review would occupy the front page or whether the book section would be torn apart and new material used. On October 14, after I had appeared on a TV program, "To Tell the Truth," in which a panel of judges sought to pick "the real Edwin Way Teale" from among three contestants, I called Phelps Platt from a wall telephone at the studio. The die had been cast, the decision made. *Wandering Through Winter* had been left on the front page. On the Sunday when it finally appeared, I bought a dozen copies of the paper. I had to use a wheelbarrow to transport them from the garage to the house at Trail Wood.

During the fall of the year in which each of the books was published, I had the sensation of being swept along toward the brink of some Niagara. The current speeded up, the excitement mounted, until, with the Christmas season, I went over the falls in a swirl of speeches and appearances. Then, on the other side of New Year's, the roar faded away and I found myself once more, in some quiet backwater, working on another book. The author who is writing the kind of books he wants to write, about the things that mean much to him, about things he believes in and thinks are important, never wants to retire. He wants to keep on writing to the fifty-ninth minute of the final hour. For me, I hope, as long as I live, when someone asks me what I am doing, I can always answer: "Writing a book."

One evening when I was nearing the end of the winter manuscript, a man from St. Louis called me long distance to ask me to give a lecture. I explained I had quit giving lectures. I needed all my time for books. He ended the conversation by exploding: "If you could always get a fee as big as this for a lecture, you wouldn't *have* to write books!" Of course, he missed the point by a million miles. The one thing I wanted to do *was* to write books. It was Hilaire Belloc's contention that very little prose would be written if wealth were better distributed. The monetary motive in writing is, of necessity, important to the author who wishes to continue being an author. But in the seasons books it was something else that took precedence over the "much gold" and "much fame" of youthful Boswell's dream.

A TV interviewer once asked me what my purpose was in writing my books. I had to stop and think—what was my purpose? I suppose, if I answered truthfully, I would have to say that the first purpose was to preserve—as insects are sometimes preserved, with every wing-venation intact, in pieces of transparent amber—portions of our lives that seem especially precious to us. But there are secondary considerations. In the chronicle of our travels with the seasons, I tried to mirror nature faithfully in all its beauty and strength and endurance. I tried to record a picture of wild nature in America at a certain time in its history. In my writings I have thought of myself less as a teacher than as a Pied Piper leading people into the out-of-doors. And running through these volumes, as through all my books, there has been an undercurrent of an unstated hope, the hope of stirring to life a sense of wonder.

Many readers who have traveled with Nellie and me through the four seasons apparently have come to regard us as old friends. In various ways, in thousands of letters, they have indicated the feeling that we have experienced it all together. And in an unexpected number of reviews a similar viewpoint has been expressed. In 1974, when the book about our sanctuary-farm, Trail Wood—*A Naturalist Buys an Old Farm*—appeared, one reviewer, as though writing about those known intimately for years, ended: "We rejoice that their lives have fallen in such pleasant places for Mr. Teale and his Nellie have come to seem dear old friends." This sense of personal relationship engendered by the books has been a remarkable feature of their publication. Over the years, readers have sent us presents ranging from paintings to fruit-cakes, from leather-bound books to sorghum molasses, from paper-weights to birdbaths, from an ornamental bird from India to a stone scarab carved in Egypt to a "real red cent"—a kopek mailed from Moscow by a businessman who had taken along one of my books to read on a visit to Russia.

When a book is published nobody knows where or when it will be read, or who will read it. Friends of ours who were sent to the Orient by the government, wrote that a section from one of my books was being used in a class in English in Katmandu, in Nepal. From Nairobi, in Africa, a reader wrote suggesting that I come to Kenya and write a book about the seasons there. One correspondent wrote me from an Indian trading post in the Southwest, another from Churchill, on Hudson Bay in northern Canada, a third from a houseboat on Puget Sound. Letters have arrived bearing Chinese stamps, New Zealand and Australian stamps, South American and African stamps, and stamps from most of the countries of Europe.

So they have come in, at times as many as ten or even twenty letters a day—letters so pleasant to receive, so interesting to read, but so great a problem to answer. Sometimes when I have looked at the pile of mail accumulating like a snowdrift on my desk, I have repeated to myself an imaginary conversation: "He is an author." "What does he write?" "Letters."

A number of the envelopes have contained accounts of following our trails. One year a Cincinnati physician made a hobby of spending weekends driving east to trace short sections of our travels coming north with the spring. In the Northwest, a retired couple started out in a camper to follow all our routes through the four seasons, using the books as guides. Other letters have asked for details on exactly where we stopped along the way. The writers desired to stay at the identical cabins. Other correspondents have written of their delight in traveling with us for thousands of miles via the pages of a book and then suddenly finding themselves journeying down the very road that ran past their homes. One of these lived on "Wonderful Eighty-Three" in North Dakota. Most of those who have written have expressed, in one way or another, an appreciation for obtaining from the books a heightened awareness, a greater understanding and an increased interest in nature. They have opened their eyes and found a new world around them.

A certain proportion of the letters have requested factual information. After asking a question about birds, one woman added that she had never consulted a naturalist before but she thought it was like consulting a doctor so she was enclosing a check for the amount of an office call. On a few occasions correspondents have made requests I have not been inclined to grant. Once a woman in upstate New York asked me to send her some of my manuscripts. She explained she was a member of the International Grapho Analysis Society and wanted to analyze my handwriting so that if she ever encountered anyone with similar handwriting she could steer them into a career of nature writing. Another letter of the kind arrived from Colorado. A young man there wrote that he had found a Shangri-la valley far back in the mountains. He and a friend planned to move there and escape from a world gone insane and likely to blow itself up. All he needed was a truck to transport their belongings. He wondered if I would send him the money to buy the truck.

Readers are fine but rereaders are better. It seems to me that all the people who have written saying they read the seasons books over and over are paying me the finest of possible compliments. Fifteen years ago, a correspondent reported reading *North With the Spring* eight times and *Autumn Across America* six times. A recent writer in a small town in New Hampshire told of each year reading again the four books in their respective seasons. From the Library of Congress, a librarian once wrote me of the countless times she had taken down one of these books from the shelf to reread some special page or paragraph during a lull in her daily work. Another librarian, in Bowling Green, Ohio, noted that she had at home a hardcover set of the four books and a paperback set—the hardcover set for "sitting-up rereading" and the paperbacks for "bedtime snacks, so to speak." Then there was the member of the mathematics faculty at Duke University who reported that for years she had been rereading the seasons books for relaxation and the professor of theological history in the divinity school at Yale who wrote that he made a practice of regularly rereading the four books to keep him "in touch with the natural world."

One aspect of the correspondence that has brought special satisfaction is the number of letters I have received from people who have found in rereading the books some solace or relief in times of trouble or grief or intolerable strain. Losing themselves in the journeys, they have felt drawn closer to the calmness and steadiness and timelessness of nature.

Over New York City, some years ago, two huge airliners collided in one of the most spectacular crashes of American aviation history. One plunged among Brooklyn apartment houses, the other onto Staten Island. There were no survivors. A month or two later I received a letter from a woman in Iowa. One of the pilots had been her brother whom she had reared as a small boy. Day after day in that time of grief and shock, she said, she found a measure of relief in reading on and on in the spring and autumn books. From Detroit, the head of the research laboratory of one of America's leading automobile manufacturers wrote that the four seasons books, which he had read aloud, had helped his wife through the last year of a fatal illness. Those immobilized by serious heart attacks have written they have found a substitute for activity by vicariously traveling with us through the seasons. One, a reader in the middle west, was told she had but a short time to live. She had just discovered *North With the Spring.* "I am not going to die now," she told the doctor, "just when I have learned how to live." She did not and in subsequent years has gone far in natural history. A Harvard ornithologist once recalled that, in a time of stress and resulting insomnia, he used to get up in the night and read a chapter, such as "A Hundred Miles of Warblers," in one of my books. The effect was calming like walking in the open air and helped him get to sleep. In fact, for patients suffering from nervous tension, one Boston specialist, I am told, used to prescribe the four books as "therapeutic reading."

As Henry Thoreau rejoiced in the fact he had been born in Concord —"and just in the nick of time, too"—Nellie and I rejoice in our great good fortune in being able to make the trips when we made them— "and just in the nick of time, too." Already so much we saw is no longer there to see. Changes innumerable have taken place along our varied routes. The wildflowers and the insectivorous plants of the wide Burgaw Savannah of the Cape Fear region of North Carolina have disappeared, uprooted by the plow and replaced by rows of blueberry bushes. The mayfly storms of Kelley's Island, since we saw them, have become largely a memory. Industrial wastes poured into Lake Erie have poisoned the water and mud of the shallow western end, destroying the burrowing nymphs. The bald eagles we watched in Florida have been reduced to but a remnant of their former numbers. The rare Venus's-flytrap that Darwin thought was the most wonderful plant in the world has virtually disappeared from the small region of its North Carolina range. And stilled now is the mighty roar of Celilo Falls on the Columbia River. The plunging water where we watched Indians in their ancient harvest of the salmon is buried far beneath the surface of a dammed-up lake. All along our routes, wild spots we visited are now no longer wild.

But the image of their wildness is preserved in the pages of the books. The four volumes on the four seasons record, in a kind of mosaic, a picture of nature as it was in this land at the time we saw it. We never, as has so often been pointed out, cross the same river twice. The river of water and the river of time flow on. But the printed page does not change. It is the river we can cross again. It possesses the power, as Thomas Hardy once phrased it, to "make the clock of the years run backward"; to bring to life the conditions and surroundings of a former time. A number of the reviewers have noted that as earlier books, such as Francis Parkman's *The Oregon Trail* and John James Audubon's Missouri River journals, have preserved a record of wild America in earlier periods, the four seasons books have provided a picture of nature as it existed midway in the twentieth century. Eventually, read in sequence, a succession of such books, set down in different periods of history, will—like a time-lapse moving picture—provide us with a running record of the sweeping alterations that the years have brought and will bring to nature in America.

EDWIN WAY TEALE

CONTENTS

CONTENTS

Wandering Through Winter

ILLUSTRATIONS

· *xxiii* ·

NORTH WITH
THE SPRING

Where Spring Begins

BARE trees imprinted the black lace of their twigs on a gray and somber sky. Dingy with soot, snowdrifts had melted into slush and were freezing again. Behind us, as we drove south, city pallor was increasing. Tempers were growing short in the dead air of underventilated offices. That quiet desperation, which Thoreau says characterizes the mass of men, was taking on new intensity. February, at once the shortest and the longest month of the twelve, had outstayed its welcome. The year seemed stuck on the ridge of winter.

At such a time, when you look with dread upon the winter weeks that lie before you, have you ever dreamed—in office or kitchen or school—of leaving winter behind, of meeting spring under far-southern skies, of following its triumphal pilgrimage up the map with flowers all the way, with singing birds and soft air, green grass and trees newclothed, of coming north with the spring? That is a dream of the winter-weary. And, for nearly a decade, it was, for Nellie and me, both a dream and a plan.

The seasons, like greater tides, ebb and flow across the continents. Spring advances up the United States at the average rate of about fifteen miles a day. It ascends mountainsides at the rate of about a hundred feet a day. It sweeps ahead like a flood of water, racing down the long valleys, creeping up hillsides in a rising tide. Most of us, like the man who lives on the bank of a river and watches the stream flow by, see only one phase of the movement of spring. Each year the season advances toward us out of the south, sweeps around us, goes flooding away into the north. We see all phases of a single phase, all variations of this one chapter in the Odyssey of Spring. My wife and I dreamed of knowing something of all phases, of reading all possible chapters, of seeing, firsthand, the long northward flow of the season.

Over and over again we laid out routes, calculated costs, made lists of things to take along. But obligations and responsibilities pushed the dream unrealized before us. Season followed season and year followed year. And while we waited, the world changed and our lives changed with it. The spring trip was something we looked forward to during

the terrible years of World War II, during all the strain and grief of losing David, our only son, in battle.

When we talked over our plans with friends we discovered that our
dream was a universal dream. They, too, had beguiled themselves, on
days when winter seemed invincible, with thoughts of lifting anchor
and, leaving everyday responsibilities behind, drifting north with the
spring.

Our plan was to start where spring begins for the North American
continent, somewhere south of Lake Okeechobee in that no man's land
of the seasons, the Everglades. There, amid the sawgrass seas and ham-
mocks, under the high, cloud-filled sky of southern Florida, spring
gathers its forces. There, the first stirrings of the season become apparent. Working north, we would keep pace with its progress, zigzagging
by car behind its advancing front. I ruled off a map into zones, each
zone representing roughly a week's advance in the northward movement of the season. This provided, in general, the timetable of our trip.

Ours would be no conventional tour. It would include wild and
remote places the usual tourist avoids. We would see spring come to
dunes and tarns and seashell islands, to caves and underground rivers,
to estuaries and savannas. For 17,000 miles we would travel with a
season. In 23 different states we would witness the defeat of winter, see
the homecoming of the birds, watch the return of the wildflowers. This
was the long spring. It would extend from February to June. The trip,
for me, would have added pleasure because my companion, after years
of married life, was the most congenial person still.

And so, on the 14th of February, we packed our black Buick, stuffed
the glove compartment full of marked maps, stored away bird glasses,
field guides, cameras and stoutly-bound record books. We eased ourselves into the front seat like a racing pilot squeezing into the cramped
cockpit of a speedplane and waved goodby to our neighbors. I switched
on the engine and we started south for our rendezvous with a season.

Long Island was hard with frost when we left. New York was a
world of windows tight shut. Across New Jersey, the distant winter
woods were smoky blue and, in Virginia, side roads cut away between
brown hills, rutted and red. We saw the white sand of South Carolina

pinelands replaced by the coppercolored soil of Georgia. We watched mistletoe give way to Spanish moss and Spanish moss give way to air plants in the cypress swamps of southern Florida. Our descent of the map ended south of the Tamiami Trail, at the little community of Everglades, near the Ten Thousand Islands of the wild Gulf coast. Here we reached the beginning of our travels with the spring.

WE FIRST SMELLED SMOKE as we came creeping down a long green tunnel under overarching trees on a narrow road pockmarked with holes. Somewhere south of the Tamiami Trail we were driving north through a swampy stretch, picking our way with care. We felt uneasy. The air ahead became tinged with blue and the acrid smell of fire grew stronger. It stirred primitive emotions of alarm. But as yet there was no sight or sound of flames.

I looked at Nellie. She looked at the roadsides—muddy lowland on one hand, a brimming ditch on the other. The solid surface of the narrow roadbed offered no room to turn around. We could either back up or go ahead.

"Let's go ahead for a while longer," she suggested.

Close to the end of the tunnel I stopped the car. We listened. Somewhere ahead we could hear the faint rush and crackle of flames. Still we could see no fire. I nosed the car from beneath the trees. Under billows of blue-brown smoke, waves of flame were rolling toward us across the open country to the right. Red streamers flared from the higher grass tangles or roared skyward amid the dry fronds of the scattered palmettos. Already the fire had swept to the edge of the road ahead of us and was racing in our direction. But the flames ran down only one fringe of the roadbed and the vegetation was mainly high tangles of grass.

We decided to run the one-sided gantlet. Rolling up the car windows we charged ahead as fast as the hole-riddled road would permit. Just as the main wave of fire came abreast of us, filling the car with sudden heat, the flames touched off the fifteen-foot torch of a dry palmetto, shaggy with fronds. In one leap, from base to crown, a sheet of flame rushed upward. The fronds exploded into blazing fragments, hurled aloft to descend like pieces of a fireworks fountain around us. Then the fire was racing away behind us and we were amid blackened, smoldering acres swept clean of life.

Everywhere we went, those February days in lower Florida, fires were raging across the Everglades. Once, we counted nine great columns of smoke pouring into the sky around us. Another time, far down the Tamiami Trail, we rode toward a mile-long cumulus cloud, the only one in the sky. It was mushrooming upward at the top of a column of heated air rising from a widespread fire below. This man-made thunderhead was crowned with creamy white. But its undersides were tinted with tans and blues where smoke and vapor intermingled.

That $50,000,000 fiasco, the ill-advised drainage scheme of half a century ago, had lowered the water table of the Glades and left them a prey to endless fires. As far away as Key West visibility is sometimes reduced to 2 miles by haze and smoke from the Everglades.

In lower Florida winter is the dry season; spring the time of rainfall. During the final weeks of winter, before the spring rains begin, the water in the Everglades reaches its lowest point. Peat and grass are driest and conflagrations most frequent. Fires by night and pillars of smoke by day—these were the first and most spectacular indications we saw around us that winter's end was near and that spring was drawing close.

But there were other signs. A dozen miles or so east of Ochopee, one afternoon, we came upon clouds of tree swallows swirling over the sawgrass, thousands and thousands of the white-breasted birds skimming low, darting high, endlessly turning, feeding upon insects as they moved into the north. A black buzzard, with short tail and silver spots under its wingtips, sailed by, its shadow crisscrossing the highway as it banked and circled. Speeding hundreds of feet above it, so high they were hardly larger than houseflies to the naked eye, were the topmost tree swallows. Through our glasses we could see, to right and left over the Everglades, other swallow clouds, immense flocks, loosely knit, rising, descending, turning, expanding, contracting, always in motion.

The day before, perhaps, many of these birds had been over the sea, coming from Cuba, or among the keys off the Florida mainland. Now the air around us was filled with their liquid calling. A little farther on,

COOT feeding among spatterdock, or yellow pond lily leaves massed on the surface of dark swamp water in the Everglades.

DARK water and moss-hung trees along the banks characterize
lowland streams that flow through lower Georgia and Florida.

RING-BILLED gulls flutter about the author on a Florida beach near the beginning of the northward journey with the spring.

HOVERING in mid-air, this gull was arrested in a split-second
photograph as it settled to the sand of the Gulf Coast beach.

WATER LILY leaves form feeding platforms for a redwing and
a boat-tailed grackle along the edge of a lake in upper Florida.

ROUGHING it smoothly in jungle surroundings is possible at this manor house owned by the government on Bull's Island.

SPRING in the Great Smoky Mountains National Park is a time of white shadbushes and acres of woodland flowers in bloom.

COMMONEST of spring flowers in eastern America is the violet. More than half a hundred species grow east of the Rockies.

BABY cottontail rabbits begin life in the spring, one of a host of creatures born during the warm days at winter's end.

SEA meadows in the spring resound to the calling of the clapper rail. The bird nests in thick tangles of cord-grass.

RIPPLES extending across wide mud flats at low tide are a
familiar feature of many places along the Atlantic seaboard.

UNFOLDING leaves of spring appear on twigs above a sphagnum swamp in the solitary pine barrens of southern New Jersey.

BLOODROOT in flower is a sign of the arrival of spring in rich open woodlands all the way from upper Florida to Canada.

RACCOONS inhabit all the area covered coming north with the spring. Their range is one of the widest among American mammals.

SWAMP streams in early spring in the North flow between massed skunk cabbage leaves and the fiddleheads of ferns.

FARTHEST north in spring's journey is represented by the
top of Mt. Washington. Its spring is similar to that of Labrador.

where the roadside ditch opened into a clear stretch of water free from the massed water hyacinths, thousands of the swallows were drinking on the wing. The birds pelted down like windblown raindrops to skim or strike the surface of the ditch and scoop up mouthfuls of water. Their snow-white underplumage caught the sun each time they rose and turned to dive again. Thus as long as we watched them the swallows climbed and swooped, rose and fell, revolving in a great wheel in the sky.

Driving south, at the beginning of our trip, we had encountered other concentrations of birds. The succession of homecoming migrants is as fixed as the sequence of blooming wildflowers. Each spring the birds come back in the same order. Pintail ducks are among the first waterfowl to fly north. Bluebirds and redwings lead the procession of the songbirds. Robins are early birds in both the day and the year. And so we met concentrations, waves, of the migrants in the order in which they would move north. They were the initial ripples of that vast tide of migration that soon would be running, full flood, up the continent.

All through South Carolina, overwintering bluebirds had been everywhere. Almost every dipping telephone wire held one of these gentle birds, sitting bolt upright, appearing a little round-shouldered at a distance, leaping aloft in a sudden rise and wingover as we rushed by. Then, near Waycross, Georgia, we encountered the redwings. A detour had shunted us down a side road. As we reached a stretch of swampy woodland, a storm of sound assailed our ears. All the trees were alive with blackbirds. Thousands swarmed among the branches, filled with the excitement of migration time. They were incessantly in motion, hopping, flying, alighting, combining their voices in a deafening clamor. A dozen miles beyond we ran through another concentration of overwintering redwings. Here the birds were scattered across a wide grainfield that recent rains had turned into a glistening sea of mud.

Just south of the Florida line we had met our initial wave of robins. All that day, as we drove through drenching rain down the western edge of the Florida peninsula, we saw robins flying, robins perching, robins running across lawns, robins swarming over fire-blackened open spaces among the palmettos. For miles on end we would see robins all about us. Then their numbers would thin away only to increase once more. Near the end of their winter stay along the Gulf the myriad redbreasts would soon take off on their flight to the north.

Passing thus from concentration to concentration we seemed moving down the line of march of a parade where different groups were assembled on side streets ready to take their places in the procession at the appointed time. All things affected by the spring have their times and seasons. The stars in their courses are hardly more dependable than the sequence of appearing life, bird, flower, batrachian. If you come north by train in midspring and have an ear for the swamp music of toads and frogs, you will become aware of something interesting. You seem to be running backward in time. As the spring becomes less and less advanced as you go north, you begin with the latest-appearing of the marsh-callers and progress backward to the earliest of the peepers, reversing the normal sequence.

Each morning, during these pre-spring days, we awoke while it was still dark, to the steady throbbing of fishing boats moving out among the Ten Thousand Islands of the Gulf. With the earliest daylight came the strident alarm clock of the red-bellied woodpecker amid the palms outside our cabin at Everglades. When we stepped outside, exciting new odors were all around us in the perfumed air of the dawn. The change from north to south, from winter to a subtropical climate, is reported most vividly of all by our sense of smell. In northern states winter is a kind of olfactory desert. The odors of spring arrive with dramatic contrast. Here amid the Everglades—where spring and autumn meet and intermingle and where winter is the lost season of the year—the perfumes of life and growth are never absent.

This intermingling of the seasons is one of the most striking features of the region. Fall flowers bloom in the spring and spring flowers bloom in the fall. The unrolling of the fruiting leaves of the cinnamon fern—an event familiar to every northern spring—occurs here in autumn. Flowers of summer and flowers of spring bloom side by side in December.

We saw along the road thistles and asters, flowers that brought to mind the dusty pasture lands of a northern fall. A whole field of higher ground, near Everglades, simmered with the early-autumn sound of innumerable crickets. We came upon beautifully shaded, purple-pink grass freshly gone to seed in February. Goldenrod, carrying us back a third of a year to the previous fall, bloomed by the Tamiami Trail. A few feet away, on the brown water of a drainage canal, water hyacinths opened the pale lavender of their earliest flowers of the new season. Here, near the southern rim of that vast, shallow, tilted bowl of oölitic limestone which holds the Everglades, we were in a land where the seasons were uncertain. Like the shore between the tides, it is an area where two zones overlap, where two forces meet in a competition that is endless and indecisive.

Nobody knows exactly where spring begins. The season has no starting point like a sprinter on a track. Somewhere south of Lake Okeechobee, in the watery wilderness of the Everglades, it comes into being, swells, gains momentum. Its arrival becomes more abrupt, more striking, its line of demarcation more evident as it progresses north. Here, in this southernmost part of the United States, there is no dramatic spring awakening as there is in some New England valley, suddenly rich with bloodroot and hepatica. Here, changes are gentle. The pendulum of the seasons moves slowly and the arc of its swing is restricted. Here we were, in a way, south of spring.

Each evening we watched the strange flat land around us sink into the twilight and each night we watched the stars come out, bright and hanging low, studding the sky in a vast sweep that descended, uninterrupted by a silhouette, to the far rim of the horizon. To the green mist of the cypresses and the moving clouds of the swallows we could add the movement of the stars as a sign of the sure approach of the spring. With all its galaxies and planets and stars, the solar system was setting the stage. Daily the sun rode higher. Nightly the astronomy of spring drew closer. Far-off events were playing their part in the birth of a season.

Okeechobee Dusk

ON the highway leading north from Everglades we passed cars and cars passed us. And all to the north of us and from ocean to ocean, on that day, the highway network of restless America was streaming with other cars—speeding corpuscles in the circulation system of a nation. There is an exhilaration in motion itself. Moreover, the eternal illusion of the traveler is the feeling that he is leaving his troubles behind. So our spirits soared as we sped northward.

Our travels during this day of sunshine carried us about two degrees of latitude up the map, some 120 miles northward, from Everglades to Wachula, inland from Sarasota. The season was advancing too. Blue lupines and golden coreopsis and white sticktights ran for miles along the highways. Flame vines were brilliant orange-red at Estero.

In groves along the way the harvest of oranges and tangerines was nearing its end—another sign of coming spring. At Wachula workers in the fields were picking strawberries—a sign we were to see repeated all the way to New England. Deriving its name from the Indian word for sandhill crane, Wachula is the home of extensive frog farms. That evening, as the batrachian chorus rose from swampy tracts, we drove down a side road leading to the west. We switched on our lights in the dusk and the beams picked out, in its staggering flight, our first bat of the trip. Twenty miles to the south that day we had seen our first black swallowtail butterfly drifting from flower to flower under trees festooned with Spanish moss.

When we looked at our map before going to bed we found we were in the midst of one of those meaningless coincidences that give us momentary pause because they reflect the mysterious workings of chance. Wachula is 77 miles north of Fort Myers; the town of Everglades is 77 miles south of Fort Myers. Moreover, Everglades, midway between the two ends of the Tamiami Trail, is 77 miles from Miami on the east and 77 miles from Fort Myers on the west. If you ask people to pick any number from one to ten, a magician once told me, the number most frequently chosen will be seven. To the Ancients, the number seven had special significance: "The Seventh Day," "The Seventh

Wave," "The Seventh Son of a Seventh Son." For some little-understood reason, men through the ages have looked on seven as a number with magic in it.

The following day we drove east, circling Lake Okeechobee, and arrived at dusk at the rambling Southland Hotel in Okeechobee City, three miles north of the lake. Cloud shadows raced ahead of us at forty miles an hour down long straight roads and, by the lake shore, we followed a highway wonderful with dragonflies. Thus we skimmed along until the last two hours of the trip. They brought strain and near disaster.

Shunted off the highway onto a road under construction, we crept behind graders, starting and stopping, attaining a five-mile-an-hour pace between stops. Our engine overheated. Radiator water boiled rapidly away. The temperature needle passed the danger mark and continued its swing. There was no way to turn out, no place to get water, no chance to stop. Thus we inched along until, almost too late, we escaped onto the open highway and found water for the car.

At the hotel a room was waiting. And that was lucky. For when I took a drink of water the glass wobbled in my hand. I felt hot. Nellie unpacked the thermometer. My temperature was 102. So with hot head and icy feet I went to bed while a great storm gathered outside the window.

Sometime in the night the tempest broke, a spring torrent of near cloudburst proportions. In ten hours nearly four inches of rainfall descended. And one inch of rainfall means that 65,000 tons, or more than 15,000,000 gallons, of water, fall on each square mile. Wind and lightning came with the rain, the lightning followed by curious short claps of thunder that dissipated themselves quickly over this flat land with none of the cannonading reverberations of hilly country. The descending sheets drummed on the balcony roof outside our window. Through this main watery roar I could hear other sounds—little dripping, simmering, sobbing noises, clamor of a different tempo, the ringing reverberations of a piece of loose tin struck by falling drops. During the hours of fever and sweating I diverted myself by noting all the different sounds produced by the descending rain. The next day, the first day of March, I remained in bed while the deluge, with its echo-less thunder, slackened and increased, stopped and began again. A lid was on the sky, shutting us in all day long. After the storm of rain stopped, the storm of wind continued. But by the next morning the rain, the wind, and my fever were gone.

It was our great good fortune, while eating ham and eggs and hominy grits at breakfast, to recognize the back of a head at the far side of the Southland dining room. Richard H. Pough had come down to help Alexander Sprunt, Jr. lead Okeechobee field trips for the Audubon Society. The two had planned a side excursion of their own that afternoon to King's Bar, in Lake Okeechobee, and they invited us to go along. It was thus that we came to witness that stirring and beautiful sight, the homecoming of the glossy ibis at sunset.

Rod Chandler took us out in his shallow-draft boat, heading down the smooth, dark flow of the Kissimmee River to reach that expanse of shallow water which natives call "the Okeechobee Sea." The Kissimmee River, draining 5,000 square miles of prairie land, forms the main water supply of the lake. Its mud stains the surface two miles from shore. Only about six feet deep, Lake Okeechobee—the Seminole word for "big water"—has an area of more than seven hundred square miles. With the single exception of Lake Michigan, it is the largest body of fresh water wholly within the boundaries of the United States. Its shallow water is easily warmed by the sun so that the Okeechobee Sea provides a reservoir of warmth that prevents sudden changes in temperature; it is a balance wheel for the climate of the region.

Originally a depression in the bed of the Pamlico Sea of Pleistocene times, the lake is roughly triangular and from 25 to 30 miles across. Before dikes and canals were constructed to control the lake, its southern edge was from 6 inches to 1½ feet above the level of the Everglades. In rainy seasons the water overflowed to the south. Lake Okeechobee was then called the "Wellspring of the Everglades."

On this afternoon of calm and sun, great slicks ran across the surface of the water, producing curious illusions where they met the horizon. Sky and water were of almost the same hue; their line of meeting was all but invisible; gulls and ducks, floating on the still surface of the lake, appeared riding at rest in the sky. A mud-bar, here called a "reef," projected like a pointing finger, seemingly above the level of the lake.

As we passed one reef, fifty black skimmers—the "cut-waters" of old Mark Catesby—leaped into the air, barking like puppies. They flew low over the water, a few with long lacquer-red bills slicing the surface in their curious form of fishing. Before vegetation increased on this bar, gull-billed terns, birds with a call like a katydid's song, used to nest here.

Stopping occasionally to clear waterweeds from his propeller, Chandler worked us into shallower water. Sometimes he cut the engine and poled us down winding trails where the dark water was bordered with giant bulrushes, pickerelweed, cattails and southern cane. Every few hundred yards the "tossils" of the canes or a mass of bulrushes were knotted together—the lakeman's counterpart of the blazed tree on a forest trail. Wild celery, in coils that looked like bedsprings, rose from the bottom. Nutgrass, a favorite food of the coot, was scattered over the water. Occasionally we caught sight of one of these birds disappearing in the reeds, its head moving forward and backward in chickenlike motions as it swam. When we emerged into an open bay among the canebrakes a score of the birds rushed across the water, their feet sending up little geysers as they struggled to get into the air in heavy-bodied, tail-heavy flight.

Streaming back from the vegetation, clinging to our clothes, sailing almost invisible through the air, were silken threads of gossamer. Tiny spiderlets were ballooning in the spring sunshine just as they ride the autumn air in northern states. Spikes of arrowhead already bore their white flowers and the waves of climbing boneset were almost in bloom. Among thick stands of "wampee"—that favored food of the purple gallinule, the pickerelweed—we glimpsed snow-white masses clinging to the stems. A closer look revealed them to be the eggs of the snail *Pomacea caliginosa*. Each pearllike egg was about a quarter of an inch across. We found other masses of the eggs on cattails and on the broad leaves of the arrowhead. The snails that hatch from these eggs are hunted by the shy limpkin and the Everglade kite, that rare bird known here as the snail-hawk. Later we found some of the shells discarded by birds, roundish, dark, almost filling the hollow of a hand and with a bell-like, metallic ring when dropped on the bottom of the boat.

In one bay, surrounded by cattails, not far from Tin-Shack Cove, we slipped close to one of the most elusive birds of the region, a snail-hunting limpkin. Rod was poling silently along. Letting the boat drift, we froze at our field glasses. Nearly as large as an American bittern, with long, downcurving bill and gray plumage streaked with brown, it walked with a curious halting gait and flipped its tail in nervous jerks when at rest. Its feet were enormous, fitted for marsh walking. Watching us apprehensively with red eyes, it repeated a grating "Clock! Clock!" At one time limpkins were so abundant in the region that natives would kill a score or more on a short hunt before breakfast. Our bird suddenly launched itself over the cattails and, flying low with strokes that had a quick flip on every upbeat, dropped out of sight. Later we caught fleeting glimpses of two other limpkins. Even at a distance the peculiar flight with more rapid upward movement of the wings, distinguishes the bird.

Even more striking than its individual manner of flight is the call of the limpkin. Its local name the "crying bird" is well merited. Later, in the dusk, we heard it, a wild, catlike yowl that echoed over the darkening waters of the lake. Rod recalled one city fisherman who was unalterably convinced that he was hearing the howl of a Florida panther.

"When," he said, "you have bullfrogs and coots and limpkins all going at the same time you have got yourself a fuss!"

The sun was low when we swung around in open water to the west of King's Bar. The racket of the outboard motor ceased. Rod dropped the anchor and we rocked gently in the slow swells and waited for the ibis.

To the east of us lay an area of scattered bulrushes succeeded by a stand of cattails, then a belt of plume-topped canes beyond which we could see clusters of low willows. This was the home of the ibis. During the day, the birds scatter to hunt the crayfish, leeches, small snakes, grasshoppers, and other insects upon which they feed. But when evening comes they wing their way for many miles around back to the King's Bar willows. Our anchored boat lay in the main line of this homeward flight.

To natives of the region the glossy ibis, with its dark plumage and downcurving bill, is the "black curlew." This bird was familiar to Moses and the Pharaohs and all the dwellers in the valley of the lower

Nile. Its breeding range extends around the world. It is found in Borneo and China and Australia and Persia and Greece and Spain. Yet, curiously enough, on the North American continent the glossy ibis is—like the great white heron of the Florida keys and the Kirtland's warbler of the Michigan pine barrens—a bird with a remarkably restricted range. When sunset comes, virtually every American glossy ibis—the *Plegadis falcinellus falcinellus* of ornithologists—in North America comes home to roost among the low willows of this one bar in Lake Okeechobee. A related species, the white-faced glossy ibis, is found farther west along the Texas coast.

Now the vanguard of the returning birds appeared out of the glowing pink of the sunset clouds—a long line of black dots approaching low over the water. The dots grew in size, took shape, became a skein of dark birds. They passed us silently, flowing over the obstruction of the cattails and canes as though each bird were a link in a pliant chain. The whole line of birds seemed a unit, an entity, rather than a group of separate individuals. Against the luminous sky each glossy ibis was imprinted sharply. Over the island they curved into a great wheel and poured downward in a spiral to alight in the willow trees.

Flock followed flock. Sometimes in loosely knit V's, sometimes in straggling clusters, sometimes in long lines or skeins that stretched for a mile or more above the water, the birds poured toward us. Sometimes they came in high in the air, sometimes low over the water—so low that their wingtips seemed to miss by only a hair the metallic-tinted swells of the surface. The smallest group contained about thirty birds, the largest more than five hundred.

"Man, oh Man! *Look* at that flock!" Sprunt shouted as the skein of half a thousand birds flowed toward us in a seemingly interminable procession. Like the other lines, it swung to one side to pass the boat at a safe distance. Natural shyness has stood the glossy ibis in good stead. Above the willows of their roost the flock wound up like a length of string as the birds descended. The wheel above the trees grew smaller as it revolved until it was gone and all the birds were down.

Through our field glasses, we could see the alighting ibises hopping awkwardly from branch to branch, working downward out of sight. As flock after flock descended, it seemed impossible for the willows to hold more. Still the birds came. Their formations continually altered like flocks of flying brant. Their undulating skeins ran like slow ripples across the sky—the birds black against the sunset-tinted clouds, their reflections black amid the tinted image-clouds mirrored on the smooth surface of the lake.

By now the frog chorus was in full swing in the shallows of the bar and, at intervals, the loud caterwauling "Me-YOW!" of a limpkin cut through it. All around us was the fresh smell of the lake. Once we heard the barking of a black skimmer behind us and several times we caught overhead the thin whistle of a baldpate passing by. Long after sunset a duck hawk scudded past and was gone before we had more than time to get it well focused in our glasses. Redwings and grackles, mostly boat-tails, came pouring into the cattail stands for the night. Numerous other birds besides ibis come home to King's Bar at evening. We watched snowy egrets and American egrets, their white plumage tinted pink by the sunset, come down to land with that awkward, falling-apart motion characteristic of herons. A great blue heron—a "Poor Joe," a "John Henry" of the South—sailed in followed by a Louisiana heron and an anhinga.

Shortly afterwards, another long line of glossy ibis arrived—all wings beating, all wings set in a glide, all wings beating again—while the final bird, like a white period at the end of a long black sentence, was a lone white ibis. It wheeled with the sooty birds that were its companions, was sucked down into the funnel of descending birds, and disappeared with them into the willows. Another time a single glossy ibis appeared flying fast and low above the water. All its fellows were in flocks; it alone arrived without companions.

The sun was well below the horizon, Orion was brightening, and a full moon was silvering the lake, but still the ibis kept coming. Each wave flowed over the barrier of rushes, now growing more black and solid in the fading light. Sprunt and Pough were keeping careful count. Their tally rose steadily. Four hundred, five hundred, a thousand, fifteen hundred, two thousand glossy ibises. They were still coming after the moon was well above the horizon. Now they were almost upon us before we could see them, the dark birds merging with the darkening western sky, then becoming distinct against the luminous, moonlit east. From over Tin-Shack Cove, a final snowy egret appeared, its form, silently stealing overhead, illuminated entirely by moonlight.

The chill of the evening, the night smells of the lake, rose around us while the wildness of the scene was augmented by the outlandish calling of the limpkins, yowling like hoarse tomcats in the distance.

The last flock arrived. Alex and Dick tallied up the score. We had seen 2,307 glossy ibises, virtually the entire population of the continent, wing their way to this island roosting place. This was in excess of the last previous count. It was heartening to discover that this rare bird, familiar to man from the cradle of civilization on the shores of the Mediterranean, was doing better than holding its own in eastern America. As we headed for home through the growing chill of the night, the line of moonlight across the water—the "moonglade" of the New Englanders—moved with us. We looked back for a final time. The reef lay black and silent in the moonlight. Within its darkness the dark birds, immobile now, rested secure for the night.

Limpkin River

THE hands of my watch pointed in opposite directions—the minute hand straight up, the hour hand straight down. We watched the minute hand. It crept to 1, plodded to 2, passed the third minute mark beyond. At that instant, at thirteen minutes and twenty-two seconds past six o'clock in the morning on the 21st of March, the sun's center was directly above the equator. The vernal equinox had arrived. Night and day were of equal length. It was spring, officially spring, all over the North American continent.

It was spring where snow lay drifted under balsams in northern Maine. It was spring where crows settled on black and frozen bottom land in Illinois. It was spring where eucalyptus trees lifted shaggy trunks in sunshine, beside the Pacific. In all these places, and in tens of thousands more, people felt a lift of the spirit. Newspapers carried editorials on the coming of the favorite season of their readers. In skyscraper elevators, in country stores, in buses, on street corners, people discussed the same subject—the arrival of spring.

For us the official beginning of spring came in the panhandle of Florida, south of Tallahassee. It came on the banks of a strange wide river, born of a single spring—the Wakulla. For weeks in peninsular Florida, in a world of lost winters, we had been watching the beginnings of a season. We had lived in a pre-spring spring. These weeks had been surplus, velvet, bonus weeks. We still had all the spring on the calendar, the whole official season of the year, before us. On this day we had crossed a boundary line, a psychological equator. Now spring seemed really spring.

Woven through all our memories of that first day of the new season is the crying of the limpkins. Wherever we walked on trails along the river the wild, far-carrying wailing of these snail hunters re-echoed through the woods. Wakulla Springs is the only place I know where these rare, shy birds can be seen in numbers close at hand.

Between the calling of the limpkins in the Okeechobee dusk and the crying of the limpkins along the Wakulla there had intervened days of wandering. We had swung east and followed the St. Johns River. We had skirted the coast where masses of wiry, wind-shorn shrubs were alive with catbirds, brown thrashers, and towhees. We had rolled through pine flats where mile after mile the trees were slashed and bleeding in a spring harvest of turpentine. Not far from Jacksonville we had run through a concentration of phoebes with a flycatcher tipping its tail on almost every fence post. We had seen a puzzled Negro orange picker walking down the road, his picking sack over his shoulder, a long piece of paper—an income tax blank—in his hand. Somewhere south of Starke we had passed a farmer's wife hanging her wash on a barbed-wire fence, primly placing men's clothing on one side of a gate, women's clothing on the other. And near Florida's famous disappearing lake, Iomonia, north of Tallahassee, we had halted to delight in a cascade of blue, a flood of spring violets running down a slope amid the rusting tin cans of an abandoned dump.

Along the way cypress swamps now mirrored in their dark waters the yellow flowers of the floating bladderworts. Beneath each upright spike and bloom the leaves radiated out spokewise from the central stalk, supported by small carnivorous bladders. With the approach of spring the plants had risen to the surface for their period of blooming. We passed one swamp where the wheels of the bladderworts were so thick that the brown water seemed a vast machine filled with innumerable intermeshing cogs. Not far beyond we came to a wooden bridge. It spanned a transparent stream in which we could see each darting fish, each waving stand of eelgrass, each swirl of current-sculptured sand. Night and day half a million gallons of water a minute flowed in a wide river under this bridge. Yet less than half a mile upstream there was no river at all.

Instead, there was a great orifice, a drowned circular chasm of greenish-white limestone dropping away for 185 feet straight down into the earth. This was Wakulla Springs, the "Water of Mystery" of the aborigines, the largest and deepest spring on the face of the earth. Although the orifice descends more than 170 feet below the level of the sea, the water is untainted by salt. It pours forth, pure, transparent, its temperature remaining the same—between 70 and 72 degrees F.— winter and summer. At the rate of three or four miles an hour, the flood of 800,000,000 gallons a day flows down the 18-mile bed of the

Wakulla River, descending 13 feet on its way to join the St. Marks and pour into the Gulf of Mexico. Watching a river appear before your eyes, seeing it pulled from nature's magic hat, so to speak, is a sight so prodigious that you gaze at it hour after hour with undiminished interest.

Above the spring, looking straight down from a drifting boat, we seemed floating in a balloon over gorges and mountains. Ripple rainbows run down the water-smoothed limestone. Far below, at the bottom of the chasm, a kind of white, underwater dust drifts with the current. Little knots of bream and bass and gar and blue-hued catfish float at different depths, some darting among tree trunks that turned to stone ages ago. Mastodon and mammoth skeletons, encrusted with lime, have been taken from the walls of the spring. The wondering eyes of Ponce de León's men, no doubt, beheld them when they paddled up the Wakulla River in the sixteenth century in search of the Fountain of Eternal Youth. For De León, paradoxically, Wakulla was the Fountain of Death. It was on the river not far from the spring that he was felled by the arrow that ended his life. The Wakulla is a stream rich in history. It is unique in a number of ways. But above all, in our memory, it stands out as the River of the Limpkins.

Hardly had we stopped at the wooden bridge before we heard the wailing of the "crying bird" up and down the river. That evening the dusk was filled with its "kur-r-eeOW!" or "me-YOW!" rising to a caterwauling crescendo on the last syllable. We heard it when we awoke, during that last night of winter, in the Wakulla Springs Lodge. We heard it at dawn and we heard it above the ticking of my watch as the hands moved toward the birth moment of a new season. It followed us down trails where the sand of tiny anthills was as white as table salt and where redbud petals lay on the brown of woodland mold, on the gray-green of strands of fallen Spanish moss, on the tan carpet of live-oak leaves. It was part of the morning crescendo when the cardinals whistled, blue jays screamed, and the woods rang with the "chur-r-r!" of the red-bellied woodpeckers. Sometimes the limpkins lifted their voices singly. At other times half a dozen yowled at once.

Thus, with the crying of the limpkins around us, we spent the earliest hours of the spring.

Half a century ago these birds were common in Florida. They were relatively tame. Their natures were unsuspicious. So their slaughter was easy. In the 1920's, noting the scarcity of limpkins on a trip down the Kissimmee River to Lake Okeechobee, T. Gilbert Pearson wrote: "The bird is so easily killed, so highly esteemed as food, and is found in a state where so little attention is paid to the enforcement of the bird and game laws, that the prospects for its long survival are not at all encouraging." Under the continual pressure of persecution the limpkin, or courlan, became wary and retiring. It is now one of the shyest of southern swamp birds. The limpkins we saw at Lake Okeechobee slipped away like rails among the reeds or, with upflipping wings, scaled quickly out of sight over the rushes and cattails. Here at Wakulla, however, where the birds have been afforded years of protection, they have regained the fearlessness of their original dispositions.

No more than a hundred feet from the rail of the wooden bridge on which we leaned, one of these spotted, brownish, bittern-sized birds probed the river bottom for snails. Again and again the limpkin thrust its slightly downcurving bill, open, under the water. Minutes of searching went by. Then the probing bill located a snail. The limpkin tugged. It twisted. It dragged to the surface its prize, a large, dark snail shell to which clung fragments of waterweed. With its long neck outstretched, its slender legs hanging down, and the shell clutched in its bill, the bird flapped 10 or 15 feet to the base of a cypress tree.

Here it dropped the snail and clucked loudly. Upstream, behind us, a hidden limpkin yowled in reply. The bird with the snail moved the shell with its bill into a crevice between the cypress roots. With one of its long-toed feet it held it solidly in place. Then, hidden from our view, the tip of its bill began working away at the shell. Just behind the tip the two halves of a limpkin's bill are separated by a slight aperture. This provides a tweezerlike tip that aids in extracting snails from their shells. In some instances the bills of these snail eaters are bent slightly to one side or the other at the end. This apparently is the result of forcing them into the curving opening of the spiral shell in extracting the snail.

When the limpkin lifted its head it had succeeded in wrenching away the operculum, or "door," of the snail shell and the soft slug-body of the extracted animal was in its bill. A backward toss of the head and the snail was swallowed. Then the bird returned to its hunting. This time it teetered along a fallen branch, pushing its bill down into the shallows on either side. Hardly a minute went by before it located a second snail. Again it clucked and again, from upstream, came the answering wail of another limpkin.

We wondered if the unseen bird was the hunter's mate, brooding the eggs. For at that time a number of Wakulla limpkins were nesting. Normally the nests of these birds are hidden in vine tangles and thick marsh vegetation. One we observed from a distance of 40 feet, however, was constructed in the crotch of a sapling cypress nine feet above the water at the edge of a small island. Above the Spanish moss that draped the sides of this nest we could see the head and long bill of the brooding bird. From the blotched eggs, being warmed beneath her body, would hatch fluffy, cinnamon-brown baby limpkins. They would be able to swim, or follow their mother about like baby chicks, almost as soon as they stepped from the shell. And they would grow into adults that could clamber about in treetops, stride across lily pads, swim in open water, or, in spite of the halting gait that has given the limpkin its name, run swiftly enough to elude dogs in a maze of marsh-land paths.

The next morning, I returned to the bridge with my camera and telephoto lens to record the snail hunting of the limpkin. I focused on the cypress roots littered with empty shells. The morning light was perfect. The limpkin appeared. But so did a truck filled with shouting road menders. At that particular hour of that particular morning the powers-that-be had decided the planks of the bridge should be re-placed. Sledges clanged. Dust filled the air. My camera quivered on its tripod. Old planks were ripped out. New planks were hammered into place. In the clanging and confusion the limpkin departed and the Speed-Graphic, with film unexposed, went back into its case.

We comforted ourselves by watching the first yellow palm warbler of our trip, darting, alighting, wagging its tail among the branch-tip twigs of a live oak. We talked of some of our other "firsts," enjoying them in retrospect: our first firefly lifting its greenish light from a weed clump near Lake Okeechobee; our first bat reeling through the dusk above the road to Sarasota; our first violets on the Kissimmee Prairie; our first conehead grasshopper shrilling in the dark near Jacksonville; our first jack-in-the-pulpit rising beside the boil of a little spring in the Florida scrub.

Later, as we were leaving, we stopped by the wooden bridge once more. The road menders were gone. The limpkins were snail hunting among the eelgrass of the shallow borders. The river rang with the wildness of their calls. Theirs was a voice that spoke for an older time, a long-ago time when primitive men believed that tiny folk, four inches tall, danced in the waters of Wakulla. It was the voice of the dark, the swamp, the vast wilderness of ancient times. It links us—as it will link men and women of an even more urbanized, regimented, crowded tomorrow—with days of a lost wildness.

Barrier Island

W E passed a farm called Lonely Acres and a field where a white-haired Negro stumbled after a plow pulled by a red steer in a harness formed of strips of gunny sacking and overalls. Our road was carrying us north. Boys' kites swung back and forth in the air over country schoolyards. Dogwood, redbud, and peach trees were clothed in clouds of white and coral and pink. And all along the main highways human migrants, trailer caravans, were rolling northward in the wake of spring.

With regret we were leaving, for a final time, the colorful birds, the lush vegetation, the river-bearing springs, the seashell islands, the mysterious swamps, the fern grottoes of Florida, that state of unwearying interest for a naturalist. There a student of nature might well spend half a dozen lifetimes. No other state east of the Mississippi has as great a north and south distance as Florida. It is equal to that of all New England. We had already followed spring almost one quarter of the way to Canada by the time we reached the northern boundary of this one state.

LAND OF THE GOLDEN MOUSE, land of the unstable earth, the great Okefenokee Swamp spread away under the heat of the spring sun. From the top of the 75-foot tower on Cowhouse Island we looked down into cypress treetops where parula and myrtle warblers fluttered amid the filmy green of new foliage on frosty-white branches draped with Spanish moss. Flickers loped past in the sunshine and that greater flicker, the pileated woodpecker, drummed like a woodchopper on a hollow limb. A tufted titmouse repeated over and over again, without tiring, the "Wheedle! Wheedle! Wheedle!" of its song.

Below the trees we could see three alligators and a dozen black-shelled turtles, as large as dishpans, sunning themselves beside dark, sphagnum-filled water. Carpenter bees swept past us, fanned our faces, darted at high-flying dragonflies, hovered where the sunshine glinted on the polished, patent-leather blackness of their bodies. Spring had brought these bumblebee-sized insects from their winter hibernation in tunnels in the logs of the tower and they were as exuberantly alive as the warblers. On this day the vast shallow bog of the Okefenokee—once a depression in a prehistoric sea—was extending its 400,000 acres in an immense caldron of life, a caldron beginning to seethe as spring turned up the heat.

Spring begins in a swamp—the Everglades. The earliest sign of its approach in northern states is found in a swamp—the appearance of the skunk cabbage. All along the line of its advance the most sudden changes, the swiftest growth, the most exuberant outpourings of life occur in swamps.

While the Okefenokee has isolated areas of solid land, such as Billy's, Black Jack, and Bugaboo islands, most of it, like the *prairies tremblantes* of the Cajuns, is unstable, watery semi-land. Its depths present such eerie sights as will-o'-the-wisps and marsh-gas blowups and such visions of beauty as acres of blue flags blooming at once. Its dark lakes, its islands, its quaking prairies, its "houses" of massed vegetation, each has its own special inhabitants. Sandhill cranes nest on the prairies, their trumpeting carrying far over the lonely stretches. Since 1937 the Okefenokee has been a federal wildlife refuge. In a country where 100,000,000 acres of marshes already have been drained, this greatest swamp of the eastern seaboard promises to retain permanently the fascination of the untamed.

BEFORE DAWN we heard a low, faraway, fluttering call, musical and repeated over and over. It came through the darkness, an elfin sound, the calling of an owl mellowed by distance. During the previous days we had drifted more than two hundred miles northward from the Okefenokee. On this morning, awakening in a cabin beside Awendaw Creek, 30 miles north of Charleston, South Carolina, we were at the start of a dreamed-of week on a barrier island.

Along the coast of the Carolina low country, between the marshes and the sea, barrier islands, long and narrow, parallel the shore. They extend from the Santee delta southward more than a hundred miles. One, Sullivan's Island, is the setting for Edgar Allan Poe's *The Gold Bug*. Long a haunt of pirates and smugglers, these islands fronting the sea are still believed by some to hold buried treasure. For the naturalist they hold unburied treasure in the form of wonderfully diverse plant and animal life. And this was the season of the year when the charm of the islands is greatest. As Herbert Ravenel Sass writes: "Spring comes with especial exquisiteness to the long, narrow, barrier islands stretching up and down the low country."

At the northern end of the chain is celebrated Bull's Island. For several generations its ocean beach, its dunes, its tangled jungles, its freshwater ponds, its marshes have been a mecca for naturalists. Lying about three miles off the mainland, Bull's Island—about six miles long and three-quarters of a mile wide—is now part of the Cape Romain National Wildlife Refuge. At the time Gayer G. Dominick, New York broker, turned the island over to the government for a nominal sum, he also turned over with it a large manor house built under live oaks. Here the official in charge of the island lives and here guests, who make previous arrangements, may obtain board and lodging, roughing it smoothly in the midst of jungle surroundings.

We looked up our letter of instructions: "Turn off U.S. Highway 17 onto a dirt road known as the SeeWee Road. At the schoolhouse, turn right onto another dirt road. An abandoned telephone line of palmetto poles runs along this road. It will lead you to Moore's Landing Dock, east of Awendaw. The boat will meet you there at eight o'clock on Monday morning, April 7." Before eight we had reached the weathered jetty and a few minutes afterwards, Joseph Moffitt, a naval officer in World War II and now in charge of the island, was heading back along a tortuous channel in the Fish and Wildlife motorboat, the *Cape Romain*. Crossing the Inland Waterway, we wound past tidal flats where, among massed oyster and mussel shells, ruddy turnstones, greater yellowlegs, Hudsonian curlews, and oystercatchers, with great lacquer-red bills, fed, rose, circled, landed and fed again.

Most of the day was still before us when we docked. And beyond that was a whole week of island life in the spring. We awoke mornings to the gobbling of wild turkeys—in itself a sign of spring. We heard a Cooper's hawk give a cry almost like the high-pitched clucking of a hen as it skimmed over an opening among the trees. This, too, was a sign of the season. For spring is nesting time and calling time for Cooper's hawks. Parula warblers and yellow-throated warblers and blue-gray gnatcatchers flashed from limb to limb among the live oaks and laurel oaks, sweet gums and cucumber trees. One day there were blue-winged teal on Summerhouse Pond; the next day they were gone. They had flown north in the night. The mockingbird, South Carolina's state bird, apparently leaves the island in winter and returns in spring. Behind the beach dunes one morning, we saw the first mocker of the new season flitting through a thicket of sweet bay. All across the interior of the island trails and puddles were coated with the spring pollen of the loblolly pines. Each day our shoes grew yellow with this arboreal dust. And over masses of wax myrtle, beside the path to the ocean beach, yellow waves of blooming jessamine filled the air with the perfume of spring.

It was our good fortune to have the island visited during our stay by someone we especially wanted to meet, William Baldwin, a young field biologist with the Fish and Wildlife Service. We had heard of him as a tagger of sea turtles. In the late spring these monsters of the deep drag their ponderous bodies out of the surf and onto the sand to lay their eggs. They come from the waves in the night and disappear into the sea before dawn. This is almost their only contact with the shore. In an effort to learn more about these creatures and their travels, Baldwin had been spending spring nights on the outer beaches. Above high-tide line the loggerhead turtle, a species that sometimes reaches a weight of 450 pounds, scoops out a hole and deposits from 80 to 150 eggs. As many as 600 loggerhead egg nests are thus formed in one season on the Cape Romain beaches. When Baldwin came upon one of these turtles busy laying her eggs he would bore a small hole at the rear edge of the shell and attach a numbered aluminum band. Already he had proved something previously unknown to science, namely, that the same turtle may visit the same beach two or three times in a season to bury successive batches of eggs.

One of these returning sea turtles, revisiting the shore by moonlight, gave Baldwin an exciting few minutes on the outer beach of Cape Romain. He came upon it just as it finished covering its eggs and began dragging its ponderous bulk toward the breakers. Struggling to get the aluminum band off, Baldwin attempted to hold back the turtle. He might as well have tried to restrain a caterpillar tractor. Then he tried to roll the monster over on its back. It was too heavy, weighing more than two hundred pounds. Steadily clawing its way toward the surf, the sea turtle dragged Baldwin to the very edge of the breakers before he succeeded in freeing the band. Its number revealed that this same turtle had been tagged on this same beach a few nights before.

Baldwin's trip to Bull's Island, while we were there, was made to sample the water at various depths in Summerhouse Pond. Coontail, a fluffy, rootless waterweed, had been increasing, replacing other vegetation of greater value to wildfowl. In refuge management the forces of nature are juggled to achieve desired results. By raising or lowering the water level only a few inches, by increasing or decreasing salinity only slightly, striking changes in vegetation are achieved. Before additional salt water was pumped into the pond to control the coontail, Baldwin was making an exact check on its salinity. At the head of a tidal creek, Summerhouse Pond has been dammed off from sea water for decades.

Among its claims to distinction is the fact that it is the home of one of the biggest saurians on the Carolina coast, a bull alligator fully 14 feet long. Two years before, two Fish and Wildlife men were pushing a shallow duckboat along the edge of Summerhouse when the big gator rushed them. The boat capsized. But the men were able to splash through shallow water and cattails to safety. This was the only instance Baldwin knew of an alligator attacking a boat. He thought the craft might have been near the alligator's nest and its upsetting more an accident than a direct attack.

This was a comforting thought as we launched a jittery cockleshell of a boat and I rowed about the pond while Baldwin took samples. Near a small island where egrets perched, I had noticed a long black log floating on the water. My glasses transformed the log into the largest alligator I had ever seen. It was, Baldwin said, the "big one." Even as I watched, the saurian sank out of sight leaving hardly a ripple on the surface.

A few months before, Baldwin had come upon the front half of a large raccoon floating on the pond. The jaws of the gator had snapped shut, cutting the swimming animal cleanly in two. As we zigzagged about the pond, among banana water lilies and beside cattail thickets where Worthington's long-billed marsh wrens set up their high-pitched clatter, we watched sharply on all sides. Once we passed directly over the spot where the big alligator had disappeared. But it did not appear again. And, although I swept the pond with my glasses on other days, I never caught a second glimpse of the "long black log."

However, events of interest were occurring wherever we looked on the ponds of this barrier island. The waterfowl that overwinter here had left for the north. But other birds were coming in from the south. The heron population of the island was building up. One blustery morning at Summerhouse Pond we spent an hour watching Louisiana herons and American egrets and little blue herons come scudding hawklike down the wind to make thrilling turns, to be carried backward, to labor ahead, to parachute to a landing with downcurved wings. On another morning, calm and bright, as we stood near the masses of needle rushes that rise like great green fountains on the western shore of Moccasin Pond, a glinting of sunlight caught our eye. Through our glasses we saw an otter sporting in the sunshine, looping above the surface, appearing and disappearing like a porpoise while the water glinted and sparkled around him.

On a later day, at the far northern end of the island—where pirates once rendezvoused in Jack's Creek, where treasure hunters have dug most often on the island, and where the decaying tabby walls of an old fortification are so ancient that nobody is sure when or by whom they were built—we came upon another creature in its way as unexpected as the otter, as outstanding as the alligator. It flew up from a sandy trail with a loud chitter of parchment-dry wings. It thumped against the sounding board of a dry palmetto frond. It clung there, *Schistocerca americana*, one of the largest grasshoppers on the North American continent. With its reddish-brown body and spotted wings, this bird locust was nearly as long as my forefinger. We came upon this grasshopper only a few times, always on sandy trails. Usually it whirred away high among tree branches when we alarmed it.

Only once on the trails, during all that early-April week, did we meet another human being. This was a snake hunter from St. Louis who arrived after breakfast one morning and left with a bag of half a dozen reptiles to catch a plane home in the evening. There are only four kinds of snakes on Bull's Island: a blacksnake, a harmless watersnake, the lined chickensnake, and the cottonmouth moccasin. Only the last is poisonous. Visitors often assume that a fifth species, the copperhead, lives on the island. This is because young cottonmouths are similarly banded and colored. Lying on fallen live-oak leaves, these snakes are amazingly well camouflaged. On the Turkey Walk, leading to Summerhouse Pond, I stepped over a log and set my foot down less than fifteen inches from a coiled but sluggish young cottonmouth. Its pattern blended so perfectly with its background of small crisscrossing leaves that my eyes missed it entirely. These snakes grow darker as they grow older. Cottonmouths live as long as twenty-one years. Old individuals are often so black that all evidence of a pattern has disappeared.

The only permanent residents on Bull's Island at the time were two of the most congenial people we met on the trip, Mr. and Mrs. Moffitt. The migratory urge of spring was in the air and Moffitt was spending his spare time studying trailer catalogues. Our faith in southern cooking, badly shaken by restaurants along the way, was restored by Mrs. Moffitt's hushpuppies, conch stew, fried sea trout, and sweet potato pie. But most of all I remember one breakfast when whole-kernel hominy appeared on the table. Ever since my boyhood in the Indiana dunes, white, plump, flavorful kernels of hominy, fried in bacon fat until each is coated with a crisp, delicious shell, has been a food favored above 99 per cent of everything I have tasted. Simple, nourishing, filled with long-lasting flavor, it is a food supreme for the start of an outdoors day.

Usually after breakfast we started out with sandwiches in a knapsack to spend the whole day drifting over the island, stopping whenever something of interest caught our eye. One time it was a chameleon changing its skin; another time it was a duck hawk balancing itself in the wind at the top of a Spanish bayonet; at other times it was Florida gallinules giving grating little calls as they fed or white bluets beside the trail or a shining blacksnake that lifted its head higher and higher to watch us pass.

Day after day we paused at the same place to watch a running battle near a willow tree clothed in polleny catkins. Flies and bees hummed about the branches and they, in turn, had attracted insect hunters, lizards and birds, to the tree. A kingbird had established its perch on the dead limb of a neighboring tree. Each time it swooped to pick an insect from the air a ruby-throated hummingbird would shoot to the attack, seeking to drive it away.

Deer, raccoons, and wild turkeys had been down many of the trails ahead of us, leaving their tracks in the sand. April showers of live-oak leaves and, some days, April showers of rain sprinkled down around us. Along one moist stretch of trail near Moccasin Pond live oaks, probably rooted there when George Washington was president, spread massive, fern-covered limbs above us, while all around us the trunks were splotched with the red and pink and brown and green and purple of brilliant lichens.

The 12 miles of trails and roads on the island carried us through widely varied surroundings. In 1940 Baldwin worked out a detailed habitat map of Bull's Island. Its 5,135 acres are divided thus: woodland, 1,515; salt marsh, 2,123; brackish ponds, 685; fresh-water ponds, 213; wax myrtle brush, 284; beach, 160; dunes, 93; food patches and strips, 40; Jack's Creek dikes, 16; headquarters clearing, 5. In its wooded areas the island represents a hammock habitat.

Although we were only three miles from the mainland, with shallows and tidal flats between, the life of the island is singularly isolated. The mainland is rattlesnake country; yet not a single diamondback lives on Bull's Island. The deer we surprised along the trail or saw bounding away across marshy shallows are a distinct subspecies, the product of inbreeding, found nowhere else in the world. There are no foxes on the island because there are no marsh rabbits. Why are there no marsh rabbits? I do not know. It is a perplexing riddle why storms and other natural disasters have not carried some of these creatures across to add to the population of the island. Perhaps the fact that the most violent storms in the area sweep from the sea onto the land may offer an explanation. Or it may be that life has become so balanced on the island that a new species has special difficulty in gaining a foothold.

However, at least one creature has found a place in spite of natural restrictions. This is the dark fox squirrel that peered down at us with bright little eyes set between white nose and white ears. Every squirrel on Bull's Island has descended from one pair of fox squirrels released about twenty years before. This Adam and Eve of the island squirrels were brought from the mainland by Gayer G. Dominick. Scientists have found in this community of related rodents an opportunity to study such things as the effects of interbreeding and population spread under natural conditions.

Scientists also journeyed to Bull's Island to study another, less attractive inhabitant, the tick. In one three-month experiment to discover the best repellent for use in the armed services, half a dozen men roamed the area wearing clothing impregnated with different chemicals. The barrier island was chosen for the test because it is one of the most heavily infested spots in the country. On my first day on the island, as I was reaching for an eyed-elater beetle on a decaying stump, my wrist seemed to develop a small mahogany-colored blood blister before my eyes. A tick had dropped and already secured itself so well that my fingernail slid over its body several times before I could dislodge it. So sensitive to warmth that they can almost be said to see with their skin, the ticks cling to leaves until some warm-blooded creature passes below. If necessary, they can fast for months while they wait. Laboratory tests have shown that some species of ticks can live for years without food. All those we encountered on the island had a single small silver spot on the back. This is the mark of that widespread species, the lone-star tick, *Amblyomma americana*. Each day, as we roamed over the island, we attracted a larger accumulation of ticks. Their increasing numbers formed a kind of arachnid yardstick that measured the advance of spring.

We wondered if the frayed tip of a wild turkey feather, which we picked up on one of the trails, also recorded the advance of the season. During the winter the gobblers and the hens separate and occupy different parts of the island. With the return of spring they come together again. Along the trails we passed places where they had scratched and dusted. Once a gobbler raced across a small opening ahead of us, its neck outstretched, its head held low, its beard almost scraping the ground as it ran. At the edge of another clearing, under a great live oak at sunset, we watched the whole pomp and pageantry of gobbler courtship. Slowly the magnificent bird paced back and forth beside a feeding female. It swelled in size. Its body feathers fluffed out, shining in metallic colors in the sunset light. Its chestnut-edged tail spread like a fan. Its wings drooped until they touched the ground. Its powder-blue head lifted. Stiff legged it strutted in stately parade. From time to time it paused, uttering its loud gobbling call, then resumed its pacing.

That sound was one we heard at every sunset and at every dawn. It was the island's most arresting voice of spring. Each night, as the light faded into darkness, it ceased, to be replaced by the chorus of the frogs, swelling and diminishing, coming through the darkness like the confused clamor of thousands of flying brant. Then, far away or near at hand, sometimes where the moonlight flooded through the shaggy branches of a live oak tree just outside our window, the chuck-will's-widow began the steady repetition of its song. Our memories of those April nights are among the most vivid of all, particularly one night, the next to the last we spent on Bull's Island. It was a night on a barrier beach.

About sunset we packed our knapsack with extra sweaters, sand-wiches, oranges, and a thermos bottle of hot tea and, after a day of un-certain weather, set out for the ocean beach. Beside the road a Caro-lina wren sang, sounding loud and shrill so close at hand—as though someone were sharpening shears on a lopsided grindstone. Once we walked through an island of perfume beside a mound of jessamine, and just before we reached the shore we came to stunted trees behind a low ridge of dunes, trees with their tops sheared flat by the wind and all their twisted branches flaring away from the sea. Beyond was the bar-rier beach. It stretched away, deserted from end to end, as lonely as some primitive shore facing a pre-Columbian sea.

We sat down on the warm sand and leaned back against a beam from a wrecked ship, half buried in the beach. The play of sunset colors changed moment by moment over the expanse of water before us. Two hundred yards from shore a long raft of scaup rode the breakers, rising and falling, appearing and disappearing, as the waves rolled under them. The tide was out. Veils of falling rain, rain that had circled and missed us, increased in number over the sea. The east was serene and blue while in the west the sun was setting in a wild and broken sky.

We wandered along the shore, examining shells and gathering fire-wood for the night. Twice in succession, shells I reached for began sliding away down the wet sand, propelled by the feet of hermit crabs. High on the beach, where a dead palm tree had been thrown by storm waves, I broke off a decaying frond and discovered the massed white bodies of termites riddling the interior. Steadily the pile of wood increased beside the weathered timber. Gathering driftwood for a fire is a comforting occupation. It is direct and obvious in a world of confusing complexities. The benefits are seen at once. There are no lost or hidden links in the chain of action. Cause and effect, effort and result, are apparent at a glance.

A sprinkle of fine rain ran across the sand and then passed out to sea. A moment later the last rays of the sun streamed suddenly through a long gap in the clouds just above the black trees on the western horizon. Horizontally they shot over the sea, tinting the wave tips pink. They struck the fine shower that had passed us and the colors of a rainbow swiftly brightened. One end of the arch rested on the sea, the other on the northern end of the island. A faint band of red strengthened below the green—the beginning of a rainbow within a rainbow.

Rarely have I seen a more brilliant arch in the sky. The distinctness of its colors probably resulted from the fact that the sheet of falling rain contained an unusual number of small droplets of water. The finer and more numerous the water droplets in the air the more distinct is the rainbow, just as in a halftone illustration the finer the screen—the more and smaller the dots—the more distinct the picture.

A small cloud of shore birds scudded past us; they seemed to fly in and out of the arch of the rainbow. They were followed by three least terns, flying single file. These dainty, butterflylike creatures were so persecuted on Bull's Island, half a century ago, that feather hunters from the North, in a single season, wiped out the entire breeding colony. The scaup, more than one hundred of them among the outer breakers, rode the rise and fall of the darkening water—under the sunset, under the rainbow, as they would ride it under the stars. Finally their bobbing forms grew indistinct, part of the vast darkness that was enveloping us.

The tide had changed. The turn of the tide and the turn of the day had come at almost the same time. The waves were advancing on the shore; the night was advancing on land and sea alike. By our flickering campfire we sat on the edge of two mysterious realms, the realm of the sea and the realm of the night.

At seven-fifteen the first star became visible to our eyes. It was

Sirius, the Dog Star. From then on, the glint and glitter of the stars and planets increased. Clouds rimmed the horizon where sheet lightning brightened and faded; but the great dome overhead was clear. Infinitely far above us, lost among the stars, we heard a lonely plane thrumming across the sky. Once in the dark, as we gathered fresh firewood, we debated without decision whether a light on the ocean's rim was a rising star or a ship standing offshore. Even our field glasses failed to dispel our uncertainty. Later two ships, like luminous hyphens an inch apart, crept northward along the horizon line.

This was Saturday night. All over the country, in cities and villages, in stores and theaters and dance halls, along Main Street and Broadway, Saturday night was something special. On our barrier beach, with the sea and the dark for our companions, it was something special too. The city man, in his neon-and-mazda glare, knows nothing of nature's midnight. His electric lamps surround him with synthetic sunshine. They push back the dark. They defend him from the realities of the age-old night. A hundred years after he asked it, the answer is still "yes" to Henry Thoreau's question: "Is not the midnight like Central Africa to most of us?"

When the postmidnight hours came, faint clouds formed in streaks or furrows or shoals of vapor. They seemed thicker to the south, and above Charleston, 20 miles away, the reflected light from thousands of street lamps formed a luminous patch on the sky, a kind of celestial lighthouse marking the site of the city.

Each time we piled driftwood on our fire the flames leaped high, brilliantly colored by salts of the sea impregnating the flotsam. They lighted the dunes and the ribbed sand of the beach and the white waves of the flood tide. With our fire as the hub of our activity, we wandered north and south along the beach. Swinging the beams of flashlights over the sand, we stalked ghost crabs, watching them scuttle back into their burrows at our approach. From grass clumps fringing the dune-tops came the metallic bandsaw buzzing of seaside grasshoppers. And beyond, just over the low ridge of dunes, a chuck-will's widow called hour after hour.

It had fallen silent by the time we packed up and threw sand over the embers of our fire. The night was far gone and "the world and all the Sons of Care lay hushed in sleep." We started back through a gap in the dunes. We had gone no more than a hundred yards before a grayish, dusky bird leaped into the air from the sandy ground. It was the chuck-will's widow. I caught it in the beam of my flashlight and held it for thirty feet or so as it rose on rapidly beating wings, shining and ghostly in the spotlight.

A still stranger sight was to greet us farther on. Cottonmouth moccasins—the "mackasin snake" of William Bartram—hunt in the night. We moved with caution along the narrow road bordered on either side by water and marshy tracts. We played the beams of our two flashlights along the path ahead of us. Lizards rattled over the palmetto fronds with a dry hissing sound. Frogs leaped from the grass over our feet.

It was under such conditions that we came on a scene of eerie beauty. Twenty yards ahead of us we caught sight of a half-moon of green, glowing light shining in the darkness of the roadside. It appeared to be about the size of a silver dollar half thrust into the earth. At first I wondered if it was some animal eye reflecting back the rays of our flashlights. We swung the beams down. The spot glowed as eerily green as before.

Approaching closer, we discovered a large, whitish grub bearing luminous spots along its sides. Almost two inches long, it was nearly out of its burrow, curving in a semicircle. With both flashlight beams concentrated on it, it began backing into the ground. I pried it out with a bamboo stick. It curled up like a cutworm, lying on its side, the row of glowing dots shining as brightly as though formed of Neon tubes. We watched it for a long time, then placed it back on the soft earth where its tunnel had brought it to the surface.

This glowing apparition was the wingless, larvaform female of a beetle, a relative of the familiar firefly. To scientists it is *Phengodes*. To people in parts of the South it is the "neon worm." To us, appearing as it did when the new day was almost beginning, it was the final memory of our night on the barrier beach.

Trillium Glen

W E had driven down a dusty road that afternoon and walked past silvery trunked beeches and among robin's plantain and violets and star chickweed, into the soft, leaf-filtered light of a mountain glen. The coolness of a grotto surrounded us. The air was perfumed with the scent of thousands of woodland flowers. It was murmurous with the music of falling water. We were at Pearson's Falls, near Tryon, North Carolina, at the southern end of the Blue Ridge Mountains.

Like the leaves of a partly opened book, the walls of the narrow glen rose steeply on either hand. They were tilted flower fields, starred from top to bottom with the great waxy pink and white blooms of immense trilliums. Changing color as they grow older, these large-flowered wake-robins range from snowy white through pink to deep purple-pink before their petals wither. Our first and most lasting impression of the ravine was this trillium tapestry that ascended on either hand.

But there were other flowers too: hepatica, columbine, Dutchman's-breeches, bloodroot, lady-slipper, spring beauty, wood anemone—just to name them over is to bring to mind the sight and smell and feel of woodland loam. Nowhere else along the way did we find so glorious a wildflower garden as in this hidden nook among the North Carolina mountains.

Half a century ago John Muir tried to buy a section of prairie land at his boyhood farm in Wisconsin, hoping to turn it into a sanctuary where the pasque-flower would bloom in the spring and conditions that existed in pioneer times would be maintained for future generations to see. He was unable to acquire the land. But, more and more, local groups are carrying out Muir's idea. They are performing invaluable service by preserving representative areas in different parts of the country. Habitat areas, as well as species of birds and wildflowers, can become extinct. Conservationists have grown increasingly conscious of the importance of these small, "type-specimen" sanctuaries. There is no finer example in the country of the value of such a preserve than the glen at Pearson's Falls. Since 1931 it has been a sanctuary maintained by the Garden Club of Tryon.

Our lives touched it at this one point, at this one time in spring when its magical beauty was unrivaled. Along the path to the falls we hardly advanced a foot without pausing to delight in some new wildflower. White violets blooming among hepaticas; the umbrella leaves of the mandrake sheltering the forming May apples; the massed plants of the false Solomon's seal crowding together on a rocky ledge; the white Dutchman's-breeches and the red columbine—the Jack-in-trousers— these, each in turn, attracted our attention. We bent close to see foam flowers that enveloped their upright stems in little clouds of white. The tip of each tiny floret seemed dipped in wax of a delicate apricot hue.

Up the slopes the striped flowers of the jack-in-the-pulpit rose among the trilliums. Like the skunk cabbage, the jack-in-the-pulpit blooms before its leaves appear. It also is a plant that changes its sex, becoming female after storing up food for three or four or even five years. Another oddity among the familiar woodland flowers around us was the bloodroot. Each year it consumes the rear portion of its root and adds a new section to the front part, thus continually renewing its rootstock. Theoretically a bloodroot should be immortal. However, it requires special conditions for its existence. It dies, for instance, if the trees around it are felled.

It is no accident that most of the spring's earliest flowers bloom on the woodland floor. This is the time, before the leaves of the trees are completely unfolded and the shadows have grown dense, that the maximum amount of light for the growing season reaches the plants. It is then that they complete their most important vegetative and reproductive functions. Just as there is a direct relationship between the amount of light reaching the interior of a forest and the character of the vegetation growing there, so there is a direct relationship between the amount of light at different seasons and the time of blooming of these woodland plants. Of necessity, wildflowers of the woods bloom early.

In several places the sides of the glen were dripping like the walls of a grotto. Where a continual trickle of water ran down saturated wicks of moss on one little ledge beside the path, a half-circle of maidenhair ferns clung to the disintegrating rock. In *A Natural History of Pearson's*

Falls, an early book by Donald Culross Peattie that did much to arouse interest in preserving the glen, thirteen different ferns are listed as native to the ravine. They include the walking fern, the rattlesnake fern, the sensitive fern, and the ebony fern. Nine species of violets also grow in the glen. We saw—below the troops of trilliums, the trout lilies, and the lady-slippers—violets of many kinds: white violets, yellow violets, blue violets. During almost the whole length of our trip we found violets, like the multitudinous footprints of spring, scattered over the map before us.

At the head of the glen the path brought us to the white lace of Pearson's Falls. It is lace formed of water by gravity on a loom of granite. In a thin, foaming layer the water of Pacolet River slides down the face of successive shelves of rock. The sound of this falling water is murmurous, calming, companionable. Here is no mighty, roaring Niagara, no deep-tongued bellow. This was a sound for a glen to enclose.

Red-gold sand forms a little bar at an edge of the pool into which the cascade falls. On this bar I picked up one perfect wing of a yellow swallowtail butterfly. Perhaps it had fallen into the ravine when some bird stripped it from the body of a captured insect. Lying there in the full brilliance of its colors, it recalled the Guiana Indians, in the South American jungles, who cling to the poetic belief that the most beautiful butterflies contain the souls of their ancestors.

Night and day the falling water of Pearson's Falls generates a cool, moist breeze. It stirred the ferns and the lady-slippers and the pendant white flowers along the underside of branches of the silver-bell tree that leaned out over the pool. It blended together the perfumes of many wildflowers. Sometimes, as we slowly walked back along the trail, we came to areas where one scent predominated as when we passed strawberry bushes and caught the overwhelming spilled-wine fragrance of their dark-red flowers.

The perfume of the wildflower is never a product of the nectaries. It comes from special cells holding the essential oils that produce the fragrance. When you break open the skin of an orange you see similar cells near the surface. Oftentimes the essential oils are waste products of the plant. They are occasionally stored in scentless chemical compounds within cells in the flower buds. When the flowers unfold, the compounds are chemically changed so that they produce fragrance. The cells that contain the essential oils may be in the leaves, the petals, or even the stamens of a plant.

It is the petals of the yellow jessamine, for example, that is the source of that flower's famous perfume. Thyme, equally famous, has its oils stored on the surface of its leaves in flask-shaped cells that are easily broken. It gives off its perfume at a touch or under the hot sun. The cells of rue lie just beneath the surface of the leaf and are roofed over with a thin layer that is pierced in the middle by a narrow slit. These lids on the cells swell, bend down at the edges, and thus—at the same time—enlarge the opening and press the fragrant oil out onto the surface of the leaf.

Writing more than three hundred years ago, an English herbalist noted the earlier observation that the seat of the perfume of the musk rose was in its stamens. "Some there be," he declared in the quaint wording of his day, "that have avouched that the chiefest scent of these roses consisteth not in the leaves but in the threads of the flower." This observation has since been verified by scientific tests.

Students of orchids have discovered a curious fact about their perfume. The elaborate specialization of some of these flowers includes giving off different scents by day and by night. *Pilumna fragrans,* for instance, is said to have a vanilla smell in the morning and a narcissus smell in the evening. *Dendrobium glumaceum* suggests heliotrope during the day and lilac at night. *Cattleya bogotensis* resembles in its scent a carnation in the morning and a primrose in the evening. It is the lily-of-the-valley in the daytime and the rose in the nighttime that is suggested by *Phaloenopsis schilleriana.*

So powerful are the perfume oils of flowers that $1/120,000$th of a grain of oil of rose is all that is required to affect our sense of smell. That sense, incidentally, can be cultivated. After World War I a number of blinded French veterans were trained by Paris perfumers and became experts at analyzing scents by nose alone.

At one time, in France, it was believed that the smell of mint was the basic scent from which all others were derived. Psychologists today divide smells into six elementary odors: spicy, flowery, fruity, resinous, foul, and scorched. Because each perfume produces its own peculiar effect upon the olfactory cells, just as each musical note has its own characteristic effect upon the ear, a European scientist, several generations ago, sought to arrange all the odors of the world in a scale corresponding to a musical scale. He actually worked out such a scheme, assigning low notes to the heavy perfumes, such as vanilla, and high notes to the sharp odors, such as peppermint and citronella.

As we accompanied the river back to the mouth of the glen, with the perfume of innumerable wildflowers sweet in the air, I recalled an old inscription engraved on the tombstone of an early American naturalist:

"Lord, 'tis a pleasant thing to stand in gardens planted by Thy hand."

It was already past sunset when we walked under the beeches and among the star chickweed once more. The coolness of evening was increasing in the glen. From somewhere ahead, on a forested slope, came the bell music of a wood thrush. The memory of this rare and beautiful place we were leaving—its water music, its flower perfume and flower color—was one that often, in later recollection, brought us special pleasure.

A Hundred Miles of Warblers

FOR hours that April Friday we went in and out of spring.

Our road led through mountain country, over a long series of ridges. It rose and fell, climbed and tobogganed down again like a roller coaster a hundred miles in length. Each time the road lifted us to a new summit we found ourselves amid trees with buds hardly opened. Then, like a swimmer diving downward into foaming surf, we would swoop into a world of white dogwood, of fruit trees clouded with blooms, of grass freshly green. Spring would be all around us in some valley fragrant with flowers.

The season was advancing swiftest along the valleys; its highwater mark was lifting little by little up the mountainsides. Like floods of water, the floods of spring follow a lowland course. They race ahead down the long valleys, climb slowly, as though struggling with gravity, up the slopes. In the mountains the streams, the highways and the railroads go through the gaps together. And with them goes spring.

We had awakened early that morning in a cabin beside a rushing mountain brook, 20 miles east of Asheville. It was still dark when we heard, high overhead where the flying bird was already touched by the sunrise, the wild, lonely voice of a killdeer. Then the valley lightened and wood thrushes, mockingbirds, and cardinals sang all up the slope of the mountain that climbed steeply behind us. Their notes descended in varying volume. Those of the topmost singers reached us in fragments, during lulls in the lower chorus, as mere fairy songs, whisper songs, echoing down the slope. These were the first of innumerable birds we heard that day.

During the night a great warbler wave had poured over the Appalachians, spilling its gay, colorful migrants down the ridges that, in gigantic waves of granite, descended toward the east. The fluttering wings that had carried them from islands of the Caribbean, from Central or South America, from Mexico, had lifted them over the barrier of this ancient range. Before we had started our trip, Ludlow Griscom, Harvard's famed field ornithologist, had told us:

"Be near Asheville, North Carolina, the third week in April and you will see the warblers pour across the mountains."

This was the third week in April. And these were the warblers he had promised. Nearly one-third of all the species of warblers found east of the rockies were about us that day.

We never knew whether we were in the beginning, the middle, or the end of the wave. We drove for more than a hundred miles, from east to Asheville south to Hendersonville and west to Highlands, and there were warblers, pockets of warblers, trees swarming with warblers, warblers beyond count, along the way. These rainbow birds of spring, like other manifestations of spring, increased and decreased as our road tobogganed or climbed. They were most numerous in the valleys; absent almost entirely on the higher summits. Wood warblers come north as the leaves unfold. They feed on the forest caterpillars that feed on the new green leaves. Their northward flight keeps pace with unfolding bud and expanding leaf. The sequences of nature, the timing of the tides of migration, are exact. Buds burst, new leaves unfurl, larvae hatch, and warblers appear.

South of Asheville the road descended a long decline with climax forest on either side. For an hour we swept the hardwoods with our glasses, watching the warbler show.

No other family of North American birds travels more in mixed companies than do the wood warblers. Redstarts darted among the branches, fanning their brilliant tails. Ovenbirds called from the woodland floor. Prairie warblers endlessly went up the scale in the thin "zee-zee-zee-zee-zee-zee" of their song and chestnut-sided warblers ended on a whiplash "switch you!" As they appeared and disappeared among branches and bushes, we saw the rich lemon of yellow warblers, the black raccoon masks across the faces of Maryland yellowthroats, the flash of yellow rump patches as myrtle warblers swooped and rose. We watched hooded warblers opening and closing their tails—birds that to Frank M. Chapman seemed to say: "You must come to the woods, or you won't see me!" The final notes are almost as explosive as those of the chestnut-sided. High in the oaks and maples the parula, smallest of all North American warblers, hung from twig tips like a chickadee or flashed among the new leaves the brilliance of its yellow throat and breast, its white wing bars, and old-gold shield on its bluish back. And every bird was in perfect plumage. This was the season of the new and unmarred leaf, the time of the bird at its best. This was the unblemished world of the spring.

A little later we pulled up near a huge tulip tree. Its billowing cloud of pale-green new leaves was a world of succulent plenty for larva and warbler alike. Magnolia warblers and blackthroated blues and parulas and redstarts and myrtles swarmed through this arboreal land of plenty. Nothing in the world is more alive than a warbler in the spring. Surely it must have been a warbler that James Stephens described in *The Crock of Gold* as being "so full of all-of-a-sudden." All of a sudden a warbler starts and stops. All of a sudden it flashes from branch to branch, peers under leaves, snaps up small caterpillars, darts on again.

One black-and-white warbler, a little striped mouse of a bird, left its caterpillar hunting to hawk after a pale-brown moth gyrating beyond a lower branch. It fluttered, hovered, spurted ahead, missed the moth in its erratic course time after time. In the end it became discouraged and suddenly zoomed upward, back to the trunk among the gray-green leaves of the tulip tree. By the time we drove on, our necks ached from looking up at the strenuous little treetop birds.

In the White House, in Washington, D.C., on May 4, 1906, Theodore Roosevelt wrote to John Burroughs, at Slabsides, that he had just come in from walking around the White House grounds and had wished heartily that Burroughs had been there to tell him what the various warblers were. Most of the birds had been in the tops of the trees and he could not get good glimpses of them. But there was one with chestnut cheeks, with bright yellow behind the cheeks and a yellow breast thickly streaked with black, which had puzzled him.

This same warbler that perplexed the twenty-sixth President of the United States at the White House danced among the upper branches of a maple near the cemetery at Fletcher, North Carolina, where Bill Nye, the humorist, is buried. It was a Cape May warbler, the only one with chestnut cheeks. This warbler, incidentally, has little to do with Cape May, New Jersey. It does not breed there. I have never seen one there. Its name resulted from the fact that, during migration in 1809, the individual from which it was described happened to be shot on Cape May. Breeding almost as far north as the Great Slave Lake of northern Canada, these warblers concentrate in winter in the West Indies, especially on the island of Haiti. The path of their migration is wide at the top and funnels down to form, roughly, an inverted pyramid.

In contrast, the redstart—the "firetail," the warbler the Cubans call the "little torch"—has a particularly broad front throughout both its southward and its northward movement. As these warblers near their southern wintering grounds, their flyway still has a width of more than two thousand miles, extending all the way from Mexico on the west to the Bahamas on the east.

Near Druid Hills, North Carolina, we pulled up beside an apple orchard in bloom. The trees descended a long slope in tumbling clouds of white. Bees hummed. The air was fragrant with the perfume of the apple blossoms. Sunshine filtered among the branches, where a myriad white petals glowed, luminous in the backlighting. And here warblers—myrtles, magnolias, Maryland yellowthroats, prairies, and black-and-whites—darted amid blossom-laden boughs or flicked, in flashes of living color, from tree to tree.

There were other moments of especial beauty that day. Where a mountain road turned sharply on the way to Highlands, a black-and-white warbler flitted past us over a shining, glittering waterfall of mica that streamed down an embankment from decomposing rock. Then there was the hooded warbler we saw, singing with face lifted to the sunny sky, beside an upland pasture blue with bird's-foot violets. Once we came upon a prairie warbler, its yellow breast edged with streakings of black and its tail bobbing about, balancing itself on the fiddleleaf of a cinnamon fern. Another time a long finger of sunshine descending through a treetop spotlighted a Maryland yellowthroat, brilliant in contrasting yellow and black, swinging on a low cluster of red maple keys.

John Burroughs thought the yellowthroat's song said: "Which way, sir? Which way, sir? Which way, sir?" In a less genteel modern day it is usually set down as: "Wichity, wichity, wichity, witch." And so it sounds in the North. But here some of the birds seemed substituting an "s" sound; seemed to be singing: "Seizery, seizery, seizery." We wondered if this was a warbler dialect, a local accent given by birds that originated in the same area. Several times on our trip we encountered regional variations in song.

Blue jays in the South seemed to have a higher-pitched, thinner, less full-bodied call. Acadian flycatchers, in a cypress swamp near Wilmington, North Carolina, called "*Squeak*-it!" In Rock Creek Park, at Washington, D.C., the accent seemed shifted. There it was "Squeak-*it!*" In Europe ornithologists have recognized that chaffinches from the continent and from the British Isles sing in a different way. One is said to have an English accent, the other a Continental accent.

Later, as we drove north, we were tantalized by a ringing bird call from the woods. It was a monosyllabic "Teach! Teach! Teach!" It immediately suggested the ovenbird. But it was so different from the rounded "Teacher! Teacher! Teacher!" of the northern ovenbird that we thought it must be made by a different species. Finally, near Lynchburg, Virginia, we saw the singer in the act of singing. It was unmistakably an ovenbird. Through the southern part of its range, below the Mason and Dixon Line, the warbler drops the final syllable from its song. Roger Tory Peterson has noted that along the old canal that bypasses the Falls of the Potomac, near Glen Echo, Maryland, he can distinguish the resident from the migrant ovenbirds, when they return together in the spring, by this difference in their song.

Each time we crossed a brook among the wooded ridges, on that day of warblers, we stopped. For there we were sure to find a pocket of migrants. The trees beside such streams were always filled with the song of the spring woods, the small and varied music of the warblers.

During one such stop we were impressed by the way the bright yellow rump patches of the myrtle warblers disappeared almost instantaneously when they alighted, leaving only grayish plumage that blended with the tree bark behind it. The effect was similar to that produced by the sudden disappearance of the brightly colored underwings of an alighting *Catocala* moth. This swift eclipse of the yellow rump patches produces the impression of watching a creature vanish into thin air.

During another stop, beyond Lake Toxaway, we fell into conversation with a native of the region. He had noticed the swarms of birds that day. But he assured us that migration had nothing to do with it. Why? Because there is no such thing as migration.

"The birds are here all the time," he said.

"Why don't we see them in the winter?"

"That's simple. They're just farther back in the woods."

Surrounded by uncounted migrants, standing on one of the great, immemorial flyways of the East, he was unalterably convinced that migration did not exist. He reminded us of Thoreau's farmer who, while contending a diet of vegetables could never make bones, was being hurried along behind his oxen which, with vegetable-made bones, were jerking along both him and his heavy plow.

Somewhere near Frozen Lake we stopped for half an hour where ancient hemlocks receded into gloom beside the jumbled boulders of a mountain torrent. The trees were hoary with usnea lichen. In small gray beards, like lesser Spanish moss, it waved from branches and the rough bark of the tree trunks. Usnea is the chief nesting material of the parula warbler. And, appropriately, here we found half a dozen parulas. They danced from limb to limb, alternately in sunshine and shade, the males singing their buzzy little trill that has been aptly described as resembling the winding of a watch.

Perhaps for these warblers the hemlocks were home, the goal of their northward migration. Driving among migrating birds along the Gulf we had assumed, before we thought about it, that the earliest flocks contained the birds with the farthest to go; that those with only a short flight ahead of them would wait until last. The reverse is true. As spring moves northward, birds return home behind its advancing front. Each bird, as Ernest Mayr so well expresses it, seems attached to its breeding area by a rubber band. No matter how far the autumn migration stretches the band, when spring comes it draws the bird back home again. Georgia birds return to Georgia and Maryland birds to Maryland. The farther south their breeding ground, as a rule, the earlier they come home. Conditions are right for the return of the songbirds in Virginia weeks before they are in Massachusetts. Thus, returning migrants leapfrog up the map. Banding has shown that the successive waves in the tide of migration carry birds over and beyond those already at home.

Late starters in the migration parade tend to catch up with the spring. The yellow warbler, for example, winters in the tropics and reaches the Gulf coast about the first week in April. Some of these warblers nest as far north as Manitoba. During the last fifteen days of their journey they traverse an area that spring requires thirty-five days to cross. The average progress made by all species of spring migrants ascending the Mississippi flyway is said to be 23 miles a day. Blackpoll warblers, one of the last warblers to come north, exceed this rate by a dozen miles a day. Between Louisiana and Minnesota they average as much as 35 miles every 24 hours. Beyond Minnesota the blackpolls that nest in western Alaska increase their speed as they follow the Mackenzie Valley until they are making 200 miles a day. They require only half the time consumed by the initial 1,000 miles to cover the final 2,500.

As the road climbed nearer to Highlands, among these ancient ridges that are a relic of the early paleozoic continent, snowdrops were in bloom beside the mountain road. Riding west we seemed transported north. Hardwoods and open meadows set among dark evergreens were around us. The Low Country of the coast had the charm of the exotic; the High Country of North Carolina had the attraction of the familiar. The forest openings might well have been in Maine. But the sun was the sun of the South. Through the clear air of the heights, unhindered by vapor, its rays beat down with full intensity. This same clear atmosphere, when we came to vantage points above the valleys, enabled us to see for immense distances across the green panorama that spread away to the east.

In the dawn of that morning, what a host of warbler eyes had glimpsed that very scene!

During the hours of the night, with tiring muscles, with consumption of stored-up fat, the little birds had followed, in the dark, the sky highway of their ancestors. They had threaded through gaps, climbed over ridges, mounted to cross the continental hump of the Appalachian range. Rocks untouched by glaciers, plants of older lineage than any in the North, had passed unseen beneath their wings. Their aerial trail had cut across the path of the early Spaniards who in 1567—so many warbler generations ago—had pushed northward among the mountains. Some of the migrants, perhaps, had passed in the night above the very spot on Bear Camp Creek, near Highlands, where in 1886 Charles S. Sargent, of Harvard, rediscovered Michaux's *Shortia*, a flower that had been lost for a century.

Now the little birds were scattered over the descending ridges, feeding, resting, regaining their strength, just as their ancestors had done in pre-Columbian springs. We wondered how many times in each bird's life it stopped at the same spots while journeying from its winter quarters to its summer home. Audubon's phoebe, marked with a loop of silver wire about its leg, proved that songbirds return to the same nesting areas in the spring. White-throated sparrows, banded at Thomasville, Georgia, have returned in successive winters to the same identical garden, revealing that southward migrants also may have specific goals. But what of the vast spaces between? Do the birds tend to come down at regular stopping places, at way stations along the route?

So far as I know, no final answer is available. The area of migration is so great, the number of migrants so astronomical, the percentage of individuals banded so infinitesimally small, the chances of recovery so slight that exact and accurate information is difficult to obtain. But it seems logical to conclude that the eastern slope of the Appalachians in North Carolina is an ancient annual resting ground of the songbirds, offering sanctuary after strain. And of this we were sure: the descending ridges for many miles that day were providing food and rest and shelter and new strength for a host of homegoing warblers.

A Night in a Cloud

FIFTY miles northwest of the ridges where the warblers fed and rested, the Great Smokies straddle the North Carolina–Tennessee line. Sixteen of their peaks rise above 6,000 feet. Five overtop famed Mt. Washington. To climb the highest of these, Clingmans Dome, in the spring is equivalent to moving backward more than a month in time or jumping northward more than half a thousand miles in space.

Each hundred feet of elevation, theoretically, represents one day's advance of spring. In mountain country, however, the wheel of the seasons speeds up. Spring advances faster the higher it goes. For more than a decade Arthur Stupka, head naturalist at the Great Smoky Mountains National Park, has recorded the blooming dates of various wildflowers. This provides a simple and accurate yardstick for measuring the arrival of spring. The season we followed north, Stupka told us, had come to the valley around Gatlinburg, Tennessee, almost two weeks late. Yet by the time it reached the 5,000-foot mark in the mountains it had caught up with itself and was running on schedule.

It had come to the heights as well as to the lower slopes on the mid-May day when we arrived accompanied by a guide, philosopher, and friend, Ben Richards. During innumerable lunches, when he and I worked in the same editorial office in New York, Ben had regaled me with stories of the southern mountains. He had been born in the Cumberlands of eastern Tennessee, son of a Welsh coal engineer, and had been familiar with the region of the Great Smokies from boyhood. Our long-standing date to see the mountains together, during the spring trip, was fulfilled when he landed at the Knoxville Airport and we drove east to Gatlinburg.

A lively cricket of a man, weighing about 115 pounds, Ben Richards speaks with a ready wit and a loud, commanding voice. Once he spent three weeks on a boat trip with a deaf companion. He had to talk loud to be heard. At the end of the trip he entered a store and, without realizing it, spoke as though to his hard-of-hearing companion. Clerks snapped to attention. Service was prompt. This result was so gratifying that he has talked the same way ever since. Taking command of the situation, he had us painlessly installed in the vast, brown Mountain View Hotel by midafternoon and during the all-too-short days that followed showed us the wondrous beauty of the Great Smokies in the spring. First, with Nellie along, we walked from Clingmans Dome to Siler's Bald. Then, on the following day, Ben led me on a climb to the summit of 6,593-foot Mt. Le Conte.

WE TAKE ABOUT 2,000 STEPS to the mile. Each step makes use of a motor mechanism that weighs in the neighborhood of 80 pounds: 60 pounds of muscles and 20 pounds of bones. To balance our heads we employ 20 muscles; to balance our spines, 144; to take a step ahead, about 300. Every one of these hundreds of muscles—all 60 pounds of them—ached as I crept from bed on the morning of our ascent. I stretched. I seemed to have hardened during the night. I felt stiff as though encased in a chitin shell like an insect. Nellie winced as she rolled over. Mountain climbing by motorcar, we agreed, had been a poor conditioner for mountain climbing on foot.

Ben was depressingly chipper as we ate our early breakfast. He seemed to have no chitin shell at all. He talked with gusto of our coming climb to the top of a mountain 305 feet higher than Mt. Washington. At Newfound Gap, where Nellie drove us before returning to well-earned rest, his motor mechanism seemed all warmed up and ready to go. He started off briskly while I trailed behind, struggling up the "rises" leading to a trail mockingly named the Boulevard. Gradually I limbered up. But for the first mile or so an unusual number of things seemed to call for a pause and a closer look.

"What's the good of being a naturalist," Ben jeered, "if you can't stop and look at things and rest yourself?"

In truth, there was a wonderful variety of things to stop and see. This was the time when, in the Great Smokies, wildflowers of the forest floor were at their peak. Masses of the fringed white flowers of *Phacelia fimbriata* extended like long patches of foam beside the trail. Trilliums and violets and showy orchises intermingled in the rich loam. Twice we came around bends in the trail and found ourselves among spring beauties, acres and acres of them. The whole mountain slope, above and below us, was white with their blossoms. They swept in a wide waterfall of flowers that fell away beneath the trees, pouring down the mountainside as far as we could see.

Mountain bumblebees, queens searching for nest sites, 5,000 feet above sea level, droned past us to alight and investigate holes in the dense green carpet of moss. And once, stealing silently along the trail, we came within a few yards of a blue-headed vireo singing in a dead birch. It slid away down the slope from tree to tree, bursting into its sweet, slurring song at each new perch. Everywhere around us we saw signs of a mountain spring.

The day had started clear and sunny. Now the sky grew grayer. A lid of somber clouds extended from rim to rim of the heavens by the time we reached the shelter at Ice Water Spring. Near here the trail forked. The Boulevard mounted LeConte; the Appalachian Trail turned right. Leaving our packs at the log lean-to shelter, we started down the right-hand trail leading to Charlie's Bunion, that spetacular promontory created by a geologic slip ages ago. For a time the trail slanted downward and gravity hustled us on.

"You take the lead," Ben suggested. "Then you will get the full force of a first impression."

The trail emerged from trees and rocks. It curved in a narrow ledge around the face of a peak whose sheer side plunged in a power-dive descent more than a thousand feet to the Greenbriar Wilderness below. A knob projected out beyond this ledge with a vast chasm beneath. This was Charlie's Bunion.

Once we became accustomed to the dizzying drop we climbed onto the Bunion. Ridges, covered with red spruce and balsam fir, extended away until they blurred into dark, smudgy lines in the distance. Seen from above, mountains become different mountains in different lighting. Under top-lighting, cross-lighting, flat-lighting, back-lighting they present varying pictures to the eye. The scene changes with every movement of the sun. On this morning, under a leaden sky, in the breathless silence before a rain, the dull gray lighting stressed the wild and lonely character of our surroundings. In all the sweep of mountains and sky around us we saw no single sign of life. Almost naked rock slid downward into the chasm. Here and there some ancient, wind-polished conifer clung, its hold on the rocks unshaken by death.

Back at the shelter, Ben and I ate sandwiches and drank some of the purest, coldest water to come from any spring. Then, with the threat of rain increasing around us, we started up the Boulevard. In the distance we heard a low, muffled, reiterated sound, like faraway cannonading, increasing in tempo. It was another sign of spring—the drumming of a ruffed grouse. We heard it at intervals that afternoon, echoing through the heavy air. Once, as we rounded a trail bend, walking noiselessly on moss, there was a windy roar and two grouse launched themselves down the slope.

Our trail steadily tilted into a steeper ascent. At times it skirted the edge of abysmal drops and once it narrowed to a path along the knife-edge of a ridge where the graywacke and conglomerate of the mountain dropped away on either hand. Beyond it mounted through dark fir forests. Under the interlacing trees, mosses and lichens formed a continuous carpet, thick and russet-green. Here the silence of the evergreens was broken only infrequently by the little bells of the Carolina juncos or the long, rambling musical monologue of a winter wren.

We had almost reached the ragged lower edges of the rain cloud when the first drops pattered around us. Then we were climbing through the cloud itself. Damp and darkness enveloped us. Gradually the light increased; the mist grew luminous and thinned away. Then suddenly we were out in sunshine. Like a slowly climbing plane, we had ascended through the cloud ceiling that had darkened our sky. Below us it was raining.

A little farther up the trail we sat in the sunshine, our backs to a rock, and looked down on the shining whiteness of the mist. It filled all the valleys. It spread away to the horizon with ridges and peaks thrusting up, dark islands in a snow-white sea. As I gazed on these islands in the fog my mind somehow went back to an entry in John Josselyn's record of his voyage from London to New England in the year 1638; "June the First Day. In very thick foggie weather, we sailed by an enchanted island." I have often wondered what Josselyn saw just as I have wondered what an Eskimo hunter meant when he told Peter Freuchen, the explorer, that he sometimes roasted and ate a lemming just "for the sake of a memory."

Above us other clouds floated in a blue sky. Their shadows trailed across the fog-fields below. These cloud shadows on clouds increased in number. New masses of mist formed above us as we watched. They joined into larger masses. The cloud factory of the Great Smokies was in operation and a second ceiling, a ceiling above a ceiling, was being formed. It closed around the top of Mt. LeConte and moved down the trail to meet us. Again we labored upward in mist and the rain began in earnest.

Late in the afternoon we reached the last steep ascent. The wet woods had taken on an early gloom. Everything was saturated. Moss, growing on the rocks, on the fallen logs, on the trees from top to bottom, formed a great sponge filled to capacity. Little waterfalls descended amid the ferns. A thousand tiny rivulets ran down stringy wicks of moss. A wind was rising and we slogged along, slashed by gust-driven sheets of rain. Near the top we paused in the shelter of a massive cliff. Across its face ran brilliant, sulphur-colored lines and patches, lichen or alga growing on the rock.

Soaked and weary, we climbed the last yards on feet of lead. Somewhere amid the roaring of the wind and the drumming of the rain the strange "musical axle" song of the winter wren went on and on. At the log lodge that Jack Huff had built for overnight guests on the summit of LeConte, we dried out before the fireplace, turning around and around like chickens on a spit. Our long climb was over. Tomorrow would be easy—all downhill.

After supper I sat in the warmth of the blazing logs—my body half asleep but my mind wide awake—and listened to Huff recall Old Tom, the big black bear that tried to carry off a whole barrel of bacon and cheese, and Old Joe, the first horse to reach the summit of Mt. Le-Conte. Even before the earliest regular trail was cut up the mountainside, Huff led this sturdy pack animal to the top. Later, when the lodge was built, everything used except wood—hardware, cement, stoves, bedsprings—had to come up the 6,593-foot mountain on the backs of horses. One hundred and fifty pack trips were required to bring up the cement alone. Almost every day, during those trips, a ruffed grouse, entirely unafraid, used to appear from the woods and walk part way up the trail ahead of the horses.

Before we went to bed, about nine, we looked outdoors. Rain

smashed against the windows. Gust-driven fog swirled over us like seething breakers. We were in the heart of a cloud and in the heart of a storm. All that night, as we slept in rustic bunks on mattresses and springs that had ridden up the mountain on horseback, the storm buffeted the cabin. It was still booming outside when I awoke a little after five. The leaden-colored fog grew slowly brighter in the early dawn. Amid the storm a robin began to sing. A little later, at each lull in the great wind, I heard the sweet, bell-ringing jingle of the awakening juncos.

All night long, more than a mile above sea level, they—and we—had slept in a cloud—a cloud that enveloped us still.

After a breakfast of scrambled eggs and popovers, we sat by the fire, hoping the storm would die out and the clouds break to give us a view of the vast panorama that spreads away from this "Grandstand of the Smokies." The rain stopped and began again. The fog grew thin, then dense. About nine o'clock the clouds parted momentarily and we saw spreading away below us range on range, a grandeur of green mountains fading into blue distance. Then the window in the sky slammed shut. The clouds darkened. And the wind rose.

On the chance that the clouds might break again, Ben and I climbed over the moss amid dripping, shaggy trees, to Clifftop. At the top of this prominence the gusts were at their maximum, the fog more dense than ever. We could see only a few yards in any direction. The cliff was a windswept island in the sky. Treetops behind us, seen dimly through the blanketing fog, writhed and lashed as the immense gusts hurled themselves over the mountain. Ben's poncho streamed straight out sidewise in the wind. We held our ground by clinging to small trees and bushes. An ex-army airman, on LeConte at the time, estimated the velocity of the gusts at 70 miles an hour. The bellow of that tempest of wind and fog was so great that we had to shout, straining our lungs, to be heard a dozen feet away.

Laboring along the edge of the precipice, clinging to laurels and rhododendrons, we saw the low sand myrtle, already in bloom, tossed and pounded by the wind and rain. Dizzying plunges yawned below us at every lightening of the fog. Down there, invisible now, were coves and prongs and ridges with comb-teeth tops formed by the red spruces.

Down there was the tangled wilderness of Huggins's Hell. And straight below us, clinging somewhere to the sheer face of the cliff, was the narrow ledge along which we would have to make our way, buffeted by the wind, in descending by a different route, this time by the Alum Cave Bluff Trail.

For a long time I stood close to the brink, clinging to a stunted Frazier fir. Hardly a dozen feet high, it had been twisted and distorted by the wind. All its branches streamed in one direction, back from the edge of the escarpment. Like some green Winged Victory it clung there, bearing the brunt of the storm. I could feel the tremors running down its toughened wood as the great gusts struck. This was an old story for it. Its world was a harsher, windier world than that of the lowland trees. It was blighted, but still alive; it had endured, altered but unbroken by adversity. I have often thought of that steadfast tree. A fragment of one of its twigs lies before me as I write. On that day, with fog streaming past us, with the wind howling over us, feeling the tremors run through the fibers of its trunk and down my arm, facing the gale as it had faced so many gales, I felt an overpowering oneness with this storm-racked tree. And never have I felt myself in better or more noble company.

Exhilarated by the fury of the mountain blasts, we made our way back to the cabin. The day held little promise of better weather. So, with sandwiches and a thermos bottle of hot coffee in our packs, we started down the long descent. At first the trail led through sheltered woods where robins and juncos fed under trees that had their tops in windblown fog. Then our path skirted the cliff and cut downward across its face along a narrow ledge of rock. Above us, brown siltstone rose in a towering wall until it disappeared in the mist. Below, a precipice plunged in a vertical descent hundreds of feet beyond the limits of our fogbound vision. Between the two was the ledge on which we walked, streaming with water, frequently narrower than the breadth of my shoulders, and open to the full onslaught of the wind.

Wryly I recalled my thought of the evening before:

Tomorrow would be easy—all downhill.

Six thousand feet up, we were above the neighboring mountains. Unhindered in its sweep across the sky, the wind met the wall of rock head-on, shooting up its face in tremendous updrafts. My main concern was the possibility that a violent gust might cease suddenly, or produce a suck-back, and upset our balance on the narrow ledge. While the gusts sometimes pushed us hard against the siltstone of the wall, this was their only effect. Three times in half a mile, as we worked along the ledge, we passed through waterfalls where runoff from the storm poured down the face of the cliff. More than once we passed over spots where the rock was pegged down with iron spikes to keep it from disintegrating and once we stepped gingerly over a V gaping at the outer side where a landslip had carried away the edge. At times the ledge was no more than eighteen inches wide. The next morning I discovered that my left hand was sliced along the side and palm with tiny cuts. They had been made, without my being aware of it, as I slid my palm along the support of the wall in edging past the narrowest spots.

Every hundred feet that the trail carried us down, the wind lessened. In the shelter of a fir forest the ledge widened and became a broad and easy path. We stopped to catch our breath. Then we went on side by side. We were below the greatest wind, but even here trees were uprooted and thrown across the path. In favorable surroundings the Frazier fir of the Great Smokies becomes a magnificent tree. One such conifer attained a circumference of 6 feet 7 inches.

Our respite from the wind soon ended where the trail led out across a great landslip on the side of the mountain. From the highway to Newfound Gap, this bare spot looks like a brown patch on a green coat. I had imagined that great boulders littered the scene of the landslide. Instead, we emerged on an expanse of smooth, undulating siltstone, pitching steeply downward. Here, if a foot slipped, there was nothing on the weather-smoothed rock, streaming with running water, to halt a long descent. Once more we were out in the open, exposed to the full pounding of the wind. We moved slowly and carefully and eventually reached the protection of the trees beyond. From now on, the wind could blow as it would. There was shelter all the way.

Just before we reached Alum Cave Bluff we traversed a gloomy stretch of spruce forest. In the wet, midday twilight beneath the fog-filled trees, snails and glistening slugs fed beside the trail. Suddenly a black apparition flapped up before us. It was a turkey vulture that had been sitting out the tempest on the protected trail. Tossed and buffeted by the gusts, it struggled upward into the treetops. Here the shifting wind struck it first on one side, then on the other. Fighting to maintain its balance on a limb, it twisted, shifted position, thrust out a wing to keep itself from falling. This lightly loaded soaring bird was ill equipped for fighting storms of wind. Once it was thrown on its side among the spruce twigs; another time it lost its hold completely and tumbled to another branch. When we had gone a hundred yards or so down the trail I turned. The vulture was dropping downward to the shelter of the path once more.

Under the overhanging rock of Alum Cave Bluff we ate our lunch, protected from the veils of falling rain. Water ran from the eaves of the rock in rivulets and cascades and occasionally stones, loosened by the downpour, came crashing to the trail and in great leaps bounded away down the slope. Chickadees were in their element in the storm. They flitted past us, called, fluttered from spruce to spruce. They seemed the only thing alive; everything else was lying low.

By the time our lunch was over, the rain was a steady drumming. The drops had increased in size. They were liquid bullets fired by the wind. Fog, the smoke of the Great Smokies, veiled the scene wherever we looked. In fog we wound downward through a rhododendron slick, walking as through a tunnel and peering to either side into a wilderness of twisted trunks. Beyond, the trail ran through a natural rock garden flowering in the spring.

Hours before the time Nellie was to drive up and meet us with the car we arrived at the Alum Cave parking field. We decided to walk the ten miles to Gatlinburg. Bedraggled and soaked, with the rain slashing us in the face, in the back, and from either side as the road wound and the direction of the gusts altered in the ravines, we plodded on. The insole of one of my shoes began slipping and wrinkling under my foot. Cars raced past us, going downhill, their whirling tires filling the air with flying spray.

It was under these conditions that the Knoxville *Journal* became my favorite paper of the South. I had never seen a copy before. That didn't matter. For it was a Knoxville *Journal* truck that slowed to a stop beside us; it was a Knoxville *Journal* driver who invited us aboard. In fog, in blizzards, on icy roads, it was his job to get the papers over Newfound Gap to towns on the North Carolina side. He rode alone with the wilderness at night, returning to Knoxville by day. Not infrequently, he told us, his headlights picked out the shambling forms of black bears beside the highway. Thus entertained and vastly contented, we rode down to Gatlinburg—to a hot bath and a good supper and a long, long sleep. The next morning, bidding Ben and the Great Smokies good-bye, we moved on with the spring.

Kite Hollow

"MRS. TOY MILLER. Kite Hollow. Off Happy Valley. On the road to Blowing Rock."

I wrote it down in a spiral-ring pocket notebook.

We were in a huge rambling wooden building at Lenoir, North Carolina. Around us rose the smell of drying plants and roots and barks. The building was the headquarters of the Greer Drug Company, one of the country's largest dealers in medicinal herbs. Mountainfolk in hundreds of lonely spots were out in the spring weather gathering herbs, grubbing out roots, making a wild harvest to sell to the Greer Company. One of the most active of the Blue Ridge plant hunters is Mrs. Toy Miller. She ranges through Kite Hollow, along a mountain stream north of Happy Valley, and over the ridges beyond. I noted the directions for reaching her; for we hoped to go along on a hunt for mountain herbs.

The Greer Company, we found in looking over a price list, is in the market for such odd items as elder flowers, catnip leaves, balm of gilead buds, skunk cabbage roots, wild strawberry vines, mistletoe twigs, horse nettle berries, haircap moss, shonny haw bark, and may-pop pops. In the United States there are more than 250 species of roots, herbs, and barks of value in the manufacture of drugs. A bulletin put out by the U.S. Department of Agriculture, *American Medicinal Plants of Commercial Importance,* is a Who's Who of these salable herbs. It is also a dictionary of curious botanical folk names. The harvest of an American plant hunter may include badman's-oatmeal, truelove, tread-softly, simpler's joy, lords-and-ladies, shoofly, nature's mistake, or mad-dog skullcap. He may bring home Aaron's-rod, Noah's ark, Jacob's-ladder, or Devil's bones. Or he may return with juglans, kinni-kinnic, hackmatack, missey-moosey, daffydowndilly, hurr-burr or robin-runs-away.

In the cavernous loft of the building at Lenoir we walked among piles of white pine and wild cherry bark, mounds of mullein leaves and blackberry roots, and rows of burlap bags filled with fragrant sassafras bark—the first product of the New World shipped back to Europe by the Pilgrims. Wooden barrels held Adam and Eve roots. Star grass roots, like small onions, were drying near adjoining mounds of yellow jessamine bark and pokeweed roots. And extending across a wide carpet of cloth lay bushels of balsam poplar, or balm of Gilead, buds. More buds were coming in every day. This was spring, the harvesttime of the budpickers. A waxy substance extracted from these buds is used in salves.

Mailtime at the Greer Company brings a varied assortment of letters, penciled in unregimented spelling on odd scraps of paper by mountain plant hunters. The morning we were there, a note was deciphered suggesting that the writer should get twice the regular price for his roots because they were dug at a place "where the most dangerous snakes in the world live."

Not all the wild products handled at the Lenoir warehouse go into making drugs. Leaves of deer's-tongue are in demand for flavoring smoking tobacco. Another wild herb is necessary in the manufacture of silver polish. Sassafras bark goes into making perfumes as well as medicines. A recent development has been the collection of pollens for the treatment of allergies. One year, in less than a month, the Greer Company shipped $40,000 worth of ragweed pollen to northern pharmaceutical laboratories. In a kind of nightmare chamber for hayfever sufferers, we saw row on row of glass vials and jars filled with brightly colored dust—pollen from more than a hundred different plants.

Some of the first pollen handled by the Greer Company came from Kite Hollow. The red dirt road that leads into this side valley eluded us that day and it was afternoon before we came to the beginning of the hollow. A mile or so away we had asked directions for finding Toy Miller's house.

"Anybody down there can tell you," we were assured. "They're all kinfolk in the hollow."

The house we were hunting, gray from long weathering, clung to the foot of a steep descent. A dozen rows of peas and a small patch of catnip for the cat occupied a cleared space in the weeds at the back of the house. Chickens, dogs, cats, and children swarmed over the porch and unfenced yard. The herbwoman came to the door—thin, tired looking, her left cheek and lower lip bulging with snuff used "for the toothache." She was, she said, going up the creek that afternoon—the balm of Gilead buds were right for picking—and we were welcome to come along.

While she was getting a basket, Nellie passed around some Beechnut gum to the children. The oldest, a girl of about eight, chewed her stick solemnly for a few minutes. Then, before all the flavor was gone, she stuck it, for future enjoyment, under the arm of a cane-bottomed chair on the porch. A moment later she thought better of it. She returned, unstuck the wad, and attached it high on the frame of the front door, well out of reach of the smaller children.

We started down the hollow. The herbwoman was alert, pleasant, friendly. She had been born near Blowing Rock and was, she said, "a mountain girl from the beginning." She had a kind of natural dignity and her mountain dialect was interspersed with words of an older and better diction. She had been collecting wild plants, roots and barks for fifteen years. Once, when lumbering operations felled a stand of white pines near Kite Hollow, she and her husband skinned the bark from the logs and, in seven hours, earned $41. Another time, in two days, they earned $61—piling up more than 800 pounds of bark at 7½ cents a pound. Those were long-remembered bonanza days.

Where a decaying rail fence staggered along under a load of honeysuckle vines we stopped amid wild strawberries. The ground was white with their blossoms over an area of a hundred square yards. The herbwoman comes here to pick strawberry leaves sometimes. They sell for 20 cents a pound. But she never comes to pick strawberries. By the time they are ripe the rattlers and copperheads that live in the honeysuckle tangle are out and active.

"There's a heap of berries here," she told us, "but you can't get near 'em for snakes."

Once, back in the mountains, she was standing in thick bushes when she heard a buzzing sound and looked down in time to see the brownish body and V-shaped crossbands of a timber rattlesnake slide almost across her foot. The snake, apparently, did not see her. What did she do?

"I made tracks out of there in a hurry!"

In the main, however, when she is hunting herbs in the mountains she gives little thought to snakes.

"Hits a wonder," she observed, "I ain't all eat up."

We followed the creek, swollen with spring rains, until we came to the first of the balm of Gilead trees. Under favorable conditions these balsam poplars reach a height of 100 feet. The young twigs are hairy and the cigar-shaped leaf buds are fragrant and shining with yellow wax. Indians used this wax for sealing the seams of their birchbark canoes. Honeybees collect it to stop up cracks in the hives. Pioneers valued the wax so highly as a healing salve that they planted balm of Gileads near their cabins. It was a medicine tree. Today these "balm buds" still form the source of an important ingredient in many manufactured salves.

We pulled down branches and picked off buds. They rattled into the basket. We went from tree to tree. The sun was warm, the air filled with fragrance. Above the roar of the swollen stream, tumbling over the boulders of its bed, the calling of a cardinal carried far from his perch in the top of a willow tree. The ringing "What cheer! What cheer! What cheer!" was repeated over and over again.

"Hits got a big enough mouth," said the herbwoman succinctly.

The farthest she goes into the mountains in her plant collecting is about four miles. This is for the rarer herbs. The most sought-after of the roots grow scarcer every year. There is only one place now in the mountains where she is sure of finding ginseng. Also rapidly disappearing in the region is the "Noah's ark," the yellow lady's-slipper. Its roots, collected in autumn, sell for $1 a pound, dried. The mountains of western North Carolina supply a large part of the nation's medicinal plants. Yet even here, where at one time the supply seemed unlimited, uncontrolled collecting is having its effect. Herb hunters have to roam farther and farther into remote regions to make their harvest. Near settled communities, many species have been completely extirpated.

As we walked along, the herbwoman pointed out plants that she would visit later. Horse nettle—apple of Sodom or tread-softly—grew in a sandy place. Its berries, split and dried in autumn, bring 36 cents a pound. The dried roots bring 25 cents. The spindle-shaped roots of the yellow dock sell for only 9 cents a pound. Mullein, that plant of many names—candlewick, blanket leaf, Adam's-flannel, old-man's-flannel, hare's-beard, velvet plant, clown's lungwort—was beginning the production of the thick, felty leaves of a new year. The leaves and tender tops of the mullein, picked and dried, have a market value of 10 cents a pound. Once we passed a mound of pokeweed. This was a wild garden the herbwoman visited annually. Pokeberries bring 15 cents a pound; the roots, which unfortunately "dry up to next to nothing," bring only 10. Nearer the stream, in a boggy stretch, skunk cabbage massed its sappy green leaves. Here harvest days come in early spring. The roots and rootstocks are dug up and dried, after being split to hasten the process. The split, dried roots sell for 20 cents a pound.

One of the few things the herbwoman never collects is mistletoe. These clumps usually grow too high in trees. However, much of the mistletoe that reaches northern states during the holiday season comes from North Carolina, tons being shipped from one county alone. Some modern Daniel Boones, expert with a squirrel rifle, are said to harvest the topmost bunches in their own peculiar way, snipping off the branches with well-directed lead.

Along the creek, as we walked back, willow trees leaned, in clouds of new, pale-green leaves, far out over the rush of the mountain stream.

"I've skinned more willow bark in this place than most people think," the herbwoman volunteered.

In recent years the streamside willows have become a new source of revenue. The catkins have assumed special importance. For willow pollen has gone to market. Each spring Mrs. Miller collects bushels of the staminate catkins, sifting their floral dust through a fine cloth into a dishpan. The best time for harvesting pollen, she has found, is in the morning just after the dawn mist has evaporated.

The fluffy, greenish catkins of the black willows are as long as a little finger. Sometimes the tassels are more than three inches in length. They represent the largest pollen source with which the herbwoman deals. The smallest is the white flower of the plantain. On one of the hottest days of June, the previous year, she had followed the black-top road through Happy Valley, picking plantain flowers on either side. A score of times cars pulled up and people who thought she must be crazy wanted to know what she was doing.

When R. T. Greer, head of the Lenoir company, needs a new kind of pollen, he frequently puts Mrs. Toy Miller on its trail. Her knowledge of local plants is widely respected. Will Rogers once observed that we are all ignorant; we are just ignorant about different things. Our companion that day had had little schooling; she had never been beyond sight of one small part of the Blue Ridge Mountains. Her knowledge was narrow—but it was deep. She was an expert, an authority in her field.

A century and a half before, when André Michaux was wandering through the wilderness of the New World, collecting plants for Old World herbariums, he had recorded in his journal, in the spring of 1795, that he was "herborising in the Bleue Ridges." We too, that day, had been "herborising" in those same mountains.

As we drove away down the red dirt road heading for Statesville, we reflected on how humbling such a trip as ours eventually becomes. I remembered a famous explorer once saying to me: "The main thing I learn on every expedition is my ignorance." Everywhere we went we met new and unfamiliar things. Everywhere we went we encountered people who had spent their lives reading from one particular shelf in nature's library. They knew more about it—more about their area and their particular field—than we could ever hope to know. We could but sample the books they had time to read in detail.

We were near Hickory, North Carolina, in the sunset that evening when we caught the perfume of the first lilacs of our trip. They bloomed in a farmyard close to the road. A little farther on we ran through a great swirl of apple petals carried from a hillside orchard. And all along the way mockingbirds and cardinals sang in the failing light. It was dusk when we reached Statesville.

May at Monticello

ALL during our trip, in a hundred different places, we asked people
what first came into their minds when they thought of spring.
Their answers covered a vast range. At the top of the list stood the
blooming of violets and dogwood, the return of the bluebirds, the
songs of redwings and robins and the calling of the spring peepers. To
some people spring meant strawberry shortcake; to others, muddy
roads, plowed fields, and rivers rising. In other minds it was associated
with skunk cabbage, white butterflies, the red of swamp maples and
the peeping of baby chicks. In still others, it recalled jessamine flowers,
jack-in-the-pulpit, circus billboards, straw hats, kite flying, kittens,
calves, and housecleaning.

Spring is all things to all men. It is the bleating of lambs, the sound
of the carpenter's hammer. It is the yellow of dandelion and the green
of new grass. It is cumulus clouds and the smell of new-turned soil,
brimming ditches and miles on miles of fruit trees in bloom. This time
of shortening shadows, these months with music in them, form an
event in everyone's life, an event in the life of every animal and tree
and flowering plant in the northern hemisphere.

OUR SPEEDOMETER touched 11,000 miles on that eighty-sixth day of
our trip. We had been running west through Virginia where May had
turned locust trees into creamy clouds of white and fire-pink blazed
along embankments and lions and tigers bared their teeth on billboards
that marked the trail of the earliest circus of spring. Now, in midmorning, we were climbing the wooded mountain road that led to Monticello.

Automobiles with license plates from more than twenty states had already mounted the road ahead of us that morning. They had brought
people of varied interests and diverse outlooks to do homage to the
many-sided genius of Thomas Jefferson. Most were attracted by the
patriot, the statesman, the humanitarian. Some were interested by the
architect, the inventor, and we—in addition to all these—by the naturalist. An often-overlooked facet in the life of this extraordinary man is

his not inconsiderable contribution as a pioneer naturalist in America.

Thomas Jefferson published the first accurate and extensive list of birds in this country. He kept careful meteorological records for decades. He set down detailed facts about the trees of Virginia. He classified its animals. He recorded the comparative weights of red, gray, and black squirrels. He was the first American to make a scientific report on the fossils of the New World.

In 1787, when Jefferson published his celebrated *Notes on Virginia*, he listed all the birds known in the area. The total was fewer than 130 species. Today, according to Dr. J. J. Murray, of Lexington—editor of *The Raven*, official organ of The Virginia Society of Ornithology—the state list includes 400 species and subspecies—344 of the former and 56 of the latter. In all the United States east of the Rockies the number of full species is well under 450. So Virginia's 344 indicates the richness of bird life in that state. Driving across it, we noted down the different kinds of birds we saw as we rode along. By the time we came to Monticello our list had reached 85.

And at Monticello, birds were all around us—wood thrushes, towhees, brown thrashers, ovenbirds, yellowthroats, ruby-crowned kinglets, catbirds. We saw—to use the terminology of the Jefferson list— the lettuce bird or the goldfinch; the Virginia nightingale or the cardinal; the fieldfare of Carolina or the robin. We did not see, and no one will ever see again, two of the species on the list. Both of them—the passenger pigeon and the Carolina paroquet—have in the intervening years become extinct. But we saw two other birds not on the list and unknown in America when it was made. These were the comparatively recent introductions, the English sparrow and the starling. Jefferson, however, was one of the few Americans of his day who would have recognized them. In all probability he had seen them abroad while representing his country in Europe.

On that May morning one hundred twenty springs had passed since Jefferson died on his mountaintop overlooking the valley where he was born. One hundred sixty years had gone by since he published his *Notes on Virginia*. Yet the natural history of Monticello remained virtually unchanged. Bluebirds sang on the fence posts. Phoebes flitted in and out of the open doors of the old stables. A robin had built its nest at the top of one of the white columns of the west portico. And brown thrashers ran across the grass beneath an ancient linden tree that once provided shade for the third President of the United States.

Off to the east, beyond the mountainside where spring-clad trees stretched in a tumbling sea down the slope toward the Piedmont, a trio of turkey buzzards swung slowly, curving on the wind, hanging on the updrafts, drifting far out over the valley above tiny fields snipped from the plush of wooded hillsides, then sliding back to go riding low above Monticello. And all that morning the brilliant blue sky was filled with the metallic crackling of the chimney swifts.

Beside Jefferson's grave, we watched a chipping sparrow tilting its rusty cap this way and that as it fed on dandelion seeds. Fluttering into the air, it would alight on a bending stem and ride it to the ground. Occasionally, as it plucked the seeds, it would lift its head for a quick survey, with dandelion fluff projecting like a scraggly white mustache on either side of its bill. Before swallowing each seed, it clipped off the parachute, which floated to the ground. At the end, beneath the denuded stem the accumulated fluff looked like a little windrow of foam clinging to the grass. How many thousand dandelion seeds never take root because of the feeding of a single sparrow!

The birds of Monticello provide one of the outstanding memories of a naturalist's visit. The trees provide another. Here, rooted where Thomas Jefferson had planted them in the eighteenth century, stood ancient tulips, lindens, copper beeches, sugar maples, European larches. Here were noble trees, patriarchs that brought to mind Sir Thomas Browne's observation of long ago: "Generations pass while some trees stand and old families last not three oaks."

In beginning one of his Socratic dialogues, Plato wrote:

"Scene: Under a plane tree . . ."

Under a tree . . . That phrase recurs frequently in the history of human thought. Thinkers as diverse and as far removed as Gautama beneath his Bo tree in the Far East and Ralph Waldo Emerson under a New England pine have been associated with trees. "He spake of trees, from the cedar tree that is in Lebanon even into the hyssop that springeth out of the wall." So the Book of Kings in the Bible describes King Solomon, whose wisdom was proverbial in his time.

Around us, on this May morning, rose trees that had been associated with the thoughts of Jefferson. He had walked beneath their boughs, rested in their shade, seen them against blue sky and red sunset, watched them in wind and rain. They were part of his life when the author of the Declaration of Independence was evolving and strengthening his own eloquent philosophy of justice and human rights.

Now they were clothed in a new installment of green. For the leaves, life was new. For the trees, the events of spring represented merely an old, old sequence. One hundred twenty, one hundred fifty times, or more, a fresh mantle of leaves had taken the place of those which had fallen in autumn. Their green varied from tree to tree, almost from branch to branch. And beyond, along the mountainside, the shadings of spring were manifold. At no other time of year, except in autumn, is there greater variety of color in a woodland than in spring. A thousand and one subtle shadings of green, lost in summer, characterize the new foliage. Autumn colors are flaunting; they catch the eye. Spring tintings are delicate and often overlooked.

Every hour, under that brilliant morning sun, each square yard of outstretched leaves was manufacturing something like one fiftieth of an ounce of sugar. The broad ribbon leaves of an acre of growing corn will produce, in a single summer day, as much as two hundred pounds of sugar which is converted into the material of the plant. Leading to all the leaf factories of the trees around us was the running transportation system of the sap. Spring had increased its volume, had stimulated its flow. Coursing through the channels of trunk and branch and twig, it moved often under surprising pressures. In one laboratory experiment, scientists found that even the lowly tomato plant can produce pressures ranging up to about one hundred pounds to the square inch—sufficient to carry sap to the topmost twig of a California sequoia. Each tree at Monticello, beech, linden, maple, tulip, was being nourished by its own particular kind of sap. As in human blood groups, the fluid within tree trunks is specialized. Oak sap, for example, will not nourish a birch tree nor maple sap a beech.

From the tops of all the trees that Jefferson had planted, lightning rods project upward. This wise precaution protects them from thunderbolts in their exposed position on the mountaintop. In other ways, good sense has prevailed in keeping the house and grounds unchanged. The gardens have been laid out from sketches Jefferson made. The same fine and simple flowers he planted in the different beds—columbine, Virginia bluebells, phlox drummondi, tulips, and stock—grow there still. On this spring day—hundreds of butterfly generations after Jefferson's desire, expressed in the words: "All my wishes end where I hope my days will end, at Monticello," had come true—tiger swallowtails drifted among the garden flowers. And all along the edge of the restored fishpool, honeybees were alighting to drink the brick-red water.

We spent a long time within that noble house whose designing and building might be called Jefferson's lifelong avocation. He began it in his twenties; he was in his sixties when it was done. Everywhere we delighted in evidences of his brilliantly original mind. In turn, we became interested in his revolving study table, his "Petite Format" library, his clock that marked the days as well as the hours, his octagonal filing table with its pie-piece drawers. We had just emerged and were standing near the spot where Jefferson used to set up his telescope to watch the progress being made in building the University of Virginia, at Charlottesville in the valley below, when all the small birds feeding in the open dashed pell-mell into the bushes.

A swift gray shape skimmed past us. It was a Cooper's hawk scudding low among the trees. As it went by, from the bushes around us there arose a confused babel of bird voices. Instead of remaining silent in the presence of the hawk, all the hidden birds joined in a twittering crescendo. We were in the midst of that curious phenomenon sometimes referred to as the "confusion chorus."

The psychology of the bird of prey directs it toward an individual which it pursues. By flocking together in the air, small birds are able to divide the attention of the hawk, to distract it by many shapes in motion. As long as they keep together, and the hawk is unable to cut one individual from the flying mass, all escape. The confusion chorus appears to be a kind of flocking by sound. The calls, coming from all sides at the same time, apparently disconcert the bird of prey. At any rate, the Cooper's hawk swept on without pausing, reached the edge of the mountainside, and slid down out of sight. The twittering chorus ceased. The little birds, mostly chipping sparrows and English sparrows, flitted out of the bushes into the open. Their fright was over. The appearance of danger had set off a sequence of instinctive acts. Now that the danger was past there remained no visible remnant of haunting fear. Monticello in May was once more a place of sunshine and of peace.

In the Forest of Fountainebleau, which Jefferson often visited while American minister to the court of France, the green woodpecker is known by the apt name of the "awakener of the woods." An American bird deserving the same title is the familiar flicker, the "yucker" of Jefferson's bird list. Directly above our heads, as we were starting down the road on leaving, one of these woodpeckers burst into its strident, rolling cry. It filled all the space between the trees and was flung far out over the valley. Then, with that disconcerting suddenness that ends a flicker's call, the sound ceased. This was the last bird voice we heard at Monticello.

A hundred miles by road to the south and west, down the Blue Ridge Mountains, we came to Virginia's famed Natural Bridge, once owned by Thomas Jefferson. George Washington first surveyed it in 1750. Jefferson first called the attention of the world to it in his *Notes on Virginia*. In 1774, just two years before the American Revolution, he acquired it from King George III, of England.

The sum he paid, ironically, was almost exactly the amount we were charged for admission. Commercial interests have fenced in this natural wonder—which ages of running water and not commercial interests produced—and have turned the spot—intimately associated with great men of the nation's founding—into a moneymaking enterprise. Like Niagara Falls, the Grand Canyon, and the geysers of the Yellowstone, all such scenic marvels of the land are part of the country's heritage. The natural wonders of the nation should belong to the nation. They should be part of the park system, open for the enjoyment of all and not closed for the enrichment of a few.

Depressed by this commercialization of natural beauty, we wandered along the paths, past the oldest and largest arborvitae tree in the world—a 1,600-year-old patriarch with a trunk 56 inches in diameter—and under the great stone arch, higher than Niagara Falls, where rough-winged swallows shuttled back and forth and Louisiana water thrushes ran among the rocks, hunting for food in the shallow stream. Nellie compared the short call-note of the water thrush to the striking together of two pebbles and we fell to listing in our minds the birds we knew whose voices suggested sounds in their surroundings—from the liquid, gurgling notes of the redwing in the swamp to the call like tinkling icicles made by the tree sparrow that comes down from the Far North in winter. Thus beguiled, by and by we began to feel better.

That evening, outside a little Virginia town, the day ended with a pleasant adventure. Dusk was far advanced when a small boy came trudging down the dusty road outside our cabin. Bird voices seemed to accompany him, surrounding him and moving with him as he advanced. Whistling to himself, he was imitating robins, cardinals, orioles, bobwhites, meadowlarks. Like Thomas Jefferson, this country boy was more alert, more observant, more richly alive than most of those around him. We envied him this springtime of his interest in wild singers. "The birds of the naturalist," John Burroughs had written half a century before, "can never interest us like the thrush the farmboy heard singing in the cedars at twilight as he drove the cows to pasture or like that swallow that flew gleefully in the air above him as he picked stones from the early May meadows."

We never saw the passerby except as a small dark shape moving through the dusk. But we have often remembered that whistling boy. I fell asleep wondering about him—who he was, what he was like, what adventures life had in store for him—and wishing him well.

City Selborne

BY now we could close our eyes and see streaming toward us concrete roads, asphalt roads, gravel roads, shell roads, dirt roads; thousands of miles of roads; some red, some black, some gray; mountain roads, back-country roads, superhighways; roads thick with dust and roads drenched with rain and roads streaked with sunshine and shadow. During the days that followed Monticello we added memories of other roads. We wandered into West Virginia and across the Ohio River and back to the Skyline Drive and the run north to Washington.

The first day of June came and passed. Wind patterns now ran across fields of wheat and, from time to time, we were enveloped in that most nostalgic of outdoor perfumes, the scent of new-mown hay. From the mountaintops of the Skyline Drive we looked over vistas of apple orchards in the Shenandoah Valley—the white of blossoms gone and in its place the green of tiny fruit swelling on the stems. The famed Japanese cherry trees of the Tidal Basin, in Washington, had long since passed their blooming time and in Rock Creek Park the trees were clouded with the full green of summer foliage. After a memorable lunch with two friends, both distinguished writers on natural history— Rachel L. Carson and Louis J. Halle, Jr.—we drove northward between miles of gaudy billboards out into the Maryland countryside. That night we stopped where we had ended the first day of our trip, at Havre de Grace, at the upper end of Chesapeake Bay.

Then the woods had been bare and, in the distance, smoky blue. Now they were massed with green. Then solitary crows had flapped across barren fields. Now the singing of birds accompanied us along the way and the lushness of June lay over the fields. Climbing roses splashed their crimson against the gray clapboards of farmhouses, killdeers circled over lines of green spears lengthening in cornfields, and strawberry pickers were busy just as they had been busy so far to the south and so many days before, at Wachula, Florida. Spring, to most people, means *early* spring. It is the first swallow, the first violet, the firstborn that attracts attention. But spring is a season three months long. And these latter weeks, for us, were as filled with interest as the first.

At dawn, next day, we headed east across New Jersey, over Two-Penny Run and Killtime Brook. The fertile farms faded away. The rich dark soil grew sterile and sandy and gray. Around us, upwards of a million acres of scraggly pines and cedar swamps and acid bogs stretched away as far as we could see. We were in the pine barrens of New Jersey.

Less than seventy-five miles south of New York City, less than thirty miles straight east from Philadelphia, the barrens form a last stronghold of wildness in a long-settled region. In the years since Bartram and Audubon roamed through the barrens they have apparently changed remarkably little. In many places you can walk a dozen miles without seeing either a house or a human being. The concrete ribbon of a superhighway cuts across the barrens carrying a stream of speeding cars between Philadelphia and Atlantic City. But cars rarely stop and only a few hundred yards off the highway conditions almost primeval surround you. The "Pineys" who dwell in the barrens have a picturesque vocabulary of their own. Whirligig beetles are "coffee beans." Radiating pitcher plants are "clock dials." Pine snakes—at one time such serpents were supplied from the barrens to carnival performers all over the country—are "wompers." And king snakes are "swamp wompers." Pioneer communities in the barrens received such odd names as Chicken Bone, Double Trouble, Mt. Misery, Loveladies, Longacoming, and Ong's Hat. There is a Hurricane Brook and a Stop-the-Jade Run. In wandering over this untamed land we passed Hambone Ridge and Apple Pie Hill and Boggly Wallow.

Barrens and dunes and tundras and tarns—spring often comes with especial beauty to these austere places of the earth. Along winding wood roads, where our footfalls were muffled in the fine sand and over our heads the breeze in the pine needles sang one of the oldest songs on earth, we came upon a flower of rare, strange beauty. Emerging from a fountain of slender, arching leaves, a central stalk rose three feet in the air to be crowned by a high-piled mass of floral foam. Snow-white the flowers gleamed against their background of fallen needles and rough-barked pines. This plant is an odd member of the lily family, the turkeybeard, *Xerophyllum asphodeloides*. It was first described and named by Thomas Nuttall, whose scientific activity ranged over the two realms of botany and ornithology.

If we had been a few weeks earlier, we would have found another flower of spring, the pyxie of the pine barrens, the matted, mosslike flowering plant on which André Michaux, in 1803, bestowed the name *Pyxidanthera barbulata*. What hepatica and bloodroot are to the rich floor of the woodland, pyxie moss is to the barrens. It leads the parade of the spring flowers. One year, on the 31st of March, when the barrens were still dun and wintry, I came upon a dense mass of pyxie moss, a foot or more in diameter, across which a host of tiny, waxy-white flowers were scattered like snowflakes.

THE SKYSCRAPERS OF MANHATTAN appeared like a low mirage beyond the Jersey Meadows. We skimmed upward onto the 3½-mile bridge of the Pulaski Skyway. Smoking factories and great parking fields filled with cars slipped past below us. All seasons were the same to their asphalt and brick. But the marshy lowlands west of the Hudson were now green from end to end where, when last we saw them, they were dead, yellow, mottled with patches of dingy snow.

At the end of the Skyway we dipped into the open mouth of the Holland Tunnel, sped beneath the Hudson through a man-made burrow lined with gleaming tile, and popped up into the maelstrom of midmorning traffic in Manhattan. Among the crisscrossing canyons and the great piles of setback buildings that rose like eroding buttes in this badlands of concrete and steel and glass and brick, spring had opened office windows. Men stood on the sidewalks in shirt sleeves. In Greenwich Village flower stands were out. And along avenues a thin line of unconquered trees, struggling to survive amid the motor fumes, had put forth new leaves.

Working our way uptown, from traffic snarl to traffic snarl, we skirted the great green rectangle, walled in with high apartment buildings, that forms Central Park—a city oasis where more than two hundred different species of birds have been recorded. We paralleled the Hudson, up which long since the shad had run. We passed the park on Riverside Drive, where, in the year 1946, I saw with amazement a wild woodchuck sitting under a bush near Columbia University feeding beside its burrow with traffic streaming above and below it and lofty apartment houses rising behind it.

Well up in the Bronx, we turned aside again—at Van Cortlandt Park. Its 1,132 acres, where American and British soldiers once faced each other during the Revolutionary War, has been a haunt of big-city naturalists for generations. John James Audubon spent his last years not many miles away. E. P. Bicknell, for whom the Bicknell's thrush was named, used to wander there. A number of youthful bird watchers, destined for scientific distinction, cut their ornithological teeth in Van Cortlandt Park. The first nesting record for the king rail in the state of New York came from a small cattail swamp bordered by a railroad and across from a public golf course at the edge of this city park. One year, when breeding-bird censuses were taken in thirty-eight different areas scattered across the country, the highest count in the whole United States came from this same city cattail swamp. In its hundred acres the census takers counted 840 pairs, 1,680 adult birds.

As Nellie and I approached the marshy pond at the head of this swamp, we surprised a black-crowned night heron fishing at its edge. The bird gazed back at us with ruby eyes for fully half a minute before it flapped away with measured wingbeats, rising over the cattails with redwings in pursuit. A painted turtle slipped into the muddy water and, in a glinting flutter of wings, a metallic-blue dragonfly suspended itself for a moment in the sunshine before us, vibrantly alive, a glittering creature worlds away from the faded pinned specimen of the insect box that is a mere reminder of beauty that has vanished, a tarnished relic of something once surpassingly lovely.

We followed the path along the western edge of the swamp. Bushes closed around us. The surf sound of traffic on the parkway diminished. A catbird mewed close beside us. Then both the noise of traffic and the calling of the bird were swallowed up in the roaring clatter of a passenger train charging down the track of the Berkshire Division of the New York Central Railroad beyond the cattails. As the din receded, we emerged into an open space. At this same spot along the path, I recalled, the erudite John Kieran once had an amusing encounter with beginner's luck.

He met a lady, one spring morning, coming down the trail with bird glasses in one hand and Roger Peterson's field guide in the other. Birds were all new to her, she explained, and the sparrows were bothering her.

"How do you tell one sparrow from another?"

Kieran was beginning to explain about the rusty cap on the chipping sparrow, the snowy patch on the whitethroat, and the dark spot on the streaked breast of the song sparrow when the woman interrupted:

"What sparrow is that?"

She pointed to a bird on the ground a few yards away down the path.

"Lady," John Kieran told her, "take a long look at that bird. It is a white-crowned sparrow, the rarest one around. I haven't seen one here in the spring in years."

And if John Kieran has not seen a bird in Van Cortlandt Park, the chances are it has not been there. He has been going over the same area on almost daily walks since 1912. He was born nearby. Engineers on the railroad recognize him and wave as they go past. Twenty years ago, as he skirted the swamp weekends, he used to meet several boys plowing through the mud, clapping their hands to scare up rails and bitterns. They were members of a remarkable group, the Bronx County Bird Club. One of the boys was Roger Tory Peterson, another Joseph J. Hickey, a third Allan D. Cruickshank.

During almost forty years, while a sportswriter on *The New York Times*, a columnist on *The New York Sun*, a mainstay of radio's famous "Information Please" and a kind of one-man institution of learning, John Kieran has studied the natural history of Van Cortlandt Park. He has roamed it the way Gilbert White roamed Wolmer forest and the beech woods of the Hanger at Selborne—with unflagging interest in all the splendid commonplaces of nature. This Selborne spirit is not confined to the country; it is not limited to any land or race. It found expression with Gilbert White in the quiet of an English countryside, with John Kieran in a traffic-encircled park in one of the largest metropolises on earth. This stretch of green, an island in a sea of buildings and thoroughfares, has been his Selborne within the city.

Izaak Walton, in setting down *The Compleat Angler*, recalled pleasant hours of "such dayes and times as I have laid aside business and gone a-fishing with honest Nat and R. Roe." So, as we walked about this city park that spring morning, I remembered with delight "such dayes and times" as I have gone afield with honest J. Kieran, Fred Nagler, the artist, and the astronomer, that modest man of wide attainments, the late Dr. Clyde Fisher. Together we had stalked horned larks above those twin subterranean rivers, the old and new Croton aqueducts that flow under the park in bringing water from the Catskills. We had seen bobolinks fly over us near the site where Jacobus Van Cortlandt, once mayor of New York, built his gristmill about 1700—a building that remained standing for more than two centuries, until it was struck by lightning and destroyed in 1910. We had surprised wood ducks in the swamp and seen ant lions digging their pits in the dust under an oak tree and had come upon solitary sandpipers beside the little pond. Those were long-remembered days with good companions.

By the time Nellie and I left Van Cortlandt Park that June day and started north once more it was well past noon. For a considerable way we still rode on city streets. Fitted together into a straight line, the thoroughfares of Gotham would stretch for 5,000 miles—clear to California and beyond almost halfway to Hawaii. The parade of houses, seemingly without end, brought to mind a saying of our friend, William T. Davis, the Staten Island naturalist:

"Only a few human beings should grow to the square mile. They commonly are planted too close."

But eventually the houses thinned and we were in open country. We rode northward on the Sawmill River Parkway, crossed the Hudson on the Bear Mountain Bridge, and swung north again on the western side of the river. We passed over a small stream with the shuddery name of Murderer's Creek. We stopped on the Storm King Highway to watch a bald eagle soar by. We rode mile after mile through a pleasant river-bank country of orchards and vineyards and stone walls. Roadworkers were cutting grass beside the highway, the long, luxurious grass of spring. We stopped for the night a few miles south of the Mid-Hudson Bridge.

About sunset we drove on to West Park, the home of John Burroughs, to see his son, Julian. A mile and a half back in the hills, in

1895, Burroughs had built his famous Slabsides. And here at West Park, overlooking the Hudson, twenty years earlier, he had constructed a home of his own design, Riverby, the house that gave the title to his tenth book and the building of which is related in the chapter "Roof-Tree" in *Signs and Seasons*. Local stone, gray and weathered, went into the masonry while timbers and boards came from special trees the naturalist selected in the woods and helped fell and saw.

We never did see Julian Burroughs that evening. Along the way, fire engines passed us at high speed. As we neared Riverby, people were running down the road. Fire hoses already wound like great serpents beside the highway and down a slope, where dense, dark smoke poured into the sky and rolled out over the river. After surviving unscathed for almost three-quarters of a century, John Burroughs' Riverby was burning to the ground.

Afterwards we thought how strange a thing was the coincidence of our arrival. We had been journeying for four months. We had traveled 14,000 miles. Our plans had altered constantly. Anywhere along the course, a delay here, a speeding up there, would have changed the hour and day of our coming to West Park. Yet our long journey through time and space had brought us to Riverby at the precise hour of its tragic end.

Green Boundary

ALL along Cape Cod, sea and shore, dune and moor, bog and pond and open headland streamed and writhed before us in the gust-driven rain of a great spring storm. The wind of a nor'easter was pummeling the lower vegetation, cuffing the locust trees, belaboring creeks and inlets, lashing the waves into the seethe of towering surf. Nowhere since Mt. LeConte, in the Great Smokies, had we met so violent a storm.

Across almost the length of Massachusetts we had ridden in sunshine. The white of wild strawberry blooms, the pink of roses, the blue of flags were with us all the way. This was a land of graceful elms and of sugar maples, with their massed foliage rising above the brows of hills like cumulus clouds, green thunderheads. Pansies and snowball bushes and lilacs bloomed in dooryards and, in country gardens, rhubarb lifted the mass of its cream-white flowers. Observing how rhubarb was just beginning to bloom in the Berkshires, was in full flower at a lower elevation, we recalled the mountains and valleys of the Blue Ridges and that day when we had gone in and out of spring. Our first bobolinks rose with jingling songs from a meadow beyond a stone wall east of Ware. In quaint early natural histories, groups of creatures are given such picturesque designations as a waddling of ducks, a pride of lions, a spring of teals, an exalting of larks, and a charm of goldfinches. If there is a gaggle of geese and a clamor of rooks, why not a jingle of bobolinks? Or a flutter of terns?

"TIME is ever precious to the student of nature."

Many times during our long trip we recalled these words of John James Audubon. They returned to us with special emphasis as we drove north along the western border of Vermont. We were in the one hundred twentieth day of our trip. Only one week and one day remained of the season we had followed so long. We were living the last chapters of a book that we were reluctant to close.

North of Cape Cod spring speeds up. Like the migrating bird that increases its daily flying distance as it nears its nesting ground, the spring accelerates its advance as it sweeps into the north. And every hour of sunshine is precious across the upper reaches of the map. Plants live shorter lives and faster lives along the northern limits of their range. The same species of plants mature more quickly in New-foundland than in New England.

The growing season, as measured from the last frost of spring to the first frost of autumn, falls from about two hundred days in the vicinity of New York City to about one hundred fifty days along the St. Lawrence and to as few as seventy-five days in upper Saskatchewan. But these days are long days with maximum sunshine. At the time of the summer solstice, the end of spring, when more sunshine falls on the region of the Arctic Circle than on the equator, far-northern plants achieve phenomenal growth. Fifteen-pound cabbages, twelve-pound turnips, seven-pound cauliflowers are produced by the swift growth of a few weeks. At the delta of the Mackenzie River, 250 miles north of the Arctic Circle, potatoes planted on June 14 are often belt high and have tubers as large as hen's eggs four weeks later. Their growth is forced by days with more than twenty hours of sunshine in them.

The working day of all the plants and trees around us was lengthening as we drove northward among the great green hills of Vermont. It was lengthening all over New England, all over America, all over the Northern Hemisphere—as it had lengthened, day by day, ever since spring began. Every twenty-four hours it would be increased by added minutes of sunshine until the last day of the season, the twenty-first of June. Then the tide would turn with the longest day of the year.

In Vermont this accelerated growth of late spring was being recorded mainly in green. Spring is many-colored in the Carolinas. It is primarily one color—with infinitely varied shadings—in northern New England. We encountered scattered patches of brilliant hawkweed and robin's plantain and several times we saw the massed blue of wild flags following some moist depression down a pasture slope. But in the main we traveled through a world that was green. These were the Green Mountains. And this was the green spring.

Ferns ran in banks and waves along the ditches. They flooded away as far as we could see across the woodland floor. They fringed the cracks of rock ledges and they crowded close to granite boulders that were scattered like sleeping cattle across pasture hillsides. Here was the fernland of the East.

Here also was the heart of New England. People ended sentences on a rising inflection, a kind of vocal question mark that revealed an aversion to reckless speech and a cautious "it's-a-sheep-on-this-side" attitude of mind. People talked more about the weather and had more weather to talk about than anywhere else on our trip. Here we dined on salmon chowder and date pie and chicken shortcake. Sheds and barns and houses began to be joined together. And that night we slept in a tourist cabin equipped with lightning rods.

All the way to Lake Champlain, the next day, we passed brimming brooks and flooded lowland meadows. The fluff of willow catkins dappled the surface of streams, and on pasture walls along ferny byways wild grapevines held clusters of newformed fruit no larger than birdshot. We passed stone chimneys that stood as monuments to houses long burned, and apple trees and lilacs that marked the site of clearings since overgrown. Mountain weather alternately bathed us in brilliant sunshine and drenched us in pelting rain. Once a whole family of scarecrows loomed up on a hillside garden plot as we rounded a turn—a father, a mother, and three children represented by castoff garments flapping on their pole skeletons. Kingbirds, each a tyrant of his little field, perched on telephone wires beneath which dandelions were going to seed. In one level valley dandelions extended away in tens of thousands of white globes. For more than a mile we ran through drifting silvery fluff.

We were in a land of pastures and dairies and big barns. We were in a land of bobolink meadows. Near the lower end of Lake Champlain we passed the most memorable cows of our trip, a herd of Jerseys lying in a lush pasture, yellow with buttercups. With eyes closed they chewed their cuds, the sun warm on their backs after rain, a perfect symbol of the peace and plenty of spring. They reminded us that of all farm animals the life of the cow is one of the best. It is not overworked like draft animals. It is well fed because it is to its owner's advantage to see that it has ample food. It is allowed to go its own way most of the time. It is not killed for meat, at least not until its life has been lived. And here in the spring, amid the green rolling hills of upper Vermont, cow life seemed at its best. In the calm light of sunset the luxuriant growth of some pastures looked so tender, so juicy, so delicious a shade of green that I, myself, longed to be a grass eater.

Near Windy Top Farm, on a high slope overlooking Lake Champlain, I asked an elderly Vermonter what was the first sign of spring he noticed in the north country. He stood for a long time rasping a calloused thumb along the stubble of his jaw.

"Crows come back," he said succinctly.

Now, except for stragglers, all the birds were back that were coming back. Barn swallows, home from Brazil, skimmed over the northern pastures. Yellow warblers, home from Yucatán, darted along the roadside. Bobolinks, home from Argentina, sang on the fences. The great spring migration was over. The tide that had ceased running north would reverse its flow a few months hence and would carry with it millions of migrants now mere maturing germs of life in nests in fields and bushes and woods all along the border.

As we drew nearer the green boundary of Vermont and Canada, and zigzagged eastward across the state, the woods grew darker, evergreens increased, the forests were edged with carpets of bunchberry starred with white blossoms. Whitethroats sang all along the way. And from the dim interior of the woods we heard the voice of the hermit thrush at evening.

North of St. Johnsbury, as we neared Lake Memphremagog and the Quebec line, the country grew more grandly wild. Dark cedars and feathery larches, white birch trees and balsam firs dotted or mantled a green land of hills and ravines. Here we seemed driving through a second no-man's-land of the seasons. In southern Florida spring and winter had been intermingled and indistinguishable. In this north country at the top of the United States, an area predominantly green, summer and spring seemed already one.

A winding road—on a clear June morning after rain—carried us to a hilltop somewhere east of Memphremagog. We stopped at the rocky edge of a pasture. A little rill gurgled past us, its banks strewn with bluets. The sight of these demure flowers recalled the bluets beside the sandy road on Bull's Island and the bluets on Silers Bald. Goldfinches passed in their rocking-horse flight. We had seen our first goldfinches in a cypress swamp below the Tamiami Trail with the smell of smoke growing stronger in the air. We had seen them at the edge of the Okefenokee Swamp and above Newfound Gap. We had seen them all along our trip just as we had seen yellow swallowtails and fresh strawberries and violets. Memories of such recurring sights would knit the days of our trip together.

Beyond the hilltop lay Canada. It too was green—the bright green of pasture land, the darker green of spruce and balsam. Across the fields and hills and woods below us ran an invisible line, the political watershed between two countries. On different sides of the line the thoughts and resources of people flowed to different centers, their lives revolved about different hubs. But to the spring the line was nonexistent; it had swept across it unchecked as it rushed into the north.

For a time we debated whether to follow it across this green boundary into Canada. Instead we decided on a quick giant's swing over into Maine, along the Androscoggin River, back among the celebrated Shelburne birches and south through Pinkham Notch into the heart of the White Mountains. This hillside overlooking Canada, this green height with its goldfinches and bluets, was the point farthest north on the map touched by our long drifting journey with the spring. But our travels with the season were not finished.

As spring goes on and on, it also goes up and up. Altitude corresponds to longitude in its northward sweep. Instead of moving across the map we would move up the mountains. Instead of following spring into Canada we would follow it into the sky. By retreating 50 miles south of the border we would advance—as spring advances—the equivalent of 500 miles north of it. An ascent above timberline on Mt. Washington would coincide with the advance of spring as far north as Hudson Bay.

Timberline

W E were cloud climbers as well as mountain climbers on the next to the last day of spring. As we worked our way up the steep trail to Hermit Lake, that lonely little tarn near timberline on Mt. Washington, we ascended through successive layers of dank rain-mist. The warm saturated air was rich with the smell of forest mold. Six times, going up and coming down, we walked through showers.

In our haste to get started under the ill-humored sky, we skipped breakfast. As we began climbing we munched on two ham sandwiches, saving a lump of maple sugar for emergency rations later. There was no uncertainty about the Tuckerman Ravine trail we followed. It did not dip or level off; it kept on up and up. Much of the way we labored along a kind of roadway that nature had paved with irregular granite cobblestones. Half a mile up this trail we overtook two women from Ohio who had made even less preparation for the climb than we had. They were turning back after ascending that far along the rocky path in high-heeled, open-toed shoes. In a Sunday supplement they had read about spring skiing in Tuckerman Ravine and had set out to see it during an hour's stopover!

Paralleling our ascent, the white water of Cutler River tumbled down the mountainside toward the east. It roared or murmured as the windings of our trail carried us nearer or farther from its rocky bed. In the midst of the crash and smother of its cascading water tiny larvae were clinging by suckers at the ends of their tails to the downstream side of boulders. Their massed bodies clustered so thickly on some stones that they resembled moss. These immature insects were the larvae of that scourge of the north woods, the black fly.

All were busy sweeping microscopic bits of food from the water into their mouths with fan-shaped brushes. Some tossed at the end of silken threads to feed in the swifter current or let themselves down from rock to rock. Others were wrapped in golden-brown pupal cases fringed along the top with tracheal gills that provided oxygen for the transforming insects within. Still others were ready for the great adventure of riding a bubble of air upward through tumbling water to the surface.

This air is stored beneath the pupal skin. When the winged adult black fly, about $1/10$ inch long, is ready to emerge, the skin splits suddenly. Soaring upward encased in a bubble the fly pops forth into the aerial world in which it spends the rest of its life. In mountain streams of the North its emergence is an annual drama of spring.

All during the lower part of our climb these humpbacked insects whirled about us in a cloud, a cloud that moved along with us up the trail. They darted into our ears. They flew up our noses. We saw the trees through a maze of gyrating motes. But they were motes with red-hot pokers. They kept us slapping in spite of insect repellent. Their thirst for blood always seems greatest before a rain.

But as we ascended the black flies decreased. Finally we left the tormentors almost entirely behind. We ascended through zones of insects as well as through zones of birds and plants and trees as we made our two-mile climb that day. In Pinkham Notch, at the beginning of the trail, we passed bird or pin cherries with blossoms gone and fruit already swelling on the twigs. Ascending the mountain we passed other pin cherries, first with blossoms just fallen, then with flower clusters in full bloom. Similarly, as our climb carried us backward through the season, we saw the waxy white of bunchberry blossoms become tinged with pale green that grew progressively darker until the petallike bracts were as green as the leaves around them.

Beeches lifted their silvery trunks beside the trail at first. Then they fell away and we climbed through evergreens. The smell of balsam replaced the odor of the forest mold. Twigs became speckled or bearded with the gray of usnea lichen. In the still, heavy air the silence of the woods increased as we climbed. The constant murmuring of droplets of collected moisture falling from leaf to leaf among the deciduous trees of the lower slope had been left behind. The living carpet of the moss extended in ever-deeper plush across the rocks and fallen trees of the mountainside. Slow as was our climb, it was equivalent to shooting northward, jet propelled, across whole zones of life.

Botanists have calculated that, as far as changes in vegetation are concerned, an ascent of 1,000 feet up a mountain is equal to a northward journey of 600 miles. Our climb of about 2,000 feet to Hermit Lake carried us, botanically, to northern Labrador. An ascent to the treeless rocks at the top of Mt. Washington is—so far as plants are concerned—a trek into the north beyond the timberline, across the Great Barrens, above the Arctic Circle.

Twice as we climbed toward the low ceiling of the sky it descended to meet us, enveloped us in gray winter light, then passed on down the mountainside. Looking back we could see the tops of lower mountains rising through the fields of fog. Looking up we could see still other clouds coming down the slope toward us. All the stones underfoot, all the moss gardens and lichen gardens beside the trail, all the leaves of the wood oxalis, all the boughs of the firs and spruces glistened with moisture. Fine curtains of rain drifted through the air, coming and going in the uncertain mountain weather.

In spite of the rain, in spite of the lowering skies, we felt elated. We sat beside the trail on a granite rock sprinkled with mica and ate part of the maple sugar. A little later, on a particularly steep section of the climb, a college boy with a pack on his back overtook us. He eased his load onto a flat rock while we talked. Then he shouldered it again and started up the trail in high gear. Looking after him was like watching a man climbing a ladder from below.

Near the end of our long ascent we jumped from rock to rock to cross Cutler River close to its source. Somewhere beyond, just before we reached Tuckerman Ravine, a side path led us off to the right, past a deserted log shelter, among stunted spruces and balsam firs. Through wet hushed woods we finished our climb to Hermit Lake.

We saw it first through mist and mistlike rain, a brooding little tarn, about half an acre in extent, walled around with evergreens. Long shreds of fog clung to the shore-line trees. Somewhere in the misty woods behind us a red-breasted nuthatch blew its tiny, tinny horn. We had stood there hardly five minutes before the changeable mountain weather made another sudden shift. The drizzle ceased. The vapors parted, broke up, moved away down the mountainside. In the clearing air we saw the towering cliff of Lion Head lifting its brown bare rock high above us.

Long scars down the mountainside marked the paths of rockslips of the past. The upper half of the largest was filled with hard-packed snow. From the lower end of this glacier-in-miniature streams of water poured in bright streaks down the face of the rock. In such snow-springs above timberline mountain streams are born. On the back wall of Tuckerman Ravine—that vast, crescent-shaped, glacier-carved bowl high on Mt. Washington—the lifeblood of the melting snow runs in innumerable rivulets down the almost vertical rock to form the famous "Stream of a Thousand Falls." Watching the swift descent of the new-born brooks on Lion Head, I recalled the line from James Thomson's *The Seasons* about the mountain that "pours a sweep of rivers from its side." A little leatherbound copy of Thomson's grand old classic of the outdoors had traveled with us on our trip. I had picked it up just before the start in a secondhand bookshop on 33rd Street, in New York. We had read it little by little, at odd moments—under palms and beside the sea and along woodland trails. We were finishing it here, where our trip was ending, in the White Mountains of New Hampshire.

A single crow flapped silently across the tarn and disappeared into the evergreens beyond. Under the brightening sky other birds of the timberline were becoming active. Slate-colored juncos, trilling their bell-songs, flitted among the trees and the moldering, mossy stumps. They reminded us of those other juncos far to the south, high on Mt. LeConte and Clingmans Dome. Another singer, unseen among the trees, also transported us to those southern mountaintops. I was examining the new spring cones—purplish, almost like berries—on a stunted evergreen no higher than my waist, when the hollow of the lake and the wet woods around it were filled with the long, sweet, unwinding monologue of a winter wren, the song we had first heard in the Great Smokies.

Alone among the birds that live on the slopes of Mt. Washington, the slate-colored junco sometimes nests above timberline, constructing its little cup of grass and bark and roots on the ground among the boulders of the high rock barrens of the mountaintop. Another bird that nests close to timberline, even among the twisted, prostrate spruces of the heights, is the Bicknell's thrush. By field marks alone, this subspecies is almost indistinguishable from the gray-cheeked thrush. Yet during the spring breeding season the two birds can be told apart infallibly by their positions on the map. Only the Bicknell's thrush nests in the New England mountains. The gray-cheek,

Hylocichla minima, breeds beyond the borders of the United States, nesting mostly below treeline in northern Canada. Although the Bicknell's thrush is not a vertical migrant, it rises up mountainsides at the end of its northward spring flight in order to reach surroundings similar to those which its close relative travels far north to find.

During our slow descent of the rocky trail later that day we saw the bunchberry blossoms change from green to white again. We watched the spruce and balsam fir lose their dominance and beech and yellow birch appear once more. We descended through clouds and climbed downward amid curtains of fine rain. We discovered black flies waiting for us along the lower stretches of the trail. On our descent we also found ourselves moving through successive zones of singing birds. From the juncos and winter wrens and white-throated sparrows of the dark upper forest, we passed through a realm of thrushes, with olive-backed and hermit thrushes predominating, and came to the redstarts and myrtle warblers of the lower hardwoods. These ill-defined bands of avian life on a mountainside are most apparent in spring, during the season of song.

Among the varied bird voices along the trail we caught a lisping, sibilant, one-pitch little song, a mystery strain we had never heard before. It was in the woods around Hermit Lake. It was in the twilight of the mist. It was all along the upper reaches of the trail. But the singer evaded us. Time and again we heard the modest little song, swelling in the middle and diminishing toward the end, coming down to us from the tops of the evergreens. Finally Nellie spotted the singer. It was a male blackpoll warbler. Previously we had seen this bird only on migration, never on its high nesting and singing ground among the mountains.

Somewhere I have read that at the end of the day the average man is ¾ inch, and the average woman ½ inch, shorter than at the beginning. On this day of mountain climbing, when we reached the bottom of the trail on weary feet we felt as though we had been jolted down and shortened far beyond the average. But once more we had seen spring recede and advance in two great waves as we climbed and descended the mountain. At Hermit Lake we had found the counterpart of a far-northern spring—a tardier, shorter, speedier season. Some hours later, riding the famous cog railway up the other side of Mt. Washington, we went even higher, to the bare summit of the peak.

Sitting in the little one-coach train, with the blunderbuss smokestack of its tilted engine belching dry cinders behind us, we ground and puffed and labored upward. We were lifted one foot for every three we advanced. We were carried through a 15-degree drop in temperature, the mercury descending one degree for every 300 feet gain in altitude. In an hour's time, we were transported the equivalent of thirty days' advance in the northward sweep of spring.

The top of Mt. Washington is 6,288 feet above sea level; about 4,500 feet above the start of the cog railway. Although it is only 150 miles from Boston, the rock-strewn summit has the climate of the arctic barrens. The wind velocity there has reached 231 miles an hour, the highest mark ever officially recorded anywhere in the world. Fog blankets the peak more than 50 per cent of the year. During every month of the twelve it snows at the top of Mt. Washington. The highest summer temperature recorded there is 73 degrees. Rising higher than any other land in the Northeast, its rocky summit has a day forty minutes longer than that along the coast. In 1605, fifteen years before the Pilgrims came to Plymouth Rock, the lofty bulk of Mt. Washington was sighted from the sea.

Nearing timberline we watched the spruces and birches shrink and flatten and hug the ground. We saw them pressing close to the rocky soil in mats of twisted twigs or huddling together like sheep in a storm or cowering between rocks, rising barely an inch above the protecting ramparts of granite. A white birch with reddish bark and willows only a few inches high grow close to timberline on Mt. Washington. Wind and cold and rarefied air play their part in dwarfing the prostrate trees. One long-dead spruce had been polished by the wind until its trunk and limbs were as smooth as ivory and as shining as silver in the brilliance of the mountain sunlight. Among the diminutive living trees, all, even the smallest, had responded to the tardy coming of spring. We saw each flattened evergreen decorated with new-formed cones, soft and glistening with pitch.

As the trees grew smaller, the immense prospect of the mountain scene widened around us. A dwarfed world of lakes and forests and lesser mountains extended to the horizon, extended west to Lake Champlain, extended north to the green boundary of Canada. Just beyond a titanic ravine on the mountainside we saw a whole forest of dead, wind-polished trees. Flattened by some great wind in the past, the trunks all lay in the same direction like a swath of hay after the swing of a scythe.

Across the mountaintop ran a giant's jumble of gray rocks splotched with green lichens. When we first swept our eyes over this expanse from the vantage point of Summit House, it seemed as dead and sterile as the moon. But when we looked closer, stooping to examine the little patches of thin soil accumulated between the rocks of the fell-fields, we found gray-green mosses and lacy lichens and low-lying alpine plants already in bloom. Spring had climbed the mountain before us. By the tenth of June these flowers that bloom above the clouds have begun to open their petals.

Writing in *Appalachia* some years ago, Stuart K. Harris noted the plants he found in alpine gardens within ten minutes' walk of the Lakes-of-the-Clouds hut above timberline on Mt. Washington. His list included rhodora, spring beauty, Labrador tea, alpine azalea, crowberry, mountain heath, bog bilberry, and the evergreen moss plant with needlelike leaves—*Cassiope hypnoides*. One of the alpine plants he found on the mountaintop, *Diapensia lapponica*, is a close relative of the little pyxie moss we had seen in the sandy pine barrens of New Jersey. Like *Pyxidanthera*, it grows close to the ground in dark mosslike mats against which the white flowers stand out conspicuously.

A tribute to the beauty of such mountaintop flowers in the spring is contained in the name of the trail we saw wandering from north to south across the rock barrens of the summit. It is known as the Alpine Garden Trail. At frequent intervals along its course mounds of boulders mark the way as an aid to hikers caught in sudden fogs or blizzards on the mountain. As we were gazing down on this line of cairns from the highest rocks of the summit we became aware of a spot of bright yellow dancing toward us over the gray expanse of stones. It was a tiger swallowtail butterfly, a colorful insect we had seen all along the way from the Far South to New England. Over our heads, over the streamlined Summit House, on into the west it fluttered. We wondered what alpine blooms had fed it as it journeyed across the treeless roof of the New England mountains.

The cairn-marked path below us forms one section of the long Appalachian Trail. How many times had we crossed the track of this trail during our zigzag northward trek! Now we were looking at it for a final time. We were parting company with it as we were parting company with the season. This rocky summit represented the farthest limit of our journey with the spring—through space. One day more and we would reach the end of our journey with the spring—through time.

The Longest Day

DURING all the days of our travels—in the Everglades, on a barrier island, in the Great Smokies, amid the pine barrens and among the green hills of the border—we had wondered vaguely about this final twenty-four hours of spring. What would the day be like? Where would we be? What would we be doing? In what surroundings, bright or gloomy, would we come to the end of our travels with a season?

Now we knew the answers. This was the final day, the summit of the spring.

We awoke before four o'clock. Already a clear sky was brightening above the birchtops outside our cabin window in Crawford Notch. By four, robins were singing and the wooded steeps above us echoed with the calling of an ovenbird. Then came the pure sweet strain of the whitethroat, most moving of all the voices of this north-country choir. Long before five even the bottom of the deep ravine, where dusk comes swiftly and dawn is retarded, was filled with daylight. With this sunrise the tide of light reached its annual flood to begin the long slow rollback to the low ebb of December.

During that day—between the earliest sunrise and the latest sunset of the spring—we roamed amid the beauty and grandeur of the mountains. They formed a fitting climax for our travels with the spring. Where else except in America would that journey have carried us through such variedly impressive scenery, such altering forms of plant and animal life, such diverse events of natural history interest?

I remember we stopped for a long time that afternoon to watch the dance of the mayflies above Echo Lake and Profile Lake below the Great Stone Face. All through Franconia Notch, over the two lakes and the Pemigewasset River, these pale-yellow ephemera drifted through the air, luminous in every open space lighted by the lengthening rays of late afternoon. Half a hundred hung in a small cloud above one spot on the shore of Echo Lake. Spotlighted by long fingers of sunshine coming through the treetops, they bobbed and turned and fluttered in a shining throng that extended from about two to six feet above the ground. Here hour after hour they engaged in a curious mating performance such as we had never witnessed before.

Every few minutes one of the dancers would leave the throng and climb steeply into the air. At a height of eight or ten feet it would turn downward and plunge in an almost vertical descent through the mayfly cloud. A foot or so from the ground it would level off and curve upward again. During each swift descent, as the diving insect passed through the bobbing dancers, three or four would dart in pursuit. Apparently the plunging mayfly was the female, those that joined in the pursuit the males. All through the sunset and on into the twilight this love dance of the ephemera continued.

A mile to the north, where Lafayette Brook tumbles down a rocky ravine on a plunging descent toward Gale River, we heard the last bird chorus of the spring. All up the mountain steeps hermit thrushes and whitethroats and wood thrushes and veeries and olive-backed thrushes sang in the sunset. From time to time a small dark form fluttered into the air above the trees of the ravine. Clear and sweet, a warbling, twittering jumble of notes came down to us. We were hearing the flight song of the ovenbird—the mysterious, never-identified "night warbler" of Thoreau's *Journal.*

In this choir whitethroats predominated. We grew to recognize different singers by variations in pitch and quality. One would begin with a long, exquisite violin note and others up the ravine, some higher pitched, others lower pitched, would repeat the sad sweet overtones of their melody. It is a song of the New World, a song of hope and confidence; it is a song of the Old World, a song of wisdom and sadness. It seems to put to music the bravery of the spirit, the courage of the frail.

In an often-quoted admonition, Mark Twain advised famous men to think up their last words beforehand rather than to depend on the inspiration of the moment. If we had planned beforehand the ending of spring's longest day, nothing we could have imagined would have excelled the glory of that final sunset. From the high aerie of the bridge spanning Lafayette Brook we watched it spread across the sky over the darkening mountains that, range on range, rolled away into the west. As the warmth of the sunlight ebbed and the air grew chill in the valleys below us, rivers of mist rose above rivers of water. The winding course of every stream was marked by vapor in the air above it. Gazing down, we could trace the progress of invisible watercourses meandering through the forest below. Contour lines had been traced on the air by mist.

During one time of strange and eerie beauty, all the curls and billows of the mist glowed red, rising like slow tongues and sheets of fire above the treetops tinged by the flames of the western sky. Nowhere else on our trip except over the lonely barrier beach at Bull's Island had we encountered so memorable a sunset as this final fading of the daylight in these final hours of spring. It was the sunset of the day, the sunset of the season, the sunset of our trip with the spring.

Unseen in the brilliance of midday, a new moon—a faint greenish-silver parenthesis mark in the sky—had moved across the zenith. Now, as the colors faded in the west and the long slow twilight of the summer solstice began, it increased in brightness. Below it in the deep dusk of the valley toward Franconia, pinpoints of electric lights at farms and villages glittered in the gathering night. Here in this wild and beautiful spot amid the mountains, the dark woods, the rising mist, the new moon hanging above the silhouettes of the peaks, we waited, in spite of the night chill, until the last sunlight of the spring had ebbed from the sky.

Miles to the south, in a cabin by the Pemigewasset, later that night we built a blazing fire of birch logs in the fireplace. We sat for a long time in the warmth of this flickering hearthfire talking of our journey with a season, of our incomparable good fortune, of the adventures we had shared together. Never in our lives would there be another spring like this. It was late when we stepped out to look at the sky. From horizon to horizon the heavens were clear, filled with the glinting of the stars. And almost as we looked, in the night, under the stars, spring was gone. It was summer when we awoke.

Everywhere in the Northern Hemisphere spring had come and gone. The season had swept far to the north; it had climbed mountains; it had passed into the sky. Like a sound, spring spreads and spreads until it is swallowed up in space. Like the wind, it moves across the map invisible; we see it only in its effects. It appears like the tracks of the breeze on a field of wheat, like shadows of windblown clouds, like tossing branches that reveal the presence of the invisible, the passing of the unseen. So spring had spread from Georgia to North Carolina, from Virginia to Canada, leaving consequences beyond number in its wake. We longed for a thousand springs on the road instead of this one. For spring is like life. You never grasp it entire; you touch it here, there; you know it only in parts and fragments. Reflecting thus as we started south on that first morning of summer—on the day of the summer solstice, the longest day of the year—we were well aware that it is only on the calendar that spring comes to so sudden a termination. In reality its end is a gradual change. Season merges with season in a slow transition into another life.

Driving home to a house where all the calendars were marked February and where piles of mail recorded four months on their postmarks, we crossed the Whitestone Bridge onto Long Island. And then—so near the irrevocable end of our journey—we turned aside, we wandered about, we made delays. We followed the Jones Beach parkway to its end, we visited the Massapequa cedars, we stopped at a pond where wild ducks sunned themselves on a grassy bank, we drove nearly a hundred miles before we swung into our driveway. Even then I let the engine idle, loath to cut the switch. Reluctantly I turned the key. The sudden stopping of the motor put a period to our long adventure with the spring.

JOURNEY INTO SUMMER

Franconia Sunrise

DOWN the long drop of the mountainside Lafayette Brook trailed the white thread of its foaming waters. Its headlong descent carried it seventy feet beneath the green bridge rail against which we leaned in the June dawn. Behind us the Franconia Mountains rose darkly, flinging an immense shadow mile after mile over the outspread land below.

As we watched, the farther edge of this shadow crept stealthily toward us. No direct movement caught our eye. But each time we glanced back more of the valley lay in sunshine. Over the roads and pastures, over the barns and houses, over Gale River and Meadow Brook, the narrowing shade trailed its farther edge. The invisible sun behind us rose; the visible shadow before us shrank. The effect was a curious illusion. Dawn and the light of the day seemed advancing toward us not out of the familiar east but out of the foreign west.

Here, in another year, in this same spot, on this same bridge, just north of Franconia Notch in the White Mountains of New Hampshire, we had leaned against this same rail at the end of our journey north with the spring. That was the sundown; this was the dawn. That was the end of one journey with a season; this was the beginning of another. Here, where we had bade farewell to the last sunset of spring, we were standing in the initial sunrise of summer.

Our car, this time blue and white, stood waiting beside the road. For thousands of miles, through more than half the states of the Union, from the backbone of New England—the White Mountains—to the backbone of the continent—the Rockies—it would carry us through the second season of the year.

Spring and autumn are constantly changing, active seasons. Summer is more stable, more predictable. We tend to consider it the high point of the year, with spring moving toward it and autumn retreating from it. In summer, that season of warmth and sunshine, life is easier, food more abundant. Babies born then have a lower infant mortality rate than at any other season of the year. To the average person, summer is the friend, winter the enemy. The Twilight of the Gods, in the old Norse legend, came with years that had no summers. Instinctively summer is accepted as the normal condition of the earth, winter as the abnormal. Summer is "the way it should be."

Summer is vacation time, sweet clover time, swing and seesaw time, watermelon time, swimming and picnic and camping and Fourth-of-July time. This is the season of gardens and flowers, of haying and threshing. Summer is the period when birds have fewer feathers and furbearers have fewer hairs in their pelts. Through it runs the singing of insects, the sweetness of ripened fruit, the perfume of unnumbered blooms. It is a time of lambs and colts, kittens and puppies, a time to grow in. It is fishing time, canoeing time, baseball time. It is, for millions of Americans, "the good old summertime."

But America has many summers. Its continental span embraces the summer of the shore, the summer of the forest, the summer of the Great Plains, the summer of the mountains. We had chosen our general route to carry us through the greatest variety. We would see the season along lake shores, on the mountain heights, amid swamps, in the cool north woods and in areas where falling rain would be sucked up by the thirsty atmosphere before it reached the ground.

We had awakened that morning in the same small cabin beside the Pemigewasset River where we had sat before a fire of blazing logs that last night of spring. When at last Nellie and I climbed into our loaded car, sunshine filled all the valley. I started the engine. We were at the beginning of what the old-time writers would have called "our joyful travels" through the many summers of the land.

Smuggler's Notch

EDEN PHILLPOTTS, the English author who spent most of his life writing about lonely Dartmoor, tells of meeting a stranger at a luncheon in London. The man asked him if he knew Dartmoor.

"Not as well as I could wish," Phillpotts answered.

It developed that his companion had once motored across the sparsely settled tableland.

"Hardly a thing you would do twice, certainly."

Phillpotts suggested the next time he try walking across it. The man was greatly amused by this advice.

"Surely," he said, "no sane man would waste his time like that."

Yet Phillpotts knew that the way to become acquainted with an area intimately, to appreciate it best, is to walk over it. And the slower the walk the better. For a naturalist, the most productive pace is a snail's pace. A large part of his walk is often spent standing still. A mile an hour may well be fast enough. For his goal is different from that of the pedestrian. It is not how far he goes that counts; it is not how fast he goes; it is how much he sees.

And, in deeper truth, it is not *just* how much he sees. It is how much he appreciates, how much he feels. Nature affects our minds as light affects the photographic emulsion on a film. Some films are more sensitive than others; some minds are more receptive. To one observer a thing means much; to another the same thing means almost nothing. As the poet William Blake wrote in one of his letters: "The Tree which moves some to tears of joy is in the Eyes of others only a Green thing that stands in the way."

EACH SECTION OF THE COUNTRY stimulates some special kind of interest. The bare, dry Southwest lies outspread like the pages of a geology textbook. The clothed green hills of New England stretch away, an inviting guide to botany. Here, on the second day of our journey, at Smuggler's Notch in the Green Mountains of Vermont, it was the ferns that attracted our particular attention. They were everywhere—at the base of the gray precipices, under the trees, overhanging the edges of the springs, massed around the fallen rocks, bordering the little stream where water thrushes sang, following cracks on the sheer cliff-sides. Vermont is fernland. More than eighty different species of these graceful plants are native to the state. In the pastures and woodlands of two adjoining farms, a botanist once found thirty different kinds of ferns. Appropriately, there is a Fernville not too far from the capital of the state.

Since early days, the vicinity of Smuggler's Notch and Mt. Mansfield has been a happy hunting ground for the student of ferns. It was here, on June 15, 1876, that Cyrus G. Pringle added the beautiful green spleenwort, *Asplenium viride*, to the flora of the United States. For a long time it was thought that this rare fern grew only in Vermont. Later it was reported from a few other scattered stations in northern New England. Always it has been found rooted in the same habitat, among cool, moist and shady ledges of limestone. Its discoverer, Cyrus Pringle, was one of America's pioneer collectors. He added sixteen new species to the lists and, in his latter years, he could write: "My hands have gathered all but thirty-six of the one hundred and sixty-five species of North American ferns."

As the day advanced Nellie and I wandered along the notch among the beech ferns and the shield ferns, the polypodies and spleenworts. Their greens were infinitely varied. Their forms ranged from the sturdy to fronds so filmy they seemed made of gauze. In spaces between the green fountain sprays of the fronds, among the clumps and masses and clusters of the ferns, wildflowers grew, red trilliums and violets and the little puffs of white froth of the foam flower, *Tiarella cordifolia*. Under the overhang of one huge boulder, we found blue and white and yellow violets blooming close together.

It was afternoon when Nellie made the great discovery of the day. The name, Smuggler's Notch, dates back to the stormy period that preceded the War of 1812. Contraband goods from Canada passed through this remote defile on its way to the markets of Boston. At one point the base of the cliff is pierced by a small, dank cave where, reputedly, the smugglers stored their cargoes. We were working our way toward this cavern beside ledges, moist and mossy, the home of delicate maidenhair and long beech ferns. Moisture gleamed on the rocks

ROBIN at its nest in a northern evergreen. In their
last stages as nestlings, the young are nearly fledged.

FERNS, violets and foam flowers rooted in the moist soil of Smuggler's Notch. Here, also, the green spleenwort grows.

PAINTED trillium rising from the moldering floor of
the forest high on Mt. Mansfield, in northern Vermont.

MAYFLIES clinging to the trunk of a tree. With the coming of evening the insects rise in their aerial mating dance.

THE KANKAKEE on a summer day. During the nights of early July, fireflies flash in the darkness all along its banks.

FAWN of the white-tailed deer on the Door Peninsula of Wisconsin. Its age, when photographed, was about two weeks.

SUNSET light is reflected on the water of a slow stream
that winds in a shallow flow across this northern bog.

SHOWY lady's slipper, delicately perfumed and daintily colored, blooms in a boggy stretch of the Door Peninsula.

NELLIE searching for summer birds along a trail that
follows the overgrown summit of a ridge in Minnesota.

THUNDERHEAD lifting its tumbling vapor high into
the summer sky above a field where the wheat is ripening.

PRAIRIE DOGS in a friendly meeting below the great monolith of Devil's Tower in northeastern Wyoming.

AT EASE, this prairie dog sits upright beside its
burrow where it can plunge to safety in emergencies.

THE COLORADO ROCKIES, high in the Gunnison country near Emerald Lake, photographed late in the summer.

MOUNTAINS IN FLOWER above timberline. Late in August the tundra meadows of the Rockies are carpeted with blooms.

STORM-WRACKED spruce high on a mountainside in Colorado has been sculptured by gale winds along the timberline.

SHADOW of Pike's Peak stretches east in the last
sunset of summer until its tip reaches the horizon.

around them. Above us, in a tangle, the voice of a winter wren rambled on and on. It was then that Nellie noticed a fringing of small fern leaves following a crevice in the limestone.

We bent closer to examine them. They were daintily formed and pale green in color. We felt the stalk. It was thin and flexible. We noted its color. It was smooth and green for most of its length, scaled and brown near its base. Point by point we checked off its identification. There could be no doubt. So long after Pringle had first discovered it—in days, as he put it, "when the feelings were young and the world was new"—we were seeing the rare and beautiful green spleenwort.

The next morning found us among ferns again, winding upward between dense walls of interrupted and hay-scented ferns, following the twisting, steeply climbing dirt road that lifted us 2,000 feet and more above the green spleenwort of Smuggler's Notch to the summit of Mt. Mansfield.

This loftiest of the Green Mountains, the highest point in Vermont, rises 4,393 feet above sea level. Along the far horizon, on clear days, you can see the Adirondacks beyond Lake Champlain, even Mt. Royal overlooking the city of Montreal. On this morning the air was filled with shining haze. The radius of our view was shortened.

For five of its 255 miles, the Long Trail, Vermont's "Footpath in the Wilderness" that follows the crest of the Green Mountains from the Massachusetts line to the Canadian border, runs along the profile of Mt. Mansfield. We followed sections of it north and south. It plunged us into low forests of twisted, storm-wracked trees and carried us around boggy depressions speckled densely with the white tufts of the cottongrass, the sedge that, in the Arctic, provides Eskimos with wicks for their lamps. It led us by humus-rich banks where modest white flowers rose on slender stems above the dark green of three-lobed leaves, flowers that are fertilized almost entirely by a tiny fungus gnat. We pulled away a little of the spongy loam and revealed the roots. Against the black mold, each shone with metallic brilliance. It seemed plated with gold. Appropriately, the common name of this wildflower of the moist woodlands is goldthread.

But the flower of flowers on the mountaintop that day was the painted trillium. All through the mossy forest, under the trees and around the little glades, these great white-and-crimson blooms were scattered singly and in clusters. The three petals, waxy white, stood apart, recurved and wavy-edged. Down the center of each ran an inverted V of rich red that widened toward the base. I sat down on a fallen tree at the edge of a small opening, close beside two perfect flowers. Camera ready, I waited for the sun to emerge from a cloud overhead. Time passed and Nellie wandered away on the trail of a siren bird-sound, an unfamiliar kind of "chewy buzz" that proved to be the call of the junco on its nesting ground.

Minute after minute went by. Overhead a crown or cap of clouds floated just above the mountaintop. The cloud-maker was the mountain itself. Warmer air, rising along the slopes, reached the top, cooled and condensed to form a gray-white umbrella of vapor that remained outspread most of the day. Even when the rest of the sky became almost entirely clear, this floating cap clung stubbornly in place. All around the edges I could see the vapor constantly dissolving and reforming. Only when the sun sank below the edge of this cloud umbrella and its rays reached the deeply shaded trillium flowers, could I take the picture I desired. So I waited.

Half an hour went by. Nellie came back and started off along the trail in the opposite direction. The sun almost came out, then disappeared, then almost came out again. Each time its pale yellow disk seemed to be breaking through the thinning vapor near the edge, I raised my camera. But invariably new clouds formed swiftly, spreading outward in a swirling mass and dimming the illumination. Thus I waited for an hour, two hours, before the sun finally dropped below the crown of clouds and shone directly on the trillium.

But those two hours were among the most pleasant, the least wasted of the day. Sitting on the trunk of the uprooted tree or wandering about the little glade, surrounded by the silence of that windless June day, breathing in the pure, balsam-scented air of the mountaintop, I was on the edge of wildness and little things of interest were all around me. I investigated the minute world of a knothole with its tiny inhabitants and a microclimate of its own. I laid my ear close to the moss and moldering leaves, listening for little sounds, and once caught the Lilliputian scratchings of a beetle pulling itself over the spongy loam. I explored among the lichen-clad balsam firs, with their wind-tempered branches as unyielding as iron. Everywhere across the forest floor the pageant of decay advanced in silence, leaves moldering, soil being born, the great wheel of change endlessly turning.

The next day, continuing west, we left the ferns and flowers of Smuggler's Notch and Mt. Mansfield and all of New England behind us.

Mayfly Island

A LITTLE after eight o'clock in the morning, on the twenty-sixth of June, a street sweeper in downtown Sandusky, Ohio, was busy shoveling from the gutter into a two-wheeled cart bushels of mayflies. Warm and humid weather had followed wind and rain. From the mud bottom of the shallow western end of Lake Erie the insects, gauzy-winged and trailing threadlike tails, were emerging in numbers beyond counting. A "mayfly storm," one of the early-summer events we had hoped most to see, was building up along the Erie shore.

The shallowest, the muddiest, the warmest and next to the smallest of the five Great Lakes, Erie, over much of its bottom, is a vast incubator of mayfly life. Some years, during the height of the invasion, truckload after truckload of the frail insects is hauled away from Sandusky streets. The arrival of the mayflies varies with the temperature from year to year. The first of the insects appear sometimes as early as May 17, other times as late as June 23. For weeks thereafter the great mating flights continue.

All along the shore of this shallow inland sea, the coming of the mayflies each year brings altered habits to the dwellers in towns and cities. Merchants turn off their neon signs at dusk. Outdoor painting comes almost to a standstill because a freshly coated house soon becomes furry with adhering insects. Traffic slows down on streets that are slippery with the crushed bodies of the mayflies. Some dwellers along the lake shore disappear for a week or two at the height of the invasion. They are allergic to mayflies. With eyes swollen, red and watering, they are miserable with "Junebug fever" as long as the fluttering hosts remain. In Toledo and other Lake Erie cities, property values are sometimes lower in sections where the insects arrive annually in the greatest numbers.

The street sweeper, a wizened little Italian smoking a short-stemmed black pipe, gave me a version of the origin of the insects that I found was widely held in the region, namely, that they emerge from unfertilized fish eggs. Or, as he put it:

"When fish eggs no hatch, they fly away."

Not long afterwards I encountered a somewhat different version when I fell into conversation with the owner of a store who had just finished brushing mayflies off his awning. His explanation:

"The larvae generate in the residue of fish along the shore."

On a street corner, while waiting for a traffic light to change, an old gentleman with watery eyes confided:

"I tell you, no man knows where they hatch!"

The captain of a lake steamer, who spent his days plowing through the very water from which the mayflies emerged by the million, told me in all seriousness that the insect hosts were born in the marshes of Canada.

"They all come from Canada," he said. "They are blown clear across Lake Erie by the wind."

Near a bank on a main street, a florid man with a voice of authority proclaimed:

"The origination of the *lava* is a complete mystery!"

The same man pointed to mayflies on the sidewalk and observed:

"Once they land, they never rise again!"

Even as he spoke, mayflies were taking off around his feet without in the least disturbing his conviction of the truth of his assertion.

For a time I sat on a green park bench and watched a gray and white kitten playing with mayflies. After a while a man sat down beside me. Cats, he said, rarely eat the insects. There just isn't anything to eat.

"There is nothing to one of those Canadian Soldiers," he declared. "Nothing but wings and tail—absolutely nothing—just nothing."

This name—Canadian Soldiers—is the one most commonly applied to mayflies along the south shore of Lake Erie. Incidentally, along the north shore, in Canada, they are called Yankee Soldiers. Other names we encountered along the way were: lake flies, fish flies, June flies, Junebugs and twenty-four-hour bugs. Along the St. Lawrence they are known as eel flies and on the Mississippi they are referred to as willow bugs. A rather universal idea seemed to be that they are literally the children of a day, that they hatch—with wings—from the eggs, live exactly twenty-four hours and die.

In truth, the clouds of insects that sometimes rise like smoke from the evening waters of Lake Erie have already lived for two years unseen on the mud of the bottom. Only at the very end of their lives are they creatures of the air. Only during the last small fraction of their existence are they visible to us. Before that comes the preliminary life, long, hidden, aquatic, the slow growing up.

Thirty times and more the nymphs molt their skins as they gradually become larger. They spend their days secreted in burrows in the soft mud, coming forth to hunt for small organic matter, feeding most actively at night. Because the great pioneer microscopist, Jan Swammerdam, of Holland, always found muddy particles in the intestines of mayfly nymphs, it was believed for generations that they lived on a diet of mud. Before coming to the surface for their final aquatic molt, they develop dark wing pads. Air, which aids in splitting the shell in this last larval molt, makes the maturing insect buoyant. It rises to the surface, the shell of its skin splits along the back, the winged insect emerges. This event, multiplied a millionfold, takes place in the calm air of the early evening hours.

Three species of *Hexagenia* mayflies take part in the Erie emergences. They are *Hexagenia limbata, Hexagenia rigida* and *Hexagenia affiliata.* The first is the most abundant, accounting for more than 12 per cent of the total fauna of the lake bottom. No other insect in the waters of Lake Erie approaches the mayfly in numbers. Always the nymphs on the mud of the bottom are of two sizes. The larger one represents the brood that will next emerge while the smaller, less fully developed ones are the nymphs that will wait until the second year before coming to the surface and attaining wings.

That afternoon we rode a ferry across ten miles of water to Kelleys Island. With its maximum width of seven miles, its shoreline of about eighteen, its more than thirty miles of roads, it is the largest of that small chain of island stepping-stones that leads out into the lake above Sandusky Bay. Long ago the island's red cedar forests were felled to provide fuel for the *Walk-in-the-Water*, the first steamer to navigate Lake Erie. Centuries before that, about 1625 it is believed, the Indians of the region engraved their history in petroglyphs on what has become world famous as Inscription Rock. And infinitely long before that, granite boulders pressed down by the weight of the ice sheet had carved grooves in its softer limestone, providing geologists with "the finest examples of glacial scouring in the western hemisphere."

Around and around like the hands of a great clock that afternoon and evening Nellie and I circled the island. Mayflies clung to the tree trunks, bent down the leaves of the roadside plants. Their feet gripped the side of Inscription Rock amid the ancient petroglyphs. They fluttered above the glacial grooves, frail, gauzy, ephemeral and transient, the life of the day above rock that had known the advance and retreat of the Ice Age. Here the great cogs and the little cogs of nature were meeting and overlapping.

Here we were face to face with a paradox. Individually knowing a winged life so fleeting that it has become a symbol of the ephemeral, the mayfly, as an insect form, has endured through aeons of change. It fluttered around the dinosaurs and retreated before the glaciers. It is part of that bewildering spectacle of nature, the endurance of the frail.

At the time of our visit the human population of the island was about 600. The mayfly population was astronomical. On these offshore islands the insects sometimes collect along the waterline in windrows three feet deep. At the approach of a visitor, gray ground spiders retreat in waves over this Gargantuan feast. Dwellers on the islands often scoop up the dead insects in bushel baskets and spade them into their gardens as fertilizer. In years of greatest abundance they may see a dark wall of mayflies approaching across the water, carried toward them by the evening breeze. On almost any day during mayfly time the direction of the wind the previous evening will be found recorded in the distribution of the insect hosts on the island. They are concentrated in greatest numbers at the windward edge.

On this particular day, all across the northern portion of Kelleys Island the multitudes of the mayflies were at their high tide. Here, where the shore road left the western edge and turned toward the east, the length of a hayfield slanted down toward the sinking sun. Everywhere across it the stems and leaves of the timothy hay were bending with a burden of clinging insects. Each gauzy wing shone luminescent in the lowered sunbeams. From end to end, the field was swept by captured light, by the yellowish glow of pale, translucent wings.

All the roadsides were furred and fringed with resting insects. All the fence posts, all the telephone poles, all the tree trunks were so densely covered they seemed wearing pelts of mayfly wings. As far as we could see up into the trees, the trunks and boughs and leaves were shaggy with insects. A brown fringing of wings hung beneath each branch, and below the larger leaves clusters of threads dangled down— the filament-tails of the clinging mayflies. Each mass of thorns projecting from the trunks of the honey locusts was festooned with gauzy insects. They covered the dogwood, the poison ivy, the wild raspberries, the Queen Anne's lace, the bindweed, the sweet clover. Willows and rushes seemed lifted from the water, dripping with mayflies. Infinitesimal weight added to infinitesimal weight bent down the leaves of the cattails. Where a green rowboat was anchored near a light, bushels of the brown husks of yesterday's mayflies were heaped on the seats and bottom.

Whenever we touched a bough or bush, a sudden puff of fluttering insects filled the air. Each time I stepped among the roadside weeds to obtain some closer look, I returned covered from head to foot with their clinging forms. Never eating in their adult form, possessing only atrophied mouth parts, these ephemeral creatures neither bite nor sting. What makes them objectionable to the average person is mainly the dead-fish smell of their decaying masses and the oily brown stains, difficult to remove, that their crushed bodies leave on clothing. Before we climbed into the car we always hastily picked off the mayflies that clung to us like burs. They alighted on us almost faster than we could toss them away. The next morning we counted forty-three fluttering about inside the car.

Everywhere, on all the trees and plants, throughout all the unnumbered legions of the ephemera around us, an event was taking place that is unique. Only the mayflies, among all the hundreds of thousands of species of insects, molt again after they attain their winged, adult form. Little winged insects never become big winged insects; once they develop wings their size is fixed. However, when the mayflies lift into the air from the floating canoes of their cast nymphal skins, their bodies and wings are completely sheathed in a thin pellicle. Hours later, sometime before the great mating dance that climaxes their lives, they make a final emergence, leaving delicate molts, frail ghosts of themselves, behind.

Wherever we looked, as evening drew on, this transformation was occurring. In brighter colors, more shining bodies, the imagoes were emerging as we watched. Carefully, through a rent running back from the head, these mayflies, an inch or more in length, pulled themselves free. Last of all, the slender threads of their tails were withdrawn from the sheath of the pellicle. Here and there an impatient one took wing with its shed skin, still attached to the tail filaments, trailing behind it as it flew like a target sleeve towed by a military airplane.

The ash-gray husks of life, the little ghosts this transformation left behind, were anchored thickly on every support. The breeze stirred them and loosened the hold of many. They drifted down in a dry rain around us. They alighted weightlessly on our hands and arms. They reached the road with a sound like the soft sifting of pine needles in a forest. Where a burdock lifted the large green saucer of a leaf, its center was white with accumulated skins. Under every spreading tree the road was coated. The cast pellicles lay like tiny twigs or fruit stems, crisscrossing, piling upon one another over square yards of hardtop.

Each delicate jewel of a shed skin that we examined, now empty, had so short a time before been occupied by vibrant life. More and more of the insects, freed of this last encumbrance, rose into the air. They poured up from the grass, fluttered from the tree trunks, took wing from the leaves to join the evening dance. At times the whole island appeared moving and alive. In the wake of the dying breeze the evening was perfectly calm. The insect clouds, mounting from the vegetation, became ever more dense. The mayflies rose and dipped, zoomed and plunged. Up and down, up and down, all in constant motion, the moving bodies shimmered like super heat waves before the landscape. Cloud on cloud, each populated by an infinite number of dancers, they extended away across hundreds of acres of open land. Millions—billions—numbers lost their meaning.

More and more we saw mayflies linked together in the air. Usually these paired insects drifted away downward. But occasionally the double forms rose higher and higher among the dancers until they were lost to sight. Into the water of the lake each fertilized female ejects about 1,500 eggs which sink immediately. Usually in less than two weeks, minute nymphs, equipped with tiny gills, hatch from the eggs and burrow into the mud. The long, gradual development of another generation has begun.

Slowly we circled the island for a final time. Where the lighted south road leads to the ferry dock, each street lamp was the hub of a wheeling, spinning cloud of mayflies. On the ground beneath, the insects piled up, already heaped into mounds a foot deep. From top to bottom, an illuminated outdoor telephone booth was plastered with clinging mayflies. When we paused momentarily beneath a street lamp the white hood of our car was almost instantly covered.

What purpose is served by the mayfly's passion for the light? All around the lake that night, hundreds of thousands of lamps were holding the insects prisoners. Instinct seemed defeating itself. The pull of light seemed stronger than any other force. The fact that all these lights were man-created may supply the answer. They are only recent additions to the mayfly's world. Some instinctive predilection for the light that would, for instance, draw them higher among the trees at twilight or pull them to the lighted surface from the muddy bottom of the lake, may have played its part in the long history of their kind. Man and his inventions are, after all, comparatively modern innovations. The mayfly had lived for infinite stretches of time before either appeared. As so often is the case, what we are observing is the functioning of an age-old instinct suddenly confronted by man-produced changes, an instinct that was originally developed and adapted to a manless world.

When I glanced at my watch, I saw it was nearly ten o'clock. We hurried toward the dock. It was time for the next-to-the-last ferry to leave for the mainland. But we saw no boat. We saw no lights. Then we caught sight of a dark form moving silently away into the night. We had expected to see the glitter of many ferry lights. But there were none. The boat was departing furtively, like a vessel in wartime, stealing away with darkened decks across the mayfly-infested waters. We sat in the night, wondering if it would return, until after eleven o'clock. Suddenly it loomed out of the darkness. Plowing through water completely mantled by a churning blanket of fallen mayflies, it maneuvered to the dock. The white beam of a spotlight shot along the ramp, lighting our way. A cloud of insects swirled around it. We rolled onto a deck thickly carpeted with mayflies. The captain climbed hastily back to the pilothouse, brushing off the insects as he went, and slammed the door. Diesels throbbed below us and we pulled away. Instantly all lights, except necessary navigation lamps and a single spotlight pointing straight ahead, blinked off. So we began our darkened passage in a mayfly blackout.

The stars were bright in the sky above us. Stepping from the car, I clutched the rail just in time as my feet shot out from under me. The whole deck seemed thickly coated with grease or slippery oil. Hand over hand, as though on a ship in a storm, I made my way forward. Around the single white eye of the spotlight, the superstructure of the ferry was hidden beneath masses of hanging insects. And all over the forward deck beyond I discovered an extraordinary sight. Thousands of mayflies had landed there. But they rested in no haphazard fashion. In the manner of a partially opened fan, the multitude spread out as the path of the light widened. All the insects pointed inward toward the source of the illumination. Their bodies, each a fragment of a radiating line, suggested iron filings in a magnetic field. They all remained motionless, charmed by the sun of the single spotlight.

Even before we approached the dock, deckhands were already sweeping away the mayflies. The accumulating grease of their crushed bodies becomes progressively more dangerous as the evening advances. Each night, all through the mayfly season, the ferry is thoroughly hosed off at the end of the final run.

One o'clock had come and gone before we reached our mainland cabin. Late as it was, we were an hour or more going to sleep. Our minds still teemed with memories of all those clouds upon clouds of dancing life.

The Orchid Ridges

DAY after day now we saw no newspapers. We heard no radio. The world wagged on without us. In June how good is the news when you get it only from nature!

Up and over and down in a 1,000-mile swing, in the days that followed, we circled the edge of the Lower Peninsula of Michigan. All along the way names on the map—names with romantic, far-off pioneer associations, names that echoed in memory like Thunder Bay and Presque Isle and the Straits of Mackinac, like Manitou Island and Manistee and Charlevoix—became transformed into definite images, sharply defined scenes that would remain in our minds.

Somewhere along our way, on some nameless country road, in the valley of the Kankakee River, after we had crossed the line into Indiana, we passed a hayfield at sunset. The windrows curved away like brown rollers in a surf of sun-dried grass, each shot through with shadings of tan and gold and yellow-green. Redwings rode on the crests of these windrow-waves while grackles, hunting crickets and grasshoppers, investigated caverns in the hay. The air, resting at the end of the day, lay calm, redolent with the early-summer perfume of the drying grass. About us, all across the countryside, the whistle of the meadowlark, the jingle of the bobolink, the last song of the day for robin and vesper sparrow, carried far through the quiet air.

Later we came by this field again. The cerise glow had faded from the sky and the deep purple of twilight was merging with the velvet blackness of the night. Birds had fallen silent. The rolling waves of the windrows now stretched away unseen. The beauty of the day was gone. But the beauty of the night had replaced it. For, from end to end, the field was spangled with winking, dancing lights. They rose and fell. They flashed on and off. They waxed and waned in brilliance. At this same moment, over hundreds of square miles around us, this eerie beauty of the fairy-dance of *Wah-Wah-Taysee*, Hiawatha's little firefly, was part of the summer night.

For a long time after we had left this field behind, we followed firefly roads. We made turns, passed dark barns, went by lonely farmhouses where moths fluttered at the lighted window screens. Around us always, wherever we went, streamed the sparks of living fire. We saw them twinkling over the roadside vegetation, above the fields of grain, in the blackness of maple shade, amid the mistily white, faintly seen, flower masses of the elderberry bushes. They passed us in a constant meteor shower. So we wandered—half-lost and forgetful of time. For hours we followed little roads, roads without a name, roads we could never find again, but roads we will never forget.

Once we went by a pasture field where black-and-white cows, vaguely seen, were browsing. In the stillness of the night we could hear them cropping, pulling away mouthfuls of grass as they fed. Three or four of the animals were bending down to drink at a small pond or puddle near the fence. About them swirled the gleams of the fireflies and all around their lowered heads the surface of the pool was sprinkled with a hundred glittering, moving points of reflected light. Somewhere, far above the field, above the miles on miles of drifting sparks of heatless light, a killdeer speeding through the darkened sky repeated three times its wild and lonely call.

THE FIREFLIES OF THE KANKAKEE clung to vegetation that now lay 200 miles behind us. We had worked north, first among gravel pits and quarries, then over Illinois flatland, cereal land, with misty trees far across the prairie. We had encountered our first western meadowlark and at an intersection of superhighways beyond the suburbs of Chicago we had observed the complications of modern life epitomized in a traffic sign: "To Make a Left Turn Make Two Right Turns." Corn and wheat diminished as we rode north. Barns became bigger, cows more numerous in rolling dairy land. And on the crests of the low hills the wind swept around us honey-rich with clover perfume or laden with the scent of new-cut hay.

Beyond a town of Two Rivers and a village of Two Creeks, we angled out onto that long thumb of land that forms the Door Peninsula of northern Wisconsin. French voyageurs, centuries before, had named the dangerous passage between rocky islets at its tip, *Porte des Morts*. Hence the designation of this peninsula which, for more than seventy-five miles, forms the lower shore of Green Bay. It was here, in 1634, that the French explorer Jean Nicolet, discoverer of Lake Michigan, leaped ashore, clad in mandarin robes, firing pistols with both hands, believing he was landing on the coast of China. It was also along this shore that Père Marquette and Louis Joliet paddled on their way to the Fox River and the discovery of the Mississippi.

As it advances northward, the Door Peninsula grows steadily narrower. The water draws closer on either hand and its moderating influence is reflected in the widespread cherry orchards of the region. A paradox is produced. The northern part of the peninsula has a milder climate than the southern part. No other county in Wisconsin, not even those along the southern boundary of the state, has so long a growing period as Door County. It enjoys an annual average of 160 frost-free days. Normally at the oldest village on the peninsula, Baileys Harbor, the lake water remains open all winter long.

It was Baileys Harbor that was our goal that day. For, just beyond it, low ridges, like a succession of parallel waves, extend inland from the shore. In the boggy troughs between, orchids bloom in wild gardens that have made the region famous. Dr. Albert M. Fuller, Curator of Botany at the Milwaukee Public Museum, reports that thirty of Wisconsin's forty-five kinds of native orchids grow in Door County and that twenty-five are found in the small area of The Ridges. In the fall of 1937, these orchid bogs obtained permanent protection as a wildflower preserve when a group of local citizens organized and incorporated The Ridges Sanctuary. The work of this group was honored in 1942 when it received the Garden Club of America's annual award for the most worthy project in conservation.

It was our good fortune to ask for directions at the Baileys Harbor Library. The Librarian, Olivia Traven, we discovered, was one of the signers of the articles of incorporation for the sanctuary. She had known the area intimately for years. No one could have been more helpful than she was when, on the following day, she showed us the wooded ridges and all the unique beauty of this region which, just in time, had been saved from destruction.

The waves of sand, fifteen in number and a couple of miles long, are at most only about six feet high. They extend inland for a mile or more. Apparently they represent the long-ago shallows of the lake edge, for swimmers who wade out from shore find similar ridges beneath the water. At one point they will be only ankle-deep, a little farther on up to their chins, then ankle-deep again. On shore, the successive ridges become older and more heavily wooded as they advance inland. Conifers predominate—hemlock and balsam fir, white pine and black spruce and tamarack. Each ridge has its name: Wintergreen Ridge, Sandy Ridge, Deer Lick Ridge. And each has its own trail running down its length and overlooking the bog strips on either hand. All told, 750 acres, well over a square mile, are included within the boundaries of this wildflower preserve.

The first orchid bloom we saw amid these orchid ridges was the delicately beautiful grass pink. Then came the rattlesnake plantain and, scattered all along the sides of the ridges, the tinted slippers of the pink moccasin flower. The great spectacular orchid show of the year had come and gone during May and June. The two rarest species of the sanctuary, the Calypso and the delicate ram's-head lady's-slipper, were both now past their blooming time. Although we had arrived too late for most of the flowers, orchid plants of many kinds rose around us as we wandered down the ridge paths and along the edges of the bogs.

For here are rooted the rose pogonia, the heart-leaved tway-blade, the tall white bog orchid, the tall leafy green orchid, the white adder's-mouth orchid, and the long-bracted orchid. Here grow the large round-leaved orchid, the smaller purplefringed orchid, and the blunt-leaved orchid.

Three of the lady's-tresses—the slender, the hooded and the nodding—bloom among the ridges. And here it is also possible to find three of the coralroots—the spotted, the early and the striped; three of the rattlesnake plantains—the giant, the dwarf and the intermediate; and four of the lady's-slippers—the showy, the large yellow, the ram's-head and the pink.

Among the bogs of Wisconsin, the welfare of the lady's-slippers depends, to some extent, on what happens to the rabbits. From 1932 to 1935, Aldo Leopold once pointed out, rabbits were abundant. They browsed heavily on the bushy little bog birches, letting in the sun, opening up the bogs and benefiting the lady's-slippers. Then during the years 1936 and 1937 the rabbits reached the low point in their cycle. The bog birches grew dense and once more deeply shaded the orchids. The following year, 1938, the rabbits recovered, built up their population, mowed down the bog birches. And again the lady's-slippers were thriving in the added sunlight.

As we moved along the ridge-top trails, that day, the sky above us darkened and a quiet rain began to fall, gentle and warm. Here and there, where the ridge slope met the bog, the dwarf lake iris, *Iris lacustris*, a plant with leaves only four or five inches long, spread in dense mats over the ground. Now they were richly green. But in the spring each mat had been a pool of blue. Then the gay-wings, *Polygala paucifolia*, had been in flower and even before that the inner ridges had known the beauty of petal and perfume brought by the trailing arbutus. Around us now the leaves of the pipsissewa, the clintonia, the white-flowered shinleaf were wet and gleaming. In the slow rain, the plants of bog and forest—the red wood lilies, the snowy-headed cottongrass, the marsh anemone—all were washed and sheathed in moisture, all possessed a glowing kind of beauty even in that dull and leaden light.

Later that afternoon we were joined by Emma Toft, a remarkable woman well along in her seventies who had lived all her life among the wildflowers, the birds and the animals of an area left relatively unchanged, the pioneer homestead where she was born, Toft's Point, just north of Baileys Harbor. A long time ago an Eastern botanist had come to the Door Peninsula to collect plants. He had boarded with her family. Thus as a small child she had become fascinated by the study of wildflowers. It was an interest that never waned, an interest that had played its part in the preservation of the orchid gardens of The Ridges.

Of all we saw that day, the memory that lingers most vividly in our minds is coming suddenly upon almost half a hundred "whip-poor-will's shoes"—showy lady's-slippers—all in bloom in an area no larger than a city lot. Each waxy-white and crimson-tinted flower, delicate as a bubble, hung pendant on its stalk. All around the air was filled with a faint, indescribable perfume. Among these orchids we came upon a number with severed stalks where flowers had been nipped off by deer. The animals, browsing here, seemed to choose such flowers as a special delicacy.

Delicately formed and gracefully beautiful enough to have been nourished by flowers was the week-old fawn we met when we rode down a dirt road lined with great-leaved thimbleberries to reach the homestead on Toft's Point. Fishermen had discovered it stranded on rocks near the lake's edge. They had taken it to the local game warden who had asked Miss Toft to raise it and then set it free. As we watched, it fed ravenously on warm milk from a bottle. But already it was nosing among leaves, nibbling tentatively here and there. With its spotted sides, its slender neck, its mobile ears, its long, curving eyelashes, its liquid eyes, it seemed at the time one of the most beautiful of all the world's beautiful and appealing wild creatures.

Mysterious Maples

'"THE horror of that moment," the King went on, "I shall never, *never* forget!"

"You shall, though," the Queen said, "if you don't make a memorandum of it."

Not infrequently during our long trip with the summer, these words of the White Queen, coming down the years from behind Alice's Wonderland looking glass, recurred to my mind. I remembered them now as I slipped a pencil stub and a small spiral-ring notebook back into my pocket. The English poet, Thomas Gray, was right: For anyone interested in accurate observation, one note set down on the spot is worth a whole cartload of later reminiscences.

At that moment we were standing in the hush of the great north woods of Michigan's Upper Peninsula. Lake Superior lay only thirty miles to the north; Lake Michigan only twenty miles to the south. Close by our trail a path of claw marks ascended the silvery-barked trunk of a beech tree. It recorded a black bear's ascent in search of nuts. But it was not this tree that held our absorbed attention. Instead it was a nearby maple. At first glance it looked like all the other tens of thousands of sugar maples we had seen in recent days. But, as we drew close, Cordia Henry, manager of the Seney National Wildlife Refuge, pointed out a small patch where the bark had been scuffed away. There, scattered thickly over the bare wood, were tiny bumps. The tree, the first of its kind we had ever seen, was the rare and valuable bird's-eye maple.

If you draw a circle with a 200-mile radius, using Escanaba on the Upper Peninsula as the center, you will enclose the source of more than 90 per cent of all the bird's-eye maple in the world. It was from Escanaba, in 1936, that 100,000 square feet of this wood went to the Cunard Line in England to finish the cabins of the S.S. *Queen Mary*. All over the north country we encountered references to this maple. But only here did we see the bird's-eye wood in a living tree.

The bird's-eye maple is not a distinct species. It is not a strain of the sugar maple. Its characteristic—wood with the grain contorted and mottled with little spots or "eyes"—is not inherited, not passed on from parent tree to seed to sapling. Some years ago when one experiment station on the Upper Peninsula planted seeds from bird's-eye trees, they obtained nothing but ordinary sugar maples. Moreover, the trees never appear in groves or stands. They are scattered and individual. Around them there are always other maples with no bird's-eye characteristics at all. What makes these particular trees grow in this particular manner?

Since that morning on the forest trail, I have asked that question of many persons. I have asked it of botanists. I have asked it of lumbermen. I have asked it of research scientists. I have asked it at the world's largest processing plant for such wood, The Bird's Eye Veneer Company, of Escanaba. Everywhere the answers I received only deepened the riddle, only underscored the strangeness of the story of these mystifying trees.

On the outskirts of Escanaba, the hub of the bird's-eye maple world, the veneer plant was shutting down for the noon hour when I talked with Russell Lee, the man in charge, and Clint Paulson, the company's veteran timber cruiser who has roamed the Upper Peninsula for years in search of the rare trees. Later Paulson took me through the yard where the logs were coming in from the forest. In his sixties, square-shouldered, a bit stooped, big-handed, soft-voiced, he had the appearance of being made of iron. He had spent all his life in the north woods.

Usually, he told me, he discovers the greatest number of bird's-eye trees in rolling land where hardwoods are mixed. The characteristic is found never among soft maples, always among hard maples, sugar maples. But wherever hard maples grow, bird's-eye trees are possible. Although he has never encountered them in stands or groups, he thinks that where he finds one he has a better chance of finding another. At such a place he always inspects the surrounding trees with special care. North slopes appear to produce the most bird's-eyes. But Paulson has found such trees rising from ground that slanted downward toward all points of the compass. So the direction of the slope cannot be the deciding factor.

Could it be the kind or condition of the soil? Apparently not. Some of the bird's-eyes he has discovered have been rooted in clay soil, some have been anchored in sand, some have derived their nourishment from black loam. Gravel has been a main feature of the ground in some areas while it has been entirely absent in others. Virtually every type of soil known to the Upper Peninsula has, in one place or another, nourished bird's-eye maple trees.

As we talked, we walked about the yard among great piles of logs. Printed on the ends of many of them were the letters "B E"—signifying bird's-eye maple. Most of these logs had come from the other side of the peninsula. On Grand Island, in Lake Superior near Munising, virgin timber was being felled. Fully 90 per cent of the Michigan bird's-eye, I was told, comes from virgin stands of maples. There is relatively little bird's-eye in second-growth woods. In the course of time, Russell Lee speculated, bird's-eye maples may become largely a thing of the past.

Not only do seeds from such trees fail to produce similar trees but saplings that show bird's-eye characteristics usually develop into normal maples when they are transplanted. A generation ago, one resident of upper Michigan conceived the idea of providing a fortune for his children by planting a grove of valuable bird's-eye maple trees. He marked saplings, had workmen dig circular trenches around them in the fall and then, when the ground froze, had the small trees, with their roots in a ball of earth, transplanted onto his land. The saplings prospered but the idea did not. As they grew, virtually all of the trees lost their bird's-eye characteristics and changed into ordinary sugar maples.

In some instances a maple will grow for half a century, producing the bird's-eye formations all during that time, then change and continue to grow as a conventional tree producing conventional wood. I talked to one lumberman who had brought home, with considerable difficulty, a large log from the forest and then discovered that the side he had blazed contained bird's-eyes, as he had seen, but that the other side contained none. Sometimes the characteristic extends not only through the entire trunk but into the branches as well. In other cases the bird's-eye wood occurs in patches in the trunk, the patches separated by normal wood. The size and number of the eyes also vary greatly in different trees.

In the Seney region, a few years ago, a farmer burned bird's-eye maple in his kitchen stove most of the winter. He had felled a large tree and sawed it into short lengths for splitting into cordwood before he discovered its value. On the outside a bird's-eye and an ordinary maple look the same. Only by blazing the tree, removing a section of the bark, can the character of the wood underneath be established.

As a rule, I was told, it is the lower part of the trunk that tends to have the most bird's-eyes. Sometimes only this portion of the tree can be used in making veneer. There have been cases in which the heartwood alone contained the bird's-eye formations. Russell Lee expressed the theory that bird's-eyes may be the result of "suppressed growth." Most of the trees are found in virgin stands where the forest is thick and young trees are deeply shaded. Originally, he believes, some of these saplings received insufficient light and for a time were unable to develop normally. Misdirected growth, producing rodlike bird's-eye formations, resulted. The trunks of such trees seem filled with small, abortive "branches" that remain contained within the wood itself.

Exactly what are these "buried branches"? Are they really branches? If not, what are they? To those questions varied answers are given. The mystery of what causes the bird's-eyes in some trees and not in others is balanced by the mystery of what it is that is produced. Later, at the New York Botanical Garden, the Brooklyn Botanic Garden and among the textbooks on timbers and woods and botany in general, I sought for a final answer. But none was forthcoming. The hypotheses were contradictory. The botanists were far from being in accord. Each small circlet on the face of the maple veneer represents an enigma.

For generations the theory has been advanced that latent buds within the trees are stimulated into misdirected growth, perhaps by a virus, perhaps by a fungus, perhaps by insect injury. Somewhat in the manner that a burl or witch's broom is produced, this abnormal activity creates from the latent buds the twiglike formations that extend outward through the successive layers of the developing wood. However this "adventitious bud" theory is flatly rejected by a number of modern authorities. The Dean of the Yale University School of Forestry, Dr. Samuel J. Record, writes in his textbook on *Timbers of the New World:* "The cause of bird's-eye is not definitely known, but it is not, as so frequently stated, attributable to buds." And so we are left with questions without answers, with the double mystery that is presented by every bird's-eye maple.

As I looked at the living tree in the Seney forest that day, I wished profoundly to know its inner history, masked by bark, hidden within its roots and trunk. Silent, so far removed from our thinking minds, withdrawn into itself, its life so different, it held, without an outward hint, the secret of this twofold enigma.

Farthest North

SCATTERED across the 84,000 square miles of Minnesota, there are well over 10,000 little lakes. They represent almost one-tenth the total inland water area of the United States. Here is a Silent Lake and a Sleepy Eye Lake, a Little Dead Horse Lake and a Full of Fish Lake, a Bowstring Lake and a Disappointment Lake and a Mantrap Lake. More than 100 names are repeated five times or more and the state contains ninety-nine Long Lakes, ninety-one Mud Lakes and seventy-six Rice Lakes. In this canoe country of the north it is estimated there are fully a thousand lakes still unchristened. We amused ourselves that afternoon by conjuring up names for the unnamed lakes of Minnesota.

Through swamp and farm and forest land, we advanced during the following days. We passed International Falls and beside the Rainy River we worked west along the Canadian line toward Lake of the Woods and the Northwest Angle. This thirty-mile wedge of land and water owes its existence to the mistaken belief that it contained the source of the Mississippi. In 1783, at the Treaty of Ghent, which recognized its independence, the United States insisted on this jog in the Canadian boundary. At no other place along the border does American territory extend north so far. The tip of the Angle was for us the farthest-north point of our summer trip. This roadless land, without complete topographical maps to this day, contains even now stretches that represent the forest primeval.

It was late in the afternoon when we came to America's only port on the Lake of the Woods, Warroad on Muskeg Bay. The name commemorates the old warpath followed by the Sioux and Chippewas around the southern end of the lake. Warroad, occupying a till-plain where the waves of ancient Lake Agassiz leveled the drift deposits of the Ice Age, seems only a day or two removed from pioneer times. Still legible on the front of a weathered building is a large sign: "Homesteads Located by an Actual Settler."

We slept that night beside Muskeg Bay, and early the next morning, aboard the veteran *Resolute*, we were on our way to Angle Inlet at the far tip of the wedge. Ever since it was built on the lake shore shortly after the First World War, the sixty-two-foot *Resolute*, with Fay H. Young as owner and captain, had been threading its way among the islands each summer. And each winter it had been frozen in ice that sometimes reached a depth of six feet, carefully anchored heading north and south so the melting in spring would occur equally on either side and in this way eliminate the danger of capsizing.

A laboring diesel, one of its cylinders inactive from a burned-out piston, pushed us north past Buffalo Point and Springsteel Island, out into the width of Big Traverse Bay. With more than 200 square miles of water surface, partly in the United States and partly in Canada, the Lake of the Woods is sown with rocks and reefs and innumerable islets. It is estimated that there are 14,000 islands in the lake. These, added to the convolutions of the lake rim, are said to give the Lake of the Woods more miles of shoreline than any other body of fresh water in the world.

Storms were predicted for the day. The sky was dark and the wind was rising as we entered the Big Traverse. For thirty miles here the wind sweeps unhindered, piling up running ridges of water in rough and sudden storms. This day the long gusts came out of the east. The moving moraines of the waves swept toward us across the lake, striking the *Resolute* broadside or at a quartering angle. Clinging to the rail, we would see the opposite rail drop down and down until it almost touched the water. Then, as the boat slid into the trough and the next great wave reached us, it rose, soaring upward as we fell away. Thus, rising and falling on our aquatic teeter-totter, we crept slowly northward.

Fay Young, our seventy-year-old captain, was a fine man to have around in a storm. We could see him peering ahead through the small pilothouse windows. The throb of the diesel rose and fell, easing off on the water ridges and digging in during the momentary lull of the troughs that followed. At the end of each steep slide-down, a white burst of spray would explode upward around the bow. Once a geyser of foam shot over the top of the pilothouse. I could see Fay Young cranking the hand-operated windshield wiper to clear his windows. Across this seemingly endless procession of waves, each time the boat heeled over the bell above the pilothouse would clang once dismally, as with a tolling sound.

"This is the kind of a day you'd like to forget!" In these words the captain summed up the trip succinctly.

Only once in his forty years on the lake, he said, had he had a rougher crossing of the Big Traverse. That occurred during a near-hurricane one June several years before. On our trip, the particular yawing and slewing motion of the boat, combined with its rearing and pitching, left almost all of the dozen passengers violently seasick. Even dogs sometimes became seasick on the Lake of the Woods. Fortunately for us, Nellie had remembered a bottle of Dramamine pills. Fortified by one apiece at breakfast time, we rode out the storm hour after hour.

For a long time I clung jammed between the rail and a redpainted davit near the stern, with the spray and the wind around me, elated by the constant change, the shifts in equilibrium, the sweep up and down, this way and that, the boat continually righting itself, conquering wind and wave with bouyancy and equilibrium. Here was no steady, bumping advance of the laden wagon, no smooth, metallic run over rails. Here was fluid motion, the stability of instability, the sensation of canoe or bicycle multiplied manyfold. Here was the excitement of the lake in a storm.

All around were the steep hills of water with the snow of foam on their ridgetops. They seemed devoid of life. At long intervals a Franklin's gull or a black tern beat past us against the wind. No longer are there in these waters the incredible numbers of sturgeon that once swam here. In the single year of 1895, for example, 1,300,000 pounds of these fish were taken from the Lake of the Woods. The roe alone totaled 97,500 pounds. One giant sturgeon caught in the Big Traverse weighed 285 pounds. But the prodigal waste of an earlier time has left this natural resource depleted. The sturgeon is now ranked in the Lake of the Woods as "very scarce."

For nearly four hours the *Resolute* lurched and plunged in heavy water crossing Big Traverse Bay. Then the lake grew calmer, protected by the maze of the upper islands. At each port of call, the captain was greeted enthusiastically. To every salutation of:

"How're you, Fay?" he would mumble:

"I managed t' get this far!"

Then, with cargo discharged, he would swing away with a farewell salute—a feeble wheeze of the boat's hand-cranked whistle—and we would head north again. We were to see it all once more, this time in brilliant sunshine, when the boat headed south again next day. Now on a water frontier we advanced toward wilder land ahead. The lowering day was well along in its fourth quarter before we reached the end of our journey, Jake Colson's wharf and the few scattered cabins that form the community of Angle Inlet. Here all the traffic goes by water. The school bus is a boat. Inland, the muskeg bogs form impassable barriers except when they are solidly frozen in winter.

Three miles farther on, on the banks of the dark Bear River, at the very tip of the Northwest Angle, Lockwood Jaynes took us in for the night. A metal worker from Tulsa, Oklahoma, he and his wife have spent their summers here for years. Nearby he was building a new reinforced and insulated cabin. There they planned to live the year around, the only dwellers on this wild northland stream.

Dark brown with the leachings of the Manitoba bogs where it originated, the river moved slowly, its farther bank a hundred feet away. The main current wound back and forth along its wider bed, each meander in its serpentine advance holding within its curve shallows green with wild rice. For two hours or more in the late afternoon and the long northern twilight, Nellie and I explored upstream, almost to the Manitoba line, pushing a heavy rowboat along the windings of this river within a river.

At first I tried to take shortcuts across the rice shallows. But it was slow, laborious work. Among the multitude of the rice plants—their seed-stalks upthrust, their green leaves extended on the water—my oars became entangled at every stroke. Each time we neared the shore, as we wound with the channel, we seemed rowing in the midst of windblown trees. Disturbed by the waves and ripples my oars produced, the reflections of all the streamside aspens shortened and lengthened and swayed on the dark mirror of the water around us.

At the quiet end of this overcast day, now without wind, the river seemed tame enough. It reminded us of sketches of the sluggish Concord in Massachusetts. We kept expecting to come upon clearings and farms, to see cows and barns. But the only sign of human habitation we saw was the moldering ruins of a log cabin, built long ago, now with roof collapsed and overgrown with moss decaying like a fallen tree and being reabsorbed into the forest. Only a few nights before, Jaynes had heard timber wolves howling. And hardly a mile inland from the stream the traveler is turned back by a virtually impenetrable barrier of tangled forest and treacherous muskeg.

Beaver-felled alder and aspen sticks, stripped of their bark, floated past or lay stranded in the rice shallows. At almost every turn we came upon the remains of beaver houses. Once, as we rounded a bend, we surprised a doe more than half submerged in the stream, escaping the flies. All over the north country at this time of year the larger animals suffer from the multitudinous insects. On the boat going back to Warroad next day, an old-timer told us of coming upon a moose in the deep woods in midsummer. Even before he saw it, he said, he detected its presence by the buzzing of the flies, the sound so loud it reminded him of "an airplane in the sky."

For three days before our arrival the weather had been abnormally warm. Thermometers had risen almost to 90 degrees. Natives spoke of this as their "three-day summer." And all along the river, in the short blooming season of the north, water plants had opened their flowers. We drifted by the white globes of the bur reeds and the white, three-petaled blooms of the arrowheads. We floated among the crowfoot, that aquatic buttercup with flowers of white instead of yellow. Among all the river blooms white predominated. Chief exceptions were the yellow pealike flowers of the bladderworts and the buds and open flowers of the yellow water lilies. Where a beaver trail led away into the woods, one small bay seemed plated all around its edge with the gold of the lilies.

As we were drifting back downstream, we stopped to examine a green rush thrust above the water and coated for half a foot with an almost solid mass of aphides nearly the same identical shade of green. A little farther on, at the outer edge of a quarter of an acre of wild rice, we discovered a large gray longicorn beetle struggling in the water. I fished it aboard on the end of my paddle. For a time, like Fabre's pine processionary caterpillars, it went round and round the rim of my hat. We headed for the bank to toss it ashore. And in so doing we encountered a special little adventure of our own. For the beetle led us to a family of kingbirds during one of the most eventful hours of their lives.

Ten or eleven feet from the ground and a dozen feet from the edge of the water, a pair of these birds had made their nest where the dead stub of a branch jutted out from the trunk of an aspen tree. Five baby kingbirds, almost ready to fly, were lined up on the stub. They clamored continuously for food while the parent birds flew back and forth bringing insects. We saw a large grasshopper stuffed hastily down the gaping throat of one fledgling. Each time a parent appeared the calling rose to a crescendo. All the young birds crowded together. They opened wide their orange-yellow mouths. Their outspread wings quivered in that age-old action of supplication and hunger instinctively used by birds around the globe.

Each time the parent left, the fluttering of the wings subsided. But there came a time when, as we watched, the fourth fledgling from the end of the stub continued the movement. At first the outstretched wings pulsated as before. Then they fluttered faster and faster. The arc of their movement increased perceptibly. Suddenly it was in the air. It was launched into flight, rising to another branch two feet higher up in another tree. From the quiver of the hunger movement to the beating of wings in flight had been a smooth transition.

A little later a second fledgling similarly took wing. Then a third broke home ties, alighting in a neighboring aspen. Finally, before we drifted away downstream, a fourth had launched itself into the air in exactly the same manner. Each rose to a higher perch. Each translated the flutter of hunger into the more frenzied wing beating of the first flight.

This was something I had never realized before. It is something I have never seen mentioned in ornithological literature. The wing-fluttering apparently becomes more than a symbol of hunger for the parents. It represents something in addition to strengthening muscles of flight. It forms a vital link in the chain of instinctive behavior that leads the bird into its aerial life. In his classic experiments with the Sphex wasps of his Provençal countryside. J. Henri Fabre demonstrated how the activity of these insects forms chains of instinctive behavior, with each act in the sequence linked with and leading into the next. So among these baby birds one act merges with another in this mechanism of nature for breaking a fledgling's ties with the nest.

We were half a mile from the cabin in the still evening air when a sound like wind rushing through the trees grew louder. Immense raindrops, each producing a gleaming bubble on the dark surface of the stream, fell all around us. In this pelting shower we reached the dock and the shelter of the cabin. The rain drummed overhead as we ate with the Jayneses a late supper of homemade bread, fresh vegetables from a wilderness garden and fruits of the forest, wild strawberries and raspberries and blueberries.

Outside, on the steps of the cabin, the deluge was washing away the little piles of dandelion fluff and the scattered pulp of wild strawberries, both discarded by the chipmunks as they nipped away the seeds. While the rain without wind continued, then slackened, then ceased altogether—to be succeeded by the dripping of innumerable leaves—we talked of the Old Dawson Trail, the overland route to Winnipeg over which Red River ox carts had labored in pioneer times. Traces still remain to the west of Angle Inlet. Aside from these, the forests are largely trackless, a waste where a man without a compass would soon become lost.

Before we went to bed late that night, at the end of this full day, at the far northern point of our summer journey, we walked for a while beside the dark river. Along our path, over the water, at the edge of the dripping forest, fireflies floated by. Unlike those living sparks of the Kankakee, they neither danced nor shot upward into the air. They drifted slowly, large, glowing, greenish lamps in the velvet darkness. When we came in at last we traded the rich perfumes of the rain-soaked forest for the nostalgic smell of the kerosene lamp in our cabin room. Long after its yellow glow was gone we lay listening to the sounds of the darkness of this northland night, the hoot of a great horned owl and the slow grating call of frogs in the river shallows.

Home of the Prairie Dogs

THE Indians called him Wishtonwish. Lewis and Clark called him the barking squirrel. The French trappers dubbed him the little dog. Early travelers referred to him as the Louisiana marmot. Zoologists bestowed on him a scientific name meaning dog-mouse. But to millions of Americans, past and present, he is the prairie dog.

In the sunshine of that summer morning, at Devil's Tower in the northeastern corner of Wyoming, our first prairie-dog town—with all its life and movement, excitement and humor—spread away around us. For thirty acres or more the sparse gray-yellow grass was dotted with mounds of earth.

Once such mounds of earth spread across hundreds of millions of acres. A single dog town on the Staked Plains of upper Texas extended for 250 miles without a break. It occupied 25,000 square miles and is computed to have had 400,000,000 inhabitants. Today, the only remaining evidence of this vast mammal metropolis is a name on the map: the Prairie Dog Town Fork of the Red River in northern Texas. Like the bison, the prairie dog is a symbol of the pioneer West. And like the bison, it has been wiped out over most of its former range and forced back into last-ditch stands within national parks and similar sanctuaries.

Almost the first colony to obtain such protection was the one that spread around us now. On September 24, 1906, by presidential decree, Theodore Roosevelt established the earliest national monument at Devil's Tower. For more than fifty years, within reach of the shadow of this volcanic monolith—formed like a titanic tree stump and rearing 865 feet into the air—the colony had flourished. The animals had become accustomed to people. Under the sun, on this summer day, the events of the busy town went on as though only prairie dogs were present.

Wandering about this animated scene or sitting quietly at the top of the long, gentle slope occupied by the mounds, we watched, close at hand or through our field glasses, all the comings and goings of the prairie dogs. In size they might have been cottontail rabbits, without the rabbit ears. Instead their ears were small, rounded, close-set, giving them a flatheaded appearance. Their eyes were placed well forward so they were almost the first things to appear above the surface of the ground when an animal emerged from its hole. Plump and short-legged, all the individuals of this animal town had the disarming appearance of friendly little yellow puppy-dogs with black-tipped tails. These stubby tails they wagged vigorously, not from side to side but up and down. It is this vertical flipping motion that reveals their kinship with their smaller cousins, the ground squirrels.

Scores of the prairie dogs stretched out on the ground while companions carefully went over their fur, cleaning and dressing it, sometimes with their teeth pulling out the loose pelt for a surprising distance. A few wriggled and squirmed and rolled, taking dust baths to rid themselves of fleas and ticks. Others, mainly the smaller, younger animals, seemed engaged in games. With a great racing through the grass, one would pursue another until, like a football tackler, he bowled him over and sent him tumbling. Then their roles would be reversed; the chaser became the chased. Although their gait appeared short-legged and floundering, they covered distance with unexpected speed. About these pursuits, as about almost all the activity of the slope, there was a playful, good-natured quality.

Few other animals are so social and amicable. All that day we watched prairie dogs go visiting. Whenever they met in their foraging they paused in greeting, touching noses as though bestowing a kiss, fondling and patting one another, often sitting for some time together with the forepaws of one resting on the shoulders of the other. Once we saw two sit up facing each other, place their forepaws together with repeated pattycake motions, then drop to the ground and touch noses.

It was pleasant sitting there in the morning sunshine and for a time we closed our eyes and listened to the sounds of the animal city that came to us from every point of the compass. There were yipping notes, a churring sound, and sharp, staccato chips. The so-called bark of the prairie dog is largely a magnified squeak. Sometimes it resembles the yelp of a small puppy. But most of the time it suggests the sound of a squeezed rubber doll. A century ago, John James Audubon noted the close similarity between certain calls of the prairie dog and those of the western kingbird.

At times a yipping animal will bounce up and down as though it is on springs. When it gives its loudest, most far-carrying call, the prairie dog stands erect, lifts its forelegs as in a salaam, and throws itself upward and backward as if propelling the sound from its throat. Young animals sometimes jerk so violently they lose their balance and throw themselves over backward. This call has become recognized as a territorial bark. It broadcasts prior claims to the burrow and the ground surrounding it. Usually it is answered from other mounds nearby. On numerous occasions we saw a chain reaction of such calling run across the town, animals all down the slope rising on their hind legs, pointing their noses at the sky, throwing up their forepaws, barking their loudest, their lighter underpelts catching the sun.

One call—a repeated birdlike "Chip! Chip! Chip!"—appeared to be a note of alertness rather than of alarm. Usually when we approached a burrow, its owner would take a position lying across the opening of the hole, ready for an instant plunge to safety. There it would repeat this sound, its black-tipped puppy tail flipping up and down with every "Chip!" Every minute or so, when a prairie dog is feeding away from its burrow, it sits up and looks intently around. At the first suggestion of danger, it raises a shrill alarm. This is echoed from end to end across the colony. All the animals sit up, watchful, ready to whisk from sight. In this way a constant surveillance is maintained of the sky above and the country around. The householders of a dog town are continually kept informed by scores and hundreds of town criers calling the news.

So effective is this warning system that rarely are prairie dogs caught in the open even by such aerial enemies as golden eagles, rough-legged and red-tailed hawks. Sometimes a prairie falcon will fold up in the sky and thunderbolt down on some animal that has wandered too far away from its burrow. But such occasions are rare. One pair of falcons nested for several years high on the side of Devil's Tower. Although they hunted over the area daily, they rarely wasted time stooping on the prairie dogs. How alert these animals are to danger from the air we observed when a considerable portion of the colony disappeared when one of the larger songbirds flew overhead. It is the extremely rare black-footed ferret, racing through the maze of tunnels, and the badger, able with its shovel forefeet to dig out a burrow in as short a time as fifteen minutes, that are the archfoes of the prairie dog. Hereditary enemies such as the coyote, the fox and the wolf are usually detected long before they reach the outskirts of the city.

Most of the time the prairie dogs we saw reappeared from their burrows within a few minutes after they disappeared. A serious fright, however, will keep them underground for an hour or more. In the brains of these little mammals their burrows and safety are synonymous. Even when shot, a prairie dog will often tumble into its hole and kick itself downward in its death struggles. This led the English traveler, John Bradbury, who visited the region of the Dakotas in 1811, to report that the creatures were so quick that after they saw the flash of the gun they could dive to safety before the bullet reached them.

For a long time we watched one large prairie dog in a puzzling performance. It was working around the entrance of its burrow, patting down the earth, when first we noticed it. Then, placing its forepaws wide apart on the ground and ducking its head, it lifted its hindquarters until it was on tiptoe. It suggested a man about to stand on his hands. In this position, it lowered its head vertically and pressed its broad nose into the dirt. Over and over again we saw it repeat this odd action. The forepart of its body lifted and fell like a pile driver. Then it would shift to a new position and repeat the process. What was it doing? It appeared to us to be tamping down the earth with its nose. And that was precisely what it was doing. The mounds of dirt that mark the burrow entrances are in reality dikes. Ringing the holes and rising to a height of as much as two feet, they not only provide the animals with watchtowers but prevent the water of summer cloudbursts from pouring into the tunnels. The rarer, less social white-tailed prairie dogs of the higher mountain valleys—where drainage is better—merely pile the excavated earth beside the hole. But the black-tails of the plains carefully shape it into a protecting wall, thoroughly tamping the dirt into place. When we examined the craterlike opening where the large prairie dog had been working, we found it stippled all over with the indented prints of its nose.

The crater form of the burrow entrance has a special value for the prairie dog. He can hurl himself into it from any angle. You often see little clouds of dust puff upward as the animals strike the sides in pouring themselves at high speed down these funnels of earth. The burrow that lies below is far from a simple hole in the ground. It is, in fact, one of the most elaborate dwellings prepared by any American mammal. It begins with a plunge hole that descends almost vertically. A yard or so below the surface, a niche or shelf is cut in the side of this tunnel to form a "guard room" or listening post. Here the owner pauses when he enters and when he leaves. And here, in safety, he barks defiance to his enemies outside. Lower down, the tunnel branches into connecting passageways with spare rooms and a round sleeping chamber lined with dry grass. Not infrequently a corridor ascends straight up from the main tunnel for several feet, ending in a vacant room. This is believed to be an escape chamber in case of flooding, the air compressed upward into such a space keeping the occupant alive until the water drains away.

In the early days, during the building of one of the transcontinental railroads, a steam shovel cut straight through a prairie-dog town, laying bare the labyrinth of tunnels that descended for as far as fourteen feet and extended horizontally for as far as forty feet. In the course of their extensive burrowing, the animals plow up the soil like oversized earthworms, making it more porous and breaking up the hard, sunbaked crust of the prairie. Prairie dogs literally turn the land upside down. For they not only bring up soil from below, but their abandoned burrows gradually fill with the dust of the surface soil which, in this manner, is shifted to a lower level.

Toward noon that day, as on every summer day, the activity of the prairie dogs quieted down. More and more they drifted out of sight, retiring underground for their midday siesta. It is early in the morning and late in the afternoon that their activity is greatest. A heavy shower will always send them indoors. They are creatures of the sun, and summer is their season. During the winter, although they do not hibernate, strictly speaking, and may be seen abroad for short periods on bright days when the temperature stands at zero, they drowse away most of the months of cold. Largely they live on themselves, using up the reserves of fat stored up late in summer. Already we saw some so layered with fat that when they turned to look at us over their shoulders their sides crinkled like corrugated paper.

While the prairie dogs napped in their burrows, we ate lunch at a small restaurant at the edge of the national monument. Here little bags of dry bread were piled up under a sign reading: "Prairie Dog Food." Normally the food supply on the Devil's Tower slope would be insufficient to support so large a colony. But here the regular seed and vegetable fare is supplemented by handouts from tourists. And a fearful and wonderful assortment is included. Bread and cookies, marshmallows and popcorn, peanuts and crackers, cake and candy, even bubble gum is welcomed by the voracious prairie dogs. I saw one chewing away on a cellophane bag that had contained potato chips. So far as I could see it was devouring the cellophane with relish. Another ran its forepaw around inside the neck of an empty Pepsi-Cola bottle and licked off the sweet residue. We were told of one prairie dog that kept returning to eat more gingersnaps, although it scolded and chattered and struck its nose with its forepaws each time its tongue began to burn. As we gazed over the almost deserted slope, we wondered how many midday siestas were being disturbed by stomachaches.

That afternoon, besides distributing dry bread—and the drier it is the better the prairie dogs like it—we provided what we thought was a new taste sensation for dog town. We passed out half a dozen fig newtons. Left to themselves, the animals feed on a wide variety of grasses and herbaceous plants. We would see prairie dogs nip off grass stems and run the heads rapidly between their teeth, as through a machine, to strip away the seeds. Frequently they harvested a tiny form of milkweed that grows to a height of only a couple of inches between the burrows. Another plant they seemed to favor at Devil's Tower is a miniature mallow with the picturesque name of cowboy's delight.

In winter, when other food is scarce, prairie dogs will sometimes nibble between the spines at the flat, fleshy leaves of the prickly-pear cactus. On several occasions in the Southwest, during great grasshopper outbreaks, the animals have been seen turning from their vegetarian diet to feed voraciously on the insects, rushing this way and that, pursuing and pouncing on their active prey, sometimes even leaping into the air in an effort to catch grasshoppers on the wing.

About 75 per cent of the plants consumed by prairie dogs are considered of value for grazing. It has been calculated that 256 of the social animals will eat as much as a cow, and thirty-two will consume as much forage as a sheep. Without doubt, extensive dog towns and ranching are incompatible. Consequently every stockman's hand has been against the "little dogs" since early days. The government joined in. Tons of strychnine were dispensed free to western ranchers. Year by year it took its toll. Cyanide and poison gas added to the destruction. In Washington, officials announced triumphantly, during the 1920's, that colonies were being wiped out at a cost of seventeen cents an acre.

This war of extermination went on until on the Great Plains today the prairie dog is virtually as rare as the bison. Across vast tracts that had been filled with sound and movement and exuberant life a great stillness settled. Windblown dust filled and obliterated the ghost towns of the tunnels. Only in protected sanctuaries were these marked animals safe from persecution. In all probability it will be these sanctuaries alone that will save the species from extinction. This achievement is something to rejoice over. For no living species should be pushed to complete extinction—least of all one that so obviously enjoys its life and lives it to the full as does the friendly, sociable little prairie dog.

Toward sunset that afternoon, we sat near one of the mounds and watched its owner foraging for food. It is only on rare occasions that a prairie dog goes as far as 100 yards from its burrow. In this instance, the farthest foray of the animal carried it no more than thirty feet from its doorstep. Not infrequently it would gather a large mouthful of vegetation and then return to dine at leisure beside the entrance, both forepaws held to its mouth, its bright eyes peering over them, alert and watchful. Around every burrow the ground is almost bare, and all across the length and breadth of the colony the view is kept unobstructed. Heavy plants are almost invariably clipped off close to the ground soon after they reach a height of six inches.

The prairie dog we watched foraging in the sunset was obtaining both food and drink. Most of these animals, when living in a wild state, may never taste water in their lives. They obtain a certain amount of moisture from the vegetation they eat. But even this is not necessary. For, like pocket mice and kangaroo rats and other rodents of the dry country, their systems are able to turn the starch of dry seeds into water. One scientist fed a pet prairie dog perfectly dry food for a week and a half. It received no liquid of any kind. At the end of the period, he offered it a dish of water. It took only a perfunctory sip, no more than when it had water available all the time.

Early settlers in the West refused to believe that prairie dogs could go indefinitely without water. For decades the mistaken idea was current that the inhabitants of every dog town sank one shaft straight down to reach the flow of subterranean fountains. So convinced of this were many pioneers that they took special pains to dig their wells where prairie dogs had lived. They were baffled by the dry holes that resulted. In one instance pipes were driven to the depth of 1,000 feet without striking water.

With the going down of the sun that evening, the shadow of the towering monolith spread farther and farther across the slope and over the mounds that dotted it. To us it seemed symbolic of the protection this natural wonder had extended to the prairie dogs close by. In the shadow we saw the animals sitting up beside their burrows or visiting their neighbors for a last time or seeking some special tidbit to finish the day. Their calls became fewer; their activity lessened. Steadily their numbers decreased as more and more dropped away to sleeping quarters underground. By eight o'clock hardly a prairie dog was in sight. Quiet lay over the dog town. But it was the quiet of rest, not the stillness of death.

Dry Rain

IN THE cool of that dawn we skimmed over the rolling land like a swallow flying. We were in a slanting world. Everywhere we were going up or going down with no extended stretches of level ground between. On each successive crest our eyes' reach extended swiftly like an outstretched arm. We crossed dry creeks. We ran by snow-white patches of gypsum cropping out of the bleached yellow of the rangeland. At long intervals, coneflowers waved beside the road resembling purple daisies grown abnormally large. Past blooming now, the yuccas supported on upthrust stems the pale-green ovals of their massed seed pods. Meadowlarks, all along the way, sunned themselves on fenceposts. Nearly all were silent. For this was August. The time of the singing of birds was mainly over.

Long before midmorning we left behind the Wyoming rangeland and crossed into South Dakota. Once more we were among ponderosa pines, the conifers that make the Black Hills black. We swung southward, traversing the length of beautiful Spearfish Canyon. Near Eleventh Hour Gulch we stopped for a time to watch white-throated swifts whirl above the cliff tops and violet-green swallows flutter, alight and cling to cranny edges as they fed their young. Down the whole twenty-mile length of the gorge, down a varying ribbon of wildflowers—pale purple asters, yellow tansy, lavender bee balm—butterflies wandered. For one memorable moment around us the chasm rang with the sweet cascading song of the canyon wren. And before the face of each varicolored cliff, grasshoppers danced. The walls of rock behind them, like giant sounding boards, magnified the fluttering crackle of each insect serenade.

That night we settled down in Hot Springs. Then we were on the road again. All life, under the burning sun of midmorning, seemed lying low, keeping silent, all except the cicadas. Intoxicated by the heat, they shrilled from the sagebrush of every open slope along the way. As we went south we met the wind head-on, a dry wind that whipped the feathery sage and sent it, with the hard drive of its gusts, streaming and waving like masses of ferns. The air was hazy with heat and dust. The distant hills became more dim and vague in outline. Once we topped a rise and saw a wide valley of farming land spreading away before us. All across it what looked like clouds of yellow smoke were pouring upward from the open ground. Sweeping across the fields, swiftly drying the top of plowed or harrowed ground, the arid gale was lifting the surface of the land into the sky as dust. And beyond the valley, for a hundred miles and more to the south, all the open country was adding other billowing clouds to the tons and acres of airborne soil. We drove on and entered the dry rain of the forward fringe of our first big dust storm.

According to the United States Department of Agriculture, during the year of our summer journey 3,864,000 acres of the Great Plains were damaged by blowing. Although such storms may occur at all times of the year, they have been most destructive in early spring. In the dust-bowl areas of Nebraska, Kansas, Oklahoma, Texas, New Mexico, Colorado, Wyoming, Montana and the Dakotas, there are millions of other acres where, given the right conditions, unprotected surface soil is ready to be carried away by the wind. The long sequence of dust storms during the drought years of the early and middle thirties turned 18,000,000 acres of farming land into yellow-hued desert. In the midst of this disaster, that staple of early days that helped American pioneers endure the hardships of the frontier—the humor of exaggeration—came to the fore again. There were stories of areas so dry the cows gave powdered milk, of prairie dogs six feet in the air trying to dig their way down to the earth, of the man who poked his finger into the air and could see the spot for a week afterwards.

The quantity of soil removed in a given dust storm depends largely on the dryness of the ground and the speed of the wind. And these factors, in themselves, are interrelated. The windborne soil, on this day, rushed past us on a forty-mile-an-hour gale. A wind moving at this speed, scientific experiments have revealed, has four times the drying power it has at twenty miles an hour and sixteen times the power it possesses at ten miles an hour. The drier the air, of course, the more rapidly it sucks moisture from the ground. But in the case of the same wind, the drying effect on the surface of the soil increases as the square of its speed.

The swiftness of this drying process at times may produce astonishing sights. Later in our trip we observed a dust devil spinning down the length of a sandbar almost awash in the Cimarron River. In one Nebraska stream, a friend of ours, Dr. James Thorp, head of the geology department at Earlham College, in Indiana, once saw this process of surface drying accomplished with such dispatch that dust was blowing away from the top of a wet mudbank.

As we drew closer to the Nebraska line, the sunshine dimmed to an odd, filtered, yellowish light. The sky took on a sickly cast of yellow-gray. On every side the hills became smoky and indistinct in the wind-blown dust. Hollows, dimly seen from the crests of the rises, appeared filled with a dense, yellow-tinted fog. The dry smell of dust now was strong in the air.

Out of this murk we saw combines careening down the road. They were trying to outrun the storm, heading north toward that zebra landscape of alternating strips of gold and green, of grain and fallow land, that we could picture so well. As we continued south the rim of the prairie faded. The walls of dust pressed closer. We advanced into a steadily contracting world, meeting head-on the wind that, ever more heavily laden, came sweeping out of the south.

All across the North Dakota prairies we had seen windbreaks planted to the north or northwest of the farm buildings. In parts of Nebraska we were to see them planted to the south. One day we passed a whole grove of cottonwoods, trees forty feet high, that recorded the prevailing direction of the storm winds. Every trunk, like a partly-drawn bow, curved toward the north. That the winds of this area so often blow from the direction of the hot, dry land to the south is undoubtedly a factor in building up the dust storms of the region.

We peered into the billion-particled clouds around us. We watched the tiny, uncountable fragments of the earth sweeping past us on the wind. Where had they all come from? How far had they traveled? Some were at the very beginning of their journey. We saw new clouds of dust peeling from the length of every roadside field. And we, ourselves, added a cloud of our own when we came to a mile of construction where, looming up suddenly before us, heavy grading equipment suggested the prehistoric monsters that once roamed this land. But other components of the storm no doubt had come from farther to the south. We wondered how much of the dust around us had had its origin in that famed graveyard of the dinosaurs along the upper reaches of the Niobrara River. We wondered how much had come from those eroding bluffs where the discovery of the *Daimonelix*, the Devil's corkscrew—now believed to be the fossilized remains of the spiral burrow of some extinct rodent—set off half a century of scientific debate.

Over the instrument panel before us a fine yellowish dust had formed. I ran a forefinger across it. It had no gritty feel. The powdery material was smooth as flour. This fine dust may well have been carried northward by the wind from the famed loess regions of southern Nebraska. Formed of pulverized rock and deposited by the wind, loess, the "golden earth" of agriculture, forms the richest grain-producing areas of the world. It supports the densest populations on earth, the teeming millions of China and India. The precious yellow-brown loess of China, which colors the Yellow River and the Yellow Sea, has a depth of as much as 600 feet. Of German origin, the word means loose or open-textured. In farming land of the Midwest loess combines fertility with a capacity for absorbing rainwater like a sponge. "Golden earth" is to Nebraska what "black gold" is to the oil regions. It represents the agricultural wealth of the state.

Looking out into the swirling dust clouds, we could imagine ourselves in the very midst of the creation of these fertile lands. For it was in the wake of the northward retreat of the glaciers that winds, winds that ceased blowing millions of years ago, swept the powdered rock aloft and deposited it over the countryside. Loess has been found on the flanks of mountains 20,000 feet above the sea. Nebraska's most fertile land is derived from these dust storms of long ago, from minute airborne particles, ground in the mills of the glaciers and deposited during the Pleistocene.

One August noon, later in the trip, we stopped for lunch at the Lakeway Hotel, at Meade, in southwestern Kansas. Before I got into the car again I looked up at the third-story windows. One of those rooms had been occupied in the late summer of 1933 by a scientist, John C. Frye. At the end of a two-hour dust storm, he carefully collected samples of the material that had settled to a depth of a sixteenth of an inch on enameled surfaces in the room. Later laboratory examination of this aeolian dust revealed that almost all the particles were approximately the same size. They ranged in diameter from $\frac{1}{100}$ to $\frac{5}{100}$ of a millimeter. The wind sorts the material as it transports it. The smaller the fragment, the farther it goes. Coarse sand, for example, not over one millimeter in diameter, is usually carried no more than a mile. Fine sand may be transported several miles. Coarse silt, $\frac{1}{16}$ to $\frac{1}{32}$ of a millimeter in diameter, may travel 200 miles. Medium silt, $\frac{1}{32}$ to $\frac{1}{64}$ of a millimeter in diameter, may be wind-borne for 1,000 miles. And the finest silt, less than $\frac{1}{60}$ of a millimeter in diameter, scientists have found, may travel around the world. This difference in the distances traveled by particles of varying size accounts for the uniform character of any given area where loess is deposited.

The finer material not only travels farther but ascends higher into the sky and requires less violent winds to transport it. A study of the loess of Nebraska, which ranges in color from nearly white through yellow and olive to very pale brown, has shown that the size of the particles becomes steadily smaller as the distance increases from the original source of supply. But whatever their size, the rock-flour fragments are laid down in countless billions. One single modern dust storm it has been calculated, transported 70,000,000 tons of earth through the air.

Once carried aloft, the finest fragments are able to float on a slight breeze, to ride on the last remnants of a dying gale. It is the larger particles that progressively drop from the sky as the speed of the wind slackens. Ordinarily solid sand grains rarely rise more than a few feet above the ground. It is for this reason that travelers in desert regions often come upon strangely eroded rocks, shaped like toadstools. The sandblast of the gales, concentrated close to the ground, has eroded away a large portion of the rock to a height of several feet, leaving the upper portions relatively intact. In bare, dry land the wind becomes an abrasive tool. Its effect is like that of the sandblast that cuts grime from the stone of city buildings.

In the sweep of the dry rain that swirled around, the dust represented fragments from infinitely varied rocks. Even gold and other precious metals sometimes ride through the sky during such storms.

Around Custer, in South Dakota, the dusty air at times glints and sparkles with minute snowflakes of mica. It is when the tiny fragments of the harder rocks predominate that the abrasion of the wind-hurled particles becomes a serious problem. Windowpanes develop ground-glass exteriors. Tin is scoured from plates and cans. In some arid regions only metal telephone poles can be employed. Wooden poles are soon cut down by the erosion of the flying sand. Even steel rails, in time, may be worn thin by the sandblasting of repeated gales.

Across the rock-strewn floor of a desert this abrasive action of the wind has another significance. Here the particles produce other particles. The wind-driven sand is the principal agent in wearing away the rocks and pulverizing the fragments. While most of the rock-flour of loess was ground in the mills of the glaciers, more is being added by the action of the desert winds. Here it is the wind that creates and it is the wind that distributes that great boon to man, the fertility of loess.

It was about three in the afternoon when we entered Nebraska. The small village of Wayside, invisible behind the curtaining dust, was to our right as we crossed into the eighteenth state of the trip and turned east on our way to Chadron. From time to time a straggling car, with headlights on, groped its way toward us. In the storm, static electricity was building up. Silk crackled. Metal sparked when I touched it to the instrument panel. At the height of a great dust storm hair sometimes stands on end, barbed wire fences become charged, the ignition systems of automobiles are disrupted.

Once we were almost on a large sign when it suddenly loomed up beside the road. It notified truckers of a Nebraska "Port of Entry" that lay ahead. It struck us as a humorous note to call anything a "port" in this dry land blowing away in clouds of dust. Yet I suppose that Nebraska has more right than many states to the term. With its winding streams, it is said to rank near the top in its number of miles of river frontage. Its name, Nebraska, is an Indian word meaning "Shallow River."

As the distance to our journey's end lessened that afternoon, we took stock. We had dust in our throats, dust on our tongues, dust in our noses. Nellie was sure she could feel dust in her stomach. Our sunglasses, we found, were coated with a thin powdery layer. I discovered my eyebrows were dusty. And so we came, sometime after four o'clock, to Chadron on the northern edge of the Nebraska sandhills. We glimpsed them vaguely, indistinct and wraithlike behind billowing curtains of dust. As we saw them then they were nondescript in hue, indefinite in outline, as unreal as the hills of a dream.

Toward evening the wind slackened and the dust thinned ever so slightly. Immense and round, like a pale-gold harvest moon, the sun sank slowly. First its lower rim, then its lower half, then all became obscured behind the dense wall of airborne particles that rose above the western skyline. A delicate, golden-tinted light, new to our experience and memorably beautiful, filled all this dusty sunset.

Night of the Falling Stars

THE lonely road lay pale silvery-yellow in the moonlight. Its narrowing ribbon extended away before us across a land level and dark and outspread beneath the immense glitter of the prairie sky. It was two o'clock in the morning. We were a hundred miles west of Wichita, Kansas. Here fields were parched; farmhouses far-scattered across an arid land. No dogs barked in the night. Standing there amid the silence of the darkened prairie, we were surrounded by a scene that was nine-tenths sky. We felt, in this hill-less, tree-less region, as though we were in direct contact with the heavens, at a meeting place, on the sky-shore. The everyday life of the world had receded far away. We were alone among the stars.

And this was a night of nights to see the full sweep of the sky unimpeded by house or hill or tree. For we were now in the time of falling stars, the time of the summer Perseids, the greatest meteor show of the year. During the second week of August, each year, the orbit of the earth carries it through a celestial cloud of fragmentary matter streaming across the void at planetary speeds. Fragment after fragment, turned incandescent by friction in the earth's atmosphere, draws in a swift, bright stroke a line of fire on the firmament. For hours now, in spite of the light of a moon almost full, we had been seeing these dark stars from outer space burst into transitory brilliance and imprint for the space of seconds their flaming paths across the dome above us.

When we started out, about 10:30, the celestial show had already begun. But, as always, it was after midnight before it reached its height. Then four or five times as many meteors are visible in the heavens. After midnight we occupy the forward side of the turning globe as it sweeps through space. We encounter the meteors head-on. Their speed and brilliance increase. In the evenings hours we are at the rear of the globe. The shooting stars we see are only those that overtake us.

Standing there in the dusty road, we watched these fragments from outer space consume themselves high in the atmosphere. Their sudden trajectories lengthened and disappeared above us. We watched them drawing fiery lines across Cassiopeia and the Big Dipper. At their peak, on a clear, moonless night, the meteors of the Perseids crisscross in the sky. On this night the light of the moon no doubt competed, erasing the fainter, more distant trails. We would see three or four streaks across the sky, one coming after the other. Then there would be a lull; then a long single line, sometimes soaring overhead, sometimes cutting to the right, sometimes descending in a shallow arc to the left.

In any twenty-four hours, it has been calculated, at least 10,000,000 fragments from outer space enter the earth's atmosphere. The number has sometimes been placed as high as 4,000,000,000. Yet one astronomer computes that their average total weight would be hardly more than a ton. Most are so minute they disappear almost instantly. However, a bit of matter no larger than a pinhead will produce a faint, short-lived streak in the sky. These are the smallest objects in the solar system ever seen by the human eye.

As the hours of that night wore on, we wandered about over the level land, changing our viewpoint, standing in the dust of the side roads while the succession of quick, flaming trails shone in self-consuming brilliance in the sky above us. Several times we passed a low, darkened farmhouse, its cyclone cellar hidden in the shadows, its two weathered windmills motionless in the moonlight. Once we looked back as we turned slowly down a crossroad and saw what we thought was the most brilliant meteor of the night trace its path half across the sky, sinking gradually and fading away, from our point of view, directly over the old farmhouse. Just so, perhaps, on some long-ago night, out of just such a glitter of stars, had come to the dark acres of the surrounding land a shower of wealth from outer space.

For these acres in Kiowa County, Kansas, hold a special place in the annals of meteorite history. About one-third of all meteorites found in North America, and almost one-sixth of those recorded throughout the entire world, have come from Kansas. The plowed fields of the western half of the state have been especially productive. But none contributed more stones from the sky than this land that bordered our lonely road. It comprised a tract that has been famous for more than a half a century as the Kansas Meteorite Farm.

In 1885, a young couple from southern Iowa, Frank and Eliza Kimberly, moved here, six or seven miles from the present town of Haviland. The earliest pioneers in the region had noted that the only rocks they found were heavy and black and strewn about in a relatively small area. Homesteaders used them to weight down haystacks and fences and the covers of rain barrels. They were also employed to anchor in place the roofs of the dugouts and protect them from the violence of the wind. But nobody suspected the dramatic history of the stones until Mrs. Kimberly picked one up not long after she arrived in Kiowa County.

As a small girl in Iowa, she had been taken by a teacher to see a large meteorite that was being transported through town on its way to an eastern museum. She now recognized the object in her hand as similar to it. Day after day she hauled other heavy, black stones in from the fields. As her pile grew, she began writing to scientists trying to interest them in her find. But her farm was remote and they were skeptical. Years went by without any response. Her pile of black stones became a standing joke throughout the region. Nevertheless, year by year, she added to it.

Then, in 1890, Dr. Cragen, the head of the geology department at Washburn College, in Topeka, drove out to the pioneer home where the Kimberlys lived and was dumbfounded to discover something like a ton of piled-up meteorites. He bought some, museums bought others, and from the stone pile that was no longer the joke of the region Mrs. Kimberly realized enough to pay off the mortgage on the farm. Not only that, but she was able to buy the adjoining farm as well. When, before she died, she had become the richest woman in Kiowa County, there were no hard feelings over the money her meteorites had brought her. She was considered by her neighbors "a mighty smart woman," an opinion that was not lessened when it was learned that she had paid a lawyer one dollar for a meteorite she later sold for $500.

That afternoon, while Nellie was getting ready for our night with the stars, I had driven west from Pratt, past the dry little town of Haviland and off on dirt roads that intersect at mile intervals and cut the plains into innumerable squares of equal size. At the second crossroad I had swung west and come to the meteorite farm. Here Kimberlys still live—Oren Kimberly, a middle-aged, stocky farmer who wore a long-peaked cap indoors and out and used slow, humorous speech, and his mother, Cora Kimberly, Eliza's daughter-in-law, a slender wisp of a woman in her early eighties who had lived in this same house for more than sixty years.

Looking down from the wall, as they recalled earlier events that had brought fame to their Kansas acres, was an enlarged photograph of Eliza Kimberly. Hers was an interesting face: capable, intelligent. She was, I surmised, the kind of person who would appreciate the ironic humor of the official records that list the great discovery of her meteorites as occurring in June, 1890—that is, when a scientist finally arrived and discovered what she had discovered and the meteorites she had collected years before.

As Nellie and I watched the falling stars that night, we wondered if any we saw were reaching the earth. It is, of course, only the largest masses that survive the fall. During its long descent, a meteorite may lose as much as half its material through heat and abrasion. Stony meteorites, by far the most common kind, are almost always characterized by a black fused crust, the product of intense heat in the sky. So far as is known, the largest ever to reach the earth intact lies buried amid limestone near the town of Grootfontein, in Southwest Africa.

Somewhere in the darkened fields that spread around us, one of the biggest of all the Kansas meteorites had been discovered in the early days by the Kimberly's hired man, Jack Sanders. One evening he came in from a day watching the cattle and told Mrs. Kimberly:

" 'Liza, I saw one of those black stones you've been saving, today."

They all trooped out to look at it. But Sanders couldn't find it.

"If you ever see it again," Mrs. Kimberly told him, "you sit right down on it. Let the cattle go. Stay right there until we come and find you."

A few weeks later the Kimberlys discovered their cattle scattered all over the fields and no Jack in sight. They hunted him up and found him sitting on the ground beside a small point of black rock projecting above the surface and half hidden in the grass. Digging down at this spot they unearthed a stony meteorite that weighed 700 pounds.

At first her husband viewed her growing stone pile with tolerant humor. Later, when its value became apparent, he hastily hunted over the fields for a large meteorite he had once discarded. His wife had found it in a remote part of the farm and had put it, with several others, in an empty wagon for him to bring to the house. He decided she had enough stones and heaved it into the bushes somewhere along the way. Hunt as he would he could never find it again. Later in our trip when, in the high Rockies, Nellie became enamored of rocks and loaded the car with specimens until the springs bent and the trunk sank low, there were times when I extended a surreptitious hand to lighten the load, but, just in time, I always remembered Mr. Kimberly and his thrown-away prize.

Although Eliza Kimberly never owned a telescope, she was long interested in the study of the stars and the constellations. Her eyes, I was told, were unusually farsighted. On this August night, above our heads glittered the same stars, the same westward-wheeling constellations, that those farsighted eyes had seen. From this identical point on the spinning globe where she had watched the procession of the nocturnal sky, we were viewing it on this night of the Perseids.

For more than six decades the fields around us had continued to yield new finds. Most of them are now scattered among American museums. A few have gone to European institutions or, as Oren put it, "way over in those foreign countries." Not a few of the Kimberly meteorites have been discovered accidentally. In 1925, Oren located one that weighed 465 pounds when his plowshare struck it a glancing blow. Another time his small son picked up a stone to throw into the cattle pond, noticed how heavy it was and brought it to the house.

Varying amounts of metallic iron containing nickel are found mixed with the stony matter of most of the meteorites. More rarely they are composed of nickeliferous iron alone. After the Second World War, a man from Hutchinson, Kansas, brought down a mine detector and went over some of the fields looking for buried meteorites. The first day he excitedly dug up a tin can. But on a later day he made a real strike. Not far from the house, near the fence of the hog lot, his sensitive detecting apparatus revealed the presence of a 400-pound meteorite buried only two or three feet below the surface.

Almost all of the meteorites of the Kimberly farm were discovered on about eighty acres of the homestead. Only dust and small fragments have been picked up on the neighboring farms. Apparently, as frequently happens, a larger meteorite burst just before striking, raining the ground below. Across the Kimberly fields the path of their exploding meteor extends for something like half a mile. That night as we watched the Perseids, Nellie and I discussed the amazing coincidence that placed the one person in the region capable of recognizing the importance of these stones from the sky on the very farm where they were concentrated.

Half a mile east of the farmhouse, where a field was now planted with corn, the Kimberlys had erected their original pioneer dwelling in the 1880's. We stopped for a long time here. During the night we returned to this spot again and again. Our feet left a maze of tracks in the dust that no doubt puzzled the first person to drive that way in the morning. All around the horizon we could see a low, diaphanous gray-white wall that seemed rising upward and thinning as it rose—the dust in miles of prairie air made visible by moonlight and starlight.

Above this wall of floating dust lifted the glitter of constellations and galaxies. As our eyes wandered among them, they brought to mind old Messier, the French comet hunter, and his paradoxical claim to fame. In his nightly search of the heavens, Messier listed 103 "nuisance spots," indistinct luminous areas in the sky that interfered with his work. In the course of time, improved telescopes revealed that these luminous spots were largely galaxies, island universes, the most exciting objects in the sky. All that later astronomers had to do to locate them in the heavens was to consult Messier's chart of nuisance spots. Even today many galaxies are listed by the designating numbers he gave them. Thus the great Andromeda Galaxy is referred to by astronomers as M 31—number 31 on Messier's list. This early scientist's lifework on comets is virtually forgotten today; his astronomical fame rests on his listing of nuisances he wished to avoid.

Standing there, facing the eastern sky, we noticed that our eyes grew progressively keener, training themselves as the night advanced to catch the fainter trails of light that winked out almost as soon as they began, the paths of little meteors too short-lived to provide even a beginning for making a "wish upon a falling star." Once in the space of no more than sixty seconds, four meteors streamed in different directions across the sky. One plunged almost vertically down into the northeast. Another traveled a long way, yellow-hued and almost horizontal. The highest of the meteors shone with a bluish cast; those lower down—seen through denser atmosphere nearer the earth—marked their transitory paths with yellowish brilliance.

Half a dozen times a year, on the average, meteorites are observed, somewhere in the world, in the very act of striking the earth. One weighing 150 pounds landed within the limits of Colby, Wisconsin, on the Fourth of July, in 1917. Another on July 6, 1924, struck a highway near Johnstown, Colorado, just after a funeral procession had passed by, and its fall was observed by all those assembled at the cemetery only a few rods away. In Sylacauga, Alabama, on a September day in 1954, Mrs. Hewlett Hodges was resting on a couch when a ten-pound meteorite crashed through the roof of her house and struck her a glancing blow.

Because of the sudden increase in density of the air before them, meteors soon lose their planetary velocities in the atmosphere. They usually reach the earth at the speed of ordinary falling objects. One was once observed in Sweden striking ice only a few inches thick and bounding off without breaking through. Moreover, most of the intense heat of the meteor's flaming course through the upper atmosphere has been lost by the end of its slowed-down descent. In 1890, during a shower of meteors near Forest City, Iowa, one fragment fell on a stack of dry hay without setting it afire.

Far away, almost directly below Perseus, the few street lamps of Haviland winked in a small cluster of stars on the dark horizon line. Our car stood white and ghostly, its top and hood reflecting the glow and glimmer of the moonbeams. All around us the roads were deserted and, save for an occasional night insect singing along the way, wrapped in silence. The breeze flowed gently out of the south, bland and presaging the heat of the coming day. Once we caught the low call of a burrowing owl. Another time a killdeer went off in the moonlight with its wild plover cry. Our footfalls, silent as the moonlight, were cushioned by the carpet of dust. And as we moved about, changing our positions, our moon shadows moved with us, imprinted on the dust of the road and slowly elongating as their source descended toward the west.

Imperceptibly that night the great wheel of the constellations kept turning. The sword of Orion had long since been withdrawn from the haze along the eastern horizon. We had to look ever higher in the heavens to see Perseus. But hour after hour the meteors kept coming, those celestial sparks of running fire, mysterious and awesome in the night. It is easy to understand how their remains, objects descended from the void, the "black stars" or "thunderstones" of the ancients, were long valued and often held in superstitious reverence. More than 3,000 years ago, a Hittite king compiled a list of his treasures, noting, along with his gold and silver and bronze, "black iron of heaven from the sky." Early man, long before iron was smelted, was using the metal of meteorites in the manufacture of tools.

Although meteor showers were recorded in China as early as 650 B.C., it has been only during very recent generations that they have received serious scientific consideration. Even as late as the eighteenth century the idea of the celestial origin of meteorites was ridiculed. The great French scientist, Lavoisier, maintained that they were ordinary stones that had been struck by lightning. A leader in attacking the "superstition" of falling meteorites was the French Academy of Science. Then, in 1803, thousands of stones fell on the village of L'Aigle, not far from Paris. The Academy sent a representative to investigate. He reported there was no question about it—they were meteorites and they had fallen from the sky. Then, as is the way of the world, the French Academy of Science hailed its representative as a great explorer who had discovered the existence of meteorites.

It was not until thirty years later that the real study of meteoric phenomena began. Its impetus was a night of falling stars unparalleled in modern history, the first and never-again-approached Leonid shower of November 12, 1833. It brought terror to many parts of the world. In Boston, a fifteen-minute count indicated the meteors were flashing across the sky at the rate of nearly 30,000 an hour. A reporter in Georgia wrote that it appeared as though "worlds upon worlds from the infinity of space were rushing like a whirlwind to our globe, the stars descending like a snowfall to the earth." Even the calendar of the Sioux Indians records this night of fire in the sky. Discussed for weeks, the prodigy stimulated widespread study of the problems connected with the life and death of these heavenly bodies.

We were sitting in the car, motionless and silent, sometime after three o'clock that morning, when I looked down at the side of the road. A pinched little face was peering up at me in the moonlight. Edging uncertainly past was a half-grown, gray and white farm kitten stealing by on some nocturnal hunting expedition. I slid slowly out of the car and we made friends. The kitten waved its tail and rolled in the dust. It rubbed its back against an extended pencil that bounced up and down along the hills and hollows of its protruding spine. Gaunt and apparently half starved, it appeared to have lost most of its voice, uttering only faint, one-syllable meows. Never once did it purr. It seemed not to know how. And in truth it probably had, in its small life, little to purr about.

The only food we had in the car was a box half full of graham crackers. I opened the trunk and got them out. When I offered a piece between thumb and forefinger, the kitten seemed confused. No one, apparently, had ever fed it by hand. I laid the cracker on the ground. It fell on it ravenously. At first it appeared to lack sufficient saliva for swallowing. But then it ate and ate and ate. Never again in all its life would it encounter this taste it was experiencing for the first time during this moonlit night's adventure. How many times would its little mind remember it? If kittens dream, how often, I wondered, would the haunting taste of graham crackers return in future catnaps?

We had been there for some time, our three shadows, two large and one tiny, dark upon the dust of the road, when I became aware of a fourth shadow. A jack rabbit had joined us. Not more than twenty feet away, it was watching us with curiosity rather than fear. I flashed the beam of a hand torch over it. Its eyes gleamed huge and glowing red. But it showed no alarm. For that small time we seemed transported back to an age that antedated fear, to some lost Eden we now but vaguely remember and rarely glimpse again. That moment of silence and moonlight, of strange and lonely companionship, seemed a moment in another world.

Then the spell was broken. The kitten saw the rabbit. It flattened in the dust, ears pricked forward. In this position it remained for a minute or more. Then, one foot slowly advancing before the other, it began the cautious stalking of a quarry fully four or five times its size. Unhurried, unalarmed, confident in its speed, the jack rabbit would bound a hop or two away, then sit down again to watch the stalking approach of its adversary, a very small kitten filled with courage, ambition and graham crackers. And thus they disappeared—their forms gradually losing distinctness, fading away like a dream into the summer night.

After 4:30 that morning, just before daybreak, the meteor shower began to diminish. The last falling star I remember seeing shone bluish, brilliant, going away from us toward the north. Perseus now had ascended far over our heads. All that night the skies had been as silent as the land. We were apparently off the main flight lanes. No single plane droned overhead. Slowly around us, in the first faint light of dawn, we saw the dusty roads emerging, the whole flat prairieland rising out of the night. Minute by minute the light strengthened and the stars paled.

It was after five when we passed the meteorite farm for a final time. The weather-beaten boards, the dusty yard, the dust-grayed trees now all stood out distinctly. In the dawning of that day there were no clouds, little red, only the hard glitter of the sun ascending with a disk of burnished brass. The night, with all its magic and memories, the night of the falling stars, was over.

Stone Dragonflies

CLIMBING into the mountains west of Colorado Springs, we came to the village of Florissant and turned onto a dirt road down a narrow valley nearly 8,200 feet above sea level. In the summer sunshine that morning, the valley floor was gay with the red of Indian paintbrush and the blue of gentians. America's most famous mountain, Pike's Peak, towered in massive silhouette fifteen miles to the southeast. Less than twenty miles ahead lay the historic gold fields of Cripple Creek. Here in this pleasant valley, treasure, too, had been mined—treasure of a different sort. In museums around the world Florissant is famous as the valley of the fossil insects. It was the place we wanted to see first in all of Colorado.

Somewhere between 10,000,000 and 25,000,000 years ago, when the waters of a shallow lake covered the land, and palms and sequoias grew along the shore, the sky above was darkened by the volcanic ash of a succession of violent eruptions. Sifting down through the air and water, this fine material hardened into layers of shale, some paper-thin, on the bed of the lake. Between these layers, as on the pages of a giant illustrated book of the past, the insects of the Miocene were preserved as fossils. More than 30,000 specimens, embracing well over 1,000 different species, have been unearthed here. Approximately one out of every twelve kinds of prehistoric insects known to science have come from this one small valley in Colorado.

But the fame of Florissant—pronounced *Flor*-sent by natives of the region—rests not only in the number and variety of its fossils but on the perfection of detail they have retained. Minute features of even the frailest insects, gnats and mosquitoes and soft-bodied plant lice, have been kept through the ages. In some instances, the individual facets of the compound eyes can be detected with a simple hand lens. In others, the feathery gill tails with which nymphs of some of the smaller dragonflies obtained oxygen from water of the Miocene have been preserved in the minutest detail. Dragonflies of stone, fossil insects that darted about on veined wings in the sunshine of at least 100,000 centuries ago, have been found in half a dozen species in the layered shales of Florissant.

Fossil trees rather than fossil insects originally attracted attention to the valley. From the Ute Indians, early pioneers heard tales of great white trees of stone. They investigated and found the petrified stumps and trunks of immense sequoias, one of them credited with being the largest fossil tree in the world. In the early 1870's the first scientific group, a party of government geologists, explored the valley. Soon afterwards, Dr. Samuel Hubbard Scudder, entomologist of Cambridge, Massachusetts, and the American authority on grasshoppers, began a serious study of the insects of the Florissant shale. For decades he delved among these creatures of the Miocene. In all, Scudder gave names to 233 genera and 1,144 species of fossil insects. His classic monograph, *The Tertiary Insects of North America*, appeared in 1890.

In the intervening years, many men have come to this insect Pompeii to search for victims of those ancient volcanoes. Their finds are scattered through museums and centers of learning in many parts of the world. At present the "white trees" of the Utes, the "petrified stumps" of the pioneers, the fossil-bearing shale of Scudder, can be visited in two adjacent areas, the Colorado Petrified Forest and the Pike Petrified Forest. They lie about thirty-five miles west of Colorado Springs, near the southern extremity of the Front Range of the Rockies. Both are privately owned. For a relatively small fee, visitors can examine the trees and stumps of stone, can dig among the layers of shale and can even keep whatever specimens they find. The deposits of the ancient lake underlie many square miles of the valley, but in these two places the fossil-bearing layers are most readily accessible.

We came to them first that morning, and we were drawn back more than once during our days in Colorado. We walked among the petrified trees. We inspected the largest fossil of its kind on earth, a sequoia stump seventy-four feet in circumference. But it was the layers of shale, ranging from white to chocolate-brown, that absorbed our attention most.

Where embankments had been cut away, the strata lay exposed like the pages of a book lying on its side—pages of unequal thickness. In separating extracted pieces of the layers, visitors have employed a wide variety of impromptu aids—screwdrivers, pincers, nail files, shovels, chisels, jackknives and razor blades. On our first visit, we used a pocketknife; later we brought along a sharp-pointed prospector's pick to help pull out portions of the shale. The rock is rather soft and the most productive layers split apart easily. Not infrequently, the strata were so weakly cemented together we could pull them apart with our hands. When the shale is dry, we soon discovered, the fossils are easier to see.

The richness of the Florissant deposits has been a constant source of amazement to scientists. During one summer in the 1870's, Scudder obtained more than twice the number of fossil insects that the German scientist, Heer, found in thirty years of searching at the famed Bavarian quarries of Oeningen. In 1912, Professor H. F. Wickham, of the University of Iowa, dug a trench about twenty feet long and six feet deep. From it he obtained well over ninety species of beetles, more than forty of them new to science. On several occasions, pieces of shale no larger than an outspread hand have contained several insects preserved close together. This does not mean, of course, that every piece of shale—or every thousand pieces of shale—split apart will contribute a prize.

But nobody knows what will come next. *This* may be the one! Digging for these mementos of the past is like picking up seashells on a strange shore. It becomes an engrossing game. We lost track of time. We dug with a kind of fossil fever, prospector's excitement. With a pocket magnifying glass, we examined each spot and stain. Scudder found that the most numerous of all insects at Florissant—as they are in the world today—were the ants. He collected more than 4,000 ants of fifty different species. They represented about 25 per cent of his total. A dozen times, we thought we had discovered ants. But the magnifying glass refused to be fooled. It expanded the small, dark spot into a bit of leaf or bark.

For fossils of the prehistoric vegetation are the most common of all. In various collections, I have seen the leaves of ferns, of roses, of iris, of elm and chestnut and poplar, sumac and tree of heaven, of balloon vine and the Oregon grape, all obtained from Florissant shale. A complete cattail head, on which some ancient dragonfly may have rested, is imprinted on one rock. Nuts and pine cones and rosebuds and even the delicate petals of wildflowers are numbered among the Florissant fossils. Living representatives of some of the plants now grow in China, Mexico, Norway and the West Indies. Between the layers of shale have been found the skeletons of fish and birds—one a finch, another a plover—as well as fossil tracks and fossil feathers and the small petrified shells of fresh-water mollusks.

Each time we split away a layer of shale and revealed some fragment of an ancient plant, we were letting the first ray of light strike it in millions of years. It had been entombed, just where we found it, since before the ice ages. On the afternoon of our first day at Florissant a piece of light-hued shale produced our best botanical find. It split apart in my hands and revealed a perfect leaf, elongated and serrated. It seemed, at first glance, to have come from a birch. Later, when I compared it with the collection at the University of Colorado, at Boulder, I found it had grown on a prehistoric water elm.

As we looked up from examining this leaf, we were surprised to see a buffalo with a tan-colored calf leading twenty or so black Angus cattle across a neighboring pasture strewn with blue gentians. I glanced from the gentians to the bison to the leaf contained in the rock I had just picked up. Time was linked together in a great triangle by the flower of today, the bison, symbolic of another generation, and the leaf that had formed its chlorophyll under the sun about which this globe had whirled millions and millions of times before the fossil of its tissues had come to light again. That fossil is preserved—as are all the specimens at Florissant, both insect and plant—in the form of a thin film of carbonaceous material.

When Samuel Hubbard Scudder was bestowing scientific names on his Florissant fossils he christened one in honor of "the industrious entomologist of Colorado," T. D. A. Cockerell. Of all those who have explored among the shales of this mountain valley, without doubt the most remarkable was Theodore Dru Alison Cockerell. Born at Norwood, a suburb of London, on August 22, 1866, he was interested in natural history from childhood. His first scientific experiment, he recalled many years later, was to disprove the theory confided to him by a grown-up that yellow primroses planted upside down would come up pink. When his father died in his early thirties, young Cockerell went to work for a firm of flour merchants. Never robust, he contracted tuberculosis in the dusty atmosphere and, in the summer of 1887, at the age of twenty, he sailed for America and the mountain climate of Colorado. It was this misfortune early in his long life—he died at the age of eighty-one—that led him into the natural history of another continent and ultimately into the prehistoric world of Florissant.

In 1890, when Scudder ended his Florissant studies, it was generally assumed that the Colorado shale beds had been worked out. Thus it was not until the summer of 1906 that Cockerell first visited them. He soon decided the beds were almost inexhaustible. Year after year, he and his wife, Wilmatte Porter Cockerell, spent part of each summer exploring among insects of the remote past. During many of these expeditions, they found an average of a new species a day.

They unearthed a tsetse fly, long extinct on this continent but in Africa still the dread carrier of sleeping sickness. They found the leaves of several wild roses and once, when they split open a layer of shale, they came upon a prehistoric rosebud. Their great hope, for years, was to discover a fossil butterfly. The only specimens known to the Western Hemisphere have come from Florissant. After years of searching they were returning to the village one day by a new path. They stopped to rest where a bit of shale protruded from a hillside. Mrs. Cockerell turned over a piece and there was the long-sought fossil, a butterfly so perfectly preserved that the spots were still apparent on the wings. Cockerell named it, in honor of its discoverer, *Chloripe wilmattae.*

The great collection of Florissant fossils that these two made is now housed in the Museum of the University of Colorado. When, later on, we visited this institution at Boulder, we saw spiders and earwigs and lantern flies, cicadas and back-swimmers, a wasp that resembled a yellow jacket and a weevil with a slender snout, not unlike the beetles we find in roses today. A number of the prehistoric leaves contained the swellings of insect galls, and a small sheet of rock held the larval case within which a prehistoric caddis fly had lived in the shallow lake at Florissant.

In our own search for a fossil insect, we continued to be disappointed. I discovered the fragment of a root. Nellie found some kind of small seed. We both uncovered bits of leaves and portions of twigs. Each time we sank the prospector's pick into the soft rock and pulled out a plate of shale to split apart and examine, we hoped to expose some insect of the Miocene. We tried hard to make insect wings from bits of leaf. But we were never completely convinced.

Then I found it! I inserted the thin blade of my jackknife carefully between two layers of gray shale. They fell apart. There, revealed where it had lain since before there were human eyes on earth to see it, was the clear form of a large crane fly. One of its wings was almost perfectly preserved. The other was partially crumpled and damaged. In the long-ago days when it fluttered over the lake shore among the sequoias and palms, the span of those wings must have been at least an inch and a half. We examined our prize over and over. There was the body and there the head and there the widespread, sprawling, stiltlike legs characteristic of all the crane flies.

We sat in great content under one of the pine trees that afternoon. We let our eyes wander over the pleasant scene around us, over the thin spires of the green gentians, over the tansy asters—still blue, still pungently aromatic when crushed—over the rose-pink cranesbill with its geraniumlike bloom, over all the quiet beauty of these latter days of summer. Relaxed, we listened to the little sounds around us, to the flutter of the dancing grasshoppers and the low croon of the breeze among the pine needles. Immense cumulus clouds, snowy white in the sunshine, piled continually higher in the sky.

Just so, other clouds, black and tumbling and volcano-born, had once billowed up here. They had darkened the sky, bearing their burden of ash. We tried, as we talked, to reach back across the millions of years and visualize that day of destruction, the last day in the life of the crane fly. Then everything we now saw had been reversed. The sunshine had been extinguished. The day had been turned into night. The tumbling clouds were black instead of white. The clear air was choked with the endless, sifting fall of fine volcanic ash. Under its hardening mantle, the crane fly had slowly altered into fossil form. There it had remained unchanged through millenniums and eras, ages and epochs, while mountain ranges rose and coast lines altered and ice ages came and went. And now, at last, on this late-summer day of sunshine, we had split open two sheets of shale and the crane fly within had returned once more to the world of light.

High Tundra

MOUNTAIN flower fields. Timberline gardens. The high tundra in bloom. One of the most dramatic events of summer is the flowering of the mountain heights when Alpine plants bloom all across the lofty meadows above timberline. This we had never seen. This we had long hoped to see. And now it was all around us.

We had ascended the Trail Ridge Road that climbs to a height of 12,183 feet in crossing the Rocky Mountain National Park in the north-central part of Colorado. For four miles it runs above 12,000 feet, and nearly one-fourth of its forty-eight miles is above timberline. Following roughly an ancient trail of the Ute Indians, it is the highest continuous automobile road in America. During the summer, when the mountain flower show reaches its height in July and August, the Trail Ridge Road is the country's most spectacular path into the world of Alpine blooms. It leads across eleven miles of tundra in the sky.

Far above timberline the sweep of wiry grass and stunted herbs is comparable to the tundra beyond the tree line in the far north. The climate of these mountaintops is similar to that of Siberia and upper Alaska. We had climbed into such surroundings as we might have found beyond the Arctic Circle, at a latitude of seventy degrees instead of the forty we occupied. During our ascent from Estes Park, the temperature had dropped about three degrees for every 1,000 feet we climbed, a total of nearly fourteen degrees. Gone was the heavy heat of the Great Plains. The sparkling, rarefied air was pleasantly cool in spite of the blaze of the sun, as we wandered over the high meadows amid the unfamiliar flora of the Arctic plants.

August was departing. Blooming time was drawing to a close. We were a little late. But, among the mountains, this particular summer season was reported to be nearly two weeks behind normal. This was our good fortune. For, above timberline, plants were still rushing into bloom, swiftly maturing their seeds. Even though we had arrived near the end of the show, the glory of the Alpine meadows, of mountains in flower, spread about us.

Henry Thoreau concluded that, in the vicinity of Walden Pond, in eastern Massachusetts, nine-tenths of the wildflowers had finished their blooming by the end of July. Here, some 1,700 miles to the west, where the high-country summer was drawing so close to its early autumn, we were seeing the last small fraction of the blooms of the year. Yet how rare, how strange, how beautiful they were!

Each time we visited these treeless heights, under the drifting clouds, surrounded by mountains shining in the sunlight and mountains dark in the shadows, we made new discoveries among the wildflowers. Tufts of white, some turning pink as they grew older, were scattered widely on slender stems. They were the flowers of the bistort, a buckwheat of the high mountains. Yellow five-petaled blooms rose above leaves deeply toothed and purplish-green. They were the Arctic avens. All the cream-colored flowers of that Alpine member of the snapdragon family, *Chionophila jamesi*, the snow-lover, were concentrated—like half the feather on an arrow—along one side of the supporting stem.

Frequently we came upon the clustered floral goblets of the Arctic gentians. In a single clump, we found eighteen massed together, each greenish-white, streaked or spotted with purple. What appeared to be escaped red clover growing in dwarf form on the mountaintop caught our attention. It was the miniature rose or Parry's clover of the high meadows. Beside one Lilliputian pool on the tundra, a clump of plants lifted on short, silvery stems masses that seemed formed of dark red beads. They proved to be the almost opened buds of a sedum or stonecrop, the king's crown, *Sedum integrifolium*. A little farther down the same slope, we came upon another sedum, the rose crown, pink instead of richly red. And each day, as the sun sank lower and we looked toward it down a slope, we saw the bracts of the yellow paintbrush turned to golden-flamed torches in the backlighting. The red paintbrush predominates at lower levels, the yellow above timberline.

According to Dr. P. A. Rydberg, a specialist in the group, there are approximately 250 species of plants belonging to the strictly Alpine flora of the Rockies. In addition there are about 100 other species that occur above as well as below timberline. Few plants survive with more tenacity than these high-mountain species. Almost all are perennials. Summer is too short to complete their life cycle in a single season. In the case of some Arctic plants, years go by during their slow advance from germination to a first blooming. We gazed in awe at these small, frail-appearing, enduring plants, their slow progress gained, their growth so hardly won, now at last in the blooming time and seedtime of their lives.

Most of them hugged the earth, miniature plants with miniature blooms. We bent to look closely at a tiny spray of yellow goldenrod. It was dwarfed to a height of no more than three inches. In the shelter of a stone, Nellie discovered a minute willow—I believe it was that smallest of its kind, the Rocky Mountain snow willow. Its top rose hardly more than the length of my forefinger above its roots. Yet it was covered with white and fluffy catkins, some of them dangling down for almost half the height of the tree.

Not infrequently, the Arctic plants huddled together in dense clusters or mats. Strewn across the cushions of the moss campion were pink flowers, across those of the Alpine sandwort white flowers. Where one mat of moss campion had already bloomed and gone to seed, the low, dense plant mass, eighteen or more inches in length, appeared to flow like viscid fluid over and down between two small rocks pink with feldspar. Experiments have shown that mats of moss and darker plants, high on a mountain top, absorb sufficient solar radiation to produce at times a microclimate of their own. In one instance, the temperature of the air a few inches from the ground was only ten degrees above zero, while within a mat of dark-hued plants it was fifty degrees F.—a difference of forty degrees. Thus some of these densely clustered plants are able to grow even when the temperature of the air around them is below the freezing point.

At every step we sank into the springy layer of turf beneath our feet. How many ages of slow development from the humus of moss and lichen, from the deliberate, infinitesimal erosion of rocks, had produced the first of this mountaintop soil! Great rocks, pink-tinted, thrust up through this thin skin of vegetation. And always the cloud shadows swept across us, across the great rocks and the little rocks scattered everywhere around us, across the flowers of the tundra sod.

The Alpine bloom we wanted most to see was the little red elephant flower. Its history is curious. It was originally discovered on Greenland as its scientific name, *Pedicularis groenlandica*, indicates. Later it was found growing under the Arctic conditions of high mountaintops in the Rockies. The first of these fairyland flowers we came upon was rooted between twining threads of seeping water that advanced almost imperceptibly down the incline. Above its fine-cut, comblike leaves, it lifted a purplish-pink spike formed of many flowers. We bent close and examined it with mounting delight. Each little flower resembled a miniature elephant's head complete with flaring ears, bulging forehead and down-curving trunk. What that long-ago botanist had first seen on Greenland's Arctic tundra, we were seeing on this mountain summit in mid-America. Although separated by thousands of miles, the little red elephant flowers of Greenland and those in Colorado bloom at the same time.

Many years ago, in an Alpine garden in the Tyrol, the great student of living plants, Anton von Kerner, conducted exhaustive studies of the changes that take place when lowland plants are transferred to higher elevations. He found that those that survived tended to shorten their stems. The color of the petals becomes more intense. And most surprising of all, in spite of the fact that the growing season begins much later in the high meadows, the same species may bloom earlier on the heights than in the lowland. In the case of such European plants as *Gentiana germanica* and one of the *Parnassia*, the flowers opened among the foothills in August while, in the mountain meadows of the upper Alps, the blooms appeared in July. Mountaintops receive direct sunlight, through thin atmosphere, with few of the rays filtered out. There the life of the plant is speeded up.

One spot on the tundra we visited again and again. We left our car in a tiny mountain turnout and climbed upward for half a mile or so, first among the contorted trunks of timberline, then out upon the tundra and finally beside a lonely little snowfield nestled at the foot of a rock slide. Here we were at the edge of a great saddle, 12,000 feet high, alone, completely, intensely alone, with the rugged grandeur of the mountains spreading away peak on peak around us. We never saw signs of another human being. We never saw a footprint here other than our own. Always we had the snowfield and the flower-carpeted tundra to ourselves. It was our own special, magic place.

Here the Alpine flowers bloomed in greatest variety. They pressed close to the snowfield; they streamed away down the saddle slopes; they climbed above us, circling the fallen talus and ascending the tundra to higher, greater rocks where the marmots lived. Little flowers, demure flowers, bright flowers, flowers that were all wonderfully new, led us on and on over the treeless heights.

We often sat on low stones to see, closer at hand, the small Alpine plants around us. In two square feet of the mountain turf, I once found the yellow paintbrush, the rose-purple of little clover, the white of bistort and the yellow of the dwarf senecio. Close to timberline, Nellie discovered the pale blue flowers of Jacob's ladder, a plant that first blooms on Long Island in the spring but here was in a late flowering on the dividing line of September. Only once did we see a wand lily and rarely did we catch sight of the yellow avens.

Only a few weeks before, the Alpine avens had been the dominant flower of the high meadows. During our successive visits we found, when several days intervened, marked changes in the blooming plants. One time we returned to our little snowfield and discovered the white of new bistort strewn thickly over wide patches of the tundra. Again, green gentians seemed to have sprung up like mushrooms all down the damper stretches of the slope.

The snowfield itself changed and shrank from day to day. It was not part of the perennial snow of the high mountains. Rather it was a melting fragment of a winter drift. Close beside it we beheld the creamy yellow blooms of our first Alpine anemone. And above it, at the time of our earliest visit, a great clump of Colorado columbine, the flower of the state, leaned out over the rock slide, its pale-blue and white flowers, each fully two inches across, nodding in the breeze. We counted seventeen of these delicate, gorgeous flowers in this single cluster.

And as we gazed our delight was suddenly multiplied. For a large sphinx moth, marked with pink and subtle shadings of gray, materialized in front of the flowers. Before each in turn it hung hummingbird-wise, caught as by a spotlight in the full brilliance of the mountain sunshine. Bees and bee-fertilized flowers are largely left behind on the heights. Blooms pollinated by other insects increase.

Two miles and more above sea level, the insects we saw appeared darker in hue than species lower down. One large dragonfly, almost black, went sailing by. Even the butterflies seemed more dusky of wing. This characteristic has been noted both among Arctic and Alpine insects. Their darker colors absorb more of the heat of the sun.

In seventeenth-century London, Samuel Pepys set down in his now-famous diary the following entry: "23rd. In my black silk suit (the first day I put it on this year) to my Lord Mayor's by coach, with a great deal of honourable company, and great entertainment. At table I had very good discourse with Mr. Ashmole wherein he did assure me that many insects do often fall from the sky, ready formed."

And so they do—not because they are generated in the atmosphere as men of Pepys' day believed, but in accordance with the simple rule that what goes up must come down. Swept aloft by powerful updrafts, even wingless species are sometimes carried far. During summer months there is a continual floating population in the air and a constant rain of life from the sky. Especially is this true among the mountains.

For twenty years, Dr. Gordon Alexander of the University of Colorado studied the altitudinal distribution of grasshoppers in his state. He found that these insects outnumber all others on the high meadows of the Alpine Zone. Yet of the twenty-eight species and subspecies collected there, only eleven can be classed as residents. All the others have been carried up the slopes and deposited by the rising winds.

One dramatic consequence of these grasshopper winds of the Rockies is the formation of grasshopper glaciers. When the insects are deposited on permanent fields of snow and ice, they become numbed, frozen and often embedded in the glacier. The most famous site of the kind, in the Beartooth Range of southern Montana, a wall of ice eighty feet high and a mile long, is streaked with successive layers of insects. The lowest stratum, buried under sixty feet of ice, is centuries old. During the hottest days of summer, melting releases some of these insects from cold storage, and rosy finches—and even bears—come to feed on a banquet of grasshoppers.

Rosy finches alighted, too, on our little snowfield in search of insects. They were the brown-capped rosy finches, beaver-brown with varying shadings of red. Almost their entire breeding range is confined to Colorado. They nest above timberline and winter in the valleys. Several times, little family groups drank, within thirty feet of us, at a thin rivulet of meltwater that ran off down the slope. Several of these birds were not long from the nest. They opened their bills and fluttered their wings and followed other finches begging for food.

In several places on the melting snow we noticed small dead insects with little pits beneath them. Their darker bodies had absorbed more of the heat of the sun and concentrated melting there. It was similar pits—deeper and larger, formed beneath dead grasshoppers—that enabled the first party of Government geologists to reach the top of the Grand Tetons, in Wyoming. By using these insect-produced pits as finger holds, they pulled themselves up the last steeply-tilted sheet of ice to attain the summit.

Once, when we were bending over an Alpine flower, we heard a sudden chiming of sweet bird warbles—all the finches calling. We looked up. On slender, pointed wings, pale sandy-hued with dark patches under the base of each, a prairie falcon skimmed up and over the saddle, saw us, swerved away down above the treetops of the timberline. It was another hawk, I think, that surprised us most. Tilting this way and that, white rump patch appearing and disappearing as it turned, a marsh hawk came beating low above the tundra. Each year among the Rockies, this bird—associated in our minds with lowland fields—makes an altitudinal food migration, ascending higher and higher between August 1 and September 15 until it is foraging for mice along the summits of the mountains.

We speak of mountain weather. We should, no doubt, speak of mountain "weathers." For where else are the varieties so great, the changes so sudden? One afternoon, as we wandered above timberline, the sky darkened swiftly. A chill wind raced ahead of the storm. Thunder, in the wake of broad flashes of lightning, rumbled on and on, caught among the peaks. Beneath the black clouds, long, descending veils of rain or snow drifted in ever-parting curtains that, in turn, obscured and revealed the distant slopes. Rain was falling when we left the tundra; snow was driving around us when we reached the wind timber of tree line; hail was descending when we found a sheltered nook and a seat on an ancient spruce trunk.

Sitting there, we listened to the changing music of the wind among the branches and needles of the Engelmann spruce. Among trees the force of the wind swiftly abates. Measurements have shown that 1,000 feet within a forest the velocity of the wind drops to one-tenth its speed in the open. Around us, sheltered by the twisted trees, the delicate blue of chiming bells ran in clusters and waves along the slope. We had been there hardly a quarter of an hour when the clouds and the trailing veils of snow and rain moved away toward the east. The sky was swept clear. The sun shone. A yellow, black-capped pileolated warbler darted among the spruce needles. All in less than an hour's time, we had experienced sunshine, clouds, veils of falling vapor, rain, snow, hail, lightning and thunder; black, swollen sky, clear air and sunshine again.

At the close of another afternoon, toward sunset, we sat on a lichen-covered rock above the clump of Colorado columbine and ate our supper of sandwiches and large sweet blue plums. Over us, American pipits flew, calling their names, to alight on boulders or walk over the ground, brownish birds wagging their white-edged tails. Behind us, low shafts of sunshine streamed out of a broken sky. They picked out, as in a spotlight, distant peaks and slopes. From where we sat, we could look down over the saddle on the timberline of the mountains ranged about us. We could see the forests climbing the steep ascents, slowing down, bending forward, falling prostrate and ending in a ragged line of matted needles and contorted branches pressed against the ground.

In this area, timberline occurs at about 11,500 feet. It varies 1,000 feet between northern and southern Colorado. Where strong winds blow, the timberline may be depressed as much as 1,500 feet. Looking away below us, we could see the tree line varying with local conditions from mountain to mountain. It stood lower on the shaded than on the predominantly sunny slopes. It rarely ran in a straight line. Tiny advantages and disadvantages are sufficient to tip the scales of life and death in the harsh struggle that is unending along these upper limits of the trees.

After a time, one of the shafts of light swept the tundra slope behind us. The flowers turned luminous. Among them all, across the turf, among the rocks, in the golden mist of backlighting, shining yellow disks like sunflowers stood out. They were the single blooms of the Alpine goldflower, the sun god, the old man of the mountain, *Rydbergia grandiflora*. Some of these flower disks were four inches across, larger than many of the sunflowers on the dry plains 7,000 feet below. Furry gray stems lifted the blooms only a few inches above the ground. Anton von Kerner, long ago, pointed out that high-mountain plants, exposed to the wind, often have woolly stems and silky or felted foliage. An outer layer of sapless, airfilled, interwoven hair structures provides protection against too rapid evaporation.

As we roamed along the slope, photographing the glowing flowers, we came upon an elk horn gnawed by mice in search of calcium. At times we found ourselves in a maze of wandering, interconnecting cylinders of solid sand and pebbles. In cleaning out and enlarging their burrows at the end of winter, pocket gophers had packed the excavated material into tunnels they had made under the snow. When summer comes and the drifts melt, the resulting labyrinth of earth cores—two or two and a half inches in diameter and sometimes covering hundreds of square feet—stands out in pale yellow on the green of the tundra.

Among the jumble of great rocks that rose a quarter of a mile above us, marmots called back and forth in the sunset. In that thin, far-carrying double note, we heard some of their last whistles of the year. It was now only a matter perhaps of days, of two or three weeks at most, before they would fall into the profound, deathlike winter sleep that occupies seven of the twelve months of their year.

Steadily the shadow of the mountain behind us crept across the tundra saddle. Around us our last sunset on the heights slowly faded. By 6:30 P.M., the wind had fallen, the birds were gone, the marmots were silent. The stillness of the summit became so intense our ears seemed to hum. The soundless mountaintop resembled a country village shut up tight for the night. We started down, winding like mountain goats among the rocks, crossing a marmot run and an elk trail on our way to timberline.

When first we came to the unfamiliar world of these high peaks, they left us feeling small and lost, overawed and alien. Then we made friends with the little things, the bistort and the chiming bells, the rosy finches and the pipits, the moss campion and the snow willow, the avens and the deep purple bells of the penstemon clusters. We became familiar with fragments of the whole. We went, bit by bit, from the particular to the general. And thus, advancing inductively from the small to the large, we came to know and love the mountains.

The Great Eyrie

ONE o'clock. Snow is scudding past our cabin windows in the darkness. Five o'clock. The sky is clear and stars are shining. Seven o'clock. In the morning light, the great mountain towers above us, white-crowned with snow. Eight o'clock. The morning papers headline the weather news. All over the Rockies snow had fallen during the night. The Pike's Peak Highway is blocked by drifts at its upper end. Officials estimate it will take at least twenty-four hours to clear the road. Ten o'clock. We gaze at the mountaintop, glistening in the sun. We look at it through our field glasses. Our hopes of attaining the summit on this last day of our summer journey are gone. Eleven o'clock. We switch on the car radio. A news announcer reports that clearing operations have been speeded up. Officials have revised their estimates. The highway to the summit will be open by early afternoon.

It was two o'clock when we started up. Twenty miles of climbing loops and zigzags, switchbacks and 160-degree turns lay ahead of us. The spectucular road of graded dirt—built in 1915—carried us through four life zones. Part way up, it brought us out on top of the Front Range and we saw, 125 miles away to the west, the snow-mantled peaks of the Continental Divide. Just below timberline, seven miles from the summit, at an elevation of 11,525 feet, we stopped for a rest at the Glen Cove parking field. Ten minutes later we were climbing again.

We left the last stunted Engelmann spruce behind and crept in zigzags up across the snow-covered boulder fields above tree line. Ravens were twisting and diving away in wild aerial games. There had been wind in the lower valleys, but here on the high slopes the air was almost still. A cloudless sky stretched above us and all the panorama that spread farther and farther away as we ascended was softened by the faint blue-tinted and shining haze. Our road extended before us, tilting upward, a plowed-out lane between recently installed snow poles that marked its wandering course among the huge pink-tinted boulders. This was one of the highway's last open days. In a week, or two weeks at most, it would be closed for the season. Snowdrifts twenty-five feet deep would cover it in winter.

We pulled up the last steep incline. Our wheels rolled on the level of the summit. We were 14,110 feet high, more than two and a half miles above the level of the sea, within fifty feet of being six times as high as the average altitude of the North American continent. At Tennessee Pass, we had climbed to 10,000 feet; at Monarch Pass to 11,000 feet; on the Trail Ridge Road to 12,000 feet. Here, at more than 14,000 feet, we were at the highest point of our summer travels. From this lofty eyrie, on this last day of the season, we could look away over the land through which we had wandered.

The last thing we expected to find on the naked shingles of the mountain roof was traffic congestion. Yet for a few minutes we seemed to be in Times Square. Thirty or forty other cars were parked or milling about—old Fords and new Fords, Cadillacs and Jaguars, Chevrolets and Volkswagens and Oldsmobiles, a Rolls-Royce and a Jeep. During the month of August alone, more than 20,000 motorcars had made the long ascent. They had transported in excess of 95,000 persons to the summit. The grand total for the summer season was well over a quarter of a million. Nobody knows how many human feet have walked about on the top of this mountain that Zebulon Pike believed no mortal man would ever climb.

More than half a century has passed since the first automobile reached the summit of Pike's Peak. On August 12, 1901, using the route of the cog railway, C. A. Yont and W. B. Felker drove a two-cylinder Locomobile steamer to the top. Now buses run up and down the mountain daily and a fleet of luxury limousines—air-conditioned, pressurized Cadillacs known locally as "Sherpa Caddys"—follow all the windings of the famed ascent. Each Labor Day, drivers from many parts of the world compete in a "Race for the Clouds," the winners maintaining for the long climb, with its switchbacks and hairpin turns, an average speed of more than a mile a minute.

Visitors to the mountaintop that day ranged from a baby carried about wrapped in a blanket to an elderly couple in their eighties. One woman in the low stone Summit House, which has weathered mountain gales since it was erected in 1882, was weighing herself to see if it was really true that she would weigh less at the top of a high mountain. Most of the cars stayed only a little while before they headed back down the road again.

As the afternoon advanced and the cars drifted away, we roamed over the boulder-strewn acres that form the flattened tip of the mountain. In all directions we looked away into the pastel shadings and smoky blues of the distance—toward the serrated line of the Great Divide, up the Front Range of the Rockies toward the north where the Trail Ridge Road now was blocked with snow, to the south and west where the Sangre de Cristos hid the Great Sand Dunes at their western base, to the east out over Colorado's level land, its tawny-yellow plains cut by the fine lines of branching roads and dotted with the far-spaced clusters of its towns and villages.

It was this eastward vista, viewed from this mountaintop at sundown, that inspired Katharine Lee Bates' patriotic hymn, "America the Beautiful." Other nations have glorious mountains, breathtaking views. But none can approach the incomparable variety of wild beauty that is the heritage of this land—with its Yosemite, its Niagara, its Grand Canyon, its Old Faithful, its Carlsbad Cavern, its timberline gardens and deserts bursting into bloom, its Olympic forests and its ancient sequoias, its snow-clad peaks and all the teeming bird life of its coastal swamps. This gift of natural beauty is a rare and precious possession. The opportunity for citizens to enjoy it freely, now and in the future, is one of the inalienable rights of Americans.

As we stood discussing such things, two businessmen struck up an acquaintance nearby. They talked endlessly, loudly, always on the same subject: the clubs they had belonged to, how one had presided over a grand conclave, how the other had headed a committee that brought in twenty-two new members. All the while the great spiritual experience of the mountains was passing them by. Unseen, unfelt, unappreciated, the beauty of the land unfolded around them. The clubs of the world formed their world entire. It enclosed them like the home of a snail wherever they went. For them, the scene would have been just as moving if they had been hemmed in by billboards.

In time, the businessmen went down the mountain. One by one the cars rolled away. Nellie and I were almost alone in the stillness of the mountain heights. Far below we could see the tangled thread of the road we had climbed twisting across the boulder fields. Away to the north, through our glasses, we picked out the very ridge with its ponderosa pines where our log cabin waited with wood piled beside the fireplace. The rarefied air, in the late afternoon, grew swiftly cold. Even when, under the burning summer sun, the ground at the top of Pike's Peak reaches a temperature of 140 degrees F., the thin air five feet above it is only half as warm.

With the sinking of the sun, we stood by the tracks of the cog railway, east of the Summit House, and watched the shadow of the mountain creeping down the slope. Nineteen thousand miles away, as our course had carried us, we had seen the sunrise of the season's first day extend to the west the shadow of the New England mountains. Now the setting sun of the season's last day was casting to the east the shadow of this peak in the Rockies. Shadows to the west, shadows to the east, these enclosed our summer.

We watched the shade descend the slope, turning the snow blue among the pink rocks. We saw it grope its way among the foothills, darken the valley of Manitou Springs and the Garden of the Gods, extend out across the grid-work maze of the streets of Colorado Springs and then rush on, darker blue, over the blue plains beyond. At first its form was blunt and wide of base. Then it became more sharply triangular, ever elongating, its tip stretching out more keenly pointed. In a great spearhead, it plunged with accelerating speed across ranches and roads toward the far-off horizon. Pike's Peak rose like a titanic, 2½-mile-high sundial, its shadow, as we saw it, indicating the hour of the year, the lateness of the season.

A few minutes before six o'clock we watched the extended tip of this last of the summer shadows touch the horizon. For more than 100 miles it extended toward the east. Summer, the season of light, the season of life, was almost over. When the sun rose again it would stretch to the west the first shadows of autumn. We gazed in silence at the darkening land. Back there, in the direction the shadow finger pointed, lay the looping, twisting, backtracking course of our journey. There we had seen the painted trilliums and the mayfly storm, the mysterious maples, the fireflies of the Kankakee, the falling stars and the home of the prairie dogs. As we watched, the shadow of the peak gradually lost its sharpness, faded slowly away, became swallowed up in the universal shadow of the mountain ranges. The sun had set on the summer season. All our wandering course now lay in the shadow of autumn's eve.

Still we lingered on. We were alone on the mountaintop, the last to leave. We remained while the dusk fell, while the wall of haze, touched with green, mounted along the eastern horizon, while all the higher peaks to the west were surrounded by a darkening saffron glow. Airway beacons twinkled along the lower mountaintops when finally we left the great eyrie and started down. With headlights switched on, we descended slowly, across the boulder fields, below the timberline with its ancient, contorted trees, so slow to grow, so slow to die, so slow to waste away. Winding downward, turning constantly, we descended into the blackness of the night.

Later, in our log cabin among the pines, a dozen miles north of Pike's Peak, we piled sticks of wood into the stone fireplace and sat in the warmth of the flames. About ten o'clock, we stepped outside to listen to the sound of the wind in the long needles of the ponderosa pines. To the northeast, a patch of glowing reddish light in the heavens caught our attention. It expanded as we watched, grew more brilliant. Then we noticed to the north another patch and still another. They swelled and merged and deepened their color. Behind them, pale bands of silver rose, probing upward toward the zenith. Unable to believe our good fortune, we stared at these resplendent northern lights, a red aurora.

For more than an hour this heavenly display continued with its spearing shafts of silver and its glowing pools of red. Their intensity waxed and waned, gradually fading away, then strengthening once more. At last the silvery streamers became too faint to see. Then the red flush paled and disappeared entirely. By eleven o'clock, the ethereal pageant was over. We returned to the cabin, piled more wood on the coals and in the light of the crackling flames waited for the boundary minute of the season.

It came well after midnight, at 2:27 A.M. The fire had died down. We stood at the window looking up at the alabaster peak soaring aloft surrounded by stars. Each heavenly body, in the clear, cold mountain air, burned with a special brilliance. Orion hung almost directly over the peak. The Milky Way flowed to its right. Here were the stars we had seen so often on our trip, the stars that bring, in their courses, all the seasons and that now were bringing the summer's end. We turned away from the window. In the silence of that star-filled night, the great summer of our lives had ended.

AUTUMN
ACROSS AMERICA

Monomoy

WHERE low dunes roll their yellow waves inland from the shore on Monomoy; where the shifting blues and greens and purples of the open Atlantic stretch away unbroken to Europe from Monomoy; where slow waves trip and spill and slide in foam up the shining incline of the beach and sanderlings flow, on scurrying feet, up and back with every wave on Monomoy; there, under the late-August sun, amid the sparse marram grass and seaside goldenrod, on Cape Cod's far-eastern tide line of the continent, our long adventure with the fall began.

The tide rose to full and made its turn. And all across the continent behind us another tide, a greater tide—the tide of the seasons—was also at its turn. Summer, during these last of the August hours, was accelerating its yearly slide into autumn. Curlew and godwit, dowitcher and plover already were moving southward along the narrow flyway of the shore. And on the mainland, in the waning summer nights, bobolinks were taking wing for far-off South America. These were the early ripples of migration, ripples we would later see mount into the great waves of the autumn flight.

Not many miles from where we stood, Henry Thoreau once faced the Atlantic on an outer beach of Cape Cod and observed that there a man had put all America behind him. For us, rather, all America lay before us.

Here where Monomoy points its ten-mile finger of sand from Cape Cod toward the island of Nantucket we were at the beginning of 20,000 miles of wandering through autumn, the third season, the most colorful of the year. Before us stretched glorious days of drifting in that time described on an ancient page as "these golden weakes that doe lye between the thunderous heates of summer and the windy gloomes of winter."

Our car was packed—binoculars and cameras and field guides stowed away, marked maps cramming the glove compartment, tramping shoes and raincoats ready in the trunk. The pleasures of preparation were over. The days of dreaming, the evenings of planning, the months of anticipation were behind us. Nellie and I were starting again on an adventure with a season.

When we had come north with the spring, some years before, Monomoy had been veiled in sheets of falling rain. Now the air was shining with the haze of summer's ending and the slow beat of the sea was in our ears. In spring we had journeyed north; following the path of the season, keeping pace with its progress up the map from Florida to Canada. Now we were cutting across the advancing front of a season, across the whole continent-wide sweep of the North American autumn—across the four great flyways of the migrating birds, through the multicolored forests of the hardwoods, over the prairie fall, through the high autumn of the Rockies and the desert autumn of the salt flats and the rain-forest autumn of the Northwest. We would see a thousand moods and facets of the season. We would see new birds, new lands, new trees, all in the surroundings of fall. Nowhere in the world is autumn more beautiful than in America. And we would witness it all—across the land from east to west, as the sun shines on it, as the pioneers saw it trekking to Oregon, as the flow of American history crossed the continent.

Only in very recent years has such a trip as my wife and I planned been possible, carrying us, as it would, into out-of-the-way corners of more than half of the states in the Union, all in a single season. Audubon and Bartram and Muir traveled on foot or on horseback or by stagecoach. Many autumns—and every autumn is different—would have been required to witness the coming of the season from coast to coast. To see it in one continuous flow we depended upon innumerable innovations of the restless present, on highways and filling stations and radio weather reports. We talked that day, as we stood amid the seaside goldenrod and sparse marram grass on Monomoy, of all the people to whom we were indebted for bringing within our grasp this dreamed-of journey through autumn—the steel workers, the automobile makers, the road menders, the glass-factory technicians, even those old, old innovators, the first men to use fire and employ wheels and devise cloth and leather to keep themselves warm and dry. They all had contributed something to the travels that lay before us and to them all we were profoundly grateful.

There is a midsummer. There is a midwinter. But there is no midspring or midautumn. These are the seasons of constant change.

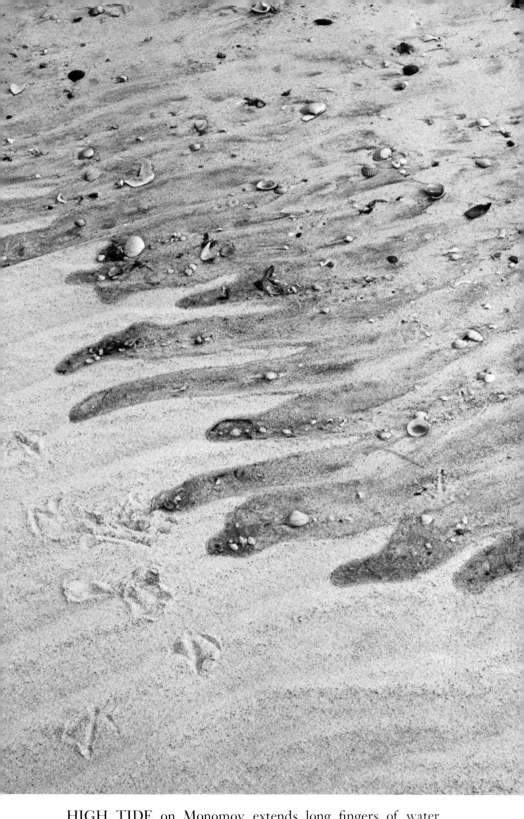

HIGH TIDE on Monomoy extends long fingers of water
among ripples left by wind on the dry sand of the upper beach.

EELGRASS rises in sinuous ribbons through the water. Many marine creatures find protection in its submerged jungles.

MORNING MIST, glowing in the slanting rays of the rising sun, is a feature of many of the early days of autumn.

HEAVY DEW often covers the leaves of plants at dawn as autumn advances. Its glitter adds its beauty to the season.

BEGINNING in this woodland brook flowing from Lake Itasca the Mississippi starts its 2,552-mile journey to the Gulf.

GOLDEN aspens run in clouds of autumn foliage among the
dark evergreens of the Uinta Mountains of northern Utah.

MOUNTAINEER birds, like this Clark's nutcracker, frequently migrate downhill into the valleys when autumn comes.

SALMON leap up the falls at Celilo on their return from
the sea. Here every autumn Indians fished with dip nets.

MISTY FOREST scenery is familiar along the paths of the
Olympic Peninsula where fog is common and rainfall heavy.

RAIN FOREST sunshine brings a glowing, misty light to the
path Nellie follows not far from the bank of the Hoh River.

STREAMLINED bushes at the top of Oregon's windswept
Cape Blanco record the direction of the prevailing gale winds.

SEA LIONS in their cavern on the Oregon coast. Here great combers enter and shatter, filling the interior with foam.

SUNSET CALM and wet, shining sand surround the towering rocks that are a feature of the picturesque Oregon coast.

GREAT SURF pounding at the foot of a headland on the
Pacific coast, gradually eroding away the lofty walls of rock.

ANCIENT bishop pines crown this hilltop on the road to
Point Reyes close to the end of our travels with autumn.

HISTORIC Point Reyes lighthouse perched high above the
sea. It is shown in the low rays of the final sunset of autumn.

Like dawn and dusk they are periods of transition. But like night and day and day and night they merge slowly, gradually. As Richard Jefferies once wrote, broken bits of summer can be found scattered far into the shortening days of fall. Only on calendars and in almanacs are the lines of division sharply defined. Just as in the far reaches of the Everglades we had found a pre-spring spring, a season that was still winter on the calendar but already showing evidences of change, so now, while summer still officially ruled, we were in a pre-autumn autumn surrounded by the signs of coming fall.

During the first days of our wanderings we followed the pointing finger of Monomoy to Nantucket where on the high moors John Kieran showed us golden plover that soon would head across the open sea with landfall on another continent—spanning, without a pause, the distance to Argentina. In the midnight stillness of a Woods Hole laboratory, Rachel Carson introduced us to plumed worms and moss animals, to the bizarre, fascinating creatures that people her book, *The Edge of the Sea*. Then, in the warm sunshine of early afternoon, we rode west on U.S. 6, the longest continuously marked highway in America. Oak leaves, here and there, had fallen and yellow was creeping into the foliage of the locust trees as we left the Cape behind.

Across New England the summer-long pageant of the wildflowers was drawing to a close. Over the lowlands spread the pinkish-purple of the joe-pye weed. Chicory blue, that bluest of blues, shone from the roadside amid the violet-blue of the New England asters. The massed yellow of goldenrod—to the English "farewell-summer"—ran up the hillsides and the madder-purple of ironweed gleamed from the higher pasturelands. These were the varied flower hues that would be replaced in the weeks to come by the blazing colors of the autumn leaves. In New England fall comes as the glorious, flaming sunset of the year.

Already, as we crossed lower Massachusetts and Rhode Island and Connecticut, we could see this brilliance in its initial stages. Scarlet enveloped an occasional sumac. Deeper red ran across the leaves of poison ivy. Along old stone walls, where chipmunks scurried with cheek pouches bulging with seeds, the berries of the bittersweet were yellow, still to split and reveal the brilliant red of the inner coating. Once we rounded a turn and came upon the glorious coloring of the branch of a sugar maple prematurely clad in autumn leaves. Although we were skirting New England along its southern border, although we were in advance of its autumn glory, we could remember from past years that beauty, unsurpassed anywhere around the world.

We could see in our mind's eye the gorgeous tapestry of its rolling countryside, the multicolored ridges curving away mile on mile, the long vistas from its mountaintops. We could see the vivid hues reflected in quiet river reaches and mirrored in the still water of the innumerable ponds and lakes of Massachusetts and Connecticut. We could see the village greens, the white-spired churches, the winding roads, all surrounded by the incomparable pageantry of the autumn leaves. Soon the elms would be scattering golden leaves across the well-cut grass of the village greens, the sugar maples would be lifting upward like sheets of flame and all the breathtaking beauty that envelops this region in the fall would be at its height.

The acid soil of New England, its wide stretches of hardwoods, its numerous sugar maples, its rolling or mountainous character, the sunshine of its autumn weather, all these contribute to the glory of this annual display. The birches of Maine, the aspens of the White Mountains, the sugar maples of Vermont, the long rainbow of the Connecticut River Valley cutting from top to bottom through New England, the Berkshires—mention these to anyone who has traveled widely through a New England fall and you will evoke instant memories of superlative beauty.

This beauty was still to come as we rode west. But other signs of the season were apparent along the coast. Beach plums were ripening close to shore and across all the sea meadows ran a wash of russet-gold. Other plums were ripening, other sea meadows were russet, when, late that day, we crossed to the far-eastern end of Long Island, riding the ferry from the Connecticut shore to Orient Point. Thirty miles away, below the Shinnecock Hills, spread the shallow waters of an extensive bay. Under its surface, as in the sea and along the tide line, fall would give rise to innumerable changes. In one of the memorable adventures of the trip—in the night, in the eelgrass jungles of the bay—I was to see some of this hidden underwater life that autumn so soon would affect.

Forests of the Sea

I ADJUSTED my face mask. Through the oval of its tempered glass I looked up at the nearly full early-September moon. Then I snapped on my underwater flashlight, took a quick, deep breath, kicked with the rubber frog-foot of a swim-fin and followed the beam of my torch down into a strange and silent forest of the sea.

It was ten o'clock at night. I was near the eastern end of Long Island. Monomoy lay 150 miles away. Between the low dark line of the seaward dunes and the high dark line of the landward hills, Shinnecock Bay extended in an expanse of moonlit waters. For more than an hour I had been alternating between this upper world of moonlight and a torch-lit submerged world where the multitudinous ribbons of the eelgrass waved in the current breezes of the bay bottom.

Acre after acre, on and on across the shallows of the bay, the eelgrass extended. Its strands, about three-eighths of an inch wide, were often a yard or more in length. And all this multitude of slender ribbons of green ascended in buoyant, sinuous curves toward the surface. My flashlight, for nearly a minute at a time, would wind among the swaying strands like a luminous eel, its beam sending a play of shadows running over the ribbons beyond. Then I would surface, see the moon through the streaming veil of water running down my face mask, stand chest-deep in the shallows, store up oxygen and dive once more. Half a hundred times I had emerged thus and descended again into the underwater night of this eelgrass jungle.

The ribbons that slid like slippery seaweed along my legs belonged to no ordinary plant. Everything connected with eelgrass—its associations, its past as well as its recent history—all are remarkable. It is not a grass. It is not related to the seaweeds. It belongs to the freshwater pondweed family. It is a flowering plant, one of the very few flowering plants found in salt water. Like the whale and the dolphin, the eelgrass, *Zostera marina*, has gone back to the sea.

Bays and estuaries where it is protected from the most violent action of the waves, shallows where the water is between two and six feet deep at high tide, a bottom that is formed of mixed mud and sand—

these provide the eelgrass with its favored habitat. But sometimes it is found at depths of more than forty feet, and where sluggish rivers join the sea it often ascends the streams to a point where the salinity of the water drops to twenty-five per cent that of the adjacent ocean.

A perennial, the plant reproduces both by seeds and by rhizomes. These creeping, jointed rootlike stems ramify until as many as 2,000 of the eelgrass ribbons may rise from a single square yard of bay bottom. Its capacity for multiplication is so great that scientists have calculated that from one seed the possible total of flowering shoots at the end of twenty-five years would be 8,388,608. The flowers are minute, naked, submerged and rarely seen. They are fertilized by currents that distribute tiny threads of pollen that have a density almost exactly that of water.

Swimming among the strands as among slender carnival streamers, I might have been anywhere in a thousand bays on either side of the Atlantic. Wherever eelgrass grows—whether it is along the coast of Europe, the northern Pacific shore of Asia or the upper part of either seaboard of North America—the underwater scene is much the same. Around the world it is a plant of many names: sea grass, ribbon grass, mallow, drew, sea wrack, bell ware, barnacle grass, sea moss, brant grass, sea oar, glass wrack and tiresome weed—the latter name bestowed, no doubt, by baymen forced to row their boats through its clinging beds or to disentangle the strands from their propellers.

The dry eelgrass that is piled in silver-brown windows on the shore by storms is variously called sea hay, sea wrack and alva marina. Analysis of ashes found on sites of ancient villages in Denmark suggest it was a source of soda and salt for early men. In Europe it has been used as fuel and fertilizer. It has gone into the thatching of French houses and into the construction of dikes in Holland. New England pioneers used it to bank their houses and barns for winter. It has been employed in the manufacture of paper, for bedding domestic animals, for packing glass and china and for stuffing mattresses and chairs. In the First World War Germany turned to eelgrass as a substitute for cotton in making nitrocellulose. During the 1920's it was rather widely employed in soundproofing and insulating. The year of maximum commercial use probably was 1929 when the Netherlands exported 3,000 tons, Nova

Scotia shipped an equal amount and production in the United States exceeded 5,000 tons.

Then disaster, a mysterious catastrophe that is still something of a riddle, brought death to the eelgrass up and down both sides of the Atlantic.

It began late in 1930. First the leaves discolored, then the stems died and finally the roots decayed. Gradually wasting away, the plants were washed ashore. Some scientists blamed the dumping of oil from ocean tankers, others thought a mycetozoan parasite was responsible, others suggested the cause was a fungus while still others maintained some highly infectious bacteria was the source of the swiftly spreading plague. By the summer of 1931 the eelgrass was dying all the way from North Carolina to Cape Cod. The following year the mysterious epidemic swept northward up the Canadian coast and, on the other side of the Atlantic, began devastating the eelgrass beds of England, Holland and France. By 1933 less than one per cent of the eelgrass along the east coast of North America—from southern Labrador to Beaufort, North Carolina—was still alive. As Clarence Cottam says in his excellent summary in the 1934 *Yearbook of Agriculture,* such rapidity of spread and destructiveness by a plant disease is unknown elsewhere in botanical history.

And as the eelgrass was stricken, creatures whose lives depended on it were stricken also. First the brant, those sea geese whose diet is often nearly ninety per cent eelgrass, were brought to starvation. Already reduced by gunning, the flocks shrank so alarmingly that the government declared a year-round closed season along the eastern seaboard. Then the scallops, those remarkable swimming clams that live largely in the eelgrass beds, grew scarce. The shellfish industry was affected. Companies that specialized in eelgrass for soundproofing and stuffing furniture went out of business. Erosion occurred in places where the matted roots previously had anchored down the mud and sand. In the vicinity of Plymouth, England, two species of small sea snails, formerly found clinging to eelgrass, disappeared entirely from the coastal waters and swans, accustomed to feed on the ribbon leaves, began appearing at remote fishing villages in search of scraps. Even some of the plankton of the coastal seas, minute organisms that had found rich fare among the detritus of eelgrass on bay bottoms, became reduced in numbers. Thus, in its effects, the catastrophe that had overwhelmed a single plant carried on and on through the innumerable links of the close-knit chains of natural life.

By the early 1940's, after ten years, the slow comeback of the eelgrass had begun. Brant, grown accustomed to eating sea lettuce, found their favorite food once more in small patches in Shinnecock Bay. For here, at the exact spot where I was exploring on this moonlit September night, the returning eelgrass had gained one of its earliest footholds. Here, in the years since its reappearance, it had spread into one of the most lush and flourishing beds on the eastern coast.

Swimming amid the maze of its sinuous strands I found that now as in the long past it signified home and food to a host of creatures. My torch-beam picked them out—a blue crab as large as my hand sculling in a swift, sidewise dash into a denser tangle; prawns, almost transparent, like creations of glass with eyes that shone pink in the glare; a baby starfish, an inch and a half across, curled around six strands of eelgrass, holding them together like a dull-gold ring on a green finger. Once I nosed out over a little opening so thickly strewn with mud snails that it seemed paved with small cobblestones. Another time I came upon a pipefish motionless and vertical and wonderfully camouflaged among the interlacing ribbons. And always, wherever I went that night, there were the drifting, insubstantial ovals of the little comb jellies, the sea walnuts, entangled like living bubbles in the strands of eelgrass.

At one place I came upon thirty or more of them caught in the upper eelgrass as though among the treetops of a forest. They ranged from half an inch to three inches in length. So transparent were they that I could see the green eelgrass beyond as though looking through clear crystal glass. When I caught one and carried it in my hand to the surface it seemed no more substantial than the white of a raw egg and just as colorless. Yet each time one of these drifting ovals came into the direct line of my flashlight, spots of metallic brilliance glowed on the slender riblike plates that ran lengthwise down the sides of the little ctenophore. Each had eight such plates with cilia, or swimming hairs, extending out from the sides like the teeth of a comb. It was these rapidly moving cilia that were breaking up the rays of light, and by refraction—somewhat as minute striations in the shards of certain beetles produce their vivid colors—were creating the metallic greenish-purple sheen I saw. In brilliant sunshine prismatic colors pass rhythmically down the length of these plates to produce a rainbow-tinted flashing as the transparent creatures propel themselves slowly and deliberately through the water.

Emerging at the end of each successive dive I would hear the band-saw chorus of the conehead grasshoppers in the beach grass a quarter of a mile away. Sometimes, farther out on the bay, I would catch the barking cry of a black skimmer winging its way just above the water, fishing in the moonlight. Then I would slip down again into that still, submerged world where the spotlight of my torch revealed noiseless movement all around me. Snail shells on the bottom advanced with sudden starts and the tiny ribbon of tracks they left behind showed they were inhabited by hermit crabs. Killifish and needlefish—with heads slender and drawn out like the noses of supersonic planes—shot away from their great hiding grounds, the denser tangles. They turned and twisted, navigating expertly the mazes between the strands, moving in unison like flocks of shorebirds on the wing. Once, where all the eelgrass tilted to one side in a current like trees leaning in a wind, and I was standing still with my flashlight pointed down into the water, the dark sliding form of an eel flowed across a small opening toward me. It was two or two and a half feet long with rounded little fins projecting out on either side just behind its head. Like an underwater blacksnake it nosed into the tangle at my feet. I shifted my weight ever so slightly and the eel was gone. One instant it was there; the next it had disappeared in a movement so fast my eye had failed to record it.

For a long time that evening I followed the wandering trail left by a boat that had plowed across the eelgrass beds earlier in the day. It led me above the tan-colored mound of a dead sponge the size of a half-bushel basket, over little openings where the green sea lettuce had collected and above the beautiful *Agardhiella* seaweed, like masses of fine red hair, the favored haunt of the sea horses. My light picked out a spiny crab making its way awkwardly over the bay bottom like something out of *The Wizard of Oz*. A little farther on it revealed the dark shell of an ancient king crab, a foot across and starred with white barnacles. One small opening became an underwater arena where I engaged in a kind of bullfight with a blue crab, heading it off in its rushes, playing a game with it, trying to touch it on the back while it sparred and veered and leaped upward with pincers wide open. A second blue crab, twenty feet away, lay on the bottom completely helpless, its shell split open around the edge. I had found it in the midst of its molt when, soft-bodied, it was emerging from the hard outer skeleton of its previous shell.

But the strangest sight I encountered along this trail through the eelgrass was one I came upon suddenly near its end. A negligent kick with a finned foot had sent me drifting slowly forward when just ahead I saw something round and dark and about the size of an apple perched on top of what looked like a mound of pure white lard. I surfaced for air and descended again. There it was in the beam of my torch, a moonsnail with its great white foot extended. I switched off the light momentarily and the moon of the moonsnail shone eerily in the moonlight of the night. At that moment so strange seemed this world of shallow water from which I had just emerged that it might well have been the setting for the old Norse myth of the fabulous wolf, Fenris, captured at last with the aid of "the breath of fishes, the noise made by a cat's footfall and the roots of stones."

I had hardly left the moon behind and descended among the eelgrass on the very first of my nocturnal dives when my flashlight picked out on the bottom of the bay what looked like a gaping mouth with thick brownish lips and, above and below, rows of shining, blue-green, gemlike eyes. The mouth was the half-open shell of a scallop. The lips were the two mantles formed of innumerable small tentacles just inside the outer edges of the upper and lower halves of the shell. The eyes were round, phosphorescent and functional. Each had a lens, retina and nerve and appeared to be located—as under an eyebrow—beneath one of the projections of the "scalloped" outer edge.

Sometimes these glowing eyes of the mollusks shone out amid the roots of the eelgrass, sometimes they flared into brilliance on the floor of little openings. Once I counted twenty scallops in an open space hardly two yards square. Many of the shellfish were furry above with brownish algae. One had a branching, red *Agardhiella* seaweed, about three inches long, growing upright from its shell. Another, an inch and a half across, carried two limpets, one partly overlapping the other. I was told later of a larger scallop brought up from the bay floor with barnacles, worm-tubes and a hydroid all firmly attached to its shell.

Between the parted lips of the mantles of a number of the scallops my beam illuminated the great central muscle that operates the two halves of the shell. It seemed to form the main contents of the interior, a shining white column like a pillar of alabaster. To the majority of men, this one muscle is all there is of interest to a scallop. It is the only part that is eaten. It forms the popular fried scallops of seafood restaurants. But there is more to scallops than "scallops." In life, the action of this muscle provides the motive power for one of the most unusual of all forms of locomotion. By opening and closing the shell it propels the clam through the water. Each time the shell is opened water rushes in; each time it is closed the fluid is expelled to drive the mollusk ahead. The scallop is a clam that swims swiftly forward or backward. It is a mollusk that can shoot through the water like a flying saucer, jet propelled.

For a long time I was puzzled as to how, exactly, this took place. I learned by what might be termed research or again might just be called the hard way. Bringing a scallop to the surface I lifted it out of the water. It opened and snapped shut with a sound like a steel trap. I dropped it in surprise. The next scallop managed to close on one of my fingers. It chewed on it rapidly, opening and closing its shell four or five times, before I got it out. After that I was careful where I held a scallop.

That lesson learned, I began to investigate the jets of ejected fluid. Swimming normally a scallop appears to be biting its way through the water. It keeps opening and clapping shut its shell—seems taking gulps of seawater—each time shooting forward with the rounded edge leading and the hinge trailing. Two streams of water, one on either side of the hinge, drive it forward. But exactly where do these twin jets emerge? I assumed they followed channels out of the "stirrups" of the hinge. Lifting out one of the shellfish and pushing back my face mask, I peered close. A stream of water shot out and caught me squarely in the right eye. Wiping away the salt water I made mental note that the jet had come, not as expected from the end of the hinge, but from the side of the shell just above the hinge where the two halves bulged slightly apart.

But that is not the only place where a scallop ejects water—as I soon discovered. I was leaning over another, with the hinge and the bulge-openings safely pointed downward, when the mantle parted slightly in the middle and an even more powerful jet squirted its stream into my left eye. I had learned my lesson and the next scallop was held edge-wise with the side of its shell toward me. If it shot up or down I would be missed. But it did not do either. It shot through an opening made in the mantle on my side, catching me squarely in the right eye again. That decided me. I knew all I needed to know about how a scallop ejects its jets of water.

These larger streams, fired through openings in the mantle, are used in emergencies. They enable the mollusk to take off in a sudden, hinge-first zoom from the floor of the bay. A single shot from these water guns will sometimes send it scaling ahead for several feet. The jets are also used to flip the shellfish over if it lands wrong side up on the sand and mud. For there is a right side and a wrong side to its shell when it comes to rest. One valve is more curved than the other. By resting on this more rounded side the scallop is lifted slightly above the bottom and so is better able to feed and to take off.

Several times when I headed with an outstretched arm toward a scallop it shot jerkily upward, clapping the two valves of its shell together and leaving a little cloud of sediment rising from the place where it had been. At other times the shellfish made no move even when I extended a hand and picked them up. Until the last moment I thought this was going to be the case when I tried to pick up a scallop where two seemed resting a few inches apart with the hinges toward each other. I had almost touched one when both disappeared in the rush of a toadfish, a rough-bodied, mud-colored creature so perfectly camouflaged that, in the beam of my torch, its body blended exactly with the gray-brown sediment around it. Only its two flat, rounded pectoral fins had caught the eye. And they, in shape and size and pat-tern and mottled coloring, in ribs and undulating outer edges, were al-most perfect imitations of the bay scallops.

A mystery connected with the swimming of the scallop concerns the mass migrations that sometimes have been observed. Great hordes of the young mollusks, all going in the same direction, swim just below the surface of the sea. Why are they moving? Where are they going? Nobody seems to know.

Born early in summer, the baby shellfish soon attach themselves with secreted filaments to ribbons of eelgrass. I found several, half an inch to three-quarters of an inch across, anchored to waving strands about two and a half feet above the bay bottom. They all were attached in the same way, hinges up. Here, in relative safety, the young scallops feed on the minutiae of the sea water and grow rapidly. Before the end of autumn they may be an inch across. Leaving their eelgrass support they begin roaming over the floor of the bay. The plant that thus offers them safety in early months also provides a measure of protection in all the seasons that follow. For unlike many plants the eelgrass remains in dense green patches throughout the winter.

There are times when the whole living world seems a vast chemical engine that is speeded up or slowed down by changes in temperature. Nature advances the throttle in spring, retards it in fall. For the snails and crabs and starfish and scallops and killifishes—for all the cold-blooded creatures of the bay bottom—the chill of autumn, now so close at hand, would bring reduced activity. The history of this time of decreased food and slowed-down growth would be written on the scale rings and shell ridges of fish and shellfish. The changes of fall would run through all this world of shallow bays. The consequences of altered temperature would be apparent among all the interlinking forms of life. But nowhere is the delicate relationship between temperature and growth more dramatically revealed than in the activity of the eelgrass itself. It is a classic example of botany.

In his exhaustive monograph, *Morphological and Phenological Notes on Zostera Marina*, published by the University of Chicago, William Albert Setchell gives the story in detail. Throughout winter the eelgrass is in a condition of cold rigor, alive but vegetatively inactive. In spring, as soon as the warming water reaches 50 degrees F., growth begins and seeds germinate. But the mercury has to rise nine more degrees, to 59 degrees, before the underwater flowers bloom. Between 59 and 68 degrees, the flowers are fertilized, seed is set and new rhizomes are produced. Then at the 68-degree mark the plant becomes inactive again, remaining in a condition of heat rigor throughout the hot months of summer. Thus, almost as though controlled by a delicate electric thermostat, its activity during these weeks of growth and reproduction is governed by the position of the mercury. Below 50 degrees the plant is quiescent; between 50 and 59 it is growing, in its vegetative period; between 59 and 68 it is flowering, in its reproductive period; above 68 it is inactive again. In the autumn the eelgrass slips from heat rigor into cold rigor without a second time of growth. This transition from one period of quiescence into another would be taking place over wide stretches of the bay bottom during the weeks to follow, weeks in which we would be moving westward across the continent-wide sweep of autumn.

Late that night when I switched off my underwater flashlight and removed my face mask and swim-fins and waded ashore, I followed for a time the moonglade that extended in a shining silver path across the water. It was a fitting trail out of these forests of the sea.

The Long Valley

STANDING in the autumn sunshine amid the lichen-spattered jumble of Tuscarora sandstone at the top of Hawk Mountain, in eastern Pennsylvania, we had watched in other years a parade of soaring migrants. On set wings the hawks had drifted or scudded by. They rode as on an invisible tide that swept them down the long ridge in a great curve toward the south. The trail they followed was the same autumn pathway their ancestors had used long before the *Santa Maria* crossed from the Old World to the New. It was a trail that, all down the Endless Mountain, provided supporting updrafts that enabled southbound hawks to cover hundreds of miles with scarcely a wingbeat.

As the migrants had grown small in the distance we had followed them in imagination. We had pictured the invisible sheets and columns of rising air on which they soared. We had felt, in fancy, the thrust of the updrafts against outspread wings. We had debated how they steered their course, choosing the aerial path best suited to their needs. We had conjured up the scene that unrolled beneath them as they sailed on and on down the length of the Great Valley, through five states, keeping to their ancient pathway through the autumn skies.

These things we had imagined. Now imagining was past. Now the ridge curved away—green below, blue in the distance—beneath our wings. Now we experienced at intervals the hard updrive of the invisible air currents. Now we were seeing, as the hawks saw, the forested wall of rock, the patchwork of valley fields moving past below us. That morning we had taken off in a lightplane from the Harrisburg airport. We were following, for a hundred miles and more, the aerial road of the hawks.

In a long curving climb Johnny Abuiso's green-bodied, silver-winged Beechcraft Bonanza carried us up to 3,000 feet. Beyond the left wing—with "N8568N" painted in black on silver—I could see the shining serpentine of the Susquehanna flowing down its corridor through the ridges. Smoking factory chimneys, rows of red- and green-roofed houses, the sooty spider web of a railroad yard steadily grew smaller below us. Like an expanding ring on water the horizon pushed back as we climbed.

At two miles a minute we headed north. Looking like some Roman aqueduct in the distance, the longest stone arch span in America, the railroad bridge over the Susquehanna at Harrisburg, drifted away behind us. Ahead, out of the hazy distance, the curving green waves of parallel ridges a thousand feet high dragged their immense lengths across the landscape—Blue Mountain, Second Mountain, Peters Mountain—with the titanic furrows of the valleys between. We crossed over the first ridge. High above it the plane lifted and dropped on swells of bumpy air, disturbed by the updrafts.

This easternmost of the ridges—the Endless Mountain or Kittatinny Ridge of the Indians, now officially called Blue Mountain—swings in an arc from east central to south central Pennsylvania. It is the most eastern of the Appalachian chain. Its towering wall of sandstone forms the escarpment of the folded Appalachian mountains. Under various names, bordering the Great Valley, it extends almost without a break from New York's Shawangunk Mountain, on the north, to Mt. Oglethorpe, in Georgia, on the south. Down the Pennsylvania length of the ridge, in former times, ran the Tuscarora Path of the Shawnee Indians. Today, the most famous of modern footpaths, the Appalachian Trail, follows its crest. And in the air—unmarked and trackless, far older than the Tuscarora Path or the Appalachian Trail—the road of the hawks parallels the ridge.

"When the wind is strong," Abuiso told us, "especially when it blows from the northwest, it is really rugged up here."

At such times the same winds that fill the pocket of Cape May with migrating birds strike the Kittatinny Ridge at right angles and shoot upward in a powerful ascending flow. The greatest hawk flights occur on such days between late August and mid-November. Then, Abuiso says, he flies high not only to be above the turbulent air but also to avoid hitting the hawks. The weight of a golden eagle or one of the larger hawks would be sufficient to damage a wing or shatter a windshield. Mostly the hawks fly low. But once, when mist hid the ground, he came abreast of a large flock of Canada geese winging south at an altitude of more than 4,500 feet.

As the warmth of the morning increased, the sky over the valley was sown with small cumulus clouds. To escape the bumps of the heated rising columns that formed them, we climbed to 5,000 feet. There we rode in a tranquil sky. We flew north, curving toward the east as the ridges curved. Across the valley below, where the cloud-shadows moved, the fields of the farms varied endlessly in shape and size and color. They seemed, viewed from the air, laid out haphazardly without rhyme or reason. Yet behind each boundary line lay the logic of topography, the weight of legal decision, the chance of inheritance, the story of expanding success or contracting misfortune.

The forested ridges were green now with only here and there an isolated splash of color. But all down their lengths, a few weeks hence, they would be gaudy with the vivid, lavish hues of autumn foliage. Far below us, along the skirts of the Kittatinny Ridge, we caught glimpses of lonely little farms snipped from the forest. At long intervals the path of a power line ran in a narrow, cleared band up and over the top. And, as the summit of this Endless Mountain moved past below our right wing, curious openings began appearing in the forest. They were sometimes square, sometimes rectangular, sometimes curving. Sometimes they turned back upon themselves. They looked like hieroglyphics or Mayan ruins on the ridgetop. They puzzled us at the time. Abuiso said he had begun to notice them only a few years before. Later I learned their meaning. The clearings were made by the Pennsylvania Game Commission to provide feeding areas along the top of the ridge for deer, wild turkeys and other forms of wildlife.

We passed Indiantown Gap and the dark Swatara River, Pine Grove and Summit Station. Hamburg and the gray line of U.S. Highway 22 lay to the southeast as we passed over the nestling village of Drehersville and crossed the coal-laden Little Schuylkill River. Then suddenly the white, tumbled sandstone of the Hawk Mountain lookout burst into view. A dozen persons stood among the rocks. Their binoculars swung in our direction. This was Hawk Mountain as tens of thousands of migrating hawks had seen it.

We cut in above the ridge and curved back, skimming out over the lip of the 1,000-foot drop. Three times we circled the promontory. Many a hawk, I remembered, had seen that rocky height we looked down upon as its last sight on earth. Within the space of this tight circle of our plane, passing hawks had been blinded, blown to pieces, maimed, or with a shattered wing had fallen through space in days when the Tuscarora slabs bristled with shotguns. Here, at this world-famous sanctuary, hawk-watchers have replaced hawk-gunners. But this promontory is but one of eleven points along the Kittatinny Ridge where the passing migrants were shot for sport. And only here has the killing stopped. The shooting still continues at all the other ten. A succession of sanctuaries, a chain of Hawk Mountains running the Pennsylvania length of the ridge, is needed to halt this autumn slaughter.

As we curved away, straightening out for the return flight, we waved to the hawk-watchers.

"If they don't see any hawks today," Nellie said. "they can put down two migrating Teales."

As a matter of fact, Maurice Broun, curator at Hawk Mountain since it was established, told us later that on that September day, eighty-three hawks passed the lookout. Forty-nine were broadwings, six sharpshins, two redtails, four marsh hawks, three ospreys and seventeen sparrowhawks. Represented by single individuals were the bald eagle and the peregrine falcon.

Flying south, down the path of the migrants, we studied the air currents. We cruised along the summit and at either side. We vaulted back and forth over the top, first from one direction then from the other. Abuiso, long experienced with the air currents of the hawk ridges, showed us where the upthrust was strongest. This came not at the exact summit but a little back of it. When a northwest wind strikes the wall of the ridge it shoots up and over in a vaulting arc. The current thus deflected sometimes rises into the sky as much as four times the height of the ridge. Beyond its high point this comber of the air drops in a swift descent. A lightplane pilot, inexperienced in the region, may narrowly escape crashing into the tree tops when caught in the grip of this powerful downdraft.

On this day the breeze was light and mainly from the north. We passed—and saw in fleeting glimpses—hawks soaring down the ridges. On such days of little wind the birds tend to follow a path farther out over the valley where the thermal currents rising from the sun-heated fields give them added lift. But whether a hawk is riding on thermals or slope-winds it is always gliding downward. The spiraling bird that mounts on set wings up and up into the sky is really descending all the time through the air. It is circling on a downward corkscrew path within a column of air that rises faster than it descends. It is like a man walking slowly down the steps of a rapidly rising escalator.

Most of the time the hawks avoid the more violent, turbulent up-drafts. In their long slide down the ridge that stretched away before us, I suspect that they set their course through rising air that will enable them to glide at normal cruising speed, so to speak, without losing altitude. Always nosing down, always using the motive power of gravity, they adjust their soaring speed by the steepness of their glide. I have watched red-tailed hawks cross the slight gap before Hawk Mountain and then, as they reached the stronger updrafts of the ridgeside, tilt slightly downward and increase their speed without loss of height. By employing the air currents that will carry them upward at the same rate that they descend, the migrating hawks ride for hundreds of miles down the valley with altitude unchanged.

The wing-loading of hawks, the relation of weight to wing surface, is a factor in their speed and in the strength of the updrafts needed to support them. Among these birds this element varies considerably. When Earl L. Poole, some years ago, published in *The Auk* the weights and wing areas of various American birds, his figures showed that a goshawk may have a wing-loading nearly twice that of a sparrowhawk and a peregrine falcon three times that of a marsh hawk. Oftentimes on days of strong winds—when the birds fly lower and closer to the ridge—the migrants pass Hawk Mountain soaring with wings partially closed, adjusting their surface and wing-loading to the conditions of the time.

Out over the valley, when we were halfway down the ridge, we saw one of the most lightly loaded of all the soaring birds, a turkey vulture. It rocked and turned among the thermals a full 1,500 feet above the ground. Even feeble updrafts will carry these broad-winged birds aloft. From one rising current to another they make long, shallow glides across the sky. But on days of heavy winds these lightly loaded birds are at a disadvantage. They lack the weight to give them ballast and stability.

A bird in the wind—that, to the average person, is one of the most confusing aspects of avian flight. "It is a well-known fact," a reader wrote in the correspondence column of *The New York Herald Tribune* in the summer of 1955, "that birds rest, when possible, by letting the winds carry them along." And in a U.S. Department of Agriculture bulletin, published in 1935, there occurs the sentence: "Even strong winds that blow in the direction of aerial travel are unfavorable for the birds, as they interfere with their balance and disarrange their feathers." Both these statements are based on a fundamental misconception of the relationship of the bird and the wind. They are derived from the viewpoint of the ground rather than from the bird's viewpoint in the air.

A bird does not drift through the sky like a thistle seed, or a gust-blown piece of paper. It does not float on the wind as a chip drifts downstream on water. It does not rest on the air: it flies by moving through it. It must maintain a certain minimum speed through the air to support it. This it achieves either by the muscular effort of moving wings or by using the power of gravity in gliding—which becomes soaring when the air around the gliding bird is moving upward as fast as or faster than the bird moves down. Only during the comparatively infrequent instances of hovering and when fluttering down to a landing does the bird drop below this minimum forward speed. It maintains it whether flying with or against the wind. And in either case its speed *through the air* is the same.

For a bird in a steady wind is like a man in the coach of a speeding express train. The car may be rushing over the rails a mile a minute. Yet as the man looks about him within the coach everything is standing still. He and the coach are moving at the same speed. So it is with the bird in the wind except that the bird cannot, like the man, sit down or remain passive. It has to maintain its minimum speed for normal flight. But this it can do moving in any direction. It advances as though in a calm, as though it were in fact flying this way and that within the moving railway coach. There is no more pressure on it when it moves in one direction than when it heads in another. When flying in and out of winds the bird feels the changing pressures. But when it is in the heart of the moving air it has no more sensation of meeting the force of the gale when it flies in the direction from which it blows than a man has of feeling the weight of the train pushing against him when he walks back along the aisle. The bird can no more be struck by the wind than the man can be struck by the train on which he is riding. The moving mass of air in a wind carries the bird with it. It may sweep it far off its course. But it does not push against the bird. There is no pressure on it when it is riding with the moving air. It is being transported by the wind as the car transports its passengers. For the bird in the wind the whole sky is moving and it is moving with it and it flies as in air that is calm.

Looking down at the ridge below our Beechcraft Bonanza, winging its way back to Harrisburg, we saw the steady slide of the trees slipping to the rear. The rate of their movement, our speed over the ground, was an entirely different matter from our speed through the air. In ground speed—both for us and for the bird—the direction and force of the wind do play an important part.

If we may return for one last time to our old friend, the man on the mile-a-minute express: Sitting still he is moving over the ground at sixty miles an hour. If he leaves his seat and walks ahead along the aisle at five miles an hour he is moving over the ground that much faster, or sixty-five miles an hour. If he turns and walks back along the aisle at the same pace he subtracts five miles from his speed over the ground, reducing it to fifty-five miles an hour. All the while the man himself in the coach is moving only five miles an hour. Similarly the bird advances at its own speed within the "coach" of the moving wind. But its rate of progress *over the ground*—as opposed to its speed through the air—leaps ahead or lags behind according to the direction of its flight and the movement of the wind.

Twenty miles from Harrisburg we crossed the ridge for a final time and curved out over the far-famed fertile fields of the Lebanon Valley. Our shadow trailed across patches of tasseled corn that looked like shaggy rugs cut into squares and rectangles; over orchards with little rows of round twig masses seen in two dimensions; down the length of a pasture where a flock of crows, no larger than flakes of soot, trailed down to land among toy cattle, red and white and black. Once, far below us, we sighted a green field strewn with a multitude of minute, white, elongated objects like kernels of rice. Only after we had flown past and looked back at an oblique angle did we see that the kernels were flocks of white hens feeding at a poultry farm.

Then the Roman aqueduct of the railroad bridge drew near, the red- and green-roofed houses spread out below us, the dark flow of the Susquehanna passed beneath our wings and, with idling engine, we soared on and on to touch at last the long black strip of the runway. I looked back at the curve of the Endless Mountain. We had seen it from the viewpoint of the airborne hawk. Now its 1,000-foot wall reared against the sky—its normal aspect for human eyes. Later that same afternoon we were to see it from still a third point of view. On the Pennsylvania Turnpike, heading west toward the Ohio line, we watched the ridge expand upward into the air ahead of us. We saw it tower directly above us. Then in a rush its exterior disappeared to be supplanted by the mole's-eye view of a tunnel that burrowed through the solid rock of its base. When we emerged on the other side and sped on, the ancient pathway of the hawks, the Kittatinny Ridge, also lay behind us.

Warbler River

IN days that followed we roamed northward through a country of inland lakes and bogs and tamarack trees. We crossed Looking Glass River. We passed Blue Gill Lake. We ran, mile on mile, never out of the sight of goldenrod and with the universal singing of the crickets in our ears. North of Clare, in Michigan's lower peninsula, the character of the country suddenly altered. Farms dropped away. Leathery sweet fern and everlasting dominated in the poorer soil. Bracken was brown and dead, already killed by heavy frosts. Here we had leaped ahead in autumn. Then in the cool of a northern evening, with the smell of aspens strong in the air, we came to Roscommon.

Some time after four o'clock the next morning we awoke in the darkness of our cabin. A clattering roar was mounting in volume outside. I looked from the window just as a stubby locomotive, belching black smoke, its headlight probing far down the single track, rushed by, dragging two dimly lit coaches behind it. Gaining momentum after a stop at Roscommon, the morning train was going north. Only two trains a day, one going north, one going south, halt at Roscommon. The southbound train arrives at midnight, the northbound at four o'clock in the morning.

We listened while the roar and clatter diminished and grew small in the night. Half a century before, standing on the platform of the Roscommon station, another man had listened to that same sound coming down the single track as that same train puffed away into the north. The man was Norman A. Wood. An enthusiastic amateur naturalist and curator-to-be of the ornithological collection at the University of Michigan, in Ann Arbor, Wood had reached Roscommon in the early dawn of the long last day of June, in the year 1903, on a singular mission.

Some fifty years before, on May 13, 1851, a small bird with striped blue-gray back and yellow underparts had been shot in a treetop on the western outskirts of Cleveland, Ohio. It was new to the leading naturalist of the region, Jared P. Kirtland, Cleveland physician, friend of Agassiz, author of valuable scientific papers and compiler of the first catalogue of Ohio birds. In honor of Kirtland, Spencer F. Baird of the Smithsonian Institution in Washington called the new bird *Sylvicola kirtlandii*, a name that has since been changed to *Dendroica kirtlandii*. This same Ohio physician is honored in the names of a mollusk, a water snake, a cherry tree, a fossil plant, a bird club and an Ohio township. Moreover, Kirtland Hall at Yale University and Kirtland, Ohio, a community east of Cleveland, derive their names from the same source as the Kirtland's warbler.

About a decade after this first specimen was collected a second was obtained—also at Cleveland and also during migration. Then in the year the Civil War ended, 1865, Baird made an astonishing discovery. In checking over specimens collected by Samuel Cabot, Jr., on a voyage to Yucatán, he came upon a perfect skin of a Kirtland's warbler. The bird had been shot at sea, near the island of Abaco in the Bahamas, in October 1841. This was almost a full ten years before the type specimen was collected in the Cleveland treetop. For a quarter of a century the warbler had gone unnoticed among the many specimens brought back by Cabot. Thus a clue to the wintering ground of the warbler was obtained decades before its northern home and breeding area were discovered. That clue was given complete substantiation when, in 1879, Charles B. Cory collected a Kirtland's warbler on Andros Island in the Bahamas.

So matters stood for the rest of the nineteenth century. At rare intervals single specimens of the migrant warblers were obtained in Ohio, in Illinois, in southern Michigan, in South Carolina. In winter they were seen on several islands of the Bahamas. But during the rest of the year the warbler disappeared. Ornithologists speculated on the mystery of its breeding range. Some thought it nested in Alaska, others picked Labrador, still others maintained it bred on the tundras of northern Canada. As late as the fall of 1898, Frank M. Chapman was writing in *The Auk* that he believed the warbler nested in the region of Hudson Bay. "Owing to its rarity and the remoteness of its probable breeding range," he added, "its nest and eggs will doubtless long remain unknown."

That prediction, however, soon went awry. By 1903, nest, eggs, breeding place all were known. And as he stood in the darkness on the Roscommon station platform that June day, Norman A. Wood was drawing near to the solution of this ornithological mystery. A friend, returning from a fishing trip on the Au Sable River, had showed him a small bird shot near a bridge in the jack-pine wilderness of Oscoda County. Wood recognized it as a Kirtland's warbler. Without delay he headed north on the Toledo, Ann Arbor and Northern Railroad for Roscommon, the nearest point by rail to the bridge where the bird had been seen. When—after a sleepless night and two changes along the way—he was set down on the deserted platform of the little lumber town, Wood was thirty-five miles overland and sixty miles by water from his destination. As soon as the sun rose and people were astir, he rented a rowboat. By seven he was afloat on the south branch of the Au Sable River, beginning a downstream ride through sixty miles of wilderness.

"This country," he later wrote, "is wild and very interesting and the songs of many birds cheered me as, with notebook in hand, I floated along."

Birds voices, no longer singing the songs of spring, were awakening in the woods around us when, a little before seven, Nellie and I stowed away our knapsacks in a canoe and—half a century after Norman A. Wood's historic journey—started down this same wild water trail he had followed into the country of the Kirtland's warbler. Dawn mist curled from the water. In nearly complete silence we stole along the winding, narrow, shadow-filled ravine down which the south branch begins its flow from Roscommon. Oscoda, Crawford and Roscommon counties all are located on the high tableland of the Lower Peninsula, 1,200 to 1,400 feet above sea level. From this plateau rivers flow east and rivers flow west, east to Lake Huron and west to Lake Michigan. The Au Sable, dropping 609 feet during its 300-mile course from Roscommon to Lake Huron, is one of the swiftest rivers of the region.

In recalling his journey down this watercourse Wood remembered how great blue herons flew downstream and landed ahead of him over and over again. Cedar waxwings were numerous all along the banks. Once he overtook a family of hooded mergansers. And another time, swinging around a sharp turn, he suddenly came upon two bald eagles fishing. By the end of the first day he had listed forty different species of birds.

We too, after a lapse of half a century, found birds everywhere along the way—phoebes and brown thrashers and whitebreasted nuthatches and spotted sandpipers and myrtle warblers and robins and ruffed grouse and red-tailed hawks. For the first mile or so, six mallards kept us company, taking off with a great skittering and quacking ahead of us as we rounded each successive turn. In a quiet stretch where a floating log had stranded among waterweeds, we came upon a spotted sandpiper sound asleep. We drifted by with paddles trailing. Just as we came abreast, the bird's eyes popped open. It was wide awake instantly. Before long the ravine widened out, the banks shallowed, the river grew lighter and the day life of the woods began.

The trilling of the waxwings accompanied us as it had accompanied Wood. Great blue herons took off and landed downstream as they had before his drifting rowboat. Instead of eagles we had kingfishers plunging into the stream before us as we rounded almost every curve. There is one turn of the river's winding course that we will always remember as Chickadee Bend. The trees were alive with darting, calling black-capped chickadees. Fully half a hundred swarmed among the branches of a large white pine. Later in the day, as we rounded a curve, we met a solitary sandpiper flying low over the water directly toward us. Apparently blinded by the sun, it saw us only at the last moment, after Nellie, in the bow, had already ducked her head. The bird veered wildly away, the black and white ladder markings on its tail brilliant in the sunshine. Of all the birds we saw, the most numerous, I think, were the flickers. We met wave after wave of the migrating woodpeckers. For several days they had been moving through, moving south, upstream along the northward-flowing river.

After the first two or three miles the riverside cabins disappeared. We were in canoe wilderness. For fully seventeen of the twenty-five miles we paddled that day we seemed cut off from the present, on a stretch of river hardly changed since Wood saw it. Mink and muskrat and otter tracks led along the mud of the stream's edge. Beaver had been at work among the aspens. Ruffed grouse shot away with a windy roaring and once three climbed steeply above the water and alighted in an overhanging tree, peering down at us with alert, round eyes as we drifted underneath. Deer drank in the shallows of many reaches. Once we came upon eight does and fawns drinking together. They stood immobile, heads lifted, water dripping from their muzzles. Then with a great splashing of mud and shooting sheets of spray they whirled in a snorting stampede for the cover of the trees. Many a deer that we failed to see, no doubt saw us as we passed by. I remember once looking to the left as we rode with rhythmic paddle strokes down a long straight stretch of the river. Behind the barricade of a fallen tree a doe peered out at us between two barkless branches—a wild cow gazing through the bars of a wild pasture gate.

Ours was a leisurely progress. Our day was as wide as the sky. We would paddle for a while with long, free-swinging strokes, then drift or swing to the bank to listen to the music of the wind in the pines or to see the kitchen middens of cone fragments left by squirrels on a mossy log or enjoy the brilliance of cardinal flowers rising from the moldering ruins of stranded driftwood. Then for long stretches we would ride the current, the sandy, gravelly bottom slipping by with every water-smoothed pebble visible below us. Sometimes where the current rippled over shallows we would run the chutes with the canoe bottom barely afloat. Then we would drift the length of some deep pool where trout—brown or brook or rainbow—shot away as the bulk of our canoe loomed over them.

In such places, Wood recalled, he would let his boat drift while he got out his fishing tackle. "As I glided along," he wrote, "I threw a cast of flies—'red ibis,' 'dark coachman' and 'white miller'—and took 'here and there a lusty trout and here and there a grayling.' "

Wood found that at many places along the banks where cedars overhung the river, the trees had been undercut and had settled into the water where they formed "sweepers" which he had to avoid carefully lest they overturn his boat. We saw hundreds of such trees, tilted outward or toppled into the stream. In passing cedar swamps we sometimes wound among a dozen or more "sweepers," many stretching half across the river. Some were ancient and weathered to shining silver; others were still alive, with tips upturned. These northern white cedars—in reality arborvitae trees—are durable, free from insect pests, long-lived. The span of their years may extend over two or even three centuries. If any of the ancient, silvered, spidery sweepers we passed that day had escaped the decades of lumbering they may well have been older than the United States. From the leaves of these trees, now known to contain vitamin C, the pioneers brewed a remedy for scurvy. From the wood—the lightest in the region, weighing only nineteen pounds to the cubic foot dry weight—the Indians formed the frameworks of their birch bark canoes.

A little after noon we pulled up on a shelving bank beneath a high bluff to eat our lunch of ham sandwiches and tomatoes. Monarch butterflies passed us—all flying upstream. Like the flickers they were following this river road south across the tableland. Deer trails ascended the side of the bluff and fanned out over the top among the sweet fern and birch clumps. In a moist spot beside one of these trails we came upon a plant with slender stems rising nearly a foot above leathery, rich-green, heart-shaped leaves. Crowning each stem was the cream-colored saucer of a five-petaled flower, each rounded petal delicately veined with lines of green. We were seeing at last the grass-of-Parnassus in bloom.

This was a great event for Nellie. Years before she had seen a picture of this plant—which, of course, is no grass at all but a member of the saxifrage family—in a botanical book. One of her ambitions was to see the herb in bloom in the wild. So long ago, the ancient Greek naturalist, Dioscorides, had named the plant after Mt. Parnassus, sacred to Apollo and the Muses. There are certain common names on the lists of botany, such names as enchanter's nightshade, viper's bugloss, tick trefoil, Venus's looking-glass, nodding pogonia, wild comfrey and pale corydalis, that have the light of another time around them. And of such is the grass-of-Parnassus. The flowers, their ovaries fertilized, would produce single-celled capsules about half an inch long and filled with small winged seeds. But now they were full blown, almost an inch across, even in the shade shining out against the green of the leaves below. Well deserved is another name for these flowers: the bog stars.

A winding road and a winding stream have special appeal. Something new, something interesting, lies around every bend. That afternoon as we drifted with the current downstream, the interest that lay around successive curves sometimes proved to be wildlife, sometimes autumn foliage. On this northern highland frosts occur every month of the year and summer may contain as few as seventy growing days between killing freezes. Here a birch and there a maple had already turned to gold or crimson. I remember one half-submerged granite rock, black and wet, mottled with brilliant splashes of yellow where the currents had plastered birch leaves all over its upstream surface. Already canoes had been reserved for a little later in the season when the autumn foliage would be at its height. "Color tours" are now a feature of the fall in many parts of the country, by stream, by road, even by air. On this day we were paddling through merely the fringes of the great autumn rainbow that we were to see in its full glory farther west and farther north, in the hardwood forests of Minnesota.

Bridges are the milestones along the Au Sable and in the course of time we reached the third bridge that was our destination, the place where we and our canoe would be picked up and taken back to Roscommon. Wood had passed this place on the first day and had traveled on to the evening of the second day when he had reached his goal, a steel bridge not far from the present village of Red Oak. There he began seven days of searching that ended on July 8, 1903 with the discovery of the first Kirtland's warbler nest and eggs and the solution of a tantalizing riddle of American ornithology.

The bridge that formed Wood's landmark in 1903 still stands. We could visualize it in our mind's eye. For, a few years before, we had driven 2,000 miles to visit the jack-pine plains of the Lower Peninsula during the breeding season of this rare and restricted warbler. Now, sitting beside the river that had carried Norman A. Wood to the heart of the warbler's secret, we recalled the events of that trip. We remembered the wonderful days with the booming of the nighthawks at dusk and the sweet crepuscular song of the wood peewee in the half light before dawn.

Oscoda County is still the most sparsely populated county in Michigan. No railroad runs through it. Until World War II it had no bus line, no dentist, no doctor. Its few scattered communities all originated as lumber camps. Over the pale-gray dirt roads that cut the endless jack-pine plains into one-mile squares, we wandered for two days, listening for the singing of an unfamiliar warbler. At the end we were pouncing on snatches of familiar songs, even slamming on the brakes at unusual squeakings of the car. That evening, frustrated, we came to Mio. As I was signing up for a cabin at a tourist camp just north of town, the manager noticed my field glasses.

"A lot of people here are interested in birds," he volunteered. "We've got a couple of bird doctors in camp right now. They come up every June."

The "bird doctors," to our great delight, turned out to be Josselyn Van Tyne, ornithologist of the University of Michigan, and Harold Mayfield, for years secretary of the American Ornithologists' Union. Van Tyne—who, like Norman A. Wood, is curator of the university's ornithological collection—has spent more time in intensive study of the Kirtland's warbler than any other scientist in the world. During many seasons he has devoted at least twenty days of every June to observing the nesting warblers, often remaining in a blind from five in the morning until six at night. For nearly a dozen years Mayfield has assisted him in his work.

At four o'clock the next morning we were sharing a breakfast of doughnuts and coffee and bread and orange juice and canned peaches and grapefruit slices with the two bird doctors. Thus fortified with vitamins we started out with Mayfield to investigate a new area that had just been reported while Van Tyne retired to his blind for another day of concentrated observation.

Normally the breeding season of the Kirtland's warbler extends from mid-May to the last of June. The birds return from the south, both males and females together, some time between the tenth and the fifteenth of May. In its yearly cycle, the warbler spends only about four of the twelve months among the jack pines of north central Michigan. But here alone—and nowhere else on earth—it nests. In half a century no nest has ever been found more than sixty miles from the spot where Wood made his initial discovery. The three counties of Oscoda, Crawford and Iosco embrace almost its whole breeding range, with a few scattered records from adjoining counties. This area, largely drained by the Au Sable, is about 60 miles wide and 100 miles long. In this relatively small spot on the face of the earth every Kirtland's warbler is born. Not only does the bird breed in no other place but even here it nests only in special spots, only in areas where new-growth pines have sprung up in the wake of a forest fire and the trees have not yet reached a height of eighteen feet. As soon as the pines attain that height the warblers desert the area. Thus this curious little bird—known to scientists around the world because of its strangely restricted breeding ground—depends, literally, upon forest fires for its nesting sites.

Most warblers are shy and elusive, appearing and disappearing to the frustration and bafflement of the bird watcher. But not so the Kirtland's. When one of the scattered colonies is discovered, the song of this warbler becomes the dominant voice of the jack pines. As we drove west that morning we heard the trill of the pine warbler, the up-scale "zee-zee-zee" of the prairie warbler and the curious drawling, insect-like "buzz-buzz-buzz, buzz, buzz" of the clay-colored sparrow. We were not prepared, when we reached the nesting site of a pair of Kirtland's, for the ringing, far-carrying song of the male. I heard it a fifth of a mile away with the breeze blowing in the wrong direction. It is the ear that first detects the site of the nesting warblers.

Repeated every ten seconds or so for minutes at a time, the song is short, lasting, as Mayfield pointed out, about as long as it takes to say: "Chattanooga choo-choo"—two seconds or less. Starting low, it progresses with an ascending "che-che-che," almost like a stammer, before suddenly bursting out in a loud and ringing "wee-wee." The song grows louder and faster as it advances until the final notes come out with an explosive rush. The final "wee-wee," heard near at hand, actually hurt our ears.

When it sings, the male appears to be in a kind of spasm. It vibrates, jerks, bobs, seems to jump up and down with the violence of its efforts. On a mild morning in June a male will sing at the rate of from five to nine songs a minute. It is rarely silent for as long as thirty minutes. Each pair of Kirtland's warblers has its own area, from one to four acres in extent, and the singing of another male in the distance seems to stimulate the male at the nesting site to greater effort. In one experiment, a recording of the song was played in the field. A male came close and appeared to sing in competition. We saw males sing, not only when perching, but also in flight. Several times we observed a male arriving at the nest with its bill crammed with small caterpillars. In spite of this impediment to song, it would pause on a branch, lift its head, and utter its notes as loudly and clearly as ever.

Sitting in the grass beside our drawn-up canoe, we recalled the appearance of the Kirtland's warbler—as arresting as its song. Conspicuous black streaks mark the bluish-gray back of the male. Its breast is lemon yellow with bold markings of black along the side. A large warbler, it measures five and three-quarters inches from bill to tail. The male has a distinctive black mask running back along the sides of its face. The female, lacking this mask, is clad in duller, grayer plumage. Both male and female have the same habit of jerking or bobbing their tails.

Another trait of this jack-pine warbler, we recalled, is its surprising fearlessness. Individuals vary but, on the whole, the Kirtland's warbler is noted for its lack of fear. One male, singing in the top of a small pine, let me take a position directly beneath him. He merely cocked his head on one side to look down at me and then took up his singing again. Even when I shook the tree he flitted only half a dozen feet away to the top of a neighboring pine. Later in the day when I had my camera set up on a tripod not far from a nest, the female perched on the extended bellows even while I was in the act of focusing and the male made a dash between the legs of the tripod in driving away a trespassing chipping sparrow.

Not far apart that day, Mayfield found two nests. Both were hidden amid sweet ferns and blueberries and dry wiry grass, little cups in the ground lined with fine grass, bark and deer hair. One nest had been deserted. We dug it up carefully later on and it now rests in the collection of bird nests at the American Museum of Natural History. The other contained four fledglings in pinfeathers. They had hatched from small white eggs speckled with brown after an incubation period of about two weeks. Ten days after hatching, these baby warblers are ready to leave the nest. When we saw them they were nearing the end of this period of rapid growth. They were ravenously hungry and the day was one long meal.

We watched the parents come and go. Hour after hour they combed the lower branches of the surrounding pines for forest caterpillars. Occasionally one of the adults would gobble down a caterpillar before it began gathering food for the nestlings. It always followed the same procedure. It cocked its head, snapped up the worm, gulped it down rapidly, then hastily wiped both sides of its bill on a twig as though whetting a knife, jerking and wagging its tail all the while.

Invariably the baby birds were fed from the same side of the nest. A little tunnel or pathway led into the bower of over-arching grass beneath which the nest was located. The bird bringing the food always landed at the entrance of the tunnel and disappeared within. When it emerged it always gave a little fluttering bound, about six or eight inches high, as it flew away. Most of the food brought to the growing warblers is formed of small caterpillars. But, as we watched that day, we saw this fare varied with an occasional adult ant-lion. Once the male came in with the gauzy wings of one of these insects extending out on either side of its bill like a long mustache. Another time the female fluttered aloft like a flycatcher to pick a passing ant-lion from the air. A curious thing about the feeding habits of the Kirtland's warbler has been noticed by Van Tyne and Mayfield. They have never seen one of these birds take a drink of water. Perhaps they obtain ample moisture from the heavy dews that are characteristic of the region or, it may be, the larvae they consume provide sufficient fluid for their needs.

In 1953, in the January issue of *The Auk*, Mayfield reported the results of the first comprehensive census of these warblers ever made. With the aid of thirty-two field observers, he surveyed all known breeding sites. The figures show that the total number of Kirtland's warblers in the world is, in all probability, less than 1,000. This census, incidentally, appears to have been the first attempt ever made anywhere in the world to count all the members of an entire species of songbirds.

On this September day of turning foliage and monarchs moving south, we had seen no bird along the way that resembled this warbler of the jack pines. For already the birds had left their curiously restricted breeding area. By the middle of September, each year, all are gone. On this day, as we drifted down the stream that had carried

Norman A. Wood to the solution of an ornithological riddle, the stream so long associated with the lives of these mysterious warblers, the stream that drains the land where every one of them first sees the light of day, the birds themselves had been far to the south. Already they were well on their way, moving in migration toward the far-off islands of their winter home.

Dusty Autumn

FOR 200 miles the next day we rode south with the long chain of the Michigan dunes on our right. The arid yellow of their tops, in an undulating horizon line, rose against the cloudless blue of the sky. Killdeers called from every plowed field and pasture land. Overcome by autumn wanderlust, woolly bear caterpillars humped across the concrete of the highway. And all down the eastern shore of Lake Michigan monarch butterflies drifted southward over the hayfields and orchards and fallow land now splotched with goldenrod and painted wine red by the tinted stems of frost-touched grasses.

Beside the road black walnut trees, almost bare of leaves, were decorated from top to bottom with the green globes of their wild harvest. Green, too, was the duckweed on black swamp water but its autumn migration down to the muddy bottom was only weeks away. Everywhere around us, from the dry fields, came the universal simmering sound of the insects, the most characteristic music of fall.

This was fruit country, orchard and vineyard land. Roadside stands were laden. Vines were redolent with their blue burden and apple trees bent low with the weight of the autumn harvest. Mile after mile we rode among gray-barked peach trees where fallen fruit on the ground below outlined the form of the trees like shadows at noontime. All through this fruit belt of western Michigan this was harvest time, payoff time, the season of profit and plenty.

The cool air of the warbler river now lay far behind us. Even before we crossed the Indiana line we were plunged into a midwestern September heat wave such as we remembered from childhood. The mercury was close to ninety-five degrees when we rolled through Michigan City and into the dune country beyond. One vivid memory remains of passing through the city. A small boy, five or six at most, had picked up a dead monarch butterfly from a pile of litter beside the street. He was standing entranced, bending forward, oblivious to all around him. It seemed as though I were looking at myself when young. A door was opening for him, a door beyond which lay all the beauty and mystery of nature. I wondered who he was and what his future would be and—

like the small boy I had heard whistling to himself in the Virginia dusk, imitating all the bird calls of the region—I wished him well.

The next day, in ninety-six degree heat, I rode the interurban to Chicago to have a balky camera shutter repaired. White and brown and red and gray, the steelmill smoke at Gary poured toward the sky. Sulphuric acid polluted the stagnant air. Overwhelmed by the heat, I stared with almost unseeing eyes at the passing miles of sunflowers along the right-of-way. Returning in the afternoon, I was depressed, deadened, left limp and half-conscious by the great city. At sunset we drove down a dusty back road and I suddenly came alive. For there, with the sundown light upon it, still green all along its upper half, was the spire of the old cedar tree that still stood where once my grandfather's gate had led to Lone Oak Farm. And in the darkening bushes all around the calling of the katydids linked the present with those summer nights long ago.

Seventy miles away, under a hazy prairie sky, the next morning we followed U.S. 6—now a thousand miles west of its Cape Cod beginning—into Joliet, Illinois. Fallen thornapples scalloped the edges of the highway with partial disks of brilliant red. Hazel nuts were plump in the dusty thickets, fox grapes were turning and hips sprinkled the wild roses. Seeds of a thousand shapes were drying on the roadside plants and the sweet smell of distant leaf fires scented the air. Autumn change was everywhere.

Beside Hickory Creek, that rocky stream on whose western bank I was born, we neared the city. Each turn recalled something of the past, memories of swimming holes and sunfish and hellgrammites under stones in the riffles, memories of butternut and walnut and hickory trees, memories of lowland stretches yellow with marsh marigolds in the wake of the melting snow, of Davison's Woods carpeted with spring beauties in the time of returning warblers.

We turned off on the side of the road and I walked back along the edge of this same woods, along the same Michigan Central Railroad tracks that once had provided a kind of highway into wilderness, a cinder-coated path leading east from the city's edge into a realm of herons and muskrats and thornapple feasts in autumn. A railroad right-of-way, to a returning native, is one of the most permanent of landmarks. A street or stream changes more. When John Burroughs revisited Polo, Illinois, a generation after he had taught school there one winter in his youth, he noted in his journal that all was so changed only one thing seemed the same, the land along the railroad. As I walked east this autumn day the tracks and their surroundings seemed hardly touched by time.

Here were the wild strawberries growing close to the cinders just as I had remembered them. Here was the hillside dropping down in tangles of wild grapes, false buckwheat, sumac and asters. Here was the hobo jungle where tramps camped all summer long. Here were the elderberry bushes laden with fruit and filled with the quick, dashing motion of feeding birds.

Every tree and bush and plant is, large or small, a kind of invisible fountain. Moisture rises from its leaves, given off by the vital processes of plant life. As the leaves slow down their activity at the end of summer, as they begin to lose their hold and drop to the ground, these fountains dry up. This is one of the reasons why autumn tends to be a time of dryness and dust.

Wherever we drove that day the dryness of the season was accentuated by the heat wave. Dust lay over the leaves of the old box elder trees in front of the house where I lived as a child. It swept across the playground at Woodland School. And all along the edges of Brown's Pond the weeds were gray with dust, autumn dust, the dust of dusty autumn.

Brown's Pond, as I remembered it from childhood, was a realm of muskrats and bullheads and cattails and willows and the singing of redwings. In the intervening quarter of a century the cattails had pushed out from shore and the willows had followed. The trash of the years, dumped from the banks, had formed shoals and bars, shallowing the bottom. In that endless seesaw of land and water, the land had encroached on the pond, pinching and contracting it until its dimensions were less than half those I recalled. Dotting its unwholesome surface were floating beer cans and whisky bottles and half-submerged auto tires. This city-edge stretch of water, that I remembered from a better time, seemed nearing the end of a long, inglorious decline.

Saddened by the sight I drove on a quarter of a mile and pulled up beside the wasteland of a long-abandoned gravel pit. It, too, I remembered well for it was the nearest wildness I knew as a boy. It had stretched away for hundreds of acres across the street from the house where I had lived. There I had found parts of fossil plants and thought them Indian beads. There, in the limestone quarries beyond I had combed the chipping piles for fragments of prehistoric ferns. The old expanse, wasteland then, was wasteland now, hardly altered by the decades. Here was the gravel, here were the enduring stones, here the remnants of the glaciers and here were the memories of boyhood.

I smiled a little ruefully at the recollection of one of my first discoveries in natural history made here in the fall. I was, at the time, in second grade. The teacher asked us to bring in brilliant autumn leaves and I found the most brilliant of all on a slope of the gravel pit. I knew my moment of triumph when I handed the large bouquet to the teacher. But it was short-lived. A few days later I was not at school. Neither was the teacher. For the bright-colored leaves were the autumn foliage of the poison ivy.

For more than an hour I wandered over this remembered gravel land, noting the narrow-leaved cattails that had obtained a foothold in the damp depressions and the dragonflies that skimmed and whirled about them. Thistledown drifted past and grasshoppers rattled away on sounding wings and crickets sang among all the low vegetation and I found myself repeating a line from a half-forgotten poem: "Oh to be a cricket in a dusty thistle thicket!"

And all the thistle thickets *were* dusty that day. Here, too, the gray autumn dust had settled. It coated my shoes. It surrounded my feet in a moving cloud when I strode through the dry vegetation. Dust—the bane of the immaculate housewife, the cause of choking and sneezing, the reducer of industrial efficiency—dust to a naturalist represents one of the great, essential ingredients in the beauty of the world.

If it were possible to banish dust from the earth, the vote probably would be overwhelmingly in favor of it. Yet subtract dust from the 5,633,000,000,000,000-ton atmosphere that surrounds the globe and you would subtract infinitely more. You would drain blue from the sky and the lake. For fine dust, as well as the molecules of vapor and the air itself, scatters the blue rays and contributes color to the heavens above and reflected color to the waters below. You would eliminate the beauty of the autumn mist and the summer cloud. For every minute droplet of moisture in fog and cloud forms about a nucleus of dust. You would halt the rain and never know the whiteness of drifted snow. For raindrops and snowflakes and hailstones also come into being about a center of airborne dust. You would remove the glory of the sunrise from the world and wipe all the flaming beauty of the sunset from the sky. For sunrise and sunset, as we know them, are the consequence of the rays passing through the hazy, dusty air near the surface of the earth where the blue rays are filtered out and the red and orange rays pass through.

Nearly as much as the scent of leaf fires in the dusk, the smell of dusty autumn weedlots is part of early memories of the fall. During our westward travels with the season I asked many people what scent first came to mind at the mention of autumn. To some it was the fragrance of ripe grapes, to others the kitchen smells of canning and jelly-making, to others the aroma of the apple harvest; to most, I think, it was the scent of burning leaves, but to more than I expected it was the mingled odor of weedlot, the smell of ragweed and sunflower and sweet clover and dust, the very breath of autumn's dryness.

That was the smell that was all around me as I climbed the slope of a gravelly ridge. Like the heavy odor of hot tar under the August sun, the scent of woodsmoke on the winter air, this was a nostalgic smell with roots that extended far back into childhood. On the low ridge side I stopped beneath a scraggly tree to fill my pockets with red thorn-apples and again beside a dusty elderberry bush to taste the autumn tonic of its dark, clustered fruit. High above the ridge three dead cottonwoods lifted barkless and silvery branches. They brought to mind another natural-history discovery made here when I was seven or so, the discovery that thick and heavy cottonwood bark is no substitute for white birch bark in making an Indian canoe.

Beyond the ridge killdeers were calling. And from toward the horizon, mellowed by distance, came that plaintive, lonesome, far-carrying sound, the sustained whistle of a locomotive. As a child I had whistles to wonder at, whistles to dream about. For a prairie boy, there is magic in the lonely, lovely music of a train whistle far off in the night.

I topped the ridge and saw spread out before me a sudden scene of strange, wild beauty. Years before, the land to the east of the ridge beyond an ancient spur of the E J & E Railroad, was an extensive expanse of low-lying peat bog. Perhaps the water level of the area sank slightly when I was nine or ten, for about that time fires broke out in the peat. Burning slowly they ate out pits and spreading troughs in the bog. By night these hollows shone red like volcano craters and the heavy, choking smoke they gave off settled over the town. Repeated efforts failed to extinguish the slowly spreading fire. It burned on and on until almost the whole area was consumed. Now in a hollow at one end of this blighted, blackened stretch, a little lake had formed. A few cattails grew there, muskrats had built their houses along the edge and the green of duckweed ran across the surface. Here, in this miniature wilderness flanked on the north by wallpaper mills and on the east by the remote houses of Logan Avenue, here nearly thirty killdeers had congregated.

I sat down and for a long time watched the coming and going of the plovers. Every muskrat house had a killdeer perching on it. Soon a sparrowhawk dropped down on the stub of a long-dead tree near the cattails. The killdeers paid no attention to this smallest of the falcons. They circled over it, swept beside it, alighted beneath it. Wherever I looked along the shore the "noisy plovers" were in motion, running, stopping, alighting, taking to the air. Their flashing wings gave vibrant life to this scene of desolation. The clamor of their calls intermingled into wild and deeply stirring music.

Sitting there, I shared for a time the autumn excitement of these beautiful birds of passage. Perhaps it was a plaintive recurring note in the killdeer's call. Perhaps it was the smell of the dusty weeds, associated in my mind with a return to city and school, with the end of summer freedom at Lone Oak. Perhaps it was the faraway, lonely, nostalgic sound of the train whistle. Perhaps it was the singing of the September insects, that dry orchestral music that carries like an overtone the thought of swiftly passing life. Perhaps it was compounded of all of them—this wave of autumn sadness that enveloped me.

In a day, a week, a month at most, the plovers would move on. All this intensity of living would leave the blighted pond. And nature—absorbed with species and averages, not with individuals—cares but little whether *these* birds return again. All the insects singing in the grass, all the leaves still spread to the sunshine, all the dusty annuals and the waning flowers—they all were living their last days and the end was moving swiftly toward them. Life would come again in the spring—but not *this* life, not to *these* flowers, not to *these* leaves, not to *these* crickets and grasshoppers.

All the multitudinous life that passes in the fall contributed to my somber mood. "Give me," Thomas Hardy wrote in a similar moment, "the roughest of spring days rather than the loveliest of autumn days for there is death in the air." This, too, is an aspect of autumn we must face and accept, an aspect that cannot be parried aside. But only here during all our travels with the fall did it intrude itself with so heavy a weight upon my mind.

I walked slowly back over the ridge. Descending the farther side my foot scuffed in the gravel. A pebble rolled away down the incline before me. What vast stretches of history were encompassed by the span of that pebble! Lying there since glacial times it had been warmed by the springs and cooled by the autumns of aeons of time. How much of human life and plover life and grasshopper life had passed away while its insensate existence had gone on and on. Yet, surely, better a single moment of awareness to enjoy the glory of the senses, a moment of knowing, of feeling, of living intensely, a moment to appreciate the sunshine and the dry smell of autumn and the dust-borne clouds above—better a thousand times even a swiftly fading, ephemeral moment of life than the epoch-long unconsciousness of the stone.

So, cheered somewhat by so simple a thing as the roll of a pebble, I regained the car. We drove away, south and west, across the rich cornlands of Illinois toward the Great River, that age-old flyway of the autumn birds, the Mississippi.

Painted Forests

ALL during my boyhood the Mississippi was a kind of unseen presence, aloof, almost legendary, lying off to the west, beyond the city, beyond the Illinois farmland that spread away to the horizon, beyond the horizon itself. I never saw it, never visited it, although it was only 120 miles away. Yet, during those years, I was always conscious of it, always aware that off there, behind the western skyline, there flowed the Father of Waters.

Now, day after day, we followed the great river upstream. As we drew nearer to its source in Minnesota, we stopped for two days at Red Wing, under Barn Bluff, on the western bank of the Mississippi. The last evening while I pored over maps beneath a lamp and Nellie, with guidebooks and a pocket magnifying glass, sought the identity of an unknown plant from the bluff top, the dusk became windless. The thermometer dropped. The stars shone with a steely glitter and lonely train whistles carried far through the frosty air. And, moment by moment, this sudden cold at the end of the day was working in the darkness, splashing new, intense and flaming colors across the already painted forests of the north.

CROW WING LAKE and Red Eye River, Hay Creek and Mantrap Valley. Chilled birds warming themselves in the sun. Snow fences rolled up at the roadside. Corn shocks extending up and over a hilltop like the last tepees of this Indian land. A farmer's wife, her shawl flapping, cleaning a stovepipe in the yard. Such things we saw as we rode north from Red Wing in the morning.

Our way threaded among swales and bogs. We were in a land of little lakes, each with a grebe or two floating on it. For more than 200 miles we followed the winding course of the Mississippi northward. That night we slept in a cabin beside Fish Hook Lake. And the next morning, not long after dawn, in the stillness of the forest, we came to the shore of Lake Itasca, to the very beginning rill of the mighty Mississippi.

All around us we saw, as Thomas Hood so long before had seen in

England, "old Autumn in the misty morn standing shadowless like silence listening to silence." This was one of the perfect moments of our trip. We seemed, in the hush of that silvered hour, very close to some inscrutable secret of the noiseless wood. Then the sun rose above the treetops, tourists arrived, cries and exclamations succeeded the silence of the dawn. People from fifteen states came that autumn day to see the wonder of Old Man River as an infant.

Twenty-five hundred and fifty-two miles from the Gulf, 1,475 feet above the level of the sea, water was overflowing from the northern tip of three-pronged Lake Itasca and gurgling away in a shallow flow among granite boulders. This was the beginning of the Mississippi. Stepping from stone to stone, we crossed it in four strides. Beyond the water-smoothed rocks the current slowed as the bed beneath it deepened suddenly into a narrow, ditchlike channel winding away amid alders and red osiers.

I stood for a long time on this first crossing of the great river. Looking down at the clear, swirling water beneath me, I reflected on the adventures that lay before those transparent drops streaming by. Some would be sucked through the gills of fish, some evaporated into the air to float as clouds, some drift downstream frozen in ice cakes. They would slide along wharves and swirl among the roots of undercut trees and rush over dams and slow down in eddies. On that long flow toward the sea they would pass towns and factories and farms and the mouths of innumerable tributaries. How many drops of this clear flow now gurgling among these granite stepping-stones, I wondered, would ever reach the salt of the sea?

My reverie was interrupted by an elderly heel-and-toe walker who came marching down the path, resolutely stepped from rock to rock in a two-way passage, observed over his shoulder, "Now I've crossed the Mississippi!" and rapidly disappeared marching back up the trail again. All day long people cross these stepping-stones or stand in the middle of this first of the innumerable crossings spanning the great river to have their pictures taken.

One woman stared around her in bewilderment.

"What's everyone coming here for?" she demanded of a companion. "There's nothing to see here but a swamp!"

It has long been my contention that there is no place on earth where there is *more* to see than in a swamp—with its immense fertility and its teeming life. But I am sure the lady would not have understood what I was talking about if I had told her so. Nellie and I wandered away along the bank of the infant river.

In my mind's eye I could see the final miles of the Mississippi as I had seen them on a spring day, flying high above the delta, watching the river's titanic flow crawling away to the sea between restraining levees. Here it was hardly wider than a beaver canal. It meandered through boggy ground thick with sphagnum moss and pitcher plants and Labrador tea. A frog leaped into the water—the first frog of the Mississippi. Whirligig beetles spun in the shelter of a tiny nook—the earliest bay of the river. A dark swamp sparrow darted from red osier dogwoods and disappeared around a turn—the initial curve in the long course of the stream. Everything here was a first—first frog, first bay, first curve. Here, in these initial wanderings, minor events were taking place that were destined to be repeated innumerable times along the 2,552-mile course of the Father of Waters.

We returned to the shore of the lake. All along the shallows, where the wild rice grew, thousands of slender stems were mirrored on the glassy stillness of tinted water. They seemed growing in the midst of the bluest of skies, rising with snow-white clouds drifting among them. This was the season of the wild-rice harvest, in Indian days a time of feasting and thanksgiving. The pale yellow-green of the seed heads had turned a delicate purple. Within, the kernels of the ripened grain were cylindrical in shape, olive green to purplish-black in color, about half an inch in length. To the Algonquin and Chippewa, they formed the staple grain of the land. Explorers, trappers and pioneers knew them by many names: Indian oats, wild oats, water oats, mad oats, Canadian rice, black rice, marsh rice, squaw rice. Linnaeus, in 1752, named the plant *Zizania aquatica*. Peter Kalm tried unsuccessfully to introduce it into Europe. The grain is, in truth, a rice and not an oat. It is a wild, New World relative of the plant so widely cultivated as a main source of food in the Orient.

Nearly 300 years ago Father Marquette noted in his journal that the finest of all Indian dishes was wild rice mixed with buffalo fat. No other grain I have ever tasted had a flavor so deliciously delicate. Its only rival among the taste sensations of our trip west with the fall was the wild and haunting flavor of pinyon nuts in the Far West. Not only did the rice nourish Indians and pioneers; it also fed and fattened the myriad waterfowl that, around the headwaters of the Mississippi, added to the overflowing abundance of autumn. Even today the wild grain is gathered by Chippewas on Minnesota lakes. Its past importance in the economy of earlier times is reflected in the fact that the names of fully ninety lakes and streams and communities, in this single state, are derived in one way or another from wild rice.

That night we slept by another forest lake. With the sinking of the sun the mercury dropped swiftly. The sturdy north-country owner of the camp observed:

"It's getting pretty chilly these nights."

"If you think this is chilly," I said, "what do you do when winter comes?"

"I go to Florida."

After an early breakfast next morning, a breakfast we will especially remember because of a sampling of another glorious food of fall—pumpkin pie—we rode once more in the dawn light down the winding roads of the 32,000-acre Itasca State Park. Itasca is not, as many persons have assumed, an Indian word. Its origin is erudite. It is formed of parts of two Latin words, the last of *veritas*, meaning truth, and the first of *caput*, meaning head or source. The man who coined this word in celebration of his discovery of the true source of the Mississippi was the remarkable Henry Rowe Schoolcraft. Geologist, Indian agent, naturalist, poet, friend and helper of Audubon, discover of the evening grosbeak, author of a monumental six-volume work on the aboriginal tribes of America, Schoolcraft had been sent into the region by President Andrew Jackson. His mission was to bring peace between the Sioux and the Chippewas. As a side activity he discovered the headwaters of the Mississippi.

One hundred and fifty-nine years after Father Marquette first sighted the river, on July 13, 1832, Schoolcraft reached the modest woodland brook that carries away the overflow from Lake Itasca. His guide was the Chippewa chief Yellow Head. After heating pitch to repair the birch-bark canoes that had been portaged over ridges, across matted tangles and through primeval forests gray with lichens, School- craft and his small band of men began the descent of those first miles of the Mississippi in which it traces a giant question mark on the map before straightening out into its southward flow. Once on the way downstream they saw overhead a bird no man now sees in Minnesota, that most graceful and beautiful of all the hawks, the swallow-tailed kite. Confined at present almost entirely to the river swamps of the Southeast, this persecuted species once ranged widely, even nested in Minnesota.

Schoolcraft enjoyed the bird's superlatively graceful flight— something we could not experience. But all around us lay superlative beauty of another kind—beauty Schoolcraft did not see during that long ago visit in July. Then it was summer and the forests were green. Now it was autumn and, surrounding the lake, running down the banks of the beginning Mississippi, extending away over the ridges were the colored leaves, the tinted trees, the painted forests of the fall.

All across the country behind us—the realm of the roundheaded hardwoods, the oaks and beeches and maples—autumn's annual chro- matic show was rising to its peak. Nowhere in the world are the hues more rich and varied than in the climax woodlands of the eastern United States. We could visualize the colors now, or soon to be, on plant and bush and tree all along the path we had followed: The pur- plish red of the Cape Cod cranberry bogs, the scarlet sheets and clouds of New England's sugar maples, the wine hue of the Cape May tupe- los, the tapestry of many colors clothing the Kittitinny Ridge, the old gold of sycamores along Ohio streams, the waves of crimson running down the swamp maples beside the warbler river, the golden mittens of the sassafras in the dune country of northern Indiana. Everywhere the leaves of the third season of the year were bringing the growth of spring and summer to a dramatic rainbow end. These were the days when the flames of autumn burned most brightly in a fleeting but memorable show.

Even overnight, it seemed, new richness had been added to the col- ors around us as we stood once more in the dawn light beside the bridge of stepping-stones. Every twig of birch and aspen was clothed in gold. Deep purple-red sheeted all the clumps of viburnum. And above our heads, stretching out over the flow of the beginning Mississippi, the branch of a maple tree extended, against the blue of the autumn sky, foliage in which scarlet and gold and orange intermingled. Not only around Lake Itasca but wherever we wandered those days through the Minnesota autumn, we were in a world of color, color subtly commingling, infinitely varied. Everywhere the life of the leaves was nearing its end. Yet there is no sadness of farewell in the foliage of autumn; all flags are flying at journey's end.

Looking about us, where the mirror of the water reflected sky and clouds and autumn leaves, we speculated on how far the stirring colors of fall go in stimulating our minds. The clear, bracing air of this third season, with its lowered humidity and its touch of chill, is given credit for the alertness and sense of well-being that characterizes our autumn mood. But is there not a corresponding lift to the mind in this riot of color, exciting and exhilarating? In the forest, fall is the season of light. The aureate leaves, the golden carpet of fallen foliage reflecting rays upward from the ground, these fill the deciduous woodlands with a luminous radiance unknown at other seasons of the year. Henri Amiel noted in his *Journal Intime:* "The scarlet autumn stands for vigorous activity; the gray autumn for meditative feeling." Later in the season there would come slaty skies, brown leaves, gray autumn. But now we wandered in the multicolored early days of fall, the time of vigor and elation.

To the red man all these tintings of fall were of miraculous origin. They came, grew in brilliance, tarnished and faded away. It has taken the researches of a host of modern scientists to decipher the story of the painted leaves. And even so this narrative of autumn change contains a number of pages that still are blurred or partly blank.

The simplest of the autumn colors to explain is yellow, the gold of the aspen and the hickory and the birch. Carotene, the pigment found so abundantly in carrots, and xanthophyll, the coloring matter found in egg yolks and the feathers of the canary, are present in these leaves all summer long. In fact there is a greater quantity of these two pigments in the green leaves of midsummer than in the yellow leaves of fall. But then these pigments are masked by the outer layers of chlorophyll.

During the warm months the tree produces and uses chlorophyll continually, with production and use balanced. Then comes the chill of autumn. It retards the production of chlorophyll more rapidly than it does its consumption. In a bleaching process that is only partly understood, the chlorophyll breaks down into colorless compounds. The green disappears from the leaf and the yellow pigments are no longer masked. Each year we see this sudden shift of autumn on elm and birch and tulip tree, the change from the green of summer to the gold of fall. The new tints we see are not new at all. They are colors that have been there all the time.

Of the two pigments, carotene and xanthophyll, autumn gold is chiefly composed of the latter. In laboratory experiments this pigment was found to be twice as abundant as carotene in yellow autumn leaves. Both together, however, represent but an infinitesimal part of the total weight of the leaf. All the sheets of golden foliage that clothe autumn boughs are the product of such small amounts of these two pigments that they have a combined weight that is only one half of 1 per cent that of the leaves they glorify.

The yellows of autumn thus are produced by subtraction, the subtraction of chlorophyll. The reds of autumn are produced by addition, the addition of something that was not present in the leaf before.

From flaming scarlet to deepest purple, the most brilliant hues of the autumn woods are the products of coloring materials known as anthocyanins. They are the "cell-sap pigments." While the green of chlorophyll and the yellows of xanthophyll and carotene are contained in the protoplasm of the cell, the anthocyanins are carried in solution in the sap. Thus all the infinitely varied shades of red, the most striking feature of autumn's greatest show, are the products of tinted sap within the leaves.

Around the world and all through the vegetable kingdom the anthocyanins are distributed. They are responsible, in stem and bud and leaf and flower, for magentas and blues as well as reds and purples. They contribute the red to red bananas in the tropics and the red to red cabbage in northern fields. The cranberry and the poppy, the grape and the violet, the radish and the poinsettia all get their colors from anthocyanins. If the cell sap is acid the plant tends to produce bright reds. If it is alkaline it tends to produce blues and purples. How intense the colors of some of these cell-sap pigments are is demonstrated by the red cabbage. All its color comes from one layer of cells within the leaves.

The production of anthocyanins is an inherited ability possessed by many plants and trees. Some, like the purple beech, possess it so abundantly that the pigment produced masks the chlorophyll even in the summer leaves. Others, like the hickories, possess it not at all and their leaves always turn to yellow. Still others, like one isolated aspen we came upon as we drove south from Lake Itasca, produce slight amounts that impart to the outer leaves a faint rose tinting. They are the leaves that receive the greatest amount of sunshine. For anthocyanins are "sun pigments" as well as "cell-sap pigments."

With very few exceptions—notably the garden beet, which produces its bright-red root underground—the coloring material develops only where sunshine strikes. Thus the stem end of a red apple is usually more brightly colored than the flower end which hangs down away from the sun. In experiments, opaque letters have been attached to the side of such an apple before it ripened and letters or words in green have been produced on its red surface where the skin, shielded from the sunshine, developed no anthocyanin pigment in its cells. Scientists have even printed simple photographs on apples, in varying shades of green and red, by attaching negatives to their sides during the period when the fruit was ripening. There are, of course, apple trees such as the greenings that never develop anthocyanins and never have red fruit.

Occasionally as we wandered through the fall we came upon a tree that was red-tinged on the outside and yellow within. The shaded leaves had failed to produce anthocyanins in sufficient quantity to make the red pigment noticeable. White oaks sometimes exhibit leaves in autumn that are reddish on top, where they have been struck by the sunshine, but whitish beneath. A breeze among such foliage produces the striking effect of an ever-shifting pattern of red and white. Again, it has been noticed that the flaming colors of the sugar maple are usually brightest at the ends of the branches, where they receive the maximum amount of sunshine.

There appears to be another reason why the red of the sugar maple is the most brilliant of all. The presence of sugar in the sap is conducive to the formation of this color. When a research worker tested bright-red leaves from a Virginia creeper, he found they contained more sugar than green leaves from the same vine collected at the same time. The leaf containing the greatest amount of sugar is believed to turn the brightest red. But all summer long there is sugar in and sunshine on the leaves of the sugar maples. Yet they remain green. Why? Another factor is missing. That is cold.

When the temperature drops to forty-five degrees F., or below, it in-terferes with the removal of sugars and other substances from the leaves and this favors the accumulation of the pigments in the sap of the cells. A sudden drop just after the sun has set—such as occurred that last evening at Red Wing—is especially productive of brilliant au-tumn leaves. So are crisp, sunny days. The high, clear skies and spar-kling weather that usually mark the third season in the New World have much to do with the many-colored splendor of the forest trees. England's autumn, with mild and cloudy weather, produces duller foliage, mainly yellows and browns. Alice in Wonderland, judging by the somber groves and copses of the English fall, remarked that she always thought a wood in autumn looked sleepy.

At one time it was believed that the frost painted the autumn leaves. Now it is known that, with or without frost, lowered temperature achieves this end. In fact a hard frost or freeze early in the fall tends to destroy the yellow pigments and prevent the formation of anthocya-nins. In such seasons the trees merely turn brownish without develop-ing the reds and yellows and the infinitely varied combinations of the two. And, as every autumn progresses, even the most colorful of the painted leaves, even those of the maples that unite the ultimate bril-liance of scarlet and gold and orange, they all—clinging to the tree or on the ground where they have fallen—tarnish and fade and lose their glory. Where do the pigments go?

Already some of the fallen leaves were brown along the paths we fol-lowed through the Minnesota woods. Others lay among them still tinted but with their colors slowly ebbing through oxidation. All the leaf pigments are unstable. Chlorophyll is the least stable of all. Next come the yellow pigments. Finally, most stable, are the anthocyanins. But even they oxidize in time, turning brown much in the manner of a slice of apple that is white when cut but takes on a brownish cast if subjected to prolonged exposure to the air.

The exact process by which the tide of autumn colors recede and browns of varying shades take their place is still imperfectly understood. Tannins, always present in the changing leaves, are believed to play a leading role. Throughout the whole chromatic parade of the fall foliage, all the tints and hues and combinations and shadings are the work of various pigments. But the universal brown that envelops the autumn leaves at last is rather the product of gradual decomposition, of chemical changes taking place little by little.

These changes—the long, slow ebbing of this forest splendor—had barely begun when we drove south again, this time through western Minnesota. Everywhere the flaming pageant was at its peak. It moved behind meadowlarks singing on a hundred fenceposts; it circled ponds where muskrat houses had been newly reinforced against the chilly nights; it trooped into the outskirts of farming towns where all along main streets the lamp posts were decorated with cornstalks; it stood in the background behind a curious stretch of rolling plowed fields where every rise was topped with silvery soil so that the farms all seemed dappled with sunshine and shadow. And so we came to the North Dakota line and Fargo and the Red River Valley. So we left one of the states we wanted least to leave—Minnesota. Before us lay the prairie; behind us stretched the thousand miles of the eastern hardwoods, now all clad in their coat of many colors. We had, in Minnesota, seen their chromatic splendor at its height, and we had, in Minnesota, come to the western border of their range.

Wonderful Eighty-Three

THIS was the prairie fall. This was the "haze on the far horizon, the infinite tender sky." And it will always come back to us as we saw it then—a long, straight road stretching like a taut string toward the south, extending away across a land rolling in great tan waves beneath the high blue of the sky. It is a road we will never forget, a road we will always remember as Wonderful Eighty-Three.

Among the hills and wooded valleys of the East, the landscape closes in like a bud. Here, on the plains, it opens out, expands like a flower full-blown. Under the height of the sky and over the waves of the land, the black line of U.S. Highway 83 carried us that day southward through two and a half degrees of latitude. It led us from beautiful Apple Creek, mentioned in Audubon's journal, to Farm Island, associated with the expedition of Lewis and Clark; from near Bismarck, the capital of North Dakota, to Pierre, the capital of South Dakota. And always, just to the west, paralleling the road, the muddy Missouri, the Smoky Water of the Mandan Indians, rolled along its winding course, moving southward too.

That day started with the uncertain crows. It ended with the cautious Canada geese. Between the two it was filled with a long succession of flocks and waves and concentrations of many kinds of birds. The full tide of migration now was flowing down the valley of the Missouri to join the mightier tide of the Mississippi Flyway. For more than 150 miles that day, we overtook and moved among wave after wave of migrants. It was as though we were riding a surfboard, sweeping ahead on the crests of the great combers of the autumn flight. This was a day, as well as a road, we will always remember.

Not far from the pioneer village of Menoken we encountered the crows. In a vast assemblage they stretched like a dark scud-cloud across an expanse of open country. The cloud elongated, contracted, shifted form continually as the birds milled about in the sky. They seemed to be at the start of migration, uncertain of mind, a democracy at the polls. Some appeared set on going north, others south. The flock split apart, rejoined, divided, returned together, the babel of cawing rising to crescendos and sinking away and then swelling once more. We stopped for a long time beside the highway to watch the outcome. For minutes at a time the birds circled, apparently in screaming debate. They were like swarming bees that had lost their queen. They rose hundreds of feet into the air, descended close to the ground; they bunched and strung out. Then at last they all rose and moved away uncertainly toward the south. This almost-human hesitance and debate and final departure was our first vivid impression of this never-to-be-forgotten day.

To the Mandan Indians who lived along this part of the Missouri in the days of Lewis and Clark, all flocking birds of autumn were going home, home to The Old Woman Who Never Dies. In their mythology this supernatural being, dwelling unseen beyond the southern horizon, was the giver of all crops and the birds were her representatives. Each fall the natives prayed and made offerings of meat and grain as the migrants departed, in order that their crops the following year might be bountiful. And in the spring when the wildfowl came back up the river the Indians greeted them as emissaries and auguries of good fortune, different birds representing success to different crops—the wild goose to the maize, the wild duck to the beans, the wild swan to the gourds.

Running south under the cloudless sky, we were at times that day in a land as lonely as the sea. We would catch glimpses of remote ranch houses across infinite stretches of country. Each surrounded by its cluster of weathered buildings, they were far-scattered, hardly more frequent than villages in the East. At times, looking ahead from the top of some rise, we would see our road, bee-lining away over the swells of land, take on a semblance to an old-fashioned spyglass seen in reverse, different sections ahead appearing beyond successive swells, suddenly narrowed by the abrupt increase in distance.

In every pond along the way muskrats were out, sleeping like kittens in the sun. A family of five slumbered in a brown cluster on top of one house no more than thirty feet from the road. They paid no attention to us. While we watched through our glasses, one lifted its head and yawned widely. Then it dozed off again. Another awoke long enough to scratch itself vigorously behind a foreleg. Two stretched, clambered down, slipped into the water and swam in a wide circle. Then they climbed out, dripping, onto the mound of yellow vegetation and curled up again, soon dry, soon part of the pile of sunlighted, shining, sleek brown fur. These were days of warmth and well-being, the days of the early-autumn sunshine.

But down the southward-leading length of Wonderful Eighty-Three it was the birds that dominated our road and our day. Here, as nowhere else, we rode the floodtide of the autumn movement. The birds increased in number, piled up in concentrations, as we advanced. Each successive pond seemed inhabited by a denser population of coot. Swimming away as we slowed to a stop, they trailed across the water behind them a multitude of spreading V's that crisscrossed endlessly until sometimes half the surface of a pond was covered with moving, ripple-bounded diamond shapes, glinting in the sun.

Scattered across one shallow pond, we saw brilliant black-and-white avocets. On slender legs, a flock of more than a hundred worked across the shallows swinging their long, upcurved bills in the water. They advanced like mowers wielding scythes in a hayfield. Then, all of a sudden, they all ceased feeding and lifted into the air. Facing the wind they sailed low over the highway, luminous birds with the sun behind them, while the multitude of their shadows—black shadows cast by black-and-white wings—trailed over and around us as they passed.

One after the other, half a dozen times in the course of the day, we overtook long, straggling, southward-drifting flocks of crows. One, like a skein of windblown smoke, was strung out for more than a mile. A whole flock had landed across one hillside, and at another place the black birds of passage were crowding around a water hole to drink. Big hawks, too, were on the move. Most seemed to be roughlegs and that hawk of the prairies, Swainson's, but a number were redtails. Usually we saw them soaring southward or circling in the sky but there was one yellow slope, descending to a swale bordered by green-black rushes, where almost every one of the gray, scattered rocks held a perching buteo.

Now we were back among killdeers again. We saw them congregated together, scattered across slopes, clustered around pasture waterholes, circling overhead, calling as they flew. Avocets and yellowlegs, both greater and lesser, swarmed around the edges of the sloughs; over one small lake 500 Franklin's gulls circled in great white wheels above the feeding shorebirds. Then there were wondrous miles when the air all around us was filled with the sweet, flutelike song of the massed meadowlarks. Somewhere in Beaver Valley, east of Fort Yates and the grave of Sitting Bull, we came upon a bird we had never seen before. Brilliant in contrasting black and white, it shot in an almost vertical climb up the steep side of a railroad embankment—our first American magpie.

It was 12:05 P.M. when we crossed the boundary between the two Dakotas. In the southern state we were about midway between the Atlantic and the Pacific and at the same time almost equidistant from the North Pole and the Equator. Hardly twenty miles inside South Dakota, in the region of Hiddenwood Lake, we encountered the largest of all the migrants that move southward through the autumn skies along the course of the Missouri. A flock of half a dozen immense white pelicans floated near the farther shore—birds with an even greater span of wing than the rare whooping crane that sometimes crosses this land in its autumn movement from the far north to the Texas coast. As we watched, one of the pelicans flapped into the air and then, with eight-foot, black-tipped wings outspread, soared on and on over the water.

As the day advanced, small, wan clouds, few and far away, formed along the edges of the burnished sky. Little twisters ran across the open land beside the highway snatching up grass and dust. And always, seen in the hazy, dusty distance, the buttes rose along the skyline, flat-topped, roofed with a layer of harder rock that protected the softer, more easily eroded material below. The time of flowers was now past and almost every plant we saw was brown of leaf and dry of stem. In the warmth of the afternoon, grasshoppers interminably crossed the road ahead of us, some walking this way, some that, as restless as the far-scattered pioneers who roamed the area in an earlier day.

In this largely treeless land we came upon a cottonwood that must have been a landmark for a generation or more. Its lower half was clad in yellow leaves, but all its upper branches were silvered and barkless and bare. As we approached, a cloud of excited blackbirds swept toward the tree, swirled around it, descended on it. Almost in an instant the migrant host covered the bare branches and the tree seemed half clad in yellow foliage, half in black. We counted the birds perching on one limb and calculated the total number. Well over 1,000 blackbirds had settled in this single tree. Their din drowned out every other sound. This was the great adventure; for many, perhaps for most, the first migration.

At the end of five minutes the concourse of birds suddenly rose into the air. For a hundred yards or so we rode parallel to one redwing. Its speed over the ground was exactly forty miles an hour. Later in the day, near Pierre, we came within sight of a vast, flowing river of birds at least five miles long—redwings and grackles and Brewer's blackbirds—crossing the sky from east to west, toward the Missouri. Tens of thousands of flocking birds were going to roost along the river.

All that day the Missouri, unseen to the west, was a dominant feature of the land. Just below the horizon, beyond the buttes to our right, it flowed, now drawing nearer, now turning farther away in its windings. We felt its presence. We saw, in dry vegetation wrapped about fenceposts, evidences of its floodwaters in the spring. For Americans, the Missouri River has more than ordinary significance. It was the Lewis and Clark roadway into the unknown. It was the path of the early fur traders. It was the water barrier crossed by the pioneers. It carried the adventurous early naturalists deeper into a wilder West.

Just over there, on this stretch of winding river between Bismarck and Pierre, the men of the Lewis and Clark Expedition had landed their fifty-five-foot keelboat, propelled by twenty-two oars, and had examined fresh tracks of a "grizzled" bear three times as large as those of a man. There, too, they had come upon great "gangues of buffalow" swimming the river. This was in the fall of the year, in October 1804.

Only seven years later, Thomas Nuttall had wandered up the banks of this same stretch of the 2,466-mile river. It was in June and along the stream and on the prairies beyond wildflowers were in bloom. "Delighted with the treasures spreading themselves out before him," as Washington Irving described him on a later trip, "he went groping and stumbling along among a wilderness of sweets, forgetful of everything but his immediate pursuits." Here he found a new cinquefoil, a new figwort, a new nightshade. Where the Cheyenne River joins the Missouri—Nuttall spelled it "Shian" in his notes—he collected a prairie pentstemon new to science. This was in the fall of 1811.

Less than two decades after Nuttall, a fur-trader's canoe, following all the windings of this part of the river, carried George Catlin, pioneer painter of Indians, upstream toward his eight years with trappers and tribes of the prairie regions. This remarkable man, working under all the hardships of primitive conditions, put down on canvas a priceless collection of aboriginal portraits. But Catlin was more than a portrait painter. He was a man of vision and nobility of spirit, a friend of red men, a defender of the persecuted. And, apparently, he was the first person in America to propose the creation of a great national park in the West.

Again, a decade and a half later, John James Audubon, painting wildlife as he went, ascended the stream that flowed just beyond our western horizon. Aboard the pioneer Missouri River steamer *Omega*, he was on his way to the Yellowstone. Also on board riding with him in the wood-burning, spark-spitting paddle-wheeler were almost 10,000 pounds of gunpowder bound for frontier trading posts. At the time Audubon was in his fifty-eighth year and was described by a reporter who interviewed him in St. Louis at the start of the expedition as "an old man with silver locks and the weight of years upon him." But the entries in the journal he kept at the time show no evidence of diminishing powers. With vitality and keenness of observation they record absorbing sidelights on wildlife—how wolves came running whenever they heard the sound of a gun being fired; how antelope were so curious by nature that they would approach close to a man who lay on his back on the prairie and kicked his legs in the air; how—above Pierre, in almost the exact portion of the river that now lay due west of us—he watched a spotted sandpiper in full flight dive under the water five or six times in escaping the pursuit of a pigeon hawk.

In an introduction to a volume of his collected poems, John Masefield, the poet laureate of England, remarks how mention of some hillside or valley or stream in the pages of a book will invest the region with special charm and how the reader feels a quickened interest when, passing that way later on, he remembers the allusion. So it was that remembered pages from the *Original Journals of the Lewis and Clark Ex-*

pedition, from *The Missouri River Journals* of Audubon, from *Travels in the Interior of North America*, by Maximilian, Prince of Wied, had enveloped this region of the Missouri with a peculiar fascination.

We came to the river again at Pierre late in the afternoon—with Wonderful Eighty-Three, that highway of birds, behind us. Turning south we followed the eastern bank downstream to sandy roads winding among cottonwoods on Farm Island. Here, in 1804, hunters of the Lewis and Clark party killed four elk. Now connected with the mainland by a short causeway, this river island, three miles long, has been set aside as a state park. Fur traders and soldiers stationed at Fort Pierre in the early days at various times raised crops here; hence the name.

A score of chickadees were trooping along the island's edge among the cottonwoods. Savanna sparrows fed on the seeds of the pigweed. And out over the river goldfinches went past, rising and falling as though on choppy waves, while, flying farther out, a flicker loped by them in great bounds, appearing to ride longer swells of the airy sea. Under the birds and past the island, brown and swirling, rolled unceasingly the muddy water of the wide and shallow Missouri River.

Sediment of many kinds made up its burden of silt. It ranged from invisible flakes of clay, only $1/25,000$ of an inch across, to sandgrains of quartz, $1/25$ of an inch in diameter, and even small pebbles of varying size. A sluggish current, moving no more than a quarter of a mile an hour, is sufficient to support the flakes of clay. At a third of a mile an hour a stream will carry fine sand. At one mile an hour it will transport gravel the size of a pea; at three miles an hour it will move along stones as big as hens' eggs. Whatever slows the current of a stream causes it to deposit its sediment, commencing with the larger elements. The minimum gradient that will keep a river flowing is a drop of six inches to the mile. If the descent becomes shallower than that all progress ceases, the water spreads out, flow and direction are lost.

Looking across the wide brown, sediment-filled flood of the river toward the dead-appearing bluffs of its farther bank, we saw nineteen slender necks stretch up along a sandbar well out from either shore. A flock of Canada geese, settling down for the night safely beyond gunshot, had seen us emerge from among the cottonwoods. Instantly they set up a deep-toned clamor, every bird on the alert. The Missouri is one of the great river highways of the migrating geese. On "10th November Satturday 1804," among the Mandans, Captain William Clark noted in his journal that "the Gees Continue to pass in gangues." Near the very spot where we stood, John James Audubon had observed these prudent birds as they were going north in spring. They were wary then; a hundred years and more later, with the number of guns arrayed against them growing year by year, they were more wary still. From their distant sandbar this band of sagacious waterfowl watched us intently, every head erect, until we left the river bank and started back toward Pierre. Those upraised heads of the cautious geese, seen in a place so long associated with movements of their kind, provided our last bird memory of this superlative day of birds.

High Autumn

THIRTY-FIVE miles from the Continental Divide. Seventy-five hundred feet above the level of the sea. In the high autumn of the Rockies. There we first encountered the charm of the pika.

It was at sunset. We were sitting amid the vast jumble of an ancient rock slide. White and marked by bubbles and seemingly formed of hardened dough, the blocks of stone ranged from a few feet in diameter to the bulk of a cabin. This rock cascade, now long stilled, had tumbled down the steep descent below a cliff of travertine. The drop plunged away below us while other rock slides ran in spreading inverted V's down the brown sides of a peak beyond. We were near the Silver Gate on Terrace Mountain, not far from Mammoth Hot Springs in the northwestern corner of Yellowstone.

We were also now in the wonderful month of October, that perfect month of fall. In October calm and sunny days prevail. High winds are almost unknown; thunderheads are rarely seen; the season of tempests and cyclones is virtually over. In October the same temperature is found over a greater portion of the United States than at any other time of year. Ellsworth Huntington of Yale, after a lifetime of research, reported that in the autumn, in October, our creative mental ability is at a peak. In this Leaf-Falling Moon of the Indians our general health is best, we feel most fit.

Sitting there on the rock slide in the calm of that October evening, in the quiet of the mountain heights, the sunset glowing above the white line of the cliff behind us, valleys and mountains—with grass embrowned and aspens golden, all in autumn dress—spread out below us, we became conscious of a sound like an elfin horn blown far away. It came down the slope across the labyrinth of rocks. We listened. It came again. This time it was answered more loudly to our right, below us to our left. Then all at once half a dozen of the elfin horns were blowing back and forth across the avalanche debris. We swept our glasses slowly from rock to rock. Almost at the same instant we discovered the diminutive horn blower. It was in the very act of sending forth the short blast of its little bleat.

Sleek, plump, brownish, about half a foot long, with short, rounded ears, with no visible tail at all, the animal sat on the flat shelf of a projecting rock. Just as it came into focus it lifted its head, opened its little mouth, stretched out its neck and then, like an old-fashioned auto horn with the rubber bulb squeezed, it jerked and propelled forth the small trumpet-note of its call.

We were looking for the first time in our lives at the animal Thomas Nuttall once described in a letter to John James Audubon—that famous haymaker of the rock slides, the pika, the cony, the calling hare, the slide rat, the little chief hare, the rock rabbit. No other animal we had ever seen, no puppy or kitten or chipmunk or flying squirrel, had ever had so much charm-at-first-glance as this little caller of the mountain tops. We saw it later in other avalanche areas, among the talus of more than one mountain cliff near timberline, and each subsequent meeting strengthened this initial impression of the endearing charm of the pika.

IN MOUNTAIN SUNSHINE, at midday, we leveled off at the top of Craig Pass, 8,262 feet above sea level. The hood of our car dipped and for the first time in thousands of miles of wandering our wheels rolled on the western side of the Great Divide.

In sunshine by day and sudden chill by night we wandered, now on one side, now on the other, along this backbone of the continent. Set aside as the first national park in the history of the United States, the Yellowstone country in the northwestern corner of Wyoming has special fascination for anyone with even the mildest interest in natural history. For hundreds of miles we wound among its hot springs and mud pots, its fumeroles and geysers. Here geology sheds its ancient, static mask. It advances to the present tense; becomes a thing active and alive. Here we were amid wildlife that, in a thousand ways, had adapted itself to this bizarre environment.

All the hours of these autumn days were spent amid shining and sometimes eerie beauty. Once, in the moonlight, we watched Old Faithful rise higher and higher until it towered in a glowing plume of white lifting 150 feet into the air. Another time, in midafternoon, we came upon the Giant Geyser in full eruption, supporting twenty tons of water in the air at one time, sending its billowing clouds of steam and scalding spray 250 feet above the ground, while in the midst of this superheated fury shone the delicate, ephemeral beauty of a rainbow.

The sudden chill of the October nights carried the mercury down as much as thirty degrees below the high point of the day. And all around the hot springs and fumeroles the clouds of steam increased. As we walked amid the bubbling kettles of the hot spring basins by moonlight we saw wherever we looked wraiths of vapor that rose and wavered and shone in the silvery light. The whole land seemed restless and alive. Chilled and shivering we would hurry from the warmth of one drifting steam cloud to the next. Only two sounds broke the stillness of the mountain night. One was the steady, uneven bumbling and bubbling of the hot springs. The other—to our amazement—was the loud and confident chirping of crickets beside the path. Their burrows in the ground were steam-heated apartments and, so far, they had defied and outlived the frosts.

These nocturnal musicians are only one of many kinds of creatures that benefit in one way or another from the heated earth and heated vapor and heated water of Yellowstone. Bird nests warmed by steam and bear dens heated by nearby springs have been observed more than once in the park. Trout are active all winter long in the warmed water of Firehole and Gibbon rivers. And every year a few kingfishers remain at Yellowstone in spite of the snow and ice and low temperatures. Their rattling call has been heard in the midst of snowstorms close to the top of the Great Divide and they have been seen diving through rising vapor of the warmed rivers when the mercury stood as low as thirty degrees below zero.

At dawn one day when all the fields of deer-colored grass were pearly with the night's heavy rime of frost, we came upon two mallards taking advantage of the Yellowstone warmth. They floated on a small, rush-bordered pool formed by the runoff of a neighboring spring. They were not feeding as they rode about with wisps of vapor curling up around them. They seemed merely enjoying the warmth. I rummaged around in the glove compartment until I found the thermometer. It showed that the temperature of the water was eighty-eight degrees F.—sixty degrees above that of the surrounding air.

In the autumn ducks come more and more to the warmed pools as the nights grow colder. Some mallards overwinter on the open rivers that carry away the flow of hot springs, on the Gardiner and Yellowstone as well as on the Firehole and the Gibbon. During some years green-winged teal and Wilson snipe, as well as mallards, winter around the warm overflow at the foot of Jupiter Terrace. Here is food and warmth even in the coldest weather. And wild ducks have been observed circling above the Giant Geyser when it was in full eruption in winter, apparently enjoying the warm air rising above it.

At Orange Mound Spring, where the deposits of years of flowing, mineral-laden water have engulfed and killed trees as a moving dune buries them among sandhills, we watched a redbreasted nuthatch obtaining a drink in an unconventional way. It darted down to the tip of a dead twig on a tree whose whole lower trunk was encased within the slanting wall of rock. Then it leaned far out and, dipping its upcurved bill into the thin sheet of descending water, drank repeatedly. I touched the flow with a forefinger. The water was warm but not hot. The largest of the birds we saw drinking at a hot spring was a magpie. It rode past us in a long toboggan, lifting or depressing its extended tail as it checked or accentuated the angle of its glide, until it dropped down beside one of the shallow pools on the terrace of Mammoth Hot Springs. There, with steam curling thinly up around it, the bird lowered its head and began to drink.

During this period when we were following the high roads of the Wyoming Rockies, everyone was talking about the wonderful fall. The days were abnormally warm and sunny. The snow that usually arrives well before the park closes officially on October 15, was still to come. In a kind of high-country Indian summer we wandered about in days of lingering warmth.

Then we drifted down into beautiful Jackson Hole below the range of the Grand Tetons. We followed the gorge of the upper Snake River over the line into the twentieth state of the trip, Idaho.

Sheep were coming down from summer pasture in the higher mountains. Children were playing in new strawstacks, and brown burlap bags of sacked potatoes ran in ragged rows across miles of open fields where killdeers circled and called. Some of the filled sacks seemed bags of cats, so large were the famed Idaho russets. We passed schools closed for a week and school buses carrying children to help in the fields.

Then we were on roads running south down the eastern edge of Idaho, in tumbleweed country, in the land of the Blackfeet, sometimes surrounded for miles by strange ebony volcanic formations. Thus we descended from the Continental Divide into the Great Basin, advancing toward Utah's desert flats, the Great Salt Lake and a day with a million ducks.

Our Million-Duck Day

ONE autumn day in the year 1824, a bullboat formed of buffalo hides stretched over a willow framework floated on the slow current out through the marshes of the Bear River delta. The lone occupant noticed his craft suddenly riding higher, gaining buoyancy. He trailed a forefinger over the side, tasted brine, and was convinced that he was drifting on the Pacific Ocean. Thus more than a century and a quarter ago Jim Bridger, pioneer trapper and scout, discovered the Great Salt Lake.

Twenty-five miles of marshes extended across the delta of the Bear River in Bridger's day. Eighteen years later, in the fall of 1842, John C. Frémont followed the tortuous channels across the marshes with Kit Carson and reported: "The whole morass was animated with multitudes of waterfowl rising for the space of a mile round about at the sound of a gun, with a noise like distant thunder." In an orgy of killing by sportsmen who complained that they got "only 325" ducks in a day's shooting and by meat-hunters who sold mallard for a dollar-and-a-half and teal for a dollar a dozen, vast numbers of the waterfowl were slaughtered in the 1890's. Today the marshes are replaced with shallow lakes rimmed by nearly forty miles of dikes. Fanning out across the delta they provide one of the greatest migratory bird refuges in the world.

We first saw this impounded water through the shining, dusty haze of afternoon. For fifteen miles west of Brigham we drove across flatlands where black-and-white cattle fed amid patches of crimson salicornia, past dark tule marshes—the home of yellow-headed blackbirds and white-faced glossy ibis—beside the Bear River, at an altitude of more than 4,000 feet meandering and brown and lazy like some lowland stream approaching the sea.

Along the dike tops twelve miles of open roads led us into a wonderland of waterfowl. Never in our lives had we seen such concentrations of birds. And we were to see still greater numbers the next day when John Bauman, refuge biologist, took us into areas closed to the casual visitor. For the Bear River delta is a kind of watershed for migrating waterfowl. In days when the ducks and geese stream southward in their autumn flight some continue south down the Great Basin, but others turn east at this point toward the Central Flyway while still others turn west toward the Pacific Coast.

Vanez T. Wilson, refuge manager, showed us that day maps and charts and some of the amazing records of birds that had been banded at Bear River. Since the refuge was established in 1928 more than 36,000 individuals have received numbered metal leg-bands. They have been recovered in twenty-nine of the forty-eight states as well as in Canada, Alaska, Mexico, Honduras, and even the Territory of Hawaii. One pintail, banded on August 15, 1942, was found eighty-three days later on the tiny island of Palmyra, far out in the Pacific. The distance between this island and Bear River is 3,600 miles.

Because this sanctuary is the most famous nesting ground of the redhead duck, individuals of this species have provided some of the most interesting records. Returns have come in from twenty-two states. They show that when autumn comes some of the redheads fly 500 miles or so west across Nevada to California and move south, beyond the Sierra, along the Pacific Coast Flyway. But others that have hatched in nests almost beside them migrate in the opposite direction, over the Continental Divide of the Rockies, to descend along the Central Flyway to the Gulf or to join flocks from Canada and move across the land to the flyway of the Atlantic Coast, three-quarters of a continent away.

It was still dark the next morning when, at 5:30, we climbed into Bauman's jeep. But by the time we had finished our ham and eggs and emerged from an all-night restaurant in Brigham the whole top of the Wasatch range was glowing in the dawn light. And a little later when we swung into the side roads of the refuge, the upper levels of the Promontory Mountains, west of Bear River Bay, were already bright with the first sunshine of the morning. Then the valley, too, became illuminated. And all across the 50,000 and more acres of the sanctuary the wings of great clouds of waterfowl shimmered and glinted in the sunrise.

Pintails predominated. Thousands at a time they leaped into the air, climbed steeply, turned in the sky or trailed in scudding clouds low above the water, or skittered along the surface as they landed amid a myriad flashing drops of thrown-up spray. This was autumn. This was the beginning of migration. The birds were immaculate in new plumage, at the peak of their powers. Everywhere we looked ducks were taking off and landing. An electric atmosphere of energy and vitality filled the air around us. Wherever we went that day—along the ridge called Molly's Stocking, past the high abandoned lookout tower where ravens have built their nest, on the dike tops, along the skirts of the mountains, tan or tawny with dry Junegrass—always we were within sight of waterfowl. Through the sunshine and drifting milkweed fluff and gossamer showers of this autumn day we saw a million ducks.

Once we climbed to the top of a hundred-foot observation tower for an eagle's-eye view of the delta. All the wide, dike-bordered ponds were stippled with the massed dots of rafts and banks and shoals of floating waterfowl. Our field glasses showed us other rafts beyond the vision of our unaided eyes and our Balscope, with its twenty-power lens, brought still more remote concentrations into view—like nebulae and galaxies and island universes thickly strewn over the reaches of outer space. A still higher eyrie is that employed by one of the refuge men who makes a weekly census of waterfowl from a lightplane that is housed in a hangar near the observation tower. Estimating with a practiced eye the number of ducks and geese below him, this flying census taker probably has more waterfowl within his sight in the course of a year than any other man in America.

Most of the redheads had already gone south on that October day. They are early migrants. So are the gadwall and the cinnamon teal. Here and there we saw a few gadwall as we saw shoveller, mallard, canvasback, baldpate and ruddy ducks. But this was the time of the pintail. And next to the pintail the green-winged teal. These beautiful, swift, vibrant forms of life, turning and flashing in the sun, darting upward, whirling in sudden circles, slanting downward in arrowy descent, moving together in perfect time and unison, these tens of thousands of small waterfowl were active all across the sanctuary. Almost all of the green-winged teal of Bear River overwinter in the Sacramento Valley of California. We saw, no doubt, some of these same birds when, weeks later, we visited that valley of the west.

For us who, among the depleted, overgunned ponds of the populous east, were accustomed to counting our flocks of migrant ducks in dozens and scores, the wonder never diminished in these thousands and tens of thousands and hundreds of thousands of waterfowl. It was, for a glorious day, a return to older times, to times when the country was new. And if the sound of the rising waterfowl was not quite like distant thunder the glint and shine of their myriad moving wings provided one of the inerasable memories of our trip.

Another link with earlier days was the dessert we had when we dined with the Baumans that noon. Wild currant pie. Then we were out on the dikes again with wildfowl all around us.

Distant objects now shimmered in the heat waves—rafts of lesser snow geese and Canada geese, long flotillas of white pelicans, the dark islands of the varied ducks. And as we looked down the dike ahead of us the dry vegetation—sunflowers, thistles, milkweed and tumbleweed-shaped *bassia*—growing on either side of the road seemed on fire. Dense black smoke appeared pouring above it, rising in twin clouds, ascending thirty feet in the air, mysteriously hanging there without changing form or size, without drifting away. What we were seeing was not smoke but billions of dark little midges hanging in the air all along the miles of vegetation, forming, when viewed down the dike's length, clouds so dense they stood out black against the sky.

Just as never before had I seen so many ducks of a kind, so never before had I seen so many insects of a kind at one time. Heads of cattails, needles of tamarisk trees, the fluff of burst milkweed pods, all were burdened with resting midges. They darkened the white-painted railings of the spillway bridges. They coated the thousands of roadside plants like a covering of dust. Along the length of every thread of stranded gossamer, midges clung like swallows sitting side by side on a telephone wire. At times the plants seemed half animal and when we disturbed one it appeared partially to dissolve into a dark cloud that puffed upward into the air. And all down the dike the living clouds merged with one another into a continuous swarm. My brain grew weary trying to calculate the astronomical number of the more than thirty-five miles of midges we saw that day.

Mile after mile the fine, high humming of the *Chironomids* accompanied us, a sound so small, so fairylike, it would have to be, I think, multiplied a thousandfold to be barely audible. But here the thousand-fold was multiplied a thousandfold. This thin, steely sound encircled every pond, ran along all the dikes, spoke of the prodigality of Nature which here, among these small creatures, had reached one of its autumn peaks.

Later in the afternoon, whenever we swung toward the lowering sun, these dark insect swarms became suddenly, in the backlighting, dancing clouds of golden motes. All the millions of midges hung in the gentle breeze like tiny minnows stemming the current of a sluggish stream. They moved forward and backward, up and down. This was their great aerial dance, their mating time, the climax of their lives. And it would continue day after day, on after sunset each day, far into the dusk.

Theirs was not the only mating flight that afternoon. For all across the delta red harvester ants drifted on wings soon to be discarded, navigating the air for the only time in their earthbound lives. And here and there in the sun we came upon dark clusters of flesh flies, insects that have increased since the mysterious "western duck sickness" first swept through Bear River forty years ago. A form of botulism, a bacterial poisoning produced by germs incubating in the mud, it has brought death to hundreds of thousands of waterfowl. We saw one great trench excavated by a bulldozer into which the bodies of dead ducks were heaped for burning. In some instances gulls have been stricken after eating contaminated flesh flies and there is one case of a red-shafted flicker falling prey to the disease as a result of feeding on flesh-fly larvae. Oftentimes if the stricken waterfowl can be transferred to fresh water in the early stages of the sickness it will recover. But many die on the outer mudbanks beyond the farthest dike. Looking out toward the shimmer of the Great Salt Lake we could see their bodies scattered across the bars and shallows waiting to be collected.

The lake beyond, a lake of brine, a dead sea so salty no fish swims in it, stretches north and south about eighty miles and east and west about forty. It is the shrunken remnant of the great Lake Bonneville of prehistoric times.

The entire flora and fauna of this lake of salt consists of one minute kind of plant life and two minute kinds of animal life. Just as in the hot springs of Yellowstone we had found brilliant-colored algae growing, so here, where the saline content of the water is almost at the saturation point, the blue-green alga, *Apanothece packardii*, makes its home. Underwater pastures of this alga provide the only food of the animal life of the lake—the quarter-inch-long brine shrimp, *Artemia gracilis*, and the larvae of two species of brine flies, *Ephydra gracilis* and *Ephydra hians*. Both shrimp and flies, in the aquatic desert to which they have adapted themselves, are free from parasites. Each summer they develop in enormous numbers. So transparent are the minute shrimp however that, although they are everywhere in the midsummer water, they are rarely noticed by bathers. It is the pupa cases of the flies that attract amazed attention.

Frémont waded ashore on the island that was later given his name through a band of these cases twenty feet wide and as much as a foot thick. Yet each brine-fly pupa is no larger than a grain of oats. Forming on the bottom of the lake and becoming buoyant with gas, they rise to the surface where hornlike projections link them together into solid floating masses, sometimes acres in extent. Although we saw none of these spectacular concentrations in October, there are years when, in July and August, the currents shape these masses into disks and ribbons and occasionally into serpentine forms as much as a mile in length. Waves toss them on the shore in great red-brown windrows. And all around these windrows are the countless hordes of the emerging adults.

J. M. Aldrich, writing in *The Journal of the New York Entomological Society* for June, 1912, reported that mile after mile along the shore in mid-July he found the big-eyed, big-headed, stubby-abdomened little brine flies resting on the surface of the water in a band almost twenty feet wide, a dark, winding ribbon of insects that he could see from a distance of several miles. So densely were they massed together that he counted twenty-five, and sometimes as many as fifty, to the square inch. We saw, in October, only small and scattered concentrations of the little flies.

At the height of their midsummer season these insects have alighted on the rails of the Southern Pacific cutoff across the Great Salt Lake in such numbers they have stalled gasoline handcars. Trainmen hastily slam down windows in coaches approaching the cutoff to prevent the clouds of flies from being sucked inside. Known locally as "buffalo gnats" or "salt flies," the tiny creatures never bite and have little interest in human beings. But for centuries before the first pioneers reached the Great Salt Lake the brine flies were the object of an autumn pilgrimage that brought Indian tribes from distant points to camp along the shore. This was "the time of kootsabe," the time when the larvae of the flies were collected, dried in the sun, and stored away like yellow kernels of grain as a staple winter food.

The coming of night amid the waterfowl of Bear River is a wild and impressive time. The water lies flat, tinted, reflecting the purple of the mountains, strewn with the constellations of the floating ducks. The clamor of the wildfowl rises and falls away. Restless flocks—pintail and green-winged teal, snow geese and white pelicans—turn in the air with the whistle of wings, their plumage stained with the red of the western sky. And all around us, under the purple-tinged mountains, on the pink-tinted water, beneath the flame-colored sky, there was the almost continuous creaking of the western grebes.

Here and there as we drifted along the dikes at sundown that evening, we came on a glowing mudflat where killdeers ran and teetered and trilled and where dowitchers fed with sewing-machine movements of their long bills. Once when I slammed the car door every dowitcher in a flock of more than fifty flipped its wings in unison but continued feeding. How amazing is the uniformity of response in such birds. Not one individual leaped into the air; not one failed to flip its wings in exactly the same manner. All the birds, and each and every one of them, was alarmed so much and no more. We wondered later about this feeding flock that reacted like a single organism composed of many cells. Were the birds so nervously alike that the same stimulus instantaneously produced an identical response? Or had we seen a contagious reaction, an imitative movement that was started by one individual and ran from bird to bird with a time-lapse so slight our eyes could not record it?

Curving into the west over our heads, their snow-white plumage suffused with glowing pink, twenty-two pelicans followed each other in single file. When these huge birds are nesting on the islands of the

Great Salt Lake they fly from 30 to 100 miles to fresh water for the fish they feed their young. Although this catch consists almost entirely of carp and other so-called "trash" fish—which by its removal actually helps the gamefish the sportsmen favor—the pelicans of Utah have been the objects of a long persecution. As late as 1918, masquerading under the often-abused term of sportsmen and with the active coopera-tion of the state fish and game department, gangs invaded the island nesting grounds and shot and clubbed to death several thousand white pelicans including the helpless nestlings.

One of the last birds we saw that night against the darkening sky was a pelican moving overhead in silent silhouette like some creature out of the prehistoric past. When we switched on our headlights and started back along the dike-top roads, out of the space ahead a black blizzard of midges continually swept toward us.

That night, as in all the months that have followed, when we closed our eyes and reviewed the scenes of that wonderful day we could see these myriad tiny forms dancing through the air just as we could see once more the rivers and constellations of the million ducks of Bear River and the shine and shimmer of waterfowl wings over the wide ex-panse of the delta.

The Long Way Home

FOR thousands of miles now far horizons had crept closer and then had slipped to the rear. Always they had been replaced by other far horizons—the low skyline of the prairies, the soaring jagged rim of the Continental Divide, the shimmering edge of the salt desert, the furry line of forest tops. Rising and falling, curving with the rivers and valleys, we had ridden over the uneven surface of the earth, moving in zigzags head-on into the roll of the spinning globe.

The far horizon on this October morning lifted in a hazy rampart against the western sky. The wilderness of the Blue Mountains of eastern Oregon rose before us, as it had risen ahead of the lumbering ox-drawn wagons of the pioneers—the final barrier before the valley of the Columbia River. Each morning, during these wonderful days in a country we had never seen before, we pulled out on "the long trail, the trail that is ever new." And on this morning we had set our watches back another hour. First in Eastern Standard Time, then in Central Standard Time, then in Rocky Mountain Standard Time and now in Pacific Standard Time—the last time zone of the continent—we had moved, as the sun moves, toward the west, toward the far edge of the American autumn.

It was past midday when we topped Deadman's Pass and came to Emigrant Hill and the switchbacks and hairpin turns that drop away down the steep slide of the western edge of the mountains. At the rim of this titanic wall we stood for a long time gazing in silence over the vast patchwork of grainfields and pastures that stretched away into the haze-dimmed distance so far below us. This land of ranches and farms was the vision the pioneers saw as they peered into the wilderness ahead. How many of them had stood at this very spot shading their eyes in the autumn sunshine, seeking a glimpse of the Columbia, that river gateway to a Promised Land!

Born amid melting icefields in the Kootenay Mountains of Canada, the Columbia winds south and west in a great serpentine about 1,400 miles long. It is the largest North American river to empty into the Pacific. Once called the Oregon, long a river of mystery, described by the red men as flowing "from a mountain of shining stones to the sunset ocean," it drains some quarter of a million square miles of land. Its flow is twice that of the Nile, eight times that of the Colorado. For more than 300 of its final miles it heads almost due west, forming a natural boundary between the states of Oregon and Washington.

We were halfway down those final miles, following the "Big Medicine Road" of the Indians—the Oregon Trail—along the south bank, when we came to Celilo and the Falls of the Columbia. Over ragged, broken walls of black basalt, the river was hurling more than 100,000 cubic feet of water a second. Lewis and Clark, in the same month of the year, had portaged around these cataracts to find congregated below the falls a great herd of sea otters.

Every fall, during uncounted centuries before the Lewis and Clark Expedition arrived, Indian tribes from many parts of what is now Oregon and Washington and Idaho had come in an autumn pilgrimage to the falls to share in the bounty of the salmon run. On this day, as in years that extended back beyond tribal memory, Indians were fishing here. Many were clad in crimson shirts; many were perched on rickety-appearing plank platforms that jutted out over the foaming water along the lip of the falls. A few, here and there, braced themselves against rocks, appearing and disappearing amid sheets of drifting spray. All held dip nets with tremendously long handles. Some leaned back, resting at ease; others probed the seething turmoil of white water at the base of the falls.

Looking down from the highway, we were seeing the twilight of an age-old custom. A dozen miles downstream, the dam at The Dalles was nearing completion. Its artificial lake, backing upstream, would soon drown out these famed Cascades of the Columbia. It would inundate all the fishing sites along the lip of the falls, stations that had been handed down from father to son by the Indian tribes to whom old treaties ironically guaranteed fishing rights here "exclusively and perpetually." Government indemnity for violation of these treaties in the not distant future willy-nilly would replace the salmon caught in this annual autumn adventure with salmon in a can.

Across the river below the falls the swirling water broke from time to time where, in an arc of glittering silver, a salmon leaped. Only once in a lifetime does the salmon face the barrier of the Celilo falls. Far inland, in some mountain tributary or high-country pool, it hatches from an egg and, as a fingerling, begins the long descent, moving with the current on its way to the sea. Often in the high water of spring, when as many as 1,600,000 cubic feet a second roar over the cascades, the baby salmon ride the torrent downstream and over the falls. For all the species of the Columbia—the coho, sockeye, humpback, chum and the king or chinook salmon—life begins and ends in fresh water. The years between are spent at sea.

We followed a dusty road that wound down to the edge of the falls past the unpainted temporary shacks of the Indian salmon hunters. The thunder of the plunging water mounted as we advanced. The air grew moist with flying spray. In the restaurant beside the highway overlooking the falls we had seen two or three of the less energetic Indians. They had been reading comic books, playing the pinball machines or dropping nickels in the jukebox. Here at the falls, we saw a different breed. The men were alert and strong, many magnificently built with shoulders like all-American fullbacks. In this natural arena they were pitting their strength and skill, risking their lives, in a dangerous game. Each year there are casualties or near escapes at Celilo. A few days after our visit an eight-year-old Indian boy slipped into the torrent and was carried over the falls. Warned by shouts from the bank, the men on their platforms swung their nets. One caught the boy like a salmon in the midst of the tumult of white water below. With the help of companions, he pulled him up, hand over hand, to safety.

Most of the men on the platforms were secured by ropes attached to the timbers. One wore a silver-colored construction worker's helmet. From rock to rock, forming limber catwalks, long planks ran above the edge of the cataract. As we watched, a white Husky dog started across one of these bridges, felt the middle sag slightly beneath its weight, froze in tense uncertainty, then turned in slow motion and carefully retraced its steps. In a spiderweb, steel cables led to the more distant rocks. Below each, supported by pulleys, hung a makeshift chair fashioned from a wooden box. Riding in such chairs, Indians hauled themselves along the cables out to their isolated fishing stations. On this day only about eighty salmon came up the river. The autumn run, which reaches its peak in September, was nearly over. One man lay on his stomach peering from the edge of his platform down into the smother of spray and white water below. Another stretched out on his back, his mouth open, sound asleep.

Downstream a salmon leaped, then another. The Indian lying on his stomach got up. The sleeper awoke. Nets began going down from rocks and platforms. Fish were nearing the falls. We saw one of the men lean forward on his platform. His net dipped, scooped downstream, emerged enclosing a struggling salmon. Dragging upward on the handle the Indian slowly hauled his heavy catch onto the planks. Even after it had been killed, the magnificent fish, nearly three feet long, lying on the wet wood, was a thing of shining, streamlined and burnished beauty. The silver of its scales seemed to catch and collect the sunshine. Other fish, shining, too, came flopping onto the rocks and platforms. A quarter of an hour passed. Then the excitement began to subside. The flurry of fish in the white water below the falls eased off, then ended.

In that water, tumbling and aerated, the salmon no doubt obtain a sudden lift in energy from the increased oxygen. This is one factor in their amazing leaps up the rocks and over the cataract. Less tangible, but even more important, is the overpowering instinctive drive that holds them to their course, heading always into the current, fighting their way always upstream no matter how raging the torrents that oppose them. No less baffling than the mechanics of bird migration is the functioning of this instinct. Each new discovery has compounded the wonder. The way of a salmon in the sea and in the river of its birth represents one of the incompletely solved mystery stories of science.

What sense are they using in finding their long way home? Is it taste? Is it smell? Is it a combination of senses? Is it some capacity or ability we do not yet fully comprehend? All of these have been suggested as solutions to the mystery.

The clearest answer yet provided by scientists is one obtained at the Wisconsin Lake Laboratory of the University of Wisconsin, 2,000 miles inland from the estuary of the Columbia. There, in 1954, Arthur D. Hasler and James A. Larsen constructed an elaborate salmon tank with four miniature fish ladders branching from a central pool. Experimenting with young salmon from the Northwest, each marked with a tiny colored bead attached to a fin, they proved the fish are equipped with both a keen sense of smell and a capacity for remembering odors. The salmon demonstrated they could tell apart, by their smells, fourteen different kinds of aquatic plants. They were able to distinguish instantly between water taken from one creek and water taken from another. By associating one odor with the reward of food and another with the punishment of a mild electric shock, the Wisconsin experimenters found they could make the salmon enter or avoid whichever fish ladder they chose. By means of odor trails they could lead them to any desired destination.

Thus, though questions innumerable still remain in connection with the life of the salmon, the work of these two research biologists has put a scientific foundation beneath much that was merely surmise in the past. The fish, they conclude, identify the river of their birth and the pool of their hatching by the distinguishing odor of the water. The "fingerprint" of the river is an olfactory one. The fish that came upstream to the Celilo falls that day, as well as all the countless generations that had preceded them, were literally smelling their way home from the sea.

A Day With the Fern Gatherers

THE red jeep whirled around turns of the river road. A green pickup truck tore along at its heels. I, in my gray car, raced close after. And behind me, thundering just back of my bumper, pounded a mud-stained logging truck. For sixteen miles this automotive comet traced the serpentine of the Toutle River. We shot through Kid Valley. We rushed by a mailbox bearing the name "Rebel Stewart." We streaked in misty light past a misty pond where wild ducks were floating. Then, twenty-five miles east of Castle Rock, Washington, halfway to Spirit Lake and Mt. St. Helens, the jeep slowed, the truck slowed, I slowed and the bellow of the timber truck eased away for a moment as, red and green and gray, the first three vehicles in this swift parade swung over a bridge to the left onto a rutted road that became mere wheel tracks across roots and moss and ended in the shadowed silence of a lofty forest. Thus amid speed and noise and nerve strain began my day in the hushed, green, tranquil world of the fern gatherers.

Out of the jeep climbed Donald Braun, square-set and in his twenties. Down from the pickup truck descended Orlo Stephens, slender and nearing sixty. Both men spend their days wandering over the forest floor, picking fronds among the dense green fountains of the sword ferns. All across the western edge of Washington and down the Oregon coast, over thousands of square miles that day, the fern harvest was in full swing. For the free-lance frond gatherers of the Northwest the peak of the year's activity comes in the fall. Daily now they were busy along remote streams, deep in rain forests, up mountainsides almost to timberline. In back-packs and horse-packs the fronds were coming out of the woods to lonely roads. Then by jeep and truck and ancient flivver many of them were rolling toward Castle Rock and the great gray Fern Barn at its eastern edge.

The day before, Nellie and I had driven fifty-three miles north from Vancouver to this community of 900 inhabitants. It was at Castle Rock, in 1906, that Sam Roake started the fern picking business in the forests of western Washington. His first shipments were trundled to the railroad station in a wheelbarrow. Today in the region there are eight major companies dealing in forest ferns. Their annual shipments to florists throughout the United States total about 20,000,000 bunches or approximately 1,000,000,000 fronds.

Ray Chapman, who manages the Fern Barn and operates the company Roake originally started, showed us the towering piles of fronds that had come in during the day. They are tied in bunches of fifty with two added to provide for breakage. First soaked in water, sometimes up to twelve hours, the ferns are kept under refrigeration, occasionally as long as ninety days. In wood or fiber or cardboard containers they go out to every state in the Union by truck, by train, by boat, even by plane. Because of their large size, the grace of their fronds, their keeping quality and the strength of their stems, the sword ferns of the West are in special demand among florists.

As we talked three men from Cougar, Washington (population 43) arrived in a battered sedan crammed with fronds. Partners—one young, one middle-aged, one old—they pick along timberline until snowfall, sometimes carrying pocket warmers or lighting chunks of pitch from time to time to keep their hands from growing numb. High on mountainsides the ferns tend to be of better quality than in the lowlands. From all sources as many as a quarter of a million fronds may come to the Fern Barn during a single autumn day. Yet, because the pickers take only part of the fronds and leave the massed roots or stools uninjured, the ferns continue to grow year after year as luxuriantly as before.

Orlo Stephens, as he and Braun shouldered their empty back-packs, recalled one stool that has remained virtually unchanged for a quarter of a century. He has been picking over the same area, along the side of the seven-mile ridge up which our trail ascended, ever since the end of the First World War. And he has noticed no lessening in the number of sword ferns growing there.

The forest closed around us, a forest of giants such as I had never entered before. We paused beside a stump, furry with moss and moldering away. It seemed, in the dim forest light, as big as a cabin. I gazed at the massive trunks of spruce and fir and hemlock. Soaring up and up, they appeared to lean together in their great height. The tops of some of them were 150 feet above us. We stole with noiseless footfalls along the mossy trail beneath these giants, three small Gullivers in an arboreal land of Brobdingnag.

Thus we advanced into the green silent depths. The air was cool and humid. It was rich with earth scents. All the leaves of the bushes were shining with a film of moisture. Our feet, at every step, sank into the deep plush of the moss. And extending away among the decayed trunks of fallen trees, lifting from the humus of the forest floor, rose the fountainlike clumps of the sword fern or dagger fern, *Polystichum mumitum*. This western relative of the eastern Christmas fern sometimes rises almost shoulder high. Its curving fronds at times reach a length of more than four feet. And as many as 200 may be rooted in a single stool. In the mild climate of the coastal Northwest the leaves stay green the year around. A new crop in the form of fiddleheads appears each spring in March. Even while the new leaves are unrolling the harvest of the old fronds continues. About ninety days are required for the spring fiddleheads to unroll, reach their full length and harden. It is mainly this supply of new fronds that is gathered in the autumn.

One of the remarkable features of the sword fern is the variety of its habitats. It grows in swamps. It clings to canyon walls. It crowds together along stream banks near sea level. It ranges as high as trees extend on mountainsides. But it is found only where it is sheltered from sun and wind. In deep, wet, misty woods, such as the one we had entered, it attains its greatest size. Most often it is associated with the vine maple, both the tree and the fern seeming to thrive under the same conditions.

For a time our trail skirted a swampy stretch where the ferns grew densely. They ran on and on, crowded together, their fountains overlapping. In this rank growth the tips of the ferns tend to be damaged and imperfect.

"We pick these alder swales last of all," Braun explained.

I gazed around. Thinking of the low alder bushes of the East, I inquired:

"Why are they called alder swales? I don't see any alders."

"You are leaning against one right now!" Stephens told me.

I looked up. The alder was a tree more than fifty feet high. Touched by that strain of giantism we saw everywhere in the forests of the

Northwest, the red alder sometimes attains a height of more than 100 feet and lives for a century.

Leaving the swale behind we climbed steeply upward, at times stooping under curtains of delicate tree moss, at other times skirting or clambering over fallen trees. Braun's cream-colored Husky dog scouted ahead, first on one side of the trail, then on the other, frequently popping from the bushes, his fur wet, his red tongue lolling out beneath his black, pointed nose. Fern hunters often take dogs into the woods with them. They are company. They warn of bears. In case of a broken leg or other serious accident they would go home and thus bring help. For the dog in the woods the days are filled with fun and adventure. Once as we rounded a turn in the trail Braun's dog made a sudden rush. There was a scuttle and airy roar of wings. Three dark ruffed grouse shot upward in a high, steep climb among hemlock branches.

We had followed the trail into the forest almost two miles before the harvest of ferns began. The men separated about an eigth of a mile and set to work. Some fern gatherers use a sharp jackknife to clip off the stems of the fronds. Others fashion a triangular cutter from a tablespoon. But most often they use a ring-knife, such as is used for cutting twine, wearing it on the middle finger of the right hand. Stephens showed me how, almost in one motion, the frond is selected and the stem clipped off within the little sickle-like curve of the cutting blade.

Only the last two feet of the fronds are harvested. The tips must be perfect, not brown or bug-eaten or curled over into a spider nest. As soon as he had clipped off twenty-six fronds, Stephens tucked them under one arm while he picked twenty-six more. Then, holding the fifty-two between his legs, he pulled a short length of white string from a bunch tied to a button of his overalls and, with a swift whirl of his practiced hand, tied the butts together. In turn each bunch was added to a green stack that began rising on the moss carpet of a small open space.

Some years ago a national magazine published an article that depicted fern picking in the Northwest as a smooth and easy road to riches. Letters poured into Castle Rock from all parts of the country. People asked for more details. They wrote they were coming from as far away as the Atlantic seaboard. Local pickers, foreseeing an invasion and a reduction in their incomes, were up in arms. Actually most fern gatherers make around forty dollars a week. But many of them spend only part of the day in the woods. About 100 bunches a day is the average harvest of a fern picker. The record, so far, was set one October a few years ago when a family of three brought in 1,700 bunches that had been collected in three days.

Families not infrequently pick together. In one instance five boys in the same family put themselves through school with spare-time fern gathering. When a husband is ill, a wife will often pick ferns to tide things over. Again, when the woods are too dry for lumbering and loggers are laid off temporarily, they may turn to harvesting ferns. Those who go to the woods during spare time, usually in summer, are known as "sunshine pickers." A comparatively recent innovation has been the leasing of exclusive picking rights in certain areas by lumber companies that own extensive forest holdings. Stephens and Braun, for example, rented each year the fern rights to 16,000 acres along the flank of the ridge where they were working.

Beginning early in October, for several weeks on dry days, the fern hunters work in moving clouds as though surrounded by fine smoke. For then, in untold billions, the spores of the sword ferns are being shed. On this day, after a shower in the night, little of this living dust was in the air. But all autumn long, after every comparatively dry day, the fern gatherer goes home from the forest embrowned from head to foot with the fine powder of the spores.

Aside from an occasional nettle, the fern gatherer has little to avoid in the forest. There is no poison oak here. He can reach down into the masses of the ferns without fear of snakes, for there are no venomous species in the region. Less than a dozen times has Stephens encountered bears in the woods. Once, some years ago, he and his wife were picking huckleberries on a mountainside when they discovered a large brown bear a couple of hundred yards away, equally busy harvesting the fruit. Using both forepaws it was raking in the berries. All that afternoon, keeping their distance, the three continued working within sight of one another. So far as is known, no fern gatherer has ever been seriously injured by a bear in the woods.

The real danger for the fern picker in the woods comes not from bears but from men. Both Stephens and Braun that day wore bright red hats. This was the deer-hunting season and there was always a chance of being shot by mistake. This is especially true because the men are bent over as they work among the clumps with a swishing and crackling of fronds. Moreover, they frequently enter tangles of vine maples and ferns where the deer are commonly found. Some protection is afforded by having a dog ranging about in the vicinity. It is likely to give warning both to the hunters and to the fern harvesters.

The two piles of ferns, where Stephens and Braun were working, mounted as the day progressed. Each bunch of fifty-two fronds weighs about a pound and a quarter. In lots of eighty bunches, weighing about 100 pounds, they are packed out of the woods. I watched Braun load his pack, placing the successive layers of bunches with the butts pointing in opposite directions. Two miles through the forest is about as far as the ferns are transported by back-pack. Beyond that distance a horse or burro is used.

As we followed the outward trail for a last time that day, the two men ahead of me were half hidden beneath their masses of ferns. Watching those fronds bobbing up and down in the packs ahead I wondered what their final destination would be. Where would they be seen for a last time? Who would see them? They might, as part of floral decorations, reach even the far side of the continent. As for myself, I knew that wherever I should see them the rest of my life, the graceful fronds would bring back vivid memories of this day—memories of towering trees and of the green fountains of the sword ferns extending away, seemingly without end, beneath them.

The Golden Squirrel

DURING autumn the earth advances nearly 150,000,000 miles on its elliptical course around the sun. Throughout all the changes of the season its unslackened speed carries it ahead nearly 1,600,000 miles each day, more than 65,000 miles each hour, more than 1,000 miles each minute, eighteen and a half miles each second. It traveled more than 100,000 miles on this November night while we wandered alone in chill and silence and moonlight in a dead forest with the glacier-clad upper slopes of Mount Rainier far above us gleaming in cold alabaster white against the depths of the night.

The Hunter's Moon of October had given way to the Mad Moon of November. The fern forests of Castle Rock lay to the west behind us. Along the slope above us, down the slope below us, rose gaunt tree trunks, dark with shadow on one side, lighted by the nearly full moon on the other. In the fall of 1947, on the night of October 1, meltwater from the Kautz Glacier had suddenly broken free. Carrying 50,000,000 cubic yards of debris into the valley below, the avalanche of water and rocks and rolling tree trunks had plunged down the steep descent. Falling trees had been shredded and pounded to pulp by the boulders. Those that remained had been killed by grinding rocks and smothering silt. Now, half a dozen years later, sparse new growth had taken root—fireweed and pearly everlasting and red alder first of all. Only after unhurried decades of healing would this long wound on the mountainside fill in and disappear.

The trails we followed among the lifeless trees led over debris twenty or thirty feet deep. And always towering far above us rose the shining mountain. Its cap of snow and glacier ice, framed by the gaunt tree trunks, at times gleamed with such brilliance in the frosty air that the whole peak seemed formed of cold and flameless light. No other mountain we have ever seen was as beautiful as Rainier appeared under that November moon.

We were looking up for a last time beside the road when, in the intense silence, I became aware of a slight scratching, scrambling sound. My ear traced it to a metal drum that park officials had placed beside a tree as a trash container. I ran the beam of a flashlight around the interior. Motionless now, staring up at me transfixed by the rays was another of those mammal mileposts of our trip, a white-footed mouse—this time the Washington white-footed mouse. I tilted down the drum and it scurried away. In Mount Rainier National Park no other animal is so numerous. One of these little rodents was even found at the very top of the peak, 14,408 feet above sea level.

Beyond the edge of the dead forest, among living trees that had escaped in the disaster of 1947, we paused that night near one of the largest Douglas firs growing on the slopes of the mountain. By its girth scientists judge that it was already towering high in the air when Christopher Columbus reached the New World. Here the shadows beneath the lofty trees were dense and inky black. A little way off, amid such shadows, a pool of moonlight lay beneath a small opening in the canopy of the forest. In this space—some thirty or forty feet across—the carpeting moss, the curving ferns, the great instep of one of the immense trees all appeared as though on a spotlighted stage. And as we watched, out from the shadows and into the light stepped two sleek and exquisite does. They moved among the ferns as graceful as the fronds. They paused. They browsed. They turned in our direction only once, their great ears uplifted, their dark, liquid eyes watching us where we stood. Then unafraid they moved out of the light and into the shadows again.

One of the annual signs of autumn on this mountainside is the movement of the Columbian black-tailed deer down from the higher levels. In spring they climb the slopes after the retreating snow. They spend the summer among the high mountain meadows free from the multitude of flies that infest the lowland woods. Some, particularly the older bucks, range even above the timberline. Then with the first heavy snows of autumn the deer move down to the valleys again. Year after year, following the same trails each time, they engage in this definite seasonal and altitudinal migration.

Although most of the 130 species of birds that have been recorded in the Mount Rainier National Park fly down the map in a long horizontal migration that carries them in autumn beyond the boundaries of the continent, a few, instead, fly down the mountain in a short vertical migration that leaves them still within sight of the peak. Each fall, about the time the deer move down, the Clark's nutcrackers, the Oregon jays, the Hepburn's rosy finches descend in an aerial toboggan to the lower levels where they find their winter food.

A few jays and nutcrackers were still haunting Paradise Valley when we climbed the twisting road that carried us to its 5,400-foot elevation the following afternoon. There, beneath our tires and under our feet, was the first snow of the trip. It lay three or four inches deep on the ground, prelude to the towering drifts that would form in this mile-high valley before the winter ended. Over it came flying a dozen jays and nutcrackers, unafraid after a summer-long contact with friendly visitors. They perched on the hood of the car and on its open door. When I bent over, a nutcracker alighted on my back. One jay hopped about inside the car looking for food. I rummaged in the trunk and found a box of crackers. The birds ate at our feet. They retrieved crumbs from the snow. They ate from our fingers. An Oregon jay landed on Nellie's arm and when there was a delay in the appearance of the next cracker crumb it would tug at her sleeve with its bill.

Into the midst of this activity there darted from a snow-covered jumble of rocks an alert, beautiful creature we had thought we were too late to see. It was an animal about ten inches long from nose to tail-tip. Down its side ran a wide white stripe bordered with black. At first glance we seemed looking at a large and brightly colored chipmunk. But here were none of the face stripings that we had seen on the little seed gatherers that had scampered along the stone walls of New England. Here the whole head, the little upright rounded ears, the forelegs were all tinged with a coppery-golden hue. This creature, darting across the snow of this far-western mountain height, was one we had long wished to know, one we had dreamed of meeting, one that by this November day we had despaired of seeing. Like the grass-of-Parnassus that we had come upon beside the warbler river, it had been an object of special interest since first we saw its name in a guidebook. Here at last was the golden squirrel. Here in Paradise Valley, close to timberline, dashing among late-lingering jays and nutcrackers, was our first mantled ground squirrel, *Citellus saturatus*, the famous mountaineer rodent of the high Cascades.

Fourteen subspecies of the mantled ground squirrel—of which *saturatus* is one—live in upper reaches in the mountains of eleven western states. Sometimes they even make their homes above timberline amid the same windswept rock slides where the pikas live. In the Sierra Nevada mountains of California, one of these ground squirrels was observed at an elevation of 10,700 feet. During summer, fruits and seeds, grasshoppers and beetles, provide most of their nourishment. Returning to their burrows from foraging expeditions they, like the eastern chipmunks, carry harvested food in bulging cheek pouches.

Perhaps it was the harsh grating calls of the nutcrackers that drew our ground squirrel from its burrow among the rocks. That call no doubt had been associated with food all during the tourist season now ending. At any rate it had left a snug little nest at the bottom of its tunnel, where it would soon fall into the deep sleep of hibernation. Such nests are usually lined with soft plant fibers or hair. In different surroundings additional material is added. One golden mantled ground squirrel was observed tearing up a brown paper bag with its feet and stuffing the fragments into its cheek pouches to carry underground. Where sheep are pastured on mountain meadows the ground squirrels of the region often collect bits of wool and carry them underground as winter lining for their nests. There they literally sleep through the months of cold tucked in a woolen blanket.

For only a short time did the squirrel stay out. Then in a sudden rush back across the snow it disappeared among the rocks again. Usually these "mantled chipmunks" remain active until the first heavy storms of autumn snow them in. Then, snug in their nests under the high-piled drifts, they sleep the winter away. This was one of our golden squirrel's last appearances above ground. Ours was a late-autumn view.

Wherever we went those days, above the flaming maples, above the rich red of the huckleberries, above the tan and russet of the upper meadows, in sunlight or moonlight, there towered above us the shining mountain. Against its immaculate whiteness the drifting clouds appeared gray as though composed of smoke. The wind at times drew into the sky from the tip of the peak long curling banners of snow. And we saw it all through the world's finest breathing space, through clear mountain air, sparkling, perfumed by evergreens, stretching away mile after mile untainted by smoke, undimmed by fog.

No other peak in America, no other peak in the world it is said, carries so great an expanse of glaciers as Mount Rainier. With an area of forty-eight square miles, its twenty-eight glaciers wind in all directions downward from its peak. Seen from the sky the ice-clad mountain resembles a multi-armed starfish or octopus, each curving arm formed by a glacier. Now in a warming climatic cycle, this ice is melting back at the rate of about seventy feet a year. Over rocks of gray granodiorite I clambered close to the snout of the Nisqually Glacier. There the water of the melting ice gushed forth to tumble down a steep valley over boulders and gravel in the foaming first mile of the Nisqually River.

Some days later we saw the last mile of this same river close to Puget Sound. Then it was moving deliberately, a wide, placid, lowland stream. And then Mount Rainier, with its gleaming ice, its snow banners, its rosy finches and its golden squirrels, lay off to the east and we were well on our way toward the Olympic Peninsula.

Land of the Windy Rain

A CIRCLE within a square—that roughly represents the Olympic Mountains. Their jagged peaks cluster around Mount Olympus and form the enduring heart of the peninsula that comprises the far northwestern corner of the United States. Rising from sea level to 5,000, 6,000, 7,000 and almost 8,000 feet in the space of less than fifty miles, the mountains lift in a great stone wall against which blows the prevailing wind from the sea. That wind has one of the highest average velocities for the entire country, more than fourteen miles an hour the year around. Like a rapidly moving conveyor belt it brings in moisture from the sea. The mountains drive it steeply upward, cool it suddenly, condense its moisture into precipitation. In effect they quickly wring the water from this ocean wind.

As a consequence the western side of the Olympics receives a greater amount of rainfall each year than any other place in America. The average is about 140 inches, approximately 2,000,000,000 gallons or 9,000,000 tons of falling rain for each square mile of land. By far the greater part of this precipitation comes between November 1 and May 1; the heaviest rains begin in autumn; the three wettest months are November, December and January. Yet during the November days we spent wandering in this land of the windy rain the silver cord that, according to Greek mythology, held gales and storms prisoner within a leather bag, remained securely tied. The sun shone. The breeze only occasionally freshened into a wind. The showers were short and infrequent or the rains came in the night. Under favoring skies in this prolonged and unusually dry autumn we roamed through the green, mossy world of a northern rain forest.

We had come up the east side of the peninsula, past red-barked, red-berried madrone trees, over the Hama Hama River, past Lilliwaup—which reminded us how often in this rainy land place-names had a wet, squashy sound, like Satsop, Lilliwaup and Tumwater. Then, based at Port Angeles, we had explored the northern coast along the Strait of Juan de Fuca. We followed roads where a rat trap dangled from a pole in front of every farmhouse to hold the brown canvas bag set out for the country postman. We continued as far as Cape Flattery and the Indian village of Neah Bay where gulls and fish crows fed in the street like sparrows. Along this wild coast we saw our first surf birds and our first black turnstones. Then we had swung south down the outside of the peninsula, down to the Hoh River and the nineteen-mile dirt road that winds into the rain forest as far as the Hoh Ranger Station and the beginning of the path that climbs eventually up to the high meadows and the glaciers of Mount Olympus. During the two succeeding days we wandered along the lower miles of this rain-forest trail.

All around us the vine maples, the towering hemlocks, the firs and the spruces were draped and bearded with moss. Great trunks rose above us green and furry as far as we could see. Branches spread over us shaggy with the primitive spikemoss, *Selaginella.* Under our feet the plush of the forest carpet grew so dense and deep we sank at times above our shoetops. In the misty light we saw it roll on and on, wave after wave, over the moldering logs, across the uneven floor of the forest. Scientists believe 100 kinds of moss grow on the Olympic Peninsula. The green carpet that covers the forest floor is formed of many species, many strands; its warp and woof are made up of a multitude of mosses.

Here and there along the path streamers of sunshine probed between the giant trees. Drawn in glowing silver lines they slanted down through the humid air. And above each spot where they reached the saturated carpet of the moss, mist curled up like smoke from a fire being started with a burning glass. And all the while the long fingers of the spikemoss, hanging from the branches like gray-green stalactites forming under the roof of a cavern, dripped endlessly. As each drop fell it entered the plush of the living carpet without a sound. It was absorbed without a trace. Moss is nature's great silencer. This was a forest soundproofed by moss.

We stopped beside a tree where the trunk had split a third of the way down from the top and half had fallen to the ground. All down the divided tree the sheathing of moss had parted as though it were a thicker shell of bark. On some trunks the coating is so dense it has the appearance of a shaggy pelt. I was told that when natives are caught in the forest overnight in the dryer summer months they sometimes strip off great sections of this moss with their hunting knives and use them as soft, thick blankets. In rare periods of comparative drought it is the tree-moss that dries out most quickly. At such times a conflagration will race ahead through the forest faster than fire-fighters can keep up with it.

An astonishing paradox in connection with the moisture of the Olympic Peninsula is the fact that less than thirty miles from the saturated forest through which we walked irrigation farming is practiced. Around Sequim, in the northeastern corner of the peninsula, rainfall is sometimes only fourteen inches a year, one-tenth that on the other side of the Olympics. There we saw troughs and ditches carrying water to dry fields lying in the rain shadow of the mountains. Coming west we had run through a succession of such areas of dryness. Prevailing winds from the west vault over the Olympics, over the Cascades, over the Rockies. Each time they leave most of their moisture on the western side of the range and little remains to water the land lying on the lee side to the east. Oregon and Washington are lush and green west of the Cascades, so dry they are often almost deserts east of the mountains. But nowhere else did we see so dramatic a demonstration of the effect of mountains on moisture as here within the narrow confines of the Olympic Peninsula.

Along our path beside the Hoh the evidences of abundant rainfall were everywhere. Combined with a mild climate and a long growing season it had produced a tropical luxuriance of growth. Immense tree trunks lifted from the moss and ferns, soared upward, towered above us, disappearing at last among the maze of the upper branches. In some cases the lowest branch was 100 feet in the air. Here in the rain forest of the Olympic Peninsula numerous trees attain their record size.

The world's largest Cascade fir grows in the wild country between the Hoh and the Bogachiel rivers and, near the mouth of the Hoh, the western red cedar reaches its maximum size in a steamed and twisted giant. On the east fork of the Quinault River the biggest known western hemlock has a girth of twenty-seven feet, two inches. Among the Douglas firs—that race of giants that with the single exception of the sequoias are the hugest trees in America—the largest of them all grows in the valley of the Queets River, south of the Hoh. Four and a half feet from the ground its circumference is fifty-three feet, four inches. And along the trail we followed, some four miles in from the ranger station on the Hoh, one of the most beautiful trees in the world, the Sitka spruce with frosted needles and silvery bark tinged with lavender and purple, reaches its maximum dimensions with a circumference of forty-one feet, six inches.

These are virgin trees in a virgin forest. Protected within the glorious living museum of this national park are some of the arboreal patriarchs of the world. Many times during our trip we felt that America's great national park system is one of its finest achievements, action by the people for the people on a high plane. Yet those who think of any national park as something permanent make a grave mistake. It can always be changed if not abolished. Its boundaries can be altered, permitting the finest of its timber to be cut. Its rules can be modified, allowing grazing here, mining there, dams destroying areas supposed to be inviolate. And because of the wonder of its trees the Olympic National Park, more than most, will always be in danger.

Decades ago John Muir declared that the Olympic Park would be attacked again and again. His prediction has been amply vindicated. Men who see no more in a tree than board feet, elected officials who refer to the nation's public lands as being "locked-up resources"—as they might refer to songbirds as being "locked-up light meat and dark"—these men we will have with us always and always they will pose a threat to our national parks. Only the vigilance of conservationists over the long haul, only an alertness to attack in a thousand guises, can prevent raids and invasions and destructions within these areas that the people believe have been permanently saved.

On June 17, 1853, Henry Thoreau noted in his journal: "If a man walks in the woods for love of them for half his days, he is esteemed a loafer; but if he spends his whole day as a speculator, shearing off those woods, he is esteemed industrious and enterprising—making earth bald before its time." That attitude is not one that disappeared when the Walden Woods were felled. It is current in every generation. It is ranged against every effort to save wild places. Those to whom the trees, the birds, the wildflowers represent only "locked-up dollars" have never known or really seen these things. They have never experienced an interest in nature for itself. Whoever stimulates a wider appreciation of nature, a wider understanding of nature, a wider love of nature for its own sake accomplishes no small thing. For from these is formed the enduring component of the conservation movement. Many people are attracted to a fight who drift away when the excitement dies down. It is only those who are deeply and fundamentally interested in nature itself who, in the long haul, the all-important continuity of effort, carry on.

Nellie and I talked of such matters under the great trees beside the Hoh and again that evening in a cabin overlooking a curving beach piled high with the flotsam of tremendous timbers. White surf thundered on the sand, swirling, seething, ripped by the offshore rocks. The sunset died beyond bleak Destruction Island while we dined on the only food we could find in a country store, crackers and corned beef and apples—saving for breakfast the sardines and oatmeal cookies and instant chocolate. Each time we awoke in our cabin we heard the roaring of the white surf in the moonlight and saw the spearheads of the spruces rising black against a starry sky. Thus passed our first night on the shore of the open Pacific.

When we left the sea and entered the forest again next morning the autumn mist was heavy among the trees. Fall is proverbially the season of ground fog and mists. The lengthening nights permit the earth to lose more of its heat, the waning strength of the sun slows down the process of warming up the ground in the morning, the lighter winds then prevailing disperse the accumulated mist less quickly. For these reasons autumn and mist are linked together in most parts of the country. Here in the moistness of the rain forest it was late in the morning before the temperature of ground and air became more nearly uniform and the heavier mist among the trees thinned away.

All along the trail winter wrens, like flitting winged mice, appeared and disappeared among the jumbles of the fallen trees. In these mossy woods they live the year around. Douglas squirrels, the chickarees with tufted ears and birdlike voices, darted off at our approach leaving behind on stump tops the kitchen middens of their cone scales. Ferns were everywhere, licorice ferns drooping like green feathers from the shaggy branches of the vine maples, deer ferns with dry fronds like antlers, oak ferns, western bracken, delicate maidenhair ferns clinging to moist, dripping embankments, lady ferns believed by generations of European peasants to produce magic seed that made the possessor invisible, clumps of sword ferns like green vases filled with fallen leaves. And here and there we came upon slashes of brilliant red and orange where slime mold, that mysterious substance that dwells on the borderline between plant and animal life, spread away across decaying wood.

All through the forest life was rising from death. Along the length of every moldering, fallen tree seedlings were rooted, young trees were growing. Often we would see four or five giant spruces rising in a perfectly straight line as though—like peas in a garden plot—their seeds had been planted along a taut string. In their case the string was six feet thick, a log perhaps 200 feet long. Many seedlings sprout on these fallen "nurse trees" but only a few survive the first years of competition. We came upon roots that extended five feet or more down the sides of moldering logs and once, where a tree had begun growing at the top of a massive stub, roots dropped fully a dozen feet to reach the mold of the forest floor.

On this day we continued farther on the trail. For eleven of its eighteen miles it threads among the trees of the rain forest following the course of the Hoh. On old maps this river appears as the Hooch, the Huch, the Hook, the Holes and the Ohahlat. It is the largest stream on the Olympic Peninsula, carrying away 85 per cent of the meltwater from the glaciers of Mount Olympus. Now in the autumn its flow had lessened greatly. The stream ran shallow, glinting and sparkling among water-smoothed stones in its wide gravel bed.

We were looking across a stretch of rapids where the river tumbled with a swifter current when Nellie caught sight of a bird balancing itself on a boulder amid the flying spray. Slaty-blue, short-tailed and chunky, it was about the size of a starling. As we watched it bobbed rapidly several times. Then it slipped down the side of the rock and plunged headfirst into the rushing torrent. It seemed inconceivable that it could escape being drowned or dashed to death against the rocks. Yet a few moments later it popped up as buoyant as a cork and mounted another rock a yard from the first. It was not only safe and sound, it was even dry. The bird we watched was the famed dipper of the West, the water ouzel of swift mountain streams. This relative of the wrens, without benefit of webbed feet or any of the other special adaptations of the water bird, is able to walk on the bed of the stream or, with the aid of its wings, swim in the swiftest current.

Time and again it disappeared in the foaming, tumbling water along the edge of a gravel bar. Once it dived into a tiny pool while on the wing. Another time it alighted on a little rug of moss between two stones. Here it turned around and around, facing first this way then that, shifting its direction a dozen times before it flitted with a rapid flutter, almost a whirring, of its wings to another perch. Not infrequently while clinging to some low stone it would thrust its head under the surface and peer about beneath the water. At last it climbed onto a rock at the end of one of its dives clutching in its bill the prize it had sought, the white larva of some aquatic insect. Tilting back its head it gulped it down. Then began one of the wonderful moments of the trip. For the first time in our lives we heard the song of the water ouzel.

It went on and on like the music of the stream. The song was clear and ringing; it was sweet and varied. On a perfectly still morning it is said the voice of the ouzel can be heard a mile away across a mountain lake. It progressed with trills and warbles, whistled notes, long cadences and flutelike phrases. It suggested the song of the mockingbird or the brown thrasher or the catbird, rich with improvising and imitating. Some notes were liquid like the gurgling of the stream, others were short and harsh like the grating together of stones. At moments we were reminded of the song of an oriole, at other moments that of a warbling vireo. Yet in its entirety it was unlike any of these. For fully ten minutes, stopping and beginning again, the bird sang to itself, and to us, as it wandered alone along the edge of the gravel bar.

The water ouzel is one of the few birds that sing the year around. Wishing the song would go on for hours, we listened entranced. But at last the music stopped and the singer darted away downstream, flying low, only inches above the tumbling water of the rapids. At Yellowstone, and again at Rainier, we had glimpsed ouzels in the mountain streams but only here, we felt, had we really come to know the bird. And only here, beside this rain-forest river, had we heard its song.

Beyond Mount Tom Creek the trail became more and more a cow-path followed by the wild cattle of the forest. Its moist earth was imprinted with a lacework of heart-shaped tracks left by the black-tailed deer. One time when we looked back we saw the antlered head of a buck lifted above distant underbrush as the animal watched us going away down the trail. And again, at the edge of an open space, we came upon two does nibbling on bright yellow fungus. Occasionally among the deer tracks in our path we discovered more oval hoof marks, suggesting the two halves of a coffee bean. These were the tracks of the Roosevelt elk.

Only once did we catch a fleeting glimpse of one of these great animals—the dark head and huge dark ears of a female gazing at us among bushes and disappearing almost as soon as we turned that way. The hunting season had already begun. Pitched in the forest around the edges of the park were the tents of the elk hunters. One herd of sixty-nine animals, fortunately still within the park, had been sighted early that morning. But the main bulk of the elk had remained on the higher slopes of the mountains. Like the Columbian blacktails of Mount Rainier, in fall these animals migrate down to the lowlands. In the mild autumn of this year the early snowstorms that start the movement had been delayed, thus, no doubt, saving the lives of many an elk. For although the total number of these animals—native only to this northwestern peninsula—is estimated to be only about 6,000 as many as 5,000 special elk-hunting licenses are issued in one season to men who roam the fringes of the forest just outside the boundaries of the park. Without the protection of this sanctuary these noble animals would face quick and certain extinction.

There were times later on when our trail swung away from the river and the sound of its running water was inaudible. Then the stillness of the forest became intense. In such a silence we rested once beside a mossy stub starred from top to bottom with oxalis. Down the trail a falling leaf, huge and yellow, descended from the lower branch of a big-leaf or Oregon maple. It rode the air in a wide serpentine, stem-first, sliding to a stop like a landing airplane. Although it was fully 100 feet away our ears caught the faint scraping of its stem along the ground and among the already fallen leaves. In that profound silence we could even hear the lisping, sibilant whisper of the dry needles sifting down from the Sitka spruces.

On the outward trail later that afternoon we found ourselves in a small opening covered with the brown of autumn bracken. Golden-crowned kinglets darted among the surrounding trees, their wiry, lisping little calls coming from here, from there, from everywhere around us. It was while we were watching them that a small black-capped bird with a rufous back caught our attention—our first chestnut-backed chickadee.

In the depths of the forest, in the twilight of its shadows, birds are comparatively few. Here the varied thrush sings and here the sooty grouse makes its home. Most dwellers in dusky forests are, like this grouse, particularly dark in color. Once on our way out we saw a sparrow, with plumage almost black, flitting among the bushes. It was the sooty song sparrow of the rain forest. Pelts of the now extinct Olympic wolf show that it, too, was so dark it was almost black. If you know the rainfall of a region you can make a pretty accurate guess as to the density of color of its wildlife inhabitants. For evolution favors dark-hued creatures in the deep woods just as it favors light-colored creatures on the open desert.

It was after sunset that day when we rounded a turn on the endlessly winding road that leads down the west side of the peninsula and came upon another dark tenant of the rain forest. A dusky cottontail bolted from the shadowed roadside. Even in the distance its actions appeared peculiar. It hopped first this way, then that, as though unable to make up its mind. It would stop, then hurry on in aimless zigzag fashion, then pause again irresolute. As we drew close what appeared to be a squirrel came bounding from the roadside bushes a hundred feet or so behind the rabbit. It halted, seemed to break in two, the front half reared up, light beneath, flat-headed like a cobra, teeth showing in a weasel grin.

This was the bloodthirsty cause of the rabbit's distraction. So terrified was the cottontail it seemed literally out of its mind. In a matter of minutes it could have leaped away in a straight line and outdistanced its short-legged pursuer completely. But it appeared incapable of effective action, bereft of all powers of decision. Many times I have remembered that silent nightmare in the dusk. It was a terrible thing to see a living creature with nerves unstrung and wits departed, stupefied by terror and delivered by fear into the hands of its enemy. We were almost abreast of the rabbit before the spell was broken. Then the weasel whirled and darted into the bushes. The cottontail, in a sudden awakening to sanity, bolted away down the road in swift, effective flight.

Tidepools

WE peered through a gray curtain of falling rain. Beside the road the leaves of a poplar tree, all gold above and silver beneath, fluttered in the wind. They were washed by the downpour, gyrated by the gusts. Even in the hooded light of the overcast they shone with metallic brilliance. And at every blast waves of gold and silver intermingling ran along the boughs. Behind the tree extended the width of a drowned river, gray under the gray sky and crawling slowly toward the sea. Here the Columbia was nearing its mouth. Not many miles ahead lay Astoria.

Out on the river near this spot, almost a century and a half before, a man in a dugout canoe had rested a travel-worn notebook on his knee and had written these words:

"Ocian in view! O! the joy!"

In that simple entry, dramatically eloquent in its understatement, Captain William Clark had recorded the goal attained in that long, laborious, heroic, pioneer westward trek "over the Shining Mountains to Everywhere-Salt-Water."

On the coast south of Astoria, next day, where the Necanicum River curves in a shallow flow across the sands to the sea, we paused again, this time at the last spot we would meet associated with Lewis and Clark. Here they had found the stranded whale—the one thing among all her adventures that Sacajawea talked about in later years—and near here the men had boiled sea water in iron kettles to obtain salt during that "wet and stormy" winter at Fort Clatsop.

When we started on again there stretched away to the south before us nearly 400 miles of Oregon coast—its great black rocks and creamy surf, its towering headlands, its tidepools and wave-cut caverns making it one of the world's most picturesque meeting places of land and sea.

The sands were many-colored when we approached Agate Beach. Metallic blues and browns and reds were woven by the waves into intricate patterns on the shore. These lines of color intersected endlessly. At times their mingled hues produced an effect that suggested the blended coloring of a moth's wing. Again for long stretches bluish sand

· 279 ·

ran before us in wavering lines like oil stains on the shore. At other times we walked as though on fine emery dust or amid specks that glittered in the sun like disintegrated mica.

Farther south, on an ebbing tide at Yachats Beach, we moved through emerging gardens of those animal-flowers, the sea anemones. Great combers cannonaded on the lower ledges and exploded over the upper tidepools. Between waves the sea anemones appeared all down the dripping rocks. Then they were blotted out by foam and rushing water. Over and over again tidepools would be filled with a solid lid of foam. Then, growing thin, it would part like clouds, revealing the starfish and the sea anemones adhering to the rock. With the gradual descent and retreat of the sea the upper tidepools became quiet.

In these Oregon pools most of the blossomlike creatures, with their spreading rosettes of tentacles, exhibited a beautiful pastel shade of green. Other species are tinted orange and rose and coral pink and white and blue and yellow and purple. In color as well as in form the sea anemones resemble flowers. Yet some of these bright-hued creatures live where bright sunlight never penetrates, as much as 300 feet below the surface of the ocean.

With the tip of a forefinger I touched the orifice of one of the green sea anemones. With surprising suddenness all the petals of the tentacles turned inward, closing on my finger. The sensation was similar to one I experienced long ago when, as a boy, I let a calf suck my finger. The grip of the sea anemone was a solid, sucking pressure. I slowly pulled my finger free. A small fish or other tidepool creature would have scant chance of freedom once it became enmeshed within that circle of tentacles, each bearing on its surface a host of small but effective organs of suction.

One of the oddest paradoxes of longevity is the fact that the frail-appearing, almost protoplasmic sea anemone has a life span that may exceed that of the great leviathans, the whales that each fall, in November and December, migrate south, often within sight of these very tidepools. Even the greatest of all the whales, the blue or sulphur-bottom, a creature that is the largest animal that ever lived on earth—exceeding in bulk the prehistoric dinosaurs—is believed to have a life span of less than thirty years. Yet in at least one instance a sea anemone lived more than twice that long in an aquarium, remaining active for a period of sixty-nine years.

Over many of the headlands of this part of the coast there is thrown a dense blanket of salal, rhododendron and huckleberry. Sheared off and pressed down by the wind, it forms the famed marine gardens of the region. With infinitely varied shadings of autumn reds and browns and greens, it rolled away up and down all the slopes around us as we neared Heceta Head. When we examined closely this wiry blanket it was the salal that interested us most. A spreading shrub with glossy leaves, olive-green and leathery, it is a western relative of the wintergreen. The tiny bells of its flowers are white, tinged with a flush of pink. Oregon Indians highly valued its black, aromatic berries. We were bending down, feeling the thick, tough leaves and fingering the sturdy twigs, when we heard a clear trilling. It was the voice of an unfamiliar bird. At first we thought it might be the Oregon junco. Then we saw the singer, red and black and white—a spotted towhee.

A mile or so beyond, at the top of a towering precipice of black basalt that plunged in a sheer drop to the white surf below, we stopped at the sound of a far different voice. Strangely exciting, it came up the face of the rock, the mingled barking of many sea lions. Looking down we saw them littering the rocks, clustered together on the ledges, sunning themselves just out of reach of the breakers. A great surf-filled cavern extending back into the cliff at its base is the home of hundreds of these marine cousins of the bear.

This cave is unique. It is the only rookery of its kind along the western coast. When we descended wooden stairs to the interior of the 1,500-foot cavern, a little later on, we found it echoing with the thunder of the surf. Great combers would shadow the two doorways leading to the sea. Then a white tumult of water would roar in, tossing the swimming sea lions, tumbling the animals from the lower rocks, carrying them in a long rush toward the outer openings.

As our eyes became accustomed to the dim illumination, we could see the animals, big and little, light and dark, lying on the rocks all around the edge of the cavern. They barked incessantly, bawling in a confused clamor that rose and sank away amid the cannonading of the waves. At moments the sound suggested the calling of cattle in a barnyard; at other times it swelled around us hoarse and guttural and foreign. One sea lion lay stretched out on its stomach on a small black island that lifted just above the water in the middle of the cavern. Over and over again it was washed away by the rush of the surf. Always it scrambled back and laid itself down to rest only to be carried away again. Twice it clung to its place while weaker waves rushed over it, each time as soon as the water receded shaking itself like a puppy coming out of the rain.

More than once we saw one of the swimming animals slammed against a rock by the violence of the water. Yet they never showed any signs of injury or even of discomfort. Tough hides and a padding of fat no doubt protected them. They also protected other sea lions from even greater poundings outside the cavern where waves from the open ocean shattered against the headland. Each wave as it met the wall of rock climbed upward stories high, spent itself and fell back in a lacework of foaming waterfalls into the sea. We stopped many times as we climbed the stairs on our return to watch sea lions riding these soaring combers up and up along the rock face of the cliff in an effort to reach a slanting resting place just above the farthest reach of the waves.

Sometimes the first attempt was successful, the sea lion reaching a small, rough ledge where it could cling with its flippers while the water rushed back, then hunch itself upward, a few inches at a time, before the next wave came. But more often it had to try and try again, each time being dragged back before it could get a flipper-hold, skittering down the rocky slide in a long bumping zigzag from waterfall to waterfall as the wave fell away.

A hundred or more of the sea lions had succeeded in reaching the resting place. They stretched out, basking in the sun, some pale yellow, others so dark a brown they seemed almost black. The former were the northern, or Steller's, sea lion, the latter the California sea lion. Here the two species meet. A sign of fall, as surely as the changing color of the leaves, is the presence of the southern animals at the sea lion cave. A few come north each autumn, spend the winter at the cavern, and move south again in the spring. Another indication of the season was the absence of the pigeon guillemot. These black-and-white oceanic birds, with their brilliant red feet at breeding time, nest near the cave in summer. But each year, around Labor Day, they leave to spend the winter at sea.

Where low black rocks appeared and disappeared in the white welter of the surf we noticed what looked like miniature palm trees, each a foot or so high, scattered across the basalt. As each wave struck, they all heeled far over like trees in a hurricane. Yet always when the force of the wave had spent itself they rose upright again. These submarine palms were the remarkable seaweed, *Postelsia palmaeformis*. All down the coast as far as we went with the autumn we saw these treelike algae. And our amazement never lessened at the untiring endurance of these marine plants that, in tumultuous seas, bend and rise again, all day and all night, all the span of their surf-engulfed lives.

Threading their way among these rocks swam a shifting parade of sea lions. Often two would move side by side with noses almost touching for as much as a quarter of a mile. Others would turn over and over in the surf like children at play. Because these creatures, like the dark-eyed, trustful harbor seals, are fitted by the economy of nature to be eaters of fish—usually fish of little commercial importance, at that—they are persecuted all along the coast. The great cavern in the Oregon cliff might well have been a slaughter pen for these animals except for the incorporation of the whole headland within the boundaries of the Siuslaw National Forest.

One of the glories of this wonderful coast is the chain of public parks and sanctuaries that extends down the whole length of the Oregon shore. We came, the next morning, to what is probably the oddest link in that chain. This is the Darlingtonia State Park. It is dedicated to the preservation of a pitcher plant. Here, in the West, such carnivorous plants are represented by a single species, *Darlingtonia californica*. So restricted is its range that it is found nowhere else in the world except on this small part of the Oregon coast and in a few scattered stands over the line in northern California.

We came to this pitcher-plant sanctuary just north of the great sand dunes that rise at the mouth of the Siuslaw River. Only a few acres in extent, it is a low swampy stretch where the green, hooded pitchers grow densely. In places hundreds were massed together in almost solid stands. Commonly called cobra plants because the shape of the hood suggests the raised head of that serpent, they have been offered for sale by nurserymen as "cobra orchids." Scattered over these cowllike hoods we noticed numerous small translucent spots or windows. If the insect that once enters the tube of the pitcher tries to fly out again, it is attracted to these lighter spots, bumps against the windows and is knocked back into the tube below. There enzymes secreted by the plant digest the captured prey. Scientists who have studied these plants have noted an interesting thing—the insects that fertilize their blooms almost never lose their lives in the pitchers. These species rarely seem impelled to enter the tubes.

When we climbed the high dunes to the south we saw between us and the sea a score or more of smaller dunes all elongated, all shaped in smooth, flowing lines, all pointing in the same direction, the direction from which the prevailing winds come from the sea. A few hours later, below Bandon with its hills of spiny Irish furze, we turned west and came out on the windswept height of Cape Blanco and saw this same molding effect of the sea gales recorded in a different medium.

For half a mile across the top of this promontory ran a multitude of streamlined masses of the evergreen huckleberry, *Vaccinium ovatum*. They varied in size. Usually they were two feet or so in height near the front. But they all tapered away to the rear like the cockpits of racing planes. Each elongated mound was a solid mass of wiry twigs, twisted and intertwining. Set only a few feet apart, these hundreds of low, wind-molded huckleberry clumps were all streamlined in exactly the same way. They all pointed in exactly the same direction. They all recorded, like a multitude of wild weather vanes, the line of movement of prevailing gales from the sea.

Road menders were burning brush beside the highway that afternoon when we neared Port Orford. And all the air was filled with a strange and haunting incense. It was the perfume of one of the rarest and most beautiful trees in America. Like the Kirtland's warbler and the *Darlingtonia* pitcher plant, the Port Orford cedar is remarkable for its restricted range. It is almost entirely concentrated in a narrow strip along the coast about thirty miles wide and no more than 200 miles long. We stopped a little farther down the road to spend an hour enjoying the delicate beauty of these aromatic conifers. Each upward-slanting branch was clothed in the golden-green lace of its feathery foliage. In virgin stands these trees sometimes reach a height of 200 feet, the smooth columns of the trunks rising for a hundred feet or more devoid of branches. But here, in second growth, the fernlike fronds of the foliage descended almost to the ground.

I crushed a twig tip between my fingers and for a long time my hand was redolent with the fragrance of the tree's perfume. When we had passed a rambling gray building on Coalbank Slough at Coos Bay, earlier in the day, we had found the air all around it delightfully scented. Later we had learned that this was the sweet smell of the white, satiny, pungently perfumed wood of the Port Orford cedar. There it was being cut and processed for market. Because of its remarkable properties it is always in demand. It is light, strong, durable and resistant to acids. It rides in every automobile as separators in the battery. Sir Thomas Lipton specified that Port Orford cedar be used in the construction of all the yachts he entered in the races for the America's Cup. At one time this fragrant wood was widely used in China for making caskets. And because it takes a high polish and stains beautifully it is employed in cabinet making. Thus the cutting of this rare, restricted tree continues unabated. Unless active steps are taken for their preservation, it is estimated the last of the virgin trees will disappear in less than a quarter of a century.

Another endangered species in this region of beautiful trees is the Oregon myrtle. Ironically the same pamphlet that stressed its scarcity and the need for its protection carried at the end a directory of all the places where products made from the wood of the felled trees might be purchased. Although no two trees could be more different, the myrtle is, in its way, almost as handsome as the cedar. Instead of rising to a spire, as the cedar does, it is solid and rounded. Instead of the filmy lace of the cedar's foliage, its limbs are densely clothed with heavy, glossy leaves. At times the trees seem so solid they might have been carved from wood and painted dark, rich green. We saw them dotting the hillsides and running down the zigzags of the gullies. Where they clustered together the shadows beneath, even at midday, seemed as dark as night. Each of the heavy leaves shone as though coated with a beautiful lacquer. And so it would shine on through the months ahead.

For the Oregon myrtle is evergreen. To its glossy foliage autumn brings no change.

But elsewhere as we neared the California line—even in the prolonged Indian summer of this mild climate, even with pink wild roses still blooming beside the road—the changes of the season were apparent. On every breeze rode the cottony drift of the groundsel tree, *Baccharis*. Its early-autumn blooming was over; its late-autumn seeds were on the wind. Although we were now on the fourth great flyway of the continent the birds were few; they had traveled this way long before us. But at once the most beautiful and the most evanescent sign of the altering season was one we saw when, with the sun high in the sky behind us, we looked back up the coast where great spray-crowned combers were parading to shore. As each wave reached a certain point the fragment of a rainbow burst into brilliance low above it and moved slowly down its length to fade and vanish. Once a white gull, soaring on rigid wings, advanced along a wave in pace with the moving colors as though, in a moment of magic, it rode on a rainbow. Seen from our particular vantage point, this vision of fleeting beauty was, in itself, an evidence of the lateness of the season. It indicated how far to the south the sun had traveled.

The next afternoon we crossed the line into California.

Valley of the West

INLAND from the sea, somewhere between the Bear and the Yuba rivers in northern California, we came to a plowed field as brilliant as a flower. All its furrows stretched away in the morning sunshine a deep, rich apricot hue. Nowhere else in nearly 20,000 miles of traveling had we encountered such soil. It added another shade to the innumerable earth colors we had enjoyed. Anyone who crosses the continent by a wandering course sees not only the power and glory and wealth of America but also the exhaustless variety of its beauty—even such simple, endlessly changing beauty as the color of its soil.

During these days we meandered widely amid new, inland signs of the season. We met trucks hurrying down from mountain forests piled high with Christmas trees. We caught glimpses of the brilliant holly-red of the toyon berries. We went past boys clambering among roadside walnut trees, shaking the branches.

Here we were in the upper part of California's Great Central Valley. This titanic bowl, elliptical in shape, is about fifty miles wide and 400 miles long. Its area is greater than that of New Hampshire and Vermont combined. It stretches from near Redding, just below Mt. Shasta, to the country beyond the Kern River, south of Bakersfield. Like the Great Valley of the Appalachians, it runs north and south. Western geologists call it the California Trough.

In all its 400-mile length there is only one break through which rivers can escape to the sea. The Sacramento—carrying the waters of Grindstone Creek and Antelope Creek and Cottonwood Creek, of the Bear and Feather and Yuba rivers—flows down from the north. The San Joaquin, almost as silt-filled as the Mississippi, moves up from the south. They join near Stockton. Their united flow pours into San Pablo Bay and passes out through the Golden Gate into the Pacific. All the water draining from the length and breadth of the valley emerges through this one break almost at the exact center of the western wall.

To the pioneers, weary of mountains and canyons, this wide central valley of California was a boulevard, a land of easy traveling. Where we advanced with the aid of road maps and highway numbers, a hundred years later, they had guided themselves by the lay of the land. Still other travelers, then moving across the valley floor in an annual autumn journey, were obtaining their bearings in a different way, in a manner that is still a mystery. These were the ladybird beetles that each year take wing in uncounted millions to converge on certain mountain canyons where they mass together among the rocks in winter hibernation.

We drove for fifty miles into the wildly beautiful Feather River Canyon, north of Oroville, searching for these spectacular beetle concentrations. We stopped near red madrone trees to scan the walls of the gorge. We peered down the rocky river banks. But only once did we see what may have been a massing of the beetles, a dark-red splash of color among the higher rocks of the canyon wall. Each winter "ladybug" prospectors search this area for pockets and veins of beetles. Sometimes the insects form solid masses several feet thick. Scooped like grain into gunny sacks, they are carried down to the valley and sold by the gallon to farmers and orchardists who distribute them over their land to consume aphids and other agricultural pests. We sought to find one of these ladybug hunters—a man with the storybook name of Golden Land who lived at Feather Falls—but without success. Customers from as far away as Texas send to Oroville for consignments of ladybird beetles. One gallon—about 135,000 ladybugs—is prescribed for five acres. More than 100,000,000 of the spotted beetles are shipped from the region in the course of a year.

A dozen miles to the west of Chico, on another day, we crossed a lonely stretch of the Sacramento River. As far as we could see its winding banks were lined with yellow-leaved cottonwoods lumpy with mistletoe. For miles on the way to Orland we ran through almond groves. Then for other miles, heading south toward Williams, we were amid dikes and rice fields and level land stretching away to a low horizon. We passed a leafless tree filled with western bluebirds. We went by a dozen American egrets scattered among sheep feeding in a creekside pasture. This was the beginning of another great bird day of our lives.

For between Willows and Williams we came to the teeming Sacramento National Wildlife Refuge. This sanctuary is to the fourth great flyway of the continent what Bear River is to the third. Its 10,000 acres of marshes, ponds and flatlands provide a haven for vast numbers of migrants each fall. During the peak of the autumn concentration it may contain as many as 1,115,000 pintail at one time. The rare little Ross's goose, coming south from its nesting grounds along the arctic shore east of the Mackenzie Delta, spends the winter here. As we followed the winding trail of the dike tops the rest of that day, hundreds of thousands of ducks and geese were scattered across the sanctuary, and the sky around us was continually filled with the moving skeins and clouds of flying waterfowl.

Wherever we went the roar of waterfowl wings preceded us as mallard and pintail and baldpate and green-winged teal—perhaps some of the very birds we saw at Bear River—shot into the air from behind the curtain of the tule rushes. Coot, like thousands of dark chickens, wandered along the dike tops or strummed their odd, metallic calls amid the cattails. At times we came out on openings where, in a long white drift across yellow fields, 10,000 snow geese fed together. In other openings these birds were mixed with Canada geese, white-fronted geese and the mallard-sized cackling geese that, with their short bills, resembled snub-nosed Canadas in miniature. In these mixed flocks we noticed it was always the Canada geese that took off first of all. Here in the Great Central Valley of California, as on the sandbar opposite Farm Island in the Missouri River, they were the wary, the cautious breed.

The continuous calling of the multitudinous waterfowl came to us from all sides—from across the tannish masses of the cattails, from behind the dark green and brown stands of the tule rushes, from over the yellow plains of the rice fields. There were times when this wild chorus mingled together into a confused murmur like bees humming or water rushing over rapids in the distance. Toward the end of the afternoon, while we were still walking in brilliant sunshine, the sky to the north grew sullen. Storm clouds, swollen and slaty-blue, rose above the horizon. For a time, later on, we saw everything touched by that peculiar enchanted light that sometimes invests a countryside before a storm. Once more than 1,000 snow geese peeled from the ground together and trailed in a long procession, gleaming white and spotlighted by the sun, across the backdrop of this dark northern sky.

It was before the windstorm struck that evening that we witnessed the homecoming of the blackbirds, the event that stands out most vividly of all in our memories of that day. As early as three o'clock they began leaving the rice fields and returning to the cattail and tule marshes where they roost. At first they approached flying low and in small flocks. Then the concentrations swelled. Flock joined flock. The numbers pyramided. We were in the midst of swirling swarms of birds, flowing rivers of birds, deafened by their clamor.

We had seen huge concentrations of redwings in Florida and along the Gulf Coast in Louisiana. But nowhere had we experienced anything comparable to this. And here we had four kinds of blackbirds roosting together. We identified them all that afternoon—the common redwing with yellow bordering its scarlet epaulets; the tricolored redwing with white replacing the yellow; the bicolored redwing with red patches alone; and the Brewer's blackbird with dark plumage, white eyes and no wing patches at all.

At first we tried to estimate the numbers of the homecoming birds. But soon we lost all count. They poured over us in ever-increasing flocks. They came faster and faster. We were overwhelmed by numbers. At the very least we saw 500,000 blackbirds coming home that day. The number may well have been twice that total. Experts have calculated that there are often more than 1,000,000 individuals in these autumn concentrations. Nowhere else in America can more blackbirds be seen at one time than at the Sacramento refuge in the fall.

Before settling down for the night, the great clouds of birds—tens and hundreds of thousands of birds—turned and swooped in aerial evolutions, diving toward the marsh, zooming up again, whirling and dancing, flying in unison, seeming to enjoy the playtime after the work of the day. We saw everything around us, the skeins of white waterfowl, the horizon line of misty mountains to the west, through this storm of flying blackbirds. Flock after flock, hundreds and thousands at a time, they dropped into the marsh, blackening the cattails and sinking into the acres of crisscrossing tules. We could see them working their way downward among the rushes. And always fresh flocks whirled above them ready to descend in turn.

The sun set that day with little color, a red ball disappearing behind a low wall of slate-covered clouds. And still the blackbirds came. In the deepening dusk we could hear the rushing sound of their wings as flock succeeded flock. There were literally acres of blackbirds around us when, with the lights switched on and the storm close at hand, we started away at last. We talked about how that scene would look on a calm evening silvered by moonlight. And we planned to return next day when the storm had passed and see it all again.

But the storm did not pass. We awoke in Williams the next morning in the midst of slashing rain and fifty-mile-an-hour gale. I switched on the radio. The weather report predicted continued gales with the wind rising to as much as eighty-five miles an hour by night. We decided to move 100 miles on down the valley away from the storm.

In that wide level land the gusts at times caught us in smashing sidewise blows that sent the car veering half across the pavement. Walnuts rolled along the road where trees had been stripped in the night, and long zigzag gashes were opening on slopes as fertile soil washed away in boiling, swirling rivers of runoff water. We passed bedraggled livestock feeding tail to the wind. And once, under the ragged, dirty-skirted clouds that swept low over the land, we saw a flock of snow and Canada geese struggling to descend in an open field. Time after time gusts caught them and tossed them aloft before they finally touched the ground. What was happening, we wondered, to the blackbirds and the teeming waterfowl at the Sacramento sanctuary? This was a great emergency. But it was also a natural emergency, the kind birds have endured for ages. Wind and rain, weather at its worst, these they were equipped to meet. It was the unnatural emergencies, the pressure of shooting, the draining of nesting grounds, the destruction of wintering areas, that endangered them more.

In the calm of another evening, more than 100 miles south of the sanctuary, we climbed out of the Great Central Valley into the foothills of the Sierra Nevada mountains. Our road reared, dived, wound, wriggled upward, twisted downward to bring us, long after sunset, to a narrow valley threaded by a river that seemed half lost in the rocky maze of its floodtime bed. Coming west we had crossed many tributary streams. Some were called brooks, some creeks, some branches, some prongs, some runs. Here they were known as forks. One California stream goes by the name of the West Fork of the South Fork of the North Fork of the San Joaquin River. The stream beside which we stopped was the South Fork of the American River. And the spot where we walked along its bank was the exact site where, on January 24, 1848, James W. Marshall had glimpsed in the tailrace of Sutter's mill the yellow specks that had started the California gold rush with all its world-encircling reverberations.

A century before our visit this lonely valley had teemed with frenzied activity. But long since the fever had died away. The quiet of that evening was as profound as it had been all through the ages before Marshall's discovery. We wandered among low willows beside the stream. The dark forms of small birds flitted before us in the deeper shadows. Then one lifted its voice in a wonderful song, a minor melody, simple, plaintive, infinitely moving. In the tranquil, windless silence of that hour when it was no longer day and still not yet night, this frail and haunting strain was repeated again and again, now here, now there, perhaps always the same voice, perhaps the song of several singers.

Over the rocks, through the weeds, in deep sand, among brown mulleins, across flood debris, under the digger pines with their great fallen cones, we followed the siren song of the unknown bird. But it remained mysterious and undiscovered. We glimpsed only flitting shapes that disappeared as soon as seen. The dusk became chill, the shadows deepened, and the moon grew bright above the valley before we gave up the quest. But now, whenever we think of Sutter's mill or the gold rush or the river or the valley at twilight, we are reminded of that simple, strangely affecting song heard at the end of a late-autumn day.

We drove away in the moonlight and the silence of the night. And I remembered John Burroughs on his second visit to the Grand Canyon. After remarking how beautiful it all was, he turned away with the added words:

"But there can be only one first time."

Perhaps someday we could discover the name of our unknown

singer. Perhaps sometime we would hear its minor melody once more. But never again would it be quite so affecting. For here we had heard it—as we had experienced so many things in our autumn journey now so close to its end—as a fresh, memorable, deeply moving first time.

Mountain Snow

NOW all the days of the autumn had dwindled down to a single week. All our wandering had narrowed to one last inland swing. Then—ending as we had begun on a cape outthrust from a far edge of the continent—we would come to winter's eve. We would meet the final moment of the fall.

On the cliffs below Point Lobos, we had attained the point farthest south along the coast. Now, leaving the headlands and the windblown cypresses, the long Indian summer and all the fascinations of the Monterey region behind us, we climbed over the coastal ranges once more. We crossed the Great Central Valley with its rusty-red vineyards and its persimmon trees laden with fruit as gay as Christmas decorations. Beyond Merced, the following day, we began climbing the long uplifted block of the Sierra range.

In 1868 John Muir gained his first indelible impression of the Sierra Nevadas from the summit of Pacheco Pass. It chanced that near this same spot we, too, saw their snow-clad beauty appear under extraordinary circumstances like a revelation in the sky. The mountains had been veiled in mist when first we had come down the valley. On this afternoon near Pacheco Pass they were once more hidden, this time behind swollen, rolling clouds that sealed in the whole length and breadth of a stormy sky. We were still in dark shadow with fine rain falling around us when far out across the valley the lid of the sky began to tear apart. Streamers of sunshine slanted down through widening rents. Then in one continuous movement along the eastern horizon the clouds rolled back, the heavens opened and the "range of light" stood revealed, every high, jagged, snow-covered peak alabaster-white in the sunshine. In the center of this breathtaking vista, vertical bands of color, the foot of a rainbow, rose above the mountains and faded in the sky. For several minutes this stupendous spectacle lay spread before us across the valley. Then the sky darkened, the sun-streamers were pinched off, the clouds tumbled together, the mountains and the rainbow were gone. It was thus that we first beheld the famed central portion of the Sierra Nevada range.

When we left Merced the next morning, the mountains toward which we drove were blotted out by valley mist. At this time of year, with more moisture in the ground and with chill air descending the mountainsides at night, many California valleys are great mixing bowls of fog.

Out of the mist into the sunshine, out of the great valley into the small valley, out of the warmth of the lowland into the frosty air and mountain snow and crystalline beauty of Yosemite in December we climbed that day. At an elevation of 4,000 feet, we found ourselves in a frosted fairyland glittering in the sunshine. Here was that final aspect of fall, the autumn of December, that we had missed in the mild climate of the western coast.

Yet all along our trail from Monomoy almost to the Pacific this was the aspect of these last days of the third season. Snow lay white on the Kittatinny Ridge, ice locked in Lake Itasca and the warbler river, freezing winds swept over the badlands, drifts choked the high passes of the Rockies. Everywhere along the way we had come west, this tail end of autumn was a time of winter weather. We read of elk hunters lost in drifts, of telephone lines down in sleet storms, of trains delayed and buses stalled by snow. In a time of changing foliage we had seen the green miles turn to red and gold miles; now all had become white miles. Harvest and fulfillment were over. The affairs of the year had been wound up. Now—with the burrows of the long sleepers hidden from view, with migrants far away—the hazy, drifting hours of Indian summer had been replaced by nights of starlit frost and days of sparkling snow.

Scattered all across the roadside drifts, under Arch Rock and El Capitan and Half Dome, near the long filmy veils of the waterfalls, amid the incense cedars and ponderosa pines, frost crystals, the largest, the most complex, the most beautiful I had ever seen, glittered in the sun. Often they were massed together as dense and luxuriant as ferns on a rain-forest floor. By midafternoon these delicate frost-ferns were shrinking and fading in the slow warming up of the valley. But in the piercingly chill air of the next morning they were back again. Wherever tires had left their tread patterns in the soft snow every embossed portion of the design was richly overlaid with the shining crystalline jewels of the frost formations. Along the winding banks of the Merced River the tree trunks seemed whitewashed. To the height of ten or a dozen feet the bark of each was plated with frost.

During our days in Yosemite the sun was close to its farthest-south point in the sky. The shadow of the high southern wall, even at midday, extended far out over the floor of the valley. Sometimes the snow in this shaded portion of the park lies four feet deep when it has almost completely melted from the ground below the northern wall. At this time of year the slanting rays of the sun strike this wall more directly than they do in midsummer when the sun is overhead. They warm the rock which in turn warms the air, and this moderates the winter climate of this particular part of the valley. Wayne W. Bryant, ranger-naturalist at the park, told us of a study he once made of a cross section of the valley. Taking a strip about a mile wide, he began at the top of one wall, worked down it and across the floor of the valley to the other wall and up it. This ecological survey revealed that the vegetation of the warmer northern side varies considerably from that of the colder southern side.

We slept that night in a log cabin among incense cedars. Darkness comes early in the depths of the valley. When we walked down icy roads in the evening the black, towering trees around us ascended up and up until they appeared supporting all the spangled canopy of stars and constellations above. We breathed deeply the evergreen air, spicy and invigorating. We listened, in the stillness of the night, to the faint liquid lisping of waterfalls. Back at the cabin, the last thing we saw before we turned out the lights was a deer looking in our window.

The first thing we saw next morning was another California mule deer nibbling on a yellow-green spray of incense cedar. A little later we came upon a doe standing in a snowdrift. It was consuming the cellophane wrapper from a package of cigarettes. The curious craving of deer for tobacco is so well known that the old-time meat hunters used to lure the animals to their death by tying a bag of Bull Durham out of reach on a limb above a trail. In rainy weather drippings from the bag would draw deer to the spot as to a salt lick.

Although it was perfectly still that morning on the floor of the valley, a wind rushing along the upper portion of the northern cliffs flared the white veil of Yosemite Falls far to the west. At the time, the falling water, only about one-tenth its maximum flow, was even more filmy than usual. From the icy road that climbed to the sequoias of Wawona Grove we looked back. The sun had just edged above the southeastern wall of the valley and all across the windblown vapors of the waterfall ran glowing bands of rainbow color.

Wawona Grove, the first and most famous of the sequoia sanctuaries, was waist-deep in snow when we reached it. But the road had been plowed out as far as the Grizzly Giant. This 3,700-ton patriarch, with a trunk that has a circumference of forty-six feet 90 feet above the ground, is believed to be at least 3,800 years old. All the arts that make this printed page possible, even to the invention of paper, occurred within its lifetime. With 100 or 150 feet of its top gone, the Grizzly Giant still towers to a height of 209 feet. Six times in a single storm this tree was struck by lightning. Yet it has endured, in spite of fire and thunderbolt, for nearly forty centuries.

While the coastal redwoods were seen by the Spaniards as early as 1769, these mountain redwoods, *Sequoia gigantea,* were not discovered until 1833 when the exploring party led by Joseph Walker crossed the Sierra Nevada in the region of Yosemite. As compared to the 2,000,000 acres originally covered by the coastal trees, the total for all the high-country groves of *Sequoia gigantea* is only about 30,000 acres. Unlike the taller redwoods, the more massive and older sequoias do not grow in pure stands. They are mixed with other trees such as the great sugar pines we saw dangling their eighteen-inch cones from the tips of their upper branches. A sequoia is several hundred years old before it begins to reproduce. This it does with cones hardly two inches long. So numerous are they that two small branches were once found to hold 480. Each cone is packed with from 150 to 300 seeds so small they range from an eighth to a quarter of an inch in length. The little western chickaree with its finely tufted ears never seems to get enough sequoia seeds. In a single day one of these squirrels may cut down as much as a bushel of cones.

When we first came to the grove it was enveloped in the age-old calm of these greater redwoods, a hush that was almost complete. Blue-tinted shadows ran across the snow of open spaces, the oldest tree shadows we had ever seen, cast by the same trunks on this same portion of the earth for ten or twenty centuries before the *Golden Hinde* carried Sir Francis Drake to the Pacific. Under the snow the spreading roots of some of the titan trees extended through an acre of soil. In one place where the sun's rays descended between two shadow paths we saw a shining mote, the form of an amazingly hardy gnat, dancing in the light surrounded by the blur of its wings. Here side by side in nature's vast machine were the largest and one of the smallest of its cogs—the long, slowly revolving life cycle of the sequoia and the swiftly completed existence of the gnat.

Looking up along the grooved, cinnamon-red trunks of the many-autumned trees we saw the brilliant green of western lichen running in lines up the ridgetops of the bark. This same growth mantled the upper branches of the Grizzly Giant and here and there green blotches stood out on the snow where tufts of the lichen had fallen. At times we heard the faraway surf-sound of wind coming toward us through the tree-tops. In the changeable mountain weather it approached in single, isolated waves with a recognizable front. Each time we would hear the sound grow in volume, pass high overhead with "a rushing like the rushing of mighty waters," then sweep on and become faint in the distance, leaving the great trees once more wrapped in stillness.

Occasionally the profound hush of the forest was broken by the calling of a white-headed woodpecker, the voice of a Steller's jay or the small clinking sounds of feeding nuthatches. Whenever we remained motionless for any length of time we became aware of a slow, almost imperceptible drift of tiny bark fragments raining down from the trees. Where these particles collect in depressions on the trunks, mountain chickadees and thin-billed nuthatches sometimes take dust baths high above the ground. Woodpeckers, on occasion, excavate their nest holes entirely within the bark of the sequoias. For no other tree has so heavy an outer layer; on large trunks it may be as much as two feet thick.

One of the secrets of the sequoia's longevity is the protection against fire and injury provided by this bark. The wood of the big tree is particularly brittle. It fractures across the grain. In consequence the trunk of a felled sequoia breaks into such small sections that nearly 80 per cent of the wood is unsuitable for lumber. This characteristic, together with the remote and mountainous location of its groves, has played a major role in saving it from the axe and saw. And the abundant supply of tannin it contains brings it immunity from the attacks of insects and fungus. Wherever the trunk of a sequoia is cut the wood turns jet black as the tannin oxidizes on contact with the air. John Muir, in this very grove, used to make the ink he used by dissolving in water flakes of reddish gum obtained from the cones of the big trees. Letters he wrote with this tannin-rich sequoia ink are still legible more than seventy years later.

All through the Yosemite country, wherever you go, you cross the trail of this remarkable man and hear echoes of the days he spent here. With a sack of bread over his shoulder and a notebook tied to his belt, Muir roamed alone among the mountains making the pioneer studies on which his early books were based. It was in Wawona Grove, then known as Mariposa Grove, that Muir camped with Theodore Roosevelt in 1903. Thirty-two years earlier he had shown the same sequoias to Ralph Waldo Emerson.

"The wonder is," Emerson had remarked, "that we can see these trees and not wonder more."

When, after only a few hours' visit, the Emerson party prepared to leave the grove, Muir remonstrated:

"It is as though a photographer should remove his plate before the impression was fully made."

Always he was amazed by the rich and distinguished visitors who came to Yosemite and then rushed away again, so "time-poor" they could spare no more than a day or so to see the glories of the mountains.

"I have not yet in all my wanderings," he wrote to his sister, "found a single person so free as myself. When in the woods I sit at times for hours watching birds or squirrels or looking down into the faces of flowers without suffering any feeling of haste."

Since Muir's day the margin of time in the average man's life has widened as working hours have become shorter. Yet the demands on that time have been ever increasing. Hazlitt's wish for "a little breathing space to muse on indifferent matters" is a desire that seems each year harder to fulfill. When the famous Sierra Club was formed, one of the early members told me, a primary purpose was to induce people to come to Yosemite. Now in summer the cars move bumper to bumper and the problem is what to do with all the people who come. Time and space—time to be alone, space to move about—these may well become the great scarcities of tomorrow. Freedom as John Muir knew it, with its wealth of time, its unregimented days, its latitude of choice, such freedom seems more rare, more difficult to attain, more remote with each new generation.

We were thinking of John Muir and of space and time that day when we left the sequoias—those trees so full of years, so independent of the clock. The last of the autumn days were slipping away. In the life of the sequoia those days represented but an infinitesimal flicker of time. But to us they would round out the season. They would bring to a close our long westward pilgrimage through the fall. During this journey we had wandered as we wished. We had changed our plans to suit the day. We had, for the space of a whole glorious autumn, been time-rich.

Windy Crag

THE last full day of fall broke after a night of pounding rain. We saw the sun rise that morning 180 miles from the sequoias, 2,800 miles by airline—or 20,000 as we had wandered—from our starting point on Monomoy. The date was the twentieth of December. The place was the Point Reyes Peninsula thirty miles north of the Golden Gate.

On opposite sides of the continent, Cape Cod stretches to the east and Point Reyes extends to the west. At Monomoy low dunes faced the Atlantic. Here the outer tip of the point met the sea in a towering 600-foot cliff that thrust out into the Pacific like the prow of some immense ship of rock, continually battered by the surf and surrounded by the wind.

The better part of that day, Nellie and I roamed over this peninsula with three western friends, Woody Williams, Don Greame Kelley and his wife, Marion. We picnicked on fried chicken among driftwood on the beach where a hollow in the headlands protected us from the wind. We wandered across miles of green, rolling, almost treeless downs, pasture land, foggy land where, after the rain, fenceposts were sometimes so thickly clad in swollen moss and lichens they rose beside the road like green candles coated with drippings of wax. On the granite slope of Inverness Ridge just west of Tomales Bay—that slender arm of the sea that penetrates the peninsula for more than fifteen miles and half severs it from the mainland—we came to a grove of pines. They were flat-topped. Their bark was deeply furrowed. And encircling their branches, even their trunks, were curious bracelets of cones.

These were the rare bishop pines. Remnants of a once-widespread species, they now occur in disconnected "islands" along the western coast as far south as Baja California. Scientists believe they originated in Pleistocene times in areas sheared off from the mainland by fault lines in the earth's crust. Cones of these trees have been found in the La Brea tar pits beside the skeletons of woolly mammoths and sabre-toothed tigers. Usually these cones develop early, when the tree is twelve or fifteen years old, sometimes even when it is only five or six.

They appear first on the trunk. Later they form in circles around the main branches, as many as five to a circle with commonly two or three of these cone-bracelets to a branch. Some that we saw were green with moss. Others were bearded with lichen. They had been attached to the branches apparently for decades. For this tree is one of the "fire type" pines. It requires the heat of a forest conflagration to produce the slow opening of the cones and the shedding of the seeds. These seeds germinate rapidly in ashy soil. Thus, all at one time, they replant a stand of pines destroyed by fire.

Wherever we went among these pines of ancient lineage we heard an ancient sound, the low murmur of the distant surf. It was a sound that steadily rose in volume as we all worked our way out toward the high, gale-swept crag of the point late that afternoon.

Point Reyes is one of the windiest spots in all America. The year around, the average velocity here is more than twenty miles an hour. Once for six consecutive days, and another time for nine days, the wind blew fifty miles an hour. For a period of twenty-four hours the average stood at eighty miles. And once for five minutes it held at 110 miles. The peak velocity recorded at the point is 120 miles an hour. For more than nine months of every year, the wind sweeps in from the sea out of the northwest.

On this afternoon it blew from that direction. And as our road climbed, the wind velocity increased. By the time we came out on the top of the lofty headland we were in the midst of a fifty-mile-an-hour gale. It shook the twisted cypresses that flared inland from the cliff edge. It keened among low-set telephone wires. It pounded along the roofs of the squat cluster of houses occupied by lighthouse men. Looking between the writhing trees we saw the straight line of the ten-mile beach that runs north from below the cliff banded on the seaward side with a wide white ribbon of tumbling surf.

Since 1870 the famous Point Reyes lighthouse has occupied a ledge some 300 feet down the face of the precipice. It is reached by an exposed wooden stairway of 433 steps that angles steeply down with a thin pipe railing on one side for support. Before we started this sheer descent, we caught our breath in the lee of sandstone formations eroded like rocks in the desert by centuries of wind.

As we descended step by step the gusts battered us, took away our breath, ballooned our coats, forced us against the rail, while all the time the taut telephone wires descending to the lighthouse just above our heads screeched in a rising and falling wail. From time to time a fine sprinkling of spindrift struck our faces fully 500 feet above the sea. And always the gusts were filled with the wild roaring of the surf. We passed brilliant splotches of red on the spray-wet rock formed of the same alga that coat the cypress twigs of Point Lobos.

In the shelter of the lighthouse we regained our breath. The young coast guardsman on duty, A. D. Garrison, showed us the complicated lenses, formed of more than 1,000 pieces of glass, that once every five seconds from an hour before sunset to an hour after sunrise send forth a white stab of light visible twenty-four miles at sea. The lenses were ground in Paris in 1867. They came around Cape Horn in a sailing vessel. And they were transported to Point Reyes by ox cart. For more than eighty years they have warned ships away from the perilous rocks of the point.

The screeching and bellowing of the wind outside was never stilled. The gusts increased in violence. They seemed to shake the very lighthouse. Whenever I thrust my head around the corner of the building to glimpse the enormous seas that shattered far below, my breath was forced back down my throat. Over and over again, as though I were diving underwater, I fought my way to the railing to peer downward at the churning, detonating tumult directly below. Gust-blown spray ran like thin shadows of clouds across the hills and valleys of the waves. At times I would see an incoming roller meet some deeply submerged rock and shatter with a tongue of foam that shot back, fanned out, shining white in the depths of the water. It was like watching the explosion of a mine or depth charge in the sea below.

These waves crashing against Point Reyes struck like liquid battering rams. Each cubic foot of water weighs more than sixty-two pounds. Once, on the coast of Scotland, scientists measured the force of incoming waves in calm and storm. They found that in fine weather they struck with a force of about 600 pounds to the square foot. But during storms the crash of the combers dealt the shore a blow of more than a ton to every square foot. The power of the waves that hit Point Reyes at such times is as great as though line after line of heavy destroyers heading toward the shore side by side at forty knots hurled themselves against the rock at ten-second intervals.

Looking down from my wind-buffeted eyrie I could note but little difference in the tumultuous seas below as the water fell away to its farthest ebb. On Monomoy we had seen the full tide, the turn of the tide, the beginning of the season. Here at Point Reyes we saw the ebb of the tide—the ebb of the season's tide, the ebb of migration's tide, the ebb tide of our travels. And in the early setting of the December sun, far to the south, we saw the tide of light, too, fall back to its lowest ebb of the year.

All the while we had been working west through the advancing autumn, the northern hemisphere had been slowly "tilting away from the sun." The days had been growing shorter. On this afternoon sunset came at 5:05 P.M. Although Point Reyes is the foggiest spot on the whole California coast, the skies were clear. Only a low bank of clouds stretched along the western horizon. It flamed in the sunset and all the great expanse of tumbling, wind-worried water between was touched with dull reflections of the flame. With silent emotion we watched the sun disappear and the colors fade. This was the sundown of the day and the sundown of the season. All across the land the glory of an American autumn had come and now had almost gone. The "third act of the eternal play" was nearly completed. And never again would we know another autumn like this.

In fading light we struggled through the gale up the long stairs to the protection of the cypress trees. We rode away down the steep descent and out across the rolling downs where hills and hollows were losing their individuality in the universal enveloping dusk. The evening closed in, the last evening of fall, the one the country people of England used to call Winter's Eve.

The next morning Nellie and I returned to the bishop pines. We wandered in sunshine through the grove accompanied wherever we went by the thin sound of wind among the needles and the low, endless murmur of the outer surf. Here, so far from home, we came to the end of our autumn journey. At 1:44 P.M. on this day of the longest shadows, this shortest day of all, this twenty-first of December, the year reached its winter solstice. The sun, shining from farthest south in the heavens, "stood still" before beginning its long, slow climb to the zenith of June. One instant it was autumn, the next it was winter. In this moment in the sunshine, between breaths, fall had slipped away.

WANDERING

THROUGH WINTER

The Silver Strand

IN THE far southwestern corner of mainland America, where California joins Mexico and the land meets the sea, we watched the shortest day of the year come to an end. Lazy swells, silky smooth, drifted in from the open Pacific. Across the sheen of the wet tide line, behind each retreating wave, running sandpipers imprinted the winding ribbons of their bill marks. The air was rich with the tang of salt and seaweed.

Away to the north, off to the south, extended the Silver Strand, that narrow barrier against the sea that forms the western boundary of San Diego Bay. Nearly ten years before, Nellie and I had stood on the towering headland of Point Reyes, north of San Francisco, and watched the final sundown of autumn. Now, on this same coast, hundreds of miles to the south, we were taking up for a last time the thread of our seasonal wanderings. More than twenty years—a good part of a lifetime—had gone into that naturalist's dream, our grand project of following all the four seasons across the face of America.

Darkness comes swiftly in the Long Night Moon of December. At the end of this twenty-first day of the month, the instant came and went that marked once more the winter solstice.

As we climbed into our white car, where the trunk and rear seat were crammed with cameras and binoculars and field guides and jackets and snowshoes, we looked inland from the sea. Before us stretched another 20,000 miles of wanderings. A whole new season extended away untouched, a book of blank pages, to be filled with the events of successive days. The zigzag of our eastward path would carry us from this far southwestern corner of the land to the far northeastern corner, above Caribou, in Maine. It would complete that web of trails that our passage through the four seasons was tracing on the map.

Dorothy Wordsworth, in October 1802, wrote in her journal: "It is a pleasure to the real lover of Nature to give winter all the glory he can, for summer *will* make its own way, and speak its own praises." Of the four seasons, spring entices, summer makes you welcome, autumn gives you a lingering farewell, but winter remains aloof. We think of it as harsh and uncompromising. We speak of the dead months, the night of the year, the return of the ice age, the *winter* of our discontent.

Yet, paradoxically, in its own way, winter is a time of superlative life. Frosty air sets our blood to racing. The nip of the wind quickens our step. Creatures abroad at this season of the year live intensely, stimulated by cold, using all their powers, all their capacities, to survive. Gone is the languor of August heat waves. Winter provides the testing months, the time of fortitude and courage. For innumerable seeds and insect eggs, this period of cold is essential to sprouting or hatching. For trees, winter is a time of rest. It is also a season of hope. The days are lengthening. The sun is returning. The whole year is beginning. All nature, with bud and seed and egg, looks forward with optimism.

Alone among the seasons, winter extends across the boundary line into two calendars. It is the double season. We meet it twice in each twelve months. It embraces the end and the beginning of the year. It includes the great holiday times of Christmas and New Year's. Alone among the seasons it retains its original Anglo-Saxon spelling. Spring began as *springen*, literally "to spring" as the grass springs up; summer as *sumer*; and fall as *feallan*, referring to the falling leaves. But winter was always *winter*.

This fourth season of the year, means many things in many places. In the California deserts, it means more rainfall. In the high Rockies, it means blizzards. In New England, it means skating and skiing. It means toboggan rides and hockey games and fishing through the ice. It means the beauty of snowflakes and trees mantled in white.

Here, in the region of the Silver Strand, it has another meaning. Here it signifies the beginning of a unique sport, the sport of whale-watching. Down from the Bering Sea, swimming on a migration equivalent to a quarter of the way around the globe, gray whales begin passing along the coast during the earliest days of the new season. Before we turned inland toward the east, Nellie and I rode out to join these migrants in our first adventure of the winter.

HIBERNATING PLACE, where the first sleeping poorwill was found, is pointed out by its discoverer, Dr. Edmund C. Jaeger.

DEVIL'S CORNFIELD in Death Valley. Wind, cutting the dirt from around arrowweed, produces these shocklike clumps.

MULE DEER, with huge ears uplifted, sniffs the air amid
junipers in the snowy highlands of northeastern Arizona.

CACTUS FOREST of the saguaro at sunset. This botanical giant may weigh ten tons and live for two centuries.

CHOLLA CACTUS, lighted by the late-afternoon sun, is
scattered in glowing clumps across the floor of the desert.

ICE STORM encases teasel heads in transparent shells
and adds a hard and glittering surface to a whole countryside.

CIRCLING STARS in the northern sky on a winter
night trace concentric circles during an hour's exposure.

WHITE-FOOTED mouse peers from the entrance hole
of a birdhouse which provides it with a snug winter home.

BLIZZARD SNOW plastered on trunks and branches of a woods by the gale winds sweeping out of the north.

TRACKS across the snow left by white-footed mice among drifts covering juniper bushes on a hillside.

CURVING LINES of ice form in long serpentines on
a New England brook during a heavy midwinter freeze.

SUGARING TIME in the oldest sugarbush in Vermont,
at Pine Grove Farm, on the Connecticut River near Putney.

WHITE FOREST, its hills and hollows filled with
drifted snow, forms a fairyland of midwinter beauty.

THE WEASEL, a surplus army vehicle, rolls over four
feet of snow near a deer yard deep in the forest of Maine.

SNOWSHOE MAKER, Charles Holway, at work in the door-
way of the shop where he created special shoes for forest use.

WINTER'S END, north of Caribou, brings to a close
the fourth and final journey with an American season.

Gray Whales

TENSELY we waited. Sunshine glittered on the waves around us. Heermann's gulls, black of tail and white of head and brilliant red of bill, slanted by. Hardly 150 feet from the boat's rail against which we leaned, the water suddenly paled to a light green. It grew more gray. With a rush and a long, audible "swoosh" of pent-up air, a forty-foot whale shouldered up out of the sea into the sunshine.

Thirty-five cubic feet of air—a single exhalation greater than that expelled by 1,000 men in normal breathing—rushed from twin nostrils on the top of its head. Coming warm and moist from the lungs of the ocean mammal, it condensed in the cooler atmosphere. A fountain of mist shot upward. It hung in the air, drifted aside, slowly dissolved. Three times the gray whale emptied and filled its lungs. Then it submerged. The water closed over it, and only a widening slick marked the spot where it had so suddenly materialized. I found I had been holding my breath. I let it out and inhaled deeply.

We were just north of the Silver Strand, a mile or more at sea. Our guide, Dr. Raymond M. Gilmore, had spent more time studying gray whales than any other scientist on earth. Season after season, while biologist for the U.S. Fish and Wildlife Service, he had followed the whales south and observed them on their ancient wintering grounds along the coast of Baja California.

From La Jolla to the Silver Strand, we cruised along the highway of the journeying whales. We would pick up one migrant and follow it south, then turn north and repeat the process. Thus we traveled with them on a short segment of their long descent from the Arctic. On one occasion, we saw mist fountains rising ten or fifteen feet into the air above three whales that had surfaced at the same time. As a rule, the travelers are not gregarious going south. Most migrate singly. But once, for miles we kept pace with two that swam side by side, rhythmically diving and reappearing together. Each submergence lasted almost exactly seven minutes. A gray whale spends about eighty-five per cent of its time under water. Usually, each dive lasts between three and seven minutes. Sometimes, but only rarely, a particular whale will remain submerged for ten minutes. Of all the thousands of descents Gilmore has timed, the record stands at twelve minutes and forty seconds.

Each time we fell in line beside a new whale, Gilmore would flick on his stopwatch. Different whales have different rhythms in their breathing. Once he has clocked its underwater period, he can tell almost precisely when a given whale will reappear. To avoid alarming our quarry by changes in the sound of the engine, the speed of our boat was kept uniform. While the whale was submerged, we used up excess speed by swinging wide or advancing in a letter S or even doubling back in a figure 8. Then, when the stop watch indicated that the time for surfacing was near, we pulled back into position. Several times, we were hardly more than a boat's length away when the leviathan rose among the waves.

Along this same California coast, in the 1840's, there had moved an armada of migrating whales estimated to have been between 25,000 and 50,000 strong. Each year—then, as now—the great mammals swim as much as 14,000 miles on a round-trip migration between the Bering Sea and the warm coastal bays where they winter and breed and bear their calves.

Gold brought the forty-niners to California. The next year, in 1850, the state was admitted to the Union. Around the Horn sailed a parade of whaling ships. Lookout stations rose on all the headlands down the coast. The migrants were hunted going south and going north. The relentless pursuit went on while their numbers dwindled. Then a fresh calamity overtook the persecuted migrants.

On an evil day for the whales, a Yankee whaling captain, Charles M. Scammon, discovered what is now known as Scammon's Lagoon. As his ship sailed down the coast of Baja California, sometime in the 1850's, a lookout sighted the impossible—whales spouting on land. The columns of vapor appeared to be rising in the midst of sandhills. Investigating, Scammon came upon a hidden inlet. It led him to a wide saltwater lagoon swarming with gray whales. This was one of the chief goals of the southward-moving migrants.

For a time, Scammon's discovery was kept secret. Then other captains learned of his whale-oil bonanza. There followed a period of butchery unequalled except among the bison herds of the Great Plains. The bay became a vast slaughterhouse. Trapped within its confines, the maddened whales, swimming through water stained with blood, attacked and smashed small boats on sight. Normally peaceful and unaggressive, they became known to their persecutors as "devil fish."

In less than a decade, the gray whale became so scarce along the West Coast that hunting it was no longer profitable. The lookout towers stood abandoned. The ships sailed away. The vast armada of whales seemed gone forever. Many people believed the sea mammals had been entirely exterminated. But gradually the whales drew back from the brink of complete destruction. Slowly their numbers increased. Then, in the 1920's and 1930's, they were overwhelmed by a second massacre. A new breed of whalers, using factory ships, harpoon cannon and high-speed pursuit boats, roamed the seas. In Scammon's Lagoon, winter after winter, they fell upon the gray whales. When the killing ended, the species once more was so reduced in numbers that there appeared little hope for its recovery. Another chapter seemed to have been written in the long record of public loss for private gain.

So things stood in 1938. In that year, an international treaty, signed by Canada, Mexico, the Soviet Union and the United States, outlawed the killing of the gray whale. The hard-pressed sea migrants at last received protection. But had it come too late?

Happily the answer is no. On this day when, in the winter sunshine, we rode beyond the kelp beds of the coastal shallows, along the ancient ocean highway of the whales, Gilmore estimated that 6,000 migrants now pass the Silver Strand each year. It is his belief that their numbers will rise to about 15,000 before they level off. In the region of San Diego, one of the few indications that winter has come is the arrival of the barnacle-encrusted travelers. Whale-watching is the sport that ushers in the season.

We have just passed through an area where lobster pots were sunk to a depth of 150 feet and had watched our wake set the red, black and yellow marking buoys bobbing, when an old-timer among the whales broke the surface a few hundred feet away. We moved along the rail for a better view. Its head was white with encrusting barnacles. Even its flukes were patched and mottled with these marine crustaceans. It is the barnacle, in fact, that is largely responsible for the gray whale being called gray. Actually, its skin is dark, sometimes almost black. But it is dappled with unpigmented areas and patches of white barnacles. The latter increase with age. The older the swimmer, the more it resembles Moby Dick.

When it has reached its full growth, a gray whale may weigh more than thirty tons and have a length of forty-five feet. It is a baleen whale, a member of the group that includes the 100-foot blue whale, the largest animal, past or present, known to man. I asked Dr. Gilmore about the gray whale's life span. At one time, this was believed to be a century. Now, the maximum is thought to be between thirty and forty years. As we watched, through our binoculars, the old whale rhythmically appearing and disappearing, we noticed that a great nick had been cut from one of its flukes. These fleshy tail fins have a span of ten or twelve feet and may weigh 400 pounds. Gilmore told me of one whale he encountered that had lost almost half of one fluke. It was swimming along with no apparent trouble. He pointed out the row of bumps running along the back toward the flukes. These knobs or knuckles vary with individuals. They may provide the sea mammals with a means of recognition.

On one occasion, a whale emerged so close to our boat that we seemed to be looking down on its back. The mammal became uneasy. The next time it rose, it resorted to what is known as evasive swimming. No longer did it break the surface with a rush. No longer did it send up a high fountain of mist into the air. It remained mostly submerged and breathed out slowly. Only a telltale slick on the surface of the sea showed where it had come up for air.

When a whale is really alarmed, it sounds, plunging deeply and often veering off its course. We witnessed this awesome sight once when a small speedboat charged in, with a sudden roaring of its engine, to let one of its passengers try for a close-up snapshot. The whale sounded. All around it, the water foamed and boiled as it tilted steeply downward. Its immense flukes lifted high in the air, carrying aloft masses of seaweed. Water streamed away in cascades. The sun played across it as across a series of waterfalls. Then the whale was gone, and swirling foam and a widening whirlpool remained. The overwhelming impression of drive and bulk and power is still vivid in our minds.

Later we fell in beside what appeared to be a tiring migrant. It was nearing the end of an immense journey, 6,000 or 7,000 miles long, a journey that consumes between three and a half and four months. During all this time, the gray whale apparently never stops to eat, and sleeps no more than four hours out of the twenty-four. At times when the moon is full, the whales swim night and day without halting. For some reason still uncertain, a migration will occasionally dam up farther north and then suddenly release a wave of whales. At such times, a hundred may plow past Point Loma and the Silver Strand in the course of a single day.

Looking toward the slant of the sun, we watched the ponderous body of the weary migrant appearing and disappearing in the midst of glittering wavelets. The maximum speed of the gray whale is ten knots. Its usual cruising speed during migration is four. This individual was hardly making two. Perhaps it was heavy with young. For the vanguard of the migration, reaching the San Diego region in the first days of winter, between the twenty-second and the twenty-seventh of December, is always made up of females. Larger than the males, they breed on the wintering ground every two years. Gestation takes almost a year. About half the females that return to Baja California bear their calves soon after their arrival. At birth, the baby whale may weigh 3,000 pounds and measure seventeen feet in length. It grows rapidly on the rich milk its mother supplies. By as early as February, it is ready to start the long migration northward to the Bering Sea.

Going north and coming south, along the ancestral sea lanes of their kind, the whales apparently make use of the contours of the ocean bed to guide them. They may also employ landmarks such as high headlands along the coast. Their eyesight is excellent. On occasions, Dr. Gilmore has seen these immense mammals hurling themselves straight up, towering twenty feet in the air, momentarily standing on their tails, while they reconnoitered their surroundings.

Before our boat turned toward home that day, Nellie and I were training our glasses on the very spot among the waves where the last whale we saw broke the surface. To our magnified vision, the water cascading over its barnacle-splotched head appeared but an arm's length away. Its eye—which alternately meets the watery dimness of the depths and the glare of the open sunshine—seemed staring directly into mine. We looked at each other across a couple of hundred feet of tumbling water and across immeasurable gulfs of evolutionary time. How far back it was that our mammalian ancestors had taken different roads! How unfathomable was the chasm that separated our ways of life! For this great creature that looked at me while I looked at it, what was existence like? This insatiable desire to be inside other forms of life, to see the things that I see with their eyes and their minds—this is a thread that has run through all our seasonal wanderings. A thousand reincarnations, each as a different form of life, would be too few to satisfy this curiosity. Thoreau understood it when he wrote of the calling of the Concord frogs:

"So the frogs dream, would that I knew what!"

That night we slept for a last time beside the Pacific. Early the next morning, we turned inland. Once more, as amid the goldenrod of Monomoy at the start of the autumn trip, the width of the continent lay before us. Now we were spanning it in the opposite direction, by a new trail and in a new season. Henceforth, no matter how our route wound or twisted or zigzagged to this side or that, our course was set toward the east. It was set toward another ocean—a winter away.

The Desert Wind

"SWALLOWS certainly sleep all winter. A number of them con-
globulate together, by flying round and round, and then all in a
heap throw themselves under the water, and lie in the bed of the
river."

Thus, in the year 1768, Samuel Johnson explained the disappearance
of these birds in fall to his biographer, Boswell. He was expressing—
with Johnsonian finality—the prevalent belief of his time. In *The Natural History of Selborne*, Johnson's contemporary, Gilbert White, noted
that one eminent Swedish naturalist of the period talked "as familiarly
of swallows going under water in the beginning of September as he
would of his poultry going to roost a little before sunset." With the passage of time, the absurdity of this idea grew obvious. A better understanding of migration explained the mystifying disappearance of birds
in fall and Johnson's "conglobulating" swallows became recognized as a
classic misconception. Through the nineteenth century and the first decades of the twentieth, the belief in hibernating birds stood as a symbol
of human credulity.

It was against this background that Dr. Edmund C. Jaeger, in the
Chuckwalla Mountains of the Colorado Desert, on December 29, 1946,
discovered a hibernating bird. On this December day of a later year,
with his friend, Gregory Hitchcock at the wheel of his green jeep. we
were returning to the scene of this discovery.

In one of his books, Dr. Jaeger has observed that "the desert landscape is monotonous only to the uninformed." Mile by mile as we advanced, our surroundings became more interesting by virtue of his
comments and explanations. They were drawn from a lifetime of desert
study. In his mid-seventies, the recognized authority in his field, he retains all the passionate interest in the interrelating life of these dry
lands that has guided his activity for more than half a century.

Almost every weekend, he heads for the desert. Over a period of
more than thirty years, he once calculated, he had spent at least two or
three nights of every week in his sleeping bag. Formerly Chairman of
the Department of Zoology at Riverside Junior College, he usually

takes along on his trips two advanced students. By preference, one is a good cook, the other proficient in the handling and repair of automobiles. Thus he is left free for his studies.

In his absorption with the desert, Dr. Jaeger represents a type of natural-history specialist that is coming to have increasing importance in science. Instead of specializing vertically, as in a lifetime spent on a restricted subject like duckweed or moss animals or feather mites, such an authority will specialize horizontally. All life within an environment will be his province. He will devote himself to every aspect of his chosen area—meadow, timberline, swamp or mesa—as Dr. Jaeger has devoted himself to the life of the desert.

We had been gradually descending as we advanced. East of the Little San Bernardino Mountains, we left the Mojave behind. We were in the lower Colorado Desert when we swung off the highway onto wheel tracks that led us across a dry flatland broken here and there by immense mounds or hills of jumbled reddish rock. In the sunset, they stretched long shadows toward the higher masses of the barren Chuckwallas.

When we made camp in the protection of one of the larger piles of weathered rock, dusk had almost fallen. We fed dry twigs from creosote bushes to a campfire and added branches from a dead paloverde tree. The fragrance of wood smoke was all around us as we ate our supper of pea soup, turkey sandwiches, hot tea and cocoa. The night came quickly. The chill of the desert increased. I slipped on a sweater, then a plaid flannel shirt, then a fleece-lined jacket. I even pulled down the ear flaps of my woolen cap. Dr. Jaeger was reminded of an old Chinese who divided winter weather into "one-shirt, two-shirt and three-shirt days." Stars were out when we washed the dishes. Each time we piled wood on the fire the glare of the mounting flames danced in flickering light across the great rocks behind us.

When I crawled into my sleeping bag that night, I kept on my woolen socks, my sweater and my woolen cap, with the ear flaps down. Snug as a snail in its shell, I lay on my back looking up at the brilliant ceiling of the stars. In the dry air of the desert, they drew close. At times, the illusion was strong that they were within reach of an outstretched hand. So the hours of the night went by while I watched the parade of the winter constellations move across the sky. I was too elated, too happy, to sleep. I was alone, but alone in a wonderful way. Each moment seemed one I would recall vividly as long as memory lasted.

The desert, it has been said, is all geology by day and all astronomy by night. And I was seeing its sky in winter, in the season of stars. To most people, the winter constellations are the most familiar. We see them then in clearer air, in a time of earlier darkness, when foliage is off the trees. Here the Great Dipper was below the horizon and Orion shone higher in the sky than at home. Lying there, I stared at the Pleiades above me and at the blue star, Sirius, in Canis Major, the brightest in the night sky. Several times meteors drew swift lines of flame among the stars. I lay remembering that August night when Nellie and I stood in the dust of a lonely Kansas road while the meteor trails of a summer Perseid shower crossed and crisscrossed in the sky above us.

The night was intensely still. Once I heard a high yipping squawl or bark some way off. It probably was the voice of the smallest of our foxes, the desert creature I wanted most to see, the kit fox. After three o'clock that morning, my mind was occupied largely with the mystery of the birth and death of the desert wind. During the early part of the night, the air was calm. Then, virtually without warning, gales of erratic wind began to blow. They came in a long sequence, reaching a peak, dying away entirely, then rushing upon us once more. What brought them into being, what caused them to stop, I could not fathom. Although I have questioned many people since, the mechanics of that strange night wind remains a riddle. The broken surface of the desert floor, the proximity of the bare rock of the mountains, the innumerable canyons nearby—all these probably played a part.

We had made our camp on the south side of the mass of rocks. Gregory Hitchcock had tied a large section of heavy canvas to the side of the Jeep and we lay with our heads against this cloth wall. Thus we were doubly protected from the north. But the gusts blew not from that direction but from the west. At times, they must have struck at a speed of fifty miles an hour. I was first in line, rocked and cuffed and pummeled in the recurring gales. In the heavier onslaughts I seemed on the verge of rolling away, tumbleweedwise, in my sleeping bag.

During some of the lulls, I fumbled about and fished from my shirt pocket a small spiral-ring notebook and the stub of a pencil. Inside my sleeping bag, sight unseen, I jotted down notes. The experiment was less than a complete success. Next day when I looked at what I had written, I found I had gone forward a few pages, then back over the same pages. In the maze of writing on writing, only a few words were legible.

Toward the end of each lull, I could hear the new wind coming like an onrushing train. I would snuggle farther into my sleeping bag, pull in my neck like a turtle, and let the gale pound me as it rushed by. I timed the lulls between the gusts as the stars paled and a faint pink flush spread up from the east. They lasted about half a minute. When six o'clock came, I waited for the beginning of a lull, then leaped out of my sleeping bag, jumped into my trousers, yanked on my fleece-lined jacket and was pulling on my shoes when the next cold blast struck. Fifty yards downwind, I retrieved my plaid flannel shirt from a creosote bush. I was up and dressed in record time. A new day had begun.

That day—like the night that had preceded it—was no ordinary one. It comes back in memory, as it always will, as the day of the poorwill canyon. We ate a breakfast of scrambled eggs cooked over a windblown campfire. Then we started off. We wandered on foot among the widely scattered paloverde and smoke trees, out over the desert, along the broken front of the Chuckwallas. The night wind blew itself out. Fresh diggings in the earth and marks of paws sliding in sand showed where a kit fox had hunted in the night.

There were few signs of the season around us. Throughout much of the year, the desert has a bare and wintry look. Even living plants appear parched and yellow. We bent to examine the curiously swollen stem of a desert trumpet, *Eriogonum inflatum*. The plant, which rain would turn green again, was dry and parchmentlike. One of the small hunting wasps employs the inflated stems of this wild buckwheat as storage chambers for the paralyzed insects on which its larvae feed. It bores a hole near the top of a stem, fills the lower part of the cavity with tiny pebbles, then deposits its prey and its eggs. Over them it places more pebbles and sand. Under such strange conditions the young wasp hatches, grows, transforms into an adult and makes its way to freedom.

Also dead-appearing in their dry surroundings were many of the slender wands of spiny ocotillo which rose in clusters from the desert floor. All through the year, in a series of short growing seasons following rains, these rodlike, unbranched stems put forth small leaves. Each time, as drought conditions return, the leaves change from green to red and fall away. Once we came upon a clump in which each wand was still clothed from top to bottom with red-tinged foliage.

In pioneer times, ranchers sometimes improvised stockproof fences around corrals by cutting off the thorny stems of ocotillo and planting them in the ground where they took root. Under favorable conditions one of these wands may rise to a height of twelve or even fifteen feet. Its bark is rich in resinlike wax. One of its common names, candlewood, is derived from the fact that it burns with a steady deep yellow flame. It is in the spring, when all the wands are tipped with scarlet flowers, that the ocotillo most deserves the *splendens* of its scientific name, *Fouquieria splendens.*

Another curious wand, gray-green, smooth, waxy and limber, rose at times higher than my head from among rock jumbles of the mountainside. When prospectors roamed the western deserts with burros, these stems, strong and pliable, were used as whips. I noticed that where the skin of one wand was broken near the tip, thick, milky sap was oozing out. The gray-green wands formed the complete plant of the desert milkweed, *Asclepias albicans.* As I was looking at this naked plant, and accepting the fact that it *was* a milkweed, my mind returned—as it did more than once during these desert days—to the words of the White Queen, who remarked to Alice behind the looking-glass:

"Why, sometimes, I've believed as many as six impossible things before breakfast."

Past a dozen clusters of these slender wands, we worked our way upward among tumbled boulders that choked the mouth of a small ravine. At the top we came out on a floor of pale-gray sand between walls of granite. At the opposite end of the canyon, the entrance was even more dramatic. On one side of this mountain portal, a pinnacle, a spire of reddish rock, towered in the air. On the other, a titanic mass of similar stone had weathered into the form of a sitting woman. Only a hundred yards or so in length, only a few yards wide at the bottom, this small canyon seemed specially marked by nature as though in anticipation of some noteworthy event in which the ravine would play a part.

That event had already occurred. It had taken place in 1946. For the ravine was the site of Dr. Jaeger's historic discovery. By the merest chance, on that late-December afternoon, as he and two of his students passed through the canyon, they had caught sight of a western relative of the whippoorwill, a Nuttall's poorwill, lost in its winter sleep.

I had imagined the bird was found in some deep fissure, well hidden from sight. But when Dr. Jaeger pointed out the spot, I was amazed to see it was only a small concave depression in the granite wall, hardly larger than my cupped hand. I measured it when, on a later day, I came here again to show Nellie the poorwill canyon. It was roughly five inches high, four and a half inches wide and four inches deep. Into this rounded depression, with its head up and its tail down, the bird had pressed itself. Its mottled gray and black plumage almost perfectly matched the coloring of the rough granite.

A thing may be found many times and still be lost. It must be recognized as well as seen. The chance discovery of the poorwill was important. But a comprehension of the significance of what was found was more important. Prospectors, Indians, children, hunters, all may have come upon sleeping poorwills in the desert. The winter dormancy of the bird apparently was known to the Hopi Indians. Their name for the poorwill is "The Sleeping One."

But Dr. Jaeger was not only the first scientist to see the bird in hibernation, the first to comprehend the importance of what he found. He also followed up his discovery with careful, detailed studies. He photographed, measured, weighed and banded the bird. He returned to the canyon for additional observations many times and over a period of four winters.

On this first encounter, he touched the poorwill, stroked its feathers, even picked it up without disturbing its torpor. As he was returning it to its niche, it slowly opened one eye and sleepily closed it again. That, Dr. Jaeger told me, was the only sign he had that it was a living bird. During four hibernating seasons, extending from 1946 to 1950, the canyon was the scene of additional scientific study. The numbered aluminum band revealed that the same individual was returning year after year to sleep the winter away in the same niche in the same small ravine.

The normal temperature of a Nuttall's poorwill is about 106 degrees F. When fortnightly temperature readings were taken over a period of six weeks in 1947, they showed the body heat of the hibernating bird had sunk to 60.4 degrees. Its breathing was so shallow and infrequent that no movement of the chest walls could be noted, and when a cold metal mirror was held close to its nostrils, no moisture collected on it. Even when using a stethoscope, Dr. Jaeger was unable to detect the slightest sound of a heartbeat. So low had the flame of life sunk that bodily functions had all but ceased.

In the sand below the niche in which the poorwill had spent successive winters, I noticed the tracks of coyotes. Apparently, the narrow canyon formed a regular path followed by these predators. When I measured the distance, I found the niche was hardly more than two feet above the sand. Yet, so effective was the bird's camouflage that it had been passed and repassed while virtually on an eye level with the hunting coyotes. In its torpid state, with its organs barely functioning, it apparently gave off virtually no odor.

By night as well as by day, Dr. Jaeger studied the occupant of this poorwill canyon. On one nocturnal visit, he found the dormant bird with one of its eyes wide open. From a distance of two inches, he shone the narrow beam of a flashlight directly into the pupil of the eye. Even this violent stimulus brought no response. The eye remained unblinking and unseeing. So deep was the torpor of the bird's hibernation that a violent storm of sleet and hail—although it left some of its feathers noticeably battered—failed to arouse it. By weighing the bird repeatedly during one season of dormancy, Dr. Jaeger found that, in spite of its extremely low rate of metabolism, its weight gradually but steadily lessened. Whether all poorwills hibernate or whether only some individuals do, the rest migrating south like other members of the goatsucker family, is a question still to be answered.

Everywhere we wandered that day, I unconsciously looked into small openings, peered into crevices, hoped in vain for another miracle, another poorwill in the midst of hibernation. The chances against seeing it were astronomical. Dr. Jaeger noted that in more than forty years of wandering in the desert he had encountered only this single dormant bird. "It is doubtful," he added, "that I will see another." Only a very few persons ever encounter this ornithological rarity. Yet Nellie and I were among that lucky few.

Seven years after Dr. Jeager made his initial discovery, we were riding home at the end of our autumn trip across America. At Tucson, Arizona, we stopped to see Joseph Wood Krutch. Not long before, two workmen, while digging up an agave in the Silverbell Mountains, northwest of the city, had come upon a torpid poorwill. When we saw it, it was resting on mesquite bark in a box set half underground and covered with a sheet of glass. The weather had turned unseasonably warm for January. The day before, the thermometer had risen to eighty-seven degrees. In this abnormal warmth, the poorwill showed signs of awakening. From time to time, it would open its eyes sleepily. But soon the lids would droop and it would fall once more into the deep stupor of its hibernation. Altogether, about thirty instances of hibernating poorwills have been recorded. Some of the birds have been found sleeping between stones in the open desert, others among the mountains. Most have been reported hibernating in clefts in rocks.

For a long time, Dr. Jaeger, Gregory Hitchcock and I wandered about the poorwill canyon—which, since then, appropriately has been set aside, with 160 surrounding acres, as the Edmund C. Jaeger Nature Sanctuary. We examined the thick, leathery leaves of the goatnut. We noted the trails of pack rats under the overhanging rocks. Dr. Jaeger recalled that once, while sleeping in the desert, he was awakened by one of these animals tugging at his hair as it gathered material for building its nest. We rested on a flat rock where the scraggly branches of an ironwood overarched the ravine. And from the topmost boulder, up which we had scrambled, we surveyed the open desert spread out below us with giant heaps of rock scattered across the flat expanse like the stumps of mountains. When, at last, we descended and began crossing the expanse to break camp, I kept looking back. I wanted to see as long as possible that remarkable spot, remarkable in its singular character, in its surrounding scenery, in its association with a dramatic discovery in natural history.

Snow Tires in Death Valley

DECEMBER was nearly over when we rode north from Barstow across the Mojave Desert. Beyond the shaggy, uplifted arms of the Joshua trees, our eyes swept over illimitable stretches of arid landscape. Here we saw none of the dramatic changes so often encountered elsewhere. No forests had been felled, no sheep pastured, no irrigation ditches dug. The land seemed unchanged since the long-past days when "desert rats" with dusty burros toiled through the heat looking for gold.

U.S. Highway 6—the road we had crossed coming north with the spring, the road we had met and re-met in our summer wanderings, the road that had carried us on the first miles of our travels with autumn across America, the road that passes within three miles of Trail Wood, our sanctuary-farm among the hills of eastern Connecticut on the other side of the continent—this same highway now led us up the west side of the Owens Valley, under the wall of the southern Sierra Nevada. It brought us, at the end of the day, to Lone Pine. There, in the deepening shadows of Mt. Whitney, lights were going on. Away to the south, below the horizon, the Chuckwalla Mountains and their poorwill canyon also were sinking into the night. They lay 300 miles behind us.

We quenched our thirst that evening with snow water piped from 14,490-foot Mt. Whitney. Outside Alaska, this is the loftiest peak in the United States. Fewer than 100 miles separate this high point of the West from the lowest point in the nation, a depression near Death Valley's Bad Water, more than 280 feet below sea level. Those miles we covered next day. We crossed the Panamint Valley on a ruler-straight road. We twisted up to mile-high Townes Pass. Death Valley, with its dunes, its salt pools, its alluvial fans, its volcanic craters, its waves of chemical deposits sweeping like white breakers along its floor—all enclosed within the colors of scarred and eroded mountains—lay outspread below us. As we descended in sweeping curves of hard-topped road, we tried to imagine ourselves, a century before, riding in a heavy-wheeled covered wagon, advancing slowly, pulled by oxen, traversing that awesome chasm. The early menace of the land is reflected in such names as Bad Water, Funeral Peak, Desolation Mountains, Starvation Canyon, Furnace Creek, and Jubilee Pass.

We dropped a vertical mile to sea level at Stovepipe Wells. When we reached Furnace Creek, we were 178 feet below sea level. In this valley of desolation and hardship, associated with the suffering of forty-niners, with twenty-mule teams dragging ponderous borax wagons through the heat, the last thing we expected to encounter was too many people. Yet Furnace Creek Ranch swarmed with visitors. Cars whizzed past. Cars milled about. Cars lined up at the filling station. There were even hitchhikers beside the road. People were playing golf under the palms of the Furnace Creek oasis. Private planes took off and landed at the nearby airport. There was swimming at the Furnace Creek Inn and there was dancing at Stovepipe Wells. In the intervening years since the Jayhawker Party escaped across the Panamints, Death Valley has become a winter resort. We had arrived on New Year's weekend. The cabin we obtained at Stovepipe Wells was the last one left in the whole valley.

Among these vacationers we proved something of a curiosity. When we stopped for gasoline they strolled over to look at our rear wheels. Ours was the only passenger car equipped with snow tires. In the open winters of southern California, such tires are unneeded and largely unknown. But, for us, the roads of other winters lay ahead.

Once we were away from a few points of congestion, we found ourselves almost alone for great stretches of the valley. Running generally north and south, it extends for 140 miles. Its greatest width is sixteen miles. Wandering along its uneven floor, we encountered successive signs marking sea level. Now we were above sea level, now below, now above again. We seemed to be making porpoise leaps, miles long, down the valley. More than 500 of the nearly 3,000 square miles of this national monument lie below sea level.

Under our wheels, salty mud from prehistoric lakes and eroded rocks from the mountainsides filled the bottom of the valley with debris to a depth of as much as 7,500 feet. We moved about in a natural museum of geology. In Death Valley, the rocks of the earth take on the fascination that shells of the sea assume on the shores of Sanibel and Marco islands off the coast of Florida. Their colors are everywhere. Here they are garish and flaunting, there subdued with pastel shadings that resemble the delicate tinting of a moth's wing.

When we looked up the length of the valley from Dante's View, we stood on black Archaean rock, the oldest building material of our planet. Where the sweeping skirt of one alluvial fan extended out onto the valley floor, we found ourselves among small, squared-off reddish rocks. We seemed in a dump yard of discarded and broken bricks. At times we were in boulder fields white with desert dust, at other times among wind-rippled dunes of quartz or amid jagged pinnacles of salt or where yellow-tan deposits looked in the distance like wheat fields ready for harvest.

Among all these colored rocks, the ones that interested us most were dark brown or black. Seen against the sun, they shone as though greasy or coated with wax. When I ran a finger over one, I found its surface was smooth and hard and polished like porcelain. At times we wandered among acres of such stones. Where they were black, we seemed surrounded by chunks of shiny anthracite coal. I picked up one of the stones and examined it curiously. It suggested a meteorite. But it lacked a meteorite's weight. I held in my hand only an earthbound stone. But that stone was almost as exciting and mysterious as though it had fallen from outer space.

For the thin, glossy coating of its exterior was desert varnish. This is sometimes called desert gloss or desert glaze or desert rind. Its distribution is worldwide, and its mystery has occupied many minds. Darwin observed it in Brazil. Von Humboldt found it along the Congo and the Nile. It is not confined to deserts, although there it is most conspicuous. Chemical analysis has shown that it is formed of manganese and iron oxides. It is insoluble in water but dissolves in hot hydrochloric acid. The riddle that has occupied generations of scientists is: What brings desert varnish into being and how is it deposited?

In recent decades, lichens, those primitive, universal plants that are found in desert and jungle, on mountaintops and below sea level, have been shown to assume an active role in the development of the oxides. No climate seems too dry or wet, too hot or cold to support those "impossible plants," the lichens. Scientists working as far apart as California and Queensland, Australia, have reported corroborative evidence in connection with their role in producing the varnish. In the Mojave Desert, near Stoddard's Well, Dr. J. D. Laudermilk, of Pomona College, made hundreds of microscopic studies of a lichen so minute that, except in the mass, it is invisible to human eyes. Pioneers in breaking down rock surfaces and preparing the way for higher plants, all lichens produce acids that eat into stone. During their growth in the Mojave Desert, Dr. Laudermilk found, the plants take up iron and magnesium which is deposited again as oxides when the lichens die. Only rocks that contain these two elements are coated with desert varnish.

One of the old songs of the Paiute Indians of the Death Valley region contains the words: "The edge of the sky is the home of the river." Abundant water is far away. Rainfall is so rare an event that, in the course of a year, the average number of clear days in the valley is 283. The record is 351. It would require almost a century of Death Valley rain to equal the amount that falls in one year on parts of the Olympic Peninsula. Even in winter, the season of rain, the showers are infrequent. One had occurred not long before we arrived.

"Another rain like that," a park employee said with a grin, "and we will be hacking our way through the vegetation!"

In the course of an hour, on some occasions, a year's supply of water will be dumped on one part of the valley while the rest remains parched. Wherever we went across the gravelly outer edges of the alluvial fans, we stooped to examine the dry and yellow forms of minute plants rising among the pebbles. Those pebbles, under the full summer sun, may reach a temperature of 190 degrees F., providing a sound basis for the old Indian name for Death Valley—Ground Afire. But in the more moderate days of spring, on years when the rainfall has reached or exceeded two inches, a host of desert flowers spring up and burst into bloom across the floor of the valley.

Life, for these plants, is often telescoped. Many grow to a height of only an inch or two. Some reproduce through flowers that unfold, bloom and disappear in a single day. So specialized are the seeds of a number of desert plants that they not only require for germination a certain amount of rainfall but they need that amount in a certain number of days or hours. Even when conditions are favorable, only a small proportion of the seeds sprout. Thus, competition for moisture is reduced and the plants are spaced well apart in the arid soil.

It was after sunset when we first came to America's lowest point, Bad Water. The pool, bitter with chemical leachings, mirrored the reds and purples of the western sky, with the white summit of Telescope Peak rising against them. Behind us, far up the sheer face of a cliff, a small white sign read: "Sea Level." A few hundred feet to the northwest, a slight depression dipped to 282 feet below the level of the sea, and the earth's surface reached its lowest point on the North American continent.

As we walked about the edge of the pool, where low clumps of green and fleshy pickleweed grew, we noticed masses of tiny aquatic crustaceans sweeping outward over the bottom like reddish, windblown dust. One species of diminutive snail lives nowhere else in the world except in the bitter pool at Bad Water. Across the glowing surface of this pool, the water was speckled by the dabbing of dark little dipterous insects. At one time, the fly larvae of Bad Water and other salt pools of the valley formed a staple food of the Paiute Indians. As a kind of dessert, these Indians also ate the froth of the spittlebugs, or froghoppers, which is slightly sweet when made on certain plants.

Of all the more than 600 kinds of plants that grow within the boundaries of the Death Valley National Monument, the largest was introduced about half a century ago—the date palms of the Furnace Creek Ranch. Watered by springs, this 900-acre oasis attracts avian as well as human tourists. During our days of wandering up and down the valley, from the volcanic crater of Ubehebe, on the north, to Jubilee Pass, on the south, over the Panamints and up the valley beyond, we saw relatively few birds away from Furnace Creek. But here robins ran, with starts and stops, over the grass of the golf course. Say's phoebes fluttered under the swinging sprinklers. Red-shafted flickers flew above water pipits walking on the ground. Audubon's warblers flashed their yellow rump patches among the palms. Killdeer called and a black, red-faced Lewis's woodpecker hovered like a flycatcher to snap an insect from the air. For several weeks a Canada goose had been feeding near the ninth green of the golf course. The number of birds we saw was almost as surprising as the number of people who had converged on Death Valley on this last weekend of the year.

It was in 1917 that English or house sparrows first appeared at Furnace Creek Ranch. They have been thriving ever since. We saw them darting in and out among the palm fronds. In 1951 the starlings arrived. A decade later their numbers had risen to 800. We saw one flock perching on telephone wires, forming solid lines from pole to pole.

In the month of June, in 1893, when the temperature rose to 116 degrees F. at midday, Dr. A. K. Fisher compiled the first scientific list of the birds of Death Valley. He recorded sixty-nine species seen below sea level. Thirty years later, Dr. Joseph Grinnell raised the list to 124. By 1933 it had reached 131. Today, according to "A Survey of the Birds of Death Valley," by Roland H. Wauer, published in *The Condor* for May–June, 1962, the number of species recorded below sea level in the valley totals 232. Most of these, of course, have appeared during migration. But they include such unlikely visitors to this desert fastness as pelicans, loons, kingfishers, avocets, rails, snipe, ducks and geese. Once, for a period of half a dozen years, a great horned owl nested in the date grove.

High on the list of things we had always wanted to see and hoped to see on our winter trip were the kit fox and the desert sardine. Both are inhabitants of Death Valley. The little fish of the desert, also known as pupfish, are members of an ancient group, the *Cyprinodons*. Twenty million years ago, their ancestors swam in the freshwater lake that filled the valley. As the climate changed and the prehistoric lake disappeared, the fish retreated to pools that became more and more filled with minerals and salt. From freshwater dwellers they evolved into the species of today that live in water saltier than the sea.

So long have these fish been isolated in their separate pools and streams that they have developed the characteristics of different species. Salt Creek, in the northern part of the valley, contains *Cyprinodon salinus;* Saratoga Springs, close to the southern boundary, *Cyprinodon nevadensis nevadensis*. Related species live hundreds of miles away, in the Colorado River Basin and elsewhere, offering biological evidence that, in ancient times, water linked the widely separated present homes of the pupfish.

Why pupfish? When we watched one of these plump, dark, inch-long desert minnows swimming about in an aquarium at the excellent museum in the new monument headquarters, Nellie noticed the way its pectoral fins moved alternately like the forepaws of a swimming dog. That seemed as good an explanation as any for the name. To watch pupfish in their natural home, we drove again and again down a dusty side road and searched along Salt Creek and the encrusted pools of its headwaters. And time after time we searched in vain.

Here we were in a "chemical desert." Water was plentiful. But its salt content was greater than any but a few plants could endure. In the flora of this dry country, different species of plants have different tolerances for salt. Mesquite, for example, grows only where the water contains less than one-half of one per cent dissolved salt. Arrowweed is found where it is more than one-half of one but not more than three per cent. Pickleweed flourishes where it is more than three but not more than six per cent. A few of the seventeen kinds of saltbush found in Death Valley also can survive where the saline content of the water is as high as six per cent. Such chemical deserts, largely barren salt flats, comprise more than 300 of the 500-odd square miles of Death Valley that lie below the level of the sea.

Meandering and many-threaded, Salt Creek wandered in a shallow flow over a rippled bottom of yellow-brown sand. It sparkled in the sun. Its water was as clear as though it gushed from some sweet spring. I dipped a forefinger in the current, touched it to the tip of my tongue and felt the bite of brine.

Around the separated pools upstream, the pickleweed was heavily encrusted with salt. When I swept my foot through the vegetation, a cloud of fine white dust arose. On successive visits we worked our way from pool to pool. But it was only on our final trip that we discovered what we shall always remember as Pupfish Pool.

It was one of the topmost of these saline puddles, ten or twelve feet long and three or four feet wide. Masses of heavily encrusted, apparently lifeless, vegetation overhung the edge. I poked one such mass. Out shot a cloud of minute crustacea. Cutting through it were flashes and streaks of larger movement. Then our eyes began to focus on tiny, almost colorless fish and slightly bigger, more pigmented ones. They streaked ahead in swift and sudden rushes, then came to rest, then shot away again among the smaller creatures. At this time of year, the Death Valley pupfish are raising their families. They spend most of their time lurking in the shelter of the poolside vegetation. I had disturbed their hiding place, and young and old alike had rushed into the open water.

At one time it was thought that these little fish estivate during the hottest months of summer. Now it is known they are active the year around. For even more remarkable than the desert sardine's ability to endure salt is its ability to endure heat. William Bullard, naturalist at the monument, told me that in summer he has seen pupfish using as umbrellas the sheets of chemicals that form on the surface of the pools. Perhaps, like white suits in the tropics, such chemical deposits on and around the pools may reflect away some of the heat. In several places we came upon salt pools that were covered solidly, as with ice, by a floating layer of chemicals. They seemed frozen in for the winter. Bullard, on more than one occasion, has watched the little fish wriggle up through a hole in one of these sheets, slither across it and disappear down another hole. The ways of the pupfish are still mysterious. It is easier to measure the scales and count the fin-rays of collected specimens than to observe the living creatures in the hot griddle that Death Valley becomes in summer.

Over and over, each time I stirred the vegetation, families of pupfish shot into view. We were amazed at the speed of these diminutive swimmers. They streaked like little rockets, cut curlicues in the water, whirled like pinwheels. Occasionally one would plunge toward the bottom. We would see a tiny burst of sediment. A Lilliputian cloud would lift and hang in the water, marking the spot where the swimmer had vanished. Not infrequently, when alarmed, these desert fish dive and burrow out of sight in the soft material of the pool bottom.

On the evening of the last day of the year, we celebrated with a dinner at the Stovepipe Wells Hotel, then drove out into the desert night. The moon, in its last quarter, was late in rising. No other human being seemed abroad. The valley lay still, aloof, wrapped in darkness as New Year's Eve advanced.

We drove slowly. We stopped often. Nellie played the beam of a powerful flashlight over the land around us. Bright pebbles shot back quick stabs of reflected light. Saltbushes leaped suddenly from the darkness. We crossed dark mesquite flats. We paused beside silvery-green clumps of the beautiful desert holly, its leaves thick and soft as though cut from chamois skin or fine felt. Skirting the edge of flowing dunes, we came to the place where, in early days, a stovepipe is said to have marked the position of a well amid the shifting sand. Near here we stopped to examine a broken and weathered iron pump. It bore the still-legible words: "F & W, Kendallville, Indiana, USA. Hoosier." Later that night, for a long time, under the ceiling of the stars, we threaded our way on foot among strange, almost eerie shapes that rose all around us in the Devil's Cornfield.

Like the tepees of a great Indian encampment or like hundreds of acres of cornshocks, mounds of earth crowned with clumps of arrowweed lifted higher than our heads. This dry-country plant, *Pluchea sericea*, is a member of the sunflower family. The wands of its stiff stems provided Indians of the valley with arrow shafts and with material for the construction of primitive shelters. To pioneers, the sight of arrowweed meant water near the surface. In the Devil's Cornfield, the alkaline soil begins to be moist at the depth of only a few inches. It was among these cornshocklike clumps of the arrowweed that the long-suffering Jayhawker Party made its last Death Valley camp in 1849.

In only one other place, nearby Saline Valley, are such mounds known to exist. They all are the product of the sculpturing of the wind. Over the years, gales have eroded soil from around the clumps until they have been left growing at the top of pedestals of earth, each pedestal held together by the intertwining of the roots.

Strange by day, these upthrust masses are stranger still by night. As we walked among them, they appeared and disappeared, ghostly in the white beams of our moving flashlights. So intense was the silence that our ears caught the tiny chirping sounds of mineral fragments rubbing together beneath our feet. At each step, motes of alkali dust swarmed upward into the light. For minutes at a time we stood, torches switched off, enveloped in the dark. It was amid such memorable surroundings, on this New Year's Eve, that the second of our Death Valley wishes came true.

We had come back to the car. For a time, we sat with the motor idling. As I pulled out from the roadside, our headlights raked across a different stretch of mounds. Two shining eyes leaped into brilliance. Then, as the swing of the headlights passed the spot, they disappeared.

I halted. Nellie's powerful dry-cell flashlight snapped on. Its beam probed between the mounds. The eyes shone again. They were set in a face silvery-white, with a pointed, black-tipped nose and great uplifted ears. We were seeing, at last, the most beautiful and charming of desert mammals, the little kit fox.

Hardly larger than a house cat, weighing only about three pounds, it is the least cunning, the most confiding and inquisitive of the foxes. One camper, sleeping on the desert floor, awoke in the night to find a kit fox exploring under his pillow. As he lifted his head, it whirled so suddenly it kicked a shower of sand into his face. Sometimes, at the Death Valley campground, these playful animals have been known to slide down the canvas of tents and then race back to do it over again. So fleet of foot is the kit fox that its alternate name is the swift. Most of the moisture it obtains is believed to come from the desert rodents that form the major part of its diet. Harmless to man, the small kit fox has long been a victim of man's persecution. Guns, poisons, traps have reduced its numbers until today it is one of our vanishing species, a beautiful and trusting creature that is nearing extinction.

For a minute or more, the fox remained in sight, looking intently in our direction. Then with a graceful turn, it whirled into the shadow of the nearest mound. We saw it side-view for an instant—its pale-gray flank, its fox-face, its bushy tail. Then it was gone. With the image of that buoyant creature vivid in our minds, we drove back to our cabin. Midnight came and, in the stillness of the desert night, the old year slipped away.

New Year's weekend was over when we left Death Valley. Strengthened by stacks of "flannel" pancakes for breakfast, we headed south on desert roads where ravens were starting their own new year, south through the country of the Shadow Mountains and the Silurian Hills, through Shoshone and Baker and back to Barstow. All over the valley, that day, an exodus was in progress. Tents came down, motors started, machines rolled. Along the way, cars continually passed us. Drivers were speeding back to the city, back to school or office or factory. For them, the short vacation was over. For us, our season of freedom had hardly begun. Vacation, for us, stretched on and on, across the land, to the end of winter.

Our Idle Days in Patagonia

SOMETIMES when I have long known some magic place, I have envied those who might come upon it unprepared, suddenly, in a moment of surprise and delight. This is the way we came to Patagonia.

It happened in this manner. We left Tucson that morning on the superhighway, U.S. 80. A dozen miles southeast of the city, we pulled to the shoulder of the road and sat enjoying the vast sweep of the desert that stretched away, miles on miles of cholla and creosote bush, until the land tilted abruptly upward into a jagged horizon-line of peaks. Cars zipped past, some with a silky swish, some with a rising whine like wasps. Trucks tore by—red trucks, white trucks, blue trucks, varicolored trucks, a rainbow parade of traffic. Each thundering machine trailed a tornado of wind that struck and shook our car in passing.

We had been sitting there no more than three minutes when a trailer truck as long as a flatcar, loaded with a factory boiler, slowed to a stop beside us. Were we in trouble? Did we need any help? No. No—thanks. With a blast of power from its Diesel engine, the leviathan gained momentum and joined the rush of traffic. It occurred to us that everyone in all that stream of hurtling machines probably assumed that because we had paused we *must* be in trouble. The only comprehensible reason for halting was a car that would run no farther.

All at once we were overwhelmed by a distaste for superhighways, for miracle miles, for the thunder of traffic and the thousand whirlwinds blasting down wide ribbons of concrete. We longed for some side road, slower-paced, where we could see and enjoy our surroundings. To those whose sole need is to get from here to there, superhighways are a boon. In truth, without their aid it is doubtful that we could have seen, in a single season, all the varied aspects of winter across the continent. Yet they are part of a present paradox: the more the land is traversed, the less it is seen. Year by year, jet airliners fly higher, passenger cars on superhighways go faster. One shows the land as a distant map unrolling, the other as a landscape blurring by. Both remove us from contact. I remember Wilbur Shaw, three times winner of the Indianapolis 500-mile race, once saying to me: "The faster you go, the farther you have to look ahead." I remembered John Muir, in the California mountains, protesting that nothing could be seen traveling in a stagecoach at the rate of *forty miles a day*. Modern cars multiply that distance ten times or more. The unseen country is the land traversed at rocketing speed.

We sat there for a short time longer, thinking of leisurely roads, praising back roads, remembering the silent appeal of all the little roads whose invitation we had turned down. And as we talked, our discontent grew. We determined to turn off on the first good side road we came to, no matter where it led. While I pulled out and rejoined the torrent of traffic, Nellie studied the map.

The road we chose turned south. A name had caught our attention. It was Patagonia. Years before we had read W. H. Hudson's *Idle Days in Patagonia*. The charm of that book lingered about the name. Hudson's Patagonia extended to the southern tip of South America. Ours, a hemisphere away, lay about a dozen miles north of the Mexican border. What we would find there, we had no idea. We imagined a region of illimitable plains stretching away to the horizon.

In our autumn travels, we had cut down across the Dakotas on a highway numbered 83. We always remembered that road as "wonderful 83." Now, far to the south, we were on another highway of the same number. Even under low clouds, dragging rain veils across the slopes around us, it, too, was a "wonderful 83." Neither rain nor wind nor a sky clamped tightly shut reduced its appeal or lessened our sense of adventure.

The road climbed steadily. And as it climbed, wands of the ocotillo multiplied around us. They ranged across whole mountainsides and ran in a fringe or mane along the high horizon. Nowhere else had we observed so wide and dense a stand of ocotillo. We pictured, in our mind's eye, all those slopes at blooming time, those hundreds of thousands of wands, each tipped with the red flame of the flowers.

Along this highway we encountered hardly another car. Gone were the trailer trucks and moving vans, gone the torrent of speeding traffic. We felt elated, set free, as free as the ravens that soared on the wind beneath the scudding rain clouds. We left the ocotillo and ascended through a kind of luxurious badlands, a country cut and scarred by erosion but now richly clothed in grass. We crossed a rolling plateau, more than 4,000 feet high, where live oaks grew in the hollows. Ours was a road of superlatives. For here the beargrass, *Nolina*, grew in unparalleled profusion. All across this widespread land, where Cochise had led his Apache braves in raids on the early settlers, the range was dotted with fountainlike clusters of this fine-leaved plant.

Sonoita Creek led us south to Patagonia. Rain was falling when we came to the edge of this small town, set in a narrow valley under the height of white-robed mountains to the east. Its elevation is 4,050 feet. Both here and in South America, the name, Patagonia, is derived—presumably from the tracks of the aborigines—from the Spanish word for "large foot." The Indians themselves had a better name. To them, because of the abundance of wood and game, the area was known as "The Enchanted Land."

It was almost noon when we splashed up to the white wooden building that housed the Patagonia Post Office. Half a dozen high school sophomores were inside selling cakes and coffee and homemade candy to raise money for a trip, in their senior year, to see Los Angeles and Hollywood. This is the way of human nature. If we live in a Los Angeles, we dream of some quiet Patagonia. If we live in a Patagonia, it is the exciting Los Angeles that we long to see. Exerted in both directions is the pull of the different and faraway.

While Nellie and I drove out the chill with a hot drink and a piece of homemade cake, we learned that the whole creek bottom here is a nature sanctuary. Rare birds seek the protection of its cottonwoods. Following directions, we turned down a side street where a raven walked, with swinging body, along the edge of a sodden baseball field. We crossed a pebbly wash and turned onto a dirt road that, keeping its distance, followed the other side of the stream. It carried us into a wild park, a place of special magic, that extended for several miles along the creek bottom, open and level, with immense and ancient cottonwoods scattered down its length. A weathered sign, nailed to a tree, carried the almost illegible words: "The San Jose de Sonoita Wildlife Sanctuary." Nearby, a newer notice read: "BIRD REFUGE. No shooting. No molesting or collecting birds or eggs. *Se prohibe cazar*. Tucson Audubon Society."

The rain halted. It started up again. Then it stopped entirely. Along the creek and among the cottonwoods and under eroding cliffs, we drifted down this valley of birds. All that afternoon, experiences unfolded, piled on each other, grew better hour by hour. Birds were everywhere after the rain. Northern and southern species met and fed together. Eastern and western birds alighted in the same trees.

Over robins, running across the wet ground, Mexican jays streamed in a screaming flock. Almost side by side, a bird of the dark northern forest, a hermit thrush, and a bird of the open plains, a lark sparrow, hunted for food. We saw an eastern phoebe and its western relative, a Say's phoebe, tipping their tails on adjoining branches. Birds of the desert—phainopeplas and curve-billed thrashers—and birds familiar to New England pastures—vesper sparrows, flashing their white tail feathers, and field sparrows, with their light bills and reddish caps—all had found sanctuary in this protected valley. And where, at a turn in the road, hackberries and ash trees grew at the foot of a cliff, half a dozen black and yellow and white evening grosbeaks hopped from limb to limb with the brilliant red of a male cardinal in their midst.

We had been here no more than five minutes when our minds were made up. For the time being, our travels through winter had come to a stop. In this small valley, we would spend our own idle days in Patatagonia.

We sat on a log beside the stream and ate our lunch. A great blue heron, fishing in the shallow flow of the creek, moved away upstream with slow and stately wingbeats, and a red-shafted flicker, which we had surprised in its ant-hunting, bounded into the air and disappeared among the cottonwoods. But other birds remained all around us. Close by, a rock wren trilled again and again. Here the birds appeared to have everything—protection, shelter, food, cover, water. There were great trees, side canyons, fallen trunks, stream banks, running water. There were berries for thrushes, grass seeds for sparrows, open ground for robins. If we were winged creatures, we decided, we too would head for Patagonia. For birds also, this is The Enchanted Land.

We had drifted the length of the road and back again when we stopped near a neat cottage beside the stream. Birds darted among feeders set out in the yard. For a dozen years, we had learned, a couple from Lebanon, Ohio, the Hal Sorters, had spent their winters here. To their feeders come an amazing variety of species. Standing in one place that afternoon, Sorter pointed out two birds in succession that we never in our lives had encountered before—a bridled titmouse and an hepatic tanager.

While we were there, two cars turned into the drive. They contained four bird enthusiasts, Bill Harrison and Warren Winslow, of Nogales, and Mr. and Mrs. Frederick Hatch, who had come south for the winter from Massachusetts. Time passed swiftly as we all watched the colorful parade of birds that came and went in the yard. For us they presented a mixture of the familiar and the bizarre—chipping sparrows and ladder-backed woodpeckers, white-breasted nuthatches and Audubon's warblers, rufous-sided towhees and Lincoln's sparrows, phainopeplas and Bewick's wrens.

A few days before, more than 100 meadowlarks had alighted around the house. On dark and rainy days, Sorter has the most bird visitors. Chilled and hungry, they seek out his feeders. On this day, white-crowned sparrows were numerous. But among all the species we saw, so many rare to us, the bird that caused the most excitement, a species that had not been seen in Sorter's yard before, a bird that Harrison had never set eyes on before, was that familiar minstrel of the north woods, the little white-throated sparrow.

Following the other cars, we traversed the windings of the dirt road once more. At the foot of the cliff where we had observed the cardinal among the grosbeaks, a new surprise awaited us. In a little flock, a dozen or more Cassin's finches, the first of these high-mountain birds we had seen, flitted among the bushes, the females striped and sparrowlike, the males tinted with pale rose.

The cliff above us, the twisting dirt road, the great cottonwoods, the narrow side canyons, all the picturesque features of this little valley, we were told, had been seen by millions of people in many parts of the world. Hollywood had discovered Patagonia before us. More than one western movie had been filmed on location in this creek-bottom valley. The cliff top, in fact, was a favored place for Indians to launch their attack on covered wagons and, more than once, bandits had ridden out of the side canyon to waylay a stagecoach as it came thundering around the bend.

The next morning, after a night at Nogales, when we returned for another of our idle days in Patagonia, we wondered if the magic of the valley had sprung from our surprise, from the unexpectedness of our discovery, or from the dark, closed-in character of the day of rain and lowering clouds. Not so. The charm of the place seemed augmented in sunshine. We walked along the creek where the clear stream wound in innumerable skeins of flowing water that joined and parted, glinting and sparkling in the sun. The wind and the rain were gone. The air grew warmer as the day advanced.

Once, for a long time, while Nellie followed an elusive birdcall among the cottonwoods, I sat with my back against the rough bark of an ancient tree. Above me, and off down the valley, Gila woodpeckers and red-shafted flickers called and drummed on the dry wood of dead limbs. I could smell the moist ground after the rain. I could catch, from somewhere beyond a sycamore, the scent of willow leaves. The damp earth and the ringing call of the flickers carried me back to early spring in Indiana.

As I sat there, relaxed, thinking of nothing, warmed by the sun, aware—with animal senses—of all the world around me, my outlook, too, shifted back to an earlier, simpler time. At such a time, with awakening childhood perceptions, we walk through the out-of-doors accompanied by wonder and delight. In later years we learn the names of the things that long ago we saw and wondered at. We catalogue them in our minds. And some of the freshness fades away. Deservedly, the pursuit of factual knowledge holds a high place. Knowing the wildflowers, naming all the birds without a gun, these are admirable attainments. But there is always a residue of sadness when we learn the name and lose the wonder of the living thing itself.

We become specialists and our interests shrink. I know one woman who is interested *only* in warblers, another who is interested only in *female* ducks. There is more to the out-of-doors than a schoolroom and much has been lost when the sight of a hermit thrush stirs in our consciousness merely the scientific name *Hylocichla guttata*. The simple enjoyment of universal nature, with no other end in mind—this, too, has its importance. And fortunate indeed are those who know this enjoyment to the end of their days. Richard Jefferies, the English author of *The Story of My Heart* and *The Life of the Fields*, was one of these. Few men have ever lived whose delight in all-embracing nature was so intense. Ten years after visiting a beach on the seashore, Jefferies declared he could remember every drift of sand grains, every fragment of a shell, every pebble, and find a joy in each.

Yet, in all ages, this simple enjoyment of nature has felt the need of a disguise. Unless some trophy resulted, unless some pressed plant or dead bird or cyanided butterfly accompanied the wanderer home, he was considered an idler who had wasted his day. Never the pure enjoyment! Never the delight in nature for its own sake! To appreciate nature with singleness of heart, as the child loves it—this was felt to be a weakness, an inferior employment of time, not readily to be confessed. Only those who stuffed birds or robbed nests could claim the title of true naturalist. The simple-hearted appreciator and enjoyer of nature was considered at best a trifler. Picking flowers, collecting butterflies, stuffing birds—all these indicate a love, or at least an interest in nature. But on a plane far higher lives the one who leaves the flower blooming and the butterfly and bird flying.

One of the volumes in my library, more than a century old, is a duplicate of the entomology textbook Thoreau owned. It is *The Life of North American Insects*, by B. Jaeger, "late professor of Zoology and Botany in the College of New Jersey." To the author—as to most of his contemporaries, but not to Thoreau—a simple enjoyment of nature needed an apology. The apology most readily accepted in his time was a search for moral lessons. They were the conventional trophies required from days afield. "To every thoughtful person," the author writes in discussing the katydid, "all nature conveys some important moral lesson. The busy bee, that improves each shining hour, cannot fail of favorably impressing us with the contentment and the sure success that follows patient and persevering industry. The ever constant and faithful dog that bears us company is ever silently but surely impressing upon us the great lesson of fidelity." And so on—a thread of self-conscious moralizing ran through the nature books of a hundred years ago. In all times, the appreciator has had to have his excuses ready. Different times, different excuses. A century ago, it was looking for a moral lesson. Today, it may be a hunt for ecological significance. But, in this speeding modern world, an increasing number of people are realizing that just to stop, just to enjoy nature, has its own significance.

On this day we had the valley all to ourselves. We saw no other person as we loitered along the way, pausing often at the call of a bird or the sight of a squirrel. Again we ate our lunch beside the Sonoita. And again we wandered through a world of colorful birds. In our glasses appeared varied birds, unfamiliar birds, never-before-seen birds. And often, for surprising stretches of time, no two were alike. We saw a cardinal and a pyrrhuloxia in the same bush. We saw gray-headed juncos and Oregon juncos with black heads. We saw canyon wrens in a canyon and house finches among the cottonwoods. In a clump of mistletoe, phainopeplas and western bluebirds fed together.

Special moments of pleasure come back from those idling days in a valley of birds. Once, where bushes ascended a cliff, clinging to cracks in rocks that were mottled with lichens, a male vermilion flycatcher mounted up from bush to bush in the sunshine. It resembled a running spark or flame leaping in a zigzag path up the face of the cliff. In glimpses we followed the restless darting among twigs and branches of gray, golden-headed little verdins. And at the foot of the same cliff where we had seen the Cassin's finches and the cardinal with the evening grosbeaks, we watched a pair of brown towhees engage in what appeared to be a kind of mating performance. They fluffed their feathers, gave odd little cries, and followed one another about, ascending higher and higher among the rocks.

Before our stay in Patagonia came to an end—and we rode north again and over rolling yellow-grass country where rarely a windmill or the smoke of a ranch house peeps above a hollow—we had seen among the varied birds of this small overwintering valley three kinds of thrushes, three kinds of flycatchers, three kinds of wrens, three kinds of towhees and three kinds of woodpeckers.

Coming upon it by accident, as we did, emphasized the impression this Enchanted Land made upon us. The thoughts, the memories, the delights of this valley interlude remain with us. One of the entries in Richard Jefferies' *Nature Diaries and Notebooks* concerns a beautiful gull he once had seen. Remembering it long years after, he observed: "The gull is dead but I think of my thoughts of the gull as living on." So, for us, the valley lives on. As long as memory is with us, we shall see it vividly as we saw it then, in sunshine and in rain.

White Dunes

A HUNDRED miles beyond the Continental Divide and 400 miles east of Patagonia, we dropped in a long descent down the arid eastern slope of the Organ Mountains of New Mexico. Left behind now were the rainbow rocks, the organ pipe cacti, the Soguaro forests of Arizona. Before us, across the level floor of the Tularosa Basin, spinning funnels of brown rose hundreds of feet into the air. As many as fifty at a time, the dust devils whirled around us as we advanced. One raced along the roadside for a quarter of a mile. I kept pace with it. It was traveling at a speed of almost exactly forty miles an hour. Away from the foot of the mountains, the turbulence of the air grew less. But the strength of the wind increased. Long, trailing, yellow-brown clouds of dust extended for miles across the desert.

Beside the highway, tumbleweeds tugged at their stems. When one snapped, we saw the released globe bound away, its stiff, curving, resilient branches bouncing it like a rubber ball. Several times, instead of tumbling haphazardly, a globe would momentarily strike a balance in the wind. With the heavier stem end holding a position against the pressure of a long gust, it would spin as though revolving on an axle and go wheeling away in a long, angling run across the level surface of the roadway.

When we opened the car window for a moment to listen to the surf-sound of wind among the yuccas, a thin film of grit formed on our faces. Above the land that smoked with the swirling dust of the storm, the blanket of haze became denser. It rose higher, glowing with a dim and tinted light, a brownish shine that filtered down through the clouds of airborne soil. All living things were lying low. Once we passed a little flock of horned larks hugging the ground in the lee of a bush. They took alarm, scudded away downwind and, dim shapes in the haze, dropped into the shelter of a yucca. It was thus, whipped by the wind, abraded by the dust, riding with headlights on through the eerie midday twilight of the storm, that we first glimpsed White Sands and its miles of wind-formed gypsum dunes.

When we returned next morning, the air was clear, the sun shining, the rolling sea of dunes around us gleaming white like hills of salt. Where these gypsum mounds were crescent-shaped, they curved like drawn bows aimed toward the southwest, the source of the prevailing winds. Unlike the Indiana dunes of my boyhood, those hills of quartz on the Lake Michigan shore, the slopes and ridges here had no gritty quality. We seemed to be walking on granules of soap. Gypsum, the mineral that forms alabaster, plaster of Paris, schoolroom chalk and casts for broken limbs and plasterboard for the builders, this material is one of the softest of the minerals. A fingernail will scratch it. Only talc is softer.

One outstanding feature of these gypsum hills that impressed itself on us was their stillness. These are the silent dunes. Here there was no squeaking of quartz grains under our feet, no lisp of running sand drifting along the surface. Even when the wind rose—and there is almost always a wind in the valley in the afternoon—all this sea of rolling dunes remained hushed. I strained to catch the slightest sound. I strained in vain. As I stood there, my head cocked on one side, concentrating on a search for even the tiniest sounds, I recalled a rather famous American ornithologist of an earlier time. In his later years, not realizing he was growing deaf, he wrote a paper on "The Alarming Decrease in Small Singing Birds." Hastily I put my wristwatch to my ear and was reassured by the small but steady sound of its ticking. The silent dunes were really silent.

Across their rippled surface the paw prints of varied animals had written, as on gypsum pages, a record of nocturnal wanderings. We saw the trail of a coyote ascending a steep dune-side to a clump of rabbitbrush and then slanting away down again. When we followed the looping, zigzagging course of one rabbit, we came to a place where its tracks formed a jumble in the sand a foot or two in diameter. It seemed to have stopped and danced a jig. Not infrequently, where the top of some yucca or other plant thrust above the drift of gypsum, the sand around was embroidered with a lacework of delicate tracks left by the feet of pocket mice and kangaroo rats.

Among the rodents of the Tularosa Basin you find a dramatic instance of evolution providing inconspicuousness for creatures living in special environments. Amid the dunes themselves there lives the very pale, almost white, race of the Apache pocket mouse, *Peroganthus apache gypsi.* Not many miles away, beyond the dunes, another race of the same species lives among hills of reddish earth. There mice are nearly red. To the north, in an outcropping of black lava, the same species is almost black.

The entire flora of White Sands contains hardly more than sixty varieties of plants. Almost all of these grow at the edge of the marginal dunes. Seven species only can survive in the midst of the gypsum dunes where the sea of sand rises and falls as the hills move forward.

These seven are: the sumac, *Rhus trilobata;* the yucca, especially *Yucca elata;* the cottonwood tree, *Populus wislizeni;* the four-winged salt-bush, *Atriplex canescens*—whose stems were eaten as greens by the Apaches; the yellow-flowered rabbitbrush, *Chrysothamus;* the Mormon tea, *Ephedra;* and the mint bush, *Poliomintha incana,* with its square stem, mint odor and silvery-gray leaves which Indians employed for seasoning meat.

All seven survive in the same manner. They originally take root in the soil of the desert floor in front of the advancing dunes. They remain anchored there and obtain their nourishment less from the gypsum in which they appear to be growing than from the ground beneath the dune. While other plants around them are being overwhelmed and buried by the movement of the hills, these seven are able to elongate their stems and keep their heads above the sand. Yuccas sometimes are found in the wake of a dune with their stems drawn out to a length of as much as forty-five feet. Well up on the slopes of the higher dunes, we came upon such plants lifting their dark-green, fountain-like masses of slender leaves above the ripple marks, those miniature dunes, that form on the surface of the gypsum.

Across such ripple marks, late on an afternoon, we followed a trail of dry, windblown leaves. They led us to a cottonwood. Only its upper branches remained unburied. Yet all across its top, the leaves of another year were rolled tightly into long brown buds. We ran them between thumb and forefinger. Each, as a protection against loss of moisture, was heavily coated with wax. The cottonwood is the giant of the White Sands flora. The name of the nearest town, Alamogordo, means Big Cottonwood Tree.

Sometimes when we descended into deep troughs between the dunes, we walked on a floor almost as hard as solidified plaster of Paris. The gypsum sand, unlike quartz sand, is soluble in water. In the hollows, where moisture tended to collect, the outer layers of the gypsum had dissolved, then hardened into a kind of pavement. Where drops of rain, driven by the wind, had struck at an angle on several slopes, we noticed how each had plowed out a little groove that was floored with hardened gypsum. Only in a country like this, a land of dry atmosphere, mainly a land of winds without rain, could gypsum dunes have come into being.

Walking here, in the rain shadow of the western mountains, we came over the brow of one dune and saw with surprise on the sheltered opposite slope a drift of snow. Later, in two other protected places, we came upon other small drifts. Across one, nearly as unexpected as Friday's famous footprint on Crusoe's island, ran the runner marks of a child's sled. We decided to add an element of surprise of our own. I opened the trunk of the car and rummaging around extracted my webbed snowshoes. When I walked the length of that thin drift, I left behind what may well have been the first snowshoe tracks on snow these white dunes had ever seen.

Strange Birds Calling

WHEN we remember Rockport, Texas, we remember first of all a woman four feet, eleven and a half inches tall, weighing a hundred pounds or less, in her seventies, as intense and alert as a hummingbird—Conger Neblitt Hagar. While Connie Hagar did not make the birds of the Texas coast, she has made them known. Single-handed, she has added twenty new species to the avifaunal list of the state. Twice a day for a quarter of a century, storm or fair weather, she has patrolled the same four-by-seven-mile area beside Aransas Bay. The number of different birds she has seen in the vicinity of Rockport is now nearing the 500 mark. Her discoveries have attracted thousands of ornithologists and advanced bird watchers to her small section of the Texas Coast.

Connie Hagar was the first to find the snowy plover nesting in Texas. She was the first to report buff-breasted sandpipers and ash-throated flycatchers and mountain plover overwintering in the state. She was the first to see a cattle egret and the first to note a flamingo there. She discovered the state's first nesting pair of warbling vireos. She was the first to observe that blue-gray gnatcatchers migrate in waves down the central Gulf Coast. It was Connie Hagar who discovered that hummingbirds of nine different species—including some "not supposed to be in the state"—move southward through Rockport in the fall. Within a mile of her home, on three successive days in the spring of 1952, she observed what was unmistakably an Eskimo curlew, a bird generally considered extinct. Because, over the years, she has kept note of the numbers as well as the species, Connie Hagar's day-by-day observations provide an invaluable record in the study of the fluctuations in bird populations in the region.

At the end of our wanderings with *Autumn Across America*, on our way home from California, we had first met Connie and her husband, Jack. At the conclusion of our *Journey into Summer*, we had made the long swing south from Pikes Peak to spend another two weeks at Rockport. Now, in the midst of this last of our seasonal travels, we had come back again.

In the days that followed, on white shell roads, under live oaks bent by the sea wind, among oil wells, where bay-side houses were roofed with oyster shells, we drifted about in leisurely roaming, surrounded by birds from morning till night. No other state in the Union approaches Texas in the number of birds in its avifauna. Lying halfway between the two oceans, it is a place where eastern and western species, northern and southern species, overlap. Here birds of mountains and plains and sea intermingle. A century ago, John James Audubon, after visiting only the eastern part of the state, estimated that two thirds of all the species of birds inhabiting the United States could be observed in Texas. That prediction proved remarkably accurate. Dr. Harry C. Oberholser, in his exhaustive study of the bird life of this commonwealth, has listed more than 800 species and subspecies.

Situated at the foot of the plains and at the edge of the Gulf, Rockport receives wandering birds from both land and sea. It also lies at the small end of a vast migration funnel. During a single day in the spring following our first visit, Connie Hagar and Clarence D. Brown, of Montclair, N.J., listed 204 species seen between dawn and dusk. In the history of American bird watching, this stands as the all-time "big day" for two observers. Once, Connie told us, she counted 3,000 ruby-throated hummingbirds in her yard. Another year, upwards of 40,000 indigo buntings descended on Live Oak Peninsula, on which Rockport is situated. Each migration time, when birds pour south or birds pour north, Rockport provides a reviewing stand for one of the great avian parades of the world.

It was this fact that drew Connie Hagar to the spot. She was nearing fifty when she and Jack moved to Rockport in 1934. They came south from Corsicana, the northern Texas city christened by a man from Corsica whose wife was named Ana. It was there, in the high-pillared home of an eminent jurist, that Connie had been born on June 14, 1886. Early in her life her father interested her in nature. As a girl she set out to learn all the birds and all the wildflowers, butterflies and shrubs in her county, an area twenty-six square miles larger than Rhode Island.

Through the later events of her life—her musical education at the piano; the discovery of oil on her father's land, which opened up the first commercial petroleum field in Texas; her marriage to Jack Hagar, a New Englander who had come south selling automobiles and had stayed to invest in oil properties; her activity in numerous organizations; her prominence in Corsicana society—through all this Connie's interest in nature remained undiminished. She first saw Rockport in the early 1930's when a physician prescribed saltwater bathing for her sister. Brought up as she was on the dry, dusty prairie, the seashore and the lush bird life it supported were a revelation to her. The only water bird she was sure she recognized was the brown pelican. The next year she came back at migration time. And the following year, to the bewilderment of her friends, she left Corsicana for good and settled in Rockport. Twenty years later, one friend was still bewailing the fact that "with social eminence right in her lap, she threw it all away and went to live on the outskirts of a village *with birds!*"

To keep himself occupied, Jack bought the Rockport Cottages, a curving line of white cabins set amid palms and wind-tilted live oaks. Connie had stayed at these cabins on her first visit to the shore. At the time, the cottages were a mile and a half from Rockport, with only one house lying between. The community was so quiet, Connie recalls, that, except when it was mailtime at the post office, "you could shoot a cannon down the main street and not hit anybody." Since then, oil derricks have sprung up in the region and the town has doubled in population. Traveling salesmen and casual tourists were the earliest guests at the cottages. But as reports of Connie's ornithological discoveries spread, more and more bird people arrived. Each year at migration time, Rockport has not only an invasion of birds but an invasion of bird watchers. Visitors come from abroad, as well as from virtually every state in the Union. Many return year after year. The registry list of the cabins now is a veritable Who's Who of American ornithology.

Riding the roads of the Rockport region with Connie on successive mornings—to Redbug Corner to see a blackthroated gray warbler, to Tule Lake to watch gull-billed terns pursuing dragonflies, to the fishing piers of the Fulton Road where snowy plover fed on a low-tide beach— riding thus we heard, little by little, the story of her gradual mastery of the teeming bird life of the Gulf Coast. At first there was no one to help her, no one to consult. She used to wade in ponds in hip boots and a bathing suit, using a dip net to scoop young grebes from under water for close study in her hand. The only reference books she had were a small Reed's pocket guide with colored illustrations "some good, some terrible," and Arthur Cleveland Bent's *Life Histories of North American Waterfowl,* published by the Smithsonian Institution in Washington.

"I tell you, it was rough," she commented. "When Roger Peterson's field guide appeared, I felt let out of the cage!"

Inheriting a phenomenal memory from her father, Connie Hagar has had to make few notes. Once a detail of plumage or song or the habitual action of a bird has been observed, it seems indelibly recorded in her mind. This, in a way, is a great misfortune. The copious notes that otherwise would have formed a whole advanced bird guide were never written. For, through the years, in addition to noting the more obvious field marks, she has concentrated on all the fine points, on all those innumerable little mannerisms and differences that set similar birds apart and enable the skilled observer to recognize them instantly as we recognize a friend coming down the street by the way he swings his arm or holds his head. Such things Connie has recorded, not on paper but on the tablets of her memory.

The winter dawns at Rockport come with soft, delicious, scented air, like June dawns in the north. This is the season of the three-month calm, the time when the trade winds, the benders of the live oaks, no longer blow in from the sea. Almost on the dot of seven each morning, Connie starts off on her six-mile circuit. She has learned that she can see more and alarm birds less if she stays in her car with the motor running. Many of her comments along the way come back in recollection. We passed a farmyard swarming with birds of common species. ("Isn't it comforting to be able to look out there and say to oneself: 'I know all those birds'?") We saw a small dead animal on the road ahead. ("Never run over a dead animal. It may be a skunk.") We passed a hall where a weekly bridge club met. ("They don't understand why I won't join them. When I was forty-five I quit being a child and I refuse to return to childish ways.") She hummed a snatch of a tune as we rode along. ("Every morning I wake up with a different tune running through my head. Sometimes it is a patriotic song, sometimes a hymn, sometimes an Irish jig. This morning it was 'Pretty Redwing.' ") We stopped to study a bird that a friend of hers had long wanted to see. ("When I find a bird somebody else wants to see so badly, I feel as though I had gone to the circus and left the children at home.")

By eight Connie was back, crossing the cattle guard at the entrance of the long drive to the cottages. During the rest of the day, on roads now grown familiar, Nellie and I drifted this way and that, our hours filled with birds. This was the winter season. Yet here we were surrounded by concentrations and varieties of species hardly rivaled at home in the midst of the spring migration.

For nearly ten miles, beside shallows where herons and egrets feed, a shore road follows the winding edge of Aransas Bay. Along its length we sometimes came upon as many as 300 willets massed in a light-gray shoal where they rested on some barely submerged bar. Again we would see a hundred black skimmers in buoyant flight, their long bills cutting the surface of the water. Or we would stop to watch a marbled godwit, with food in its bill, twist and dodge and finally elude the running pursuit of ring-billed gulls.

Out in a dripping world, after a deluge of "Texas dew" one afternoon, we came to the edge of the bay just as the dark, swollen sky beyond was cut by the glowing arch of a rainbow. Beneath its curve, across the yellow-tinged water of the wind-roiled shallows, great blue herons stood hunched against the gusts, their forms extending away in long curves that, like a series of surveyor's stakes, marked the course of hidden sandbars.

Not infrequently as we followed this shore road in the sunshine, we stopped and walked about, examining the unfamiliar plants. I remember the beauty of the coral bean, its pods opened to reveal the brilliant red seeds that Indians once collected and used for making necklaces. Several times we stooped over a ground-hugging plant for a closer view of its leaves. They were round as coins and of several sizes. Children, playing store, use such leaves for money. The colloquial name for the plant is "nickels, dimes and quarters."

All across Texas, a host of other picturesque names have been bestowed on the wild plants of the state. They run from angel's trumpet, dry whiskey, dew flowers and careless weed to shame vine, barometer bush, love-in-a-puff, fluttermill, baby slippers, cloth-of-gold, lazy daisy and kiss-me-and-I'll-tell-you. On one published list that Connie let me read, I found frog fruit, good mother, tiny Tim, big-drunk bean, nimble Kate, Polly-prim, sunbonnet babies, poor man's patches, prairie lace and widow's tears. Such colorful local names represent a rich addition to our language.

Day after day, at one point along the shadows of this bird coast, we used to come to a halt to watch the antics of a reddish egret. It was the clown of our three-ringed circus. Like an awkward child burlesquing a ballet, it performed a ludicrous dance. It leaped into the air, seemed to clap its heels together, landed off balance, staggered drunkenly, minced backward a few steps, fell forward, stabbing wildly at the water. All the time it peered about with its head held at odd and comical angles, its crest feathers raised like a shock of unruly hair. Usually, during this dance, a ring-billed gull circled low or a willet edged nearer. For by playing the fool in the shallows, the egret in reality was stirring up food on the bay bottom. More than once, its wild stabbing brought it a prize.

To do justice to the Rockport region, to the fascination and variety of its wildlife, even a Texas-sized chapter will hardly suffice. Memories come crowding back, memories of tree snails strewn like white pussy willows along the branches of a bush, of a glittering metallic green scarab beetle plodding down a rangeland cattle path, and of a centipede, red of head and nearly half a foot long, flowing over the ruts of a dirt road. In that curious area of low mounds known as the Pimple Prairies, we watched sandhill cranes leaping high and parachuting down on partially opened wings, already beginning the strangely graceful, airy dance of their spring courtship. Not far from the spot where Connie had seen the Eskimo curlew, we looked out across the bay one morning and beheld nearly a thousand redhead ducks floating in long rafts on the water. Another time, without changing position, we had five species of plover within focus of our glasses.

Individual birds return in recollection. On one particular sandbar, a pugnacious little ringneck, a semipalmated plover that apparently considered the bar its private preserve, dashed endlessly this way and that, scattering smaller sandpipers and even launching an attack on an alighting willet, a bird twice its size. Each day, we saw the same vermilion flycatcher perched on a duck blind before a large live oak, standing out against its dark background like a glowing coal on a green hearth.

There were some mornings around Redbug Corner, on the way to Rattlesnake Point, when birds were so numerous and so active that branches all around us seemed jumping and vibrating with their alighting and taking off. Our eyes encountered species we had never beheld before. Connie pointed out black-crested titmice and gray-tailed cardinals. Farther afield, we saw such life-list species as white-rumped shrikes and white-tailed hawks and—out near the Tin Barn and the Lard Road, which a rain turns into gumbo—mountain plover, killdeer-sized birds with white foreheads and white showing under their wings as they flew. In the excitement of those hours I found myself referring to "Bedbug Corner," saying "cottontails" when I meant cattails, and even, as Connie and Nellie always afterwards agreed, talking about somebody's "bird guide to the mammals."

For nearly fifteen years, until his death in 1959, Patch, a black and white terrier, was Connie's companion on every trip she made. He was a bird watcher's bird-watching dog. More than once, he called Connie's attention to some hidden bird beside the road. And in the spring, when great flocks of willet suddenly reappeared and flew, a thousand at a time, over the Rockport Cottages, it was his habit to race and bark until she came out to see them.

Almost invariably when distinguished visiting ornithologists climbed into the car at the start of their first trip with Connie and Patch, they would glance in his direction. Their expression said:

"Is *he* going along?"

Then they looked resigned: "*Well, here go the birds!*"

But at the end of the trip they viewed Patch with a new expression. Usually they commented:

"I never saw such a quiet dog."

Bumps in the road made him bark. Red automobiles and garbage trucks drove him into a frenzy. But in the presence of birds he remained still and quiet. He never gave chase unless Connie clapped her hands, a signal that she wanted the birds put up in order to study them in flight. At the time of his death, Patch, without doubt, had seen more species of birds—and more species of bird watchers—than any other dog in history.

Because his life was filled with a long succession of visitors who came, stayed a few days, then disappeared, he made friends slowly. Sometimes he took a dislike to a stranger and spent the whole ride sitting in the front seat growling. Fortunately, he seemed to take to Nellie and me. I say fortunately, because I long suspected that Jack Hagar gave visitors the dog test. He tended to like people, but the ones he liked best, I felt, were the ones his dog liked too.

In the early days when Connie, pioneering in this area of avifaunal riches, began sending lists of birds she had seen to the celebrated Dr. Harry C. Oberholser, of the U.S. Fish and Wildlife Service in Washington, D.C., that careful and exact scientist became worried. She was seeing birds out of their range, birds nesting where they were not supposed to nest. He made a special trip to Rockport. All day long, as he and Connie drove about the country, he would interrupt the conversation with "What bird is that?" or, shooting out a forefinger, demanded: "Identification!" By evening, he was satisfied with Connie's care and competence and thereafter became her sponsor among professional ornithologists.

One morning, near the end of our stay, Nellie and I followed a cattle path beside Copano Bay, half a mile from Rattlesnake Point. We were looking for a new bird, the Sprague's pipit. Near this same spot, on another morning, we had watched five coyotes, probably a family, hunting jackrabbits in a pack, like a group of yellow dogs. After we had seen the pipit—small, striped and buffy—we were returning well content when a commotion at the edge of the bay attracted our attention.

A dozen white pelicans were thrashing the water with their wings. Hidden behind clumps of mesquite, we watched through our field glasses. In a ragged line, the huge birds advanced upon the shore. Their beating wings drove the fish before them. By the time the line of pelicans closed about the mouth of a small baylet, its water was swarming with prey. Then the feast began. Over and over, the birds dipped their heads and lifted them, their pouches bulging with water and fish. Other birds joined the banquet. Cormorants and egrets, both snowy and common, came flying. With the white pelicans wheeling like stately battleships and the white egrets darting about like small destroyers, they reaped an abundant harvest. For the first time in our lives, by that morning's good fortune, we were witnessing the famed cooperative fishing of the white pelicans. I remember we rode home, that day, puzzling over the mystery of how such closely related species as the white and brown pelicans could have evolved fishing techniques so different, one diving in individual hunting, the other obtaining food by cooperative endeavor.

Nearly 20,000 times, Connie Hagar has made her six-mile circuit of the roads of her four-by-seven-mile tract at Rockport. She has traveled within it in excess of 100,000 miles. This small foothold in the immensity of Texas has provided her with an interest that has never waned. When people invite her to make trips elsewhere, she always replies that she will as soon as she knows all there is to learn at Rockport.

How many hundred thousand persons do you suppose we talk to in the course of a lifetime? How many billion words do we hear spoken? Yet, how few are those we remember. One short sentence, only five words long, ending in a question mark, has returned to my mind innumerable times from our days at Rockport. For it condenses Connie Hagar's outlook. It explains the endurance of her enthusiasm.

I had commented on the fact that at Rockport you see rare species often enough and you see them in sufficient numbers to become really acquainted with them. You see them head-on and tail-to and from the side and top and bottom. You observe their characteristics. Elsewhere, after diligent search, you might find a single specimen of a rare species and see it only in a fleeting glimpse.

"The beauty of Rockport," I concluded, "is that here you have *enough* birds."

To which Connie replied:

"Are there *ever* enough birds?"

Giant Beavers

MIDWINTER, the halfway point between the beginning and the end of the season, had come and gone while we were on the Texas coast. A drifting, Indian summer quality had characterized the warm days of Rockport. Now, turning northward, we braced ourselves for a sudden leap into the deep freeze of ice and snow and winter wind. But, as we learned long ago, on such a trip as this events rarely occur exactly as we anticipate them. Instead of cold, we met warmth; instead of a deep freeze, we encountered a heat wave. Across the Gulf Coastal Plain, onto the Edwards Plateau, over the high prairies beyond, we rode with a soaring thermometer. We shed our coats. We opened all the car windows. We saw the mercury climb close to the ninety-degree mark. Almost as far as the Oklahoma line we were surrounded by a February thaw, Texas-sized.

About ten o'clock on the second morning, we crossed the Red River into the red land of Oklahoma. Almost suddenly, the far west seemed left behind. On every hand, as we advanced, we were reminded of the midwestern country we knew in childhood. Blue jays screamed in the hardwoods. Sycamores appeared in the creek bottoms. Once more we heard the nostalgic sound of midwestern spring and summer days, the clear, whistled song of the eastern meadow lark. The fascination of the strange—desert and mesa, canyon and Gulf Coast, creosote bush and saguaro—had been succeeded by the attraction of the familiar. During the next few days, as we advanced through Oklahoma and Arkansas and on into Missouri, the impression strengthened that we were coming home, that we had returned to a land we knew.

IN THE SUMMER OF 1843, when John James Audubon ascended the Missouri River in a fur-company boat loaded with 10,000 pounds of gunpowder, a trader at Fort Union told him that the largest beaver he had ever encountered weighed sixty-one pounds. Nearly 120 years later, on December 2, 1960, a farmer named Henry Mullins trapped a beaver weighing virtually half as much again on a tributary of this same river near Otterville in central Missouri. Its length was almost five feet, and it weighed ninety pounds.

A few years earlier, on December 12, 1956, a beaver weighing seventy-two and a half pounds was taken on the Roche Perce River, less than fifty miles from the capital of Missouri. On March 19, 1953, Clyde Ramsey, of Hazelgreen, trapping along the Gasconade, caught a female beaver that tipped the scales at eighty-eight pounds. It held the record until Mullins' catch seven years later. The average beaver weighs about thirty pounds. I handled the skull of Ramsey's animal and examined the huge cutting teeth, orange in front and yellow behind, when I called at the Missouri Conservation Commission to inquire about the giant beavers taken in recent years.

At one time, the beaver was almost extinct along the lower reaches of the Missouri River. Today it is common. It is found in all the tributaries as well as in the main stream. It lives in the Moreau River within the city limits of the capital. A beaver weighing sixty pounds was caught, a few fears ago, less than five miles from Jefferson City. Mike Milonski, of the State Conservation Department, showed me one den in the north bank of the Missouri within sight of the dome of the state capitol.

For nearly 100 miles, Milonski and I rode up the river and along its tributaries to view the work of these animals. In this region almost all are bank beavers. Instead of building dams and lodges, they burrow into steep banks produced by the undercutting of the river currents. The largest beavers are always found in areas of ample food, in cottonwood bottoms and where corn land runs down to the river. However, plentiful food is only a contributing factor, not the entire explanation for the larger animals. For other beavers, with exactly the same foraging opportunities, may stop growing at a weight of less than thirty pounds. No matter how ample the food supply, the animal never exceeds its individual potential for growth. Nor do the larger beavers belong to a special race. Individual beavers, like some human beings, are just larger than others. A strain of giantism appears to have cropped up among these aquatic animals of the lower Missouri.

The next morning dawn came slowly. The sky, overcast and dark, pressed low. Cold rain began falling as I left Nellie snug in a motel room on the outskirts of Jefferson City and started for Otterville. On a farm somewhere in that region lived Henry Mullins, the man who had seen and handled the ninety-pound beaver.

For fifty miles I rode west, up the Missouri. The gray falling rain added to the gray of the winter hills, the sodden cornfields, the stream-side sycamores. When I came splashing into Otterville, all of its 400 or so inhabitants were indoors. The streets were deserted. Outside a fur-niture store I spotted the one telephone booth in town. But when I looked under "M" in the directory, I found no one named Mullins. For a time I circled about on puddle-studded streets seeking the post office. When I discovered it, it was closed and empty, in the process of being repainted and renovated. Eventually I traced the temporary post office to the rear of a grocery store. Henry Mullins, I learned, no longer received his mail from Otterville. He was on another route, out of Smithton, five miles farther on. There, at the local feed store, where a dozen farmers in overalls and muddy rubber boots were swapping news on this rainy day, I received conflicting directions until the pro-prietor appeared.

"He can tell you," the farmers chorused.

He did. Go back to an orchard. Turn left on a county-line road. Go to a crossroads. Keep going to the second mailbox. That was it. It seemed easy and simple. But when I swung off on the county-line road, I stopped. It was unpaved, a road of soaked dark-brown earth. And I had already had experience with Missouri mud. However, the surface of the road seemed fairly solid, and there were fresh tire tracks coming out. So I started gingerly ahead.

The road rose and fell. In each hollow I came to, the mud seemed a little deeper. But my cleated snow tires, the tires that had caused so much comment in Death Valley, carried me through. As I neared the crossroads, a bluebird and a cardinal, flying almost side by side, ap-peared and disappeared. That fleeting glimpse of gay plumage gave a momentary brightening to the gray and misty landscape. The country grew wilder. It seemed more lonely and remote. I met no one, saw no one. Some distance beyond the crossroads I came to the first mailbox. On it red letters spelled: JOE MULLINS. A hundred yards beyond, a second mailbox bore in black letters the name; H. W. MULLINS. Opposite it wheel tracks led through a gateway. They dipped down a wide stretch of meadow, forded a stream, then lifted steeply up the slope beyond until they reached a weathered farmhouse set far back among the fields.

I looked for a long time before I started down. If I got across the stream, I would be all right. With sheets of water fanning away on either side and tires biting into mud and gravel, I shot across and reached the solid ground. All was well. At the top of the rise, I entered a narrow lane, made a right-angle turn around the house and came to the barnyard. Now there was no turning back. One low, wet spot lay ahead. All the rest was higher ground. My luck had held so far. I rushed the spot, hit it with spraying muddy water, and then, with wheels spinning, sank to the floorboards in the soft glue of the Missouri mud.

I climbed out. Nobody was in sight. Nobody came to the door. The rain fell with a soft, steady patter on the roof of the car. For a long time after I knocked at the farmhouse door, nothing happened. Then a woman in her seventies appeared. I asked for Henry Mullins.

"He can't come to the door," she told me. "He isn't well. He's in bed."

"I was interested in the big beaver he caught."

"Oh, that wasn't this Henry Mullins. That was our grandson. He doesn't live here. He's in the woods today cutting posts."

I looked at my white car splattered with mud and anchored fast in the barnyard.

"I'm afraid we can't help you any," the woman volunteered. "We are old and my husband is sick. There isn't anybody else here. I guess you'll have to just work your way out as best you can."

A few minutes later, as I stood in the rain looking at the car hopelessly mired, her husband, an elderly man with an immense white handlebar mustache, appeared from the farmhouse. He leaned on a post and surveyed the scene.

"There's only one thing to do," he told me. "Go to the next place." He waved toward the distant roof of Joe Mullins' house peeking above a hilltop. "They have a tractor. Maybe they can pull you out."

I started off with my raincoat collar turned up and my hat pulled down. The winter air was chill but not piercingly cold. The winter rain fell steadily but not in a deluge. Ascending the slope, I found it dense with dripping weeds. Before I was halfway up, I was soaked above my knees. Water sloshed in my shoes. For this higher ground, instead of being comparatively dry, was a running sheet of water. From top to bottom, a network of intertwining rivulets covered the hillside. Once, almost at my feet, a woodcock flew up from among the weeds of the sodden ground.

I was a long time making the climb. The house seemed to recede before me. It was nearly noon when I came out into a muddy barnyard where rusting machinery stood about in the rain. There was another long delay before anyone answered my knock on the farmhouse door. Then a girl of about ten explained that there was nobody there to help me. Her parents had gone to town. When would they be home? About two o'clock she thought. That frail—and, as it proved, ill-founded—hope buoyed me for a long time that day. Did any other farm around have a tractor? She didn't know. However, she thought the place back down the road might have one. How far was it? Oh, not so far. To keep warm, I decided to continue to be active, to find another tractor if I could, but at least to keep walking until her parents returned. I headed down the rutted and muddy lane toward the road. It was a long, long lane.

On the road, the mud under my feet had a particular greaselike quality. It did not ball up beneath my feet as had the mud of the black river bottom. But it let my feet slip at every step. Ascending the rises, I slid back almost half a step at the end of each forward stride. Stopping at the crest of each successive elevation, I scanned the fields around. No house was anywhere in sight. I was alone, the only human being in all that wide, deserted, dripping landscape. The sole sign of life I saw for a long time was a sow and a litter of small pigs lying in the mud of a fence corner. I paused to look at them, then plodded on. The rain increased as I advanced.

Slipping at every step, my progress was slow. It was almost one o'clock when I came to the crossroads. Now there was no bluebird, there was no cardinal. But down the side road to the right I glimpsed a house. As I drew nearer, plodding through the mud, I saw behind it well-kept farm buildings. But most important of all, under the protection of an open shed there stood, on huge mud tires, a bright-red tractor. My troubles were over! With high hopes I knocked at the door. I knocked again. I knocked and knocked and knocked, unable to believe my bad luck. Nobody was home. On this rainy winter day, every farmer in the region seemed to have gone to town.

For a long time I stood on the farmhouse porch, leaning against a post, staring at the rain, listening to it drumming on the roof, regaining some of my energy. Then I started back toward the intersection. Just visible over a hill down the side road to the left, I saw the ridgepole of another house. I plodded toward it. Water raced beside me down the ditches on every descent. When the house came into full view, I saw that it was well-painted. The farm buildings were substantial. Wires led in from poles along the road. I was thinking in terms of telephones, of the possibility of calling a garage in Otterville, seven miles away, for a tow car—of at least letting Nellie know where I was. Then I neared the house. A large, recently installed picture window stared from the front. But behind the glass I could see no furniture. The room was empty. I circled to the back. Each window revealed an empty room. The whole house was empty. At the rear I found piles of pipes and lumber. I had come to an uninhabited house, a house in the process of renovation.

Now I was completely discouraged. Slowly I retraced my steps to the crossroads. Nobody seemed to dwell in all this drenched and deserted land. I turned left along the county-line road in the direction of the far-off hard-topped highway. I could see a higher rise down this road and decided to climb to the top on the chance of sighting a house somewhere beyond. For what seemed an interminable time I struggled in the rain, slipping and sliding in the mud. From the top of the hill I swept my gaze in a great circle over the landscape. The expanse that met my eye contained nowhere a single sign of human life except wheel tracks leading away down the muddy road and the fences that bounded the immense and desolate fields. I turned away. I seemed bewitched, isolated, in a nightmare, inhabiting a land as barren of life as a moonscape.

It was now long after two o'clock. Only the thought that the Mullinses might be back from town lightened the great burden of discouragement I carried as I struggled on the slippery footing of the mud back along the county-line road, back to the crossroads, up and down over the interminable rises and descents.

My hope, my sole hope, now was pinned on their return, on the tractor I had seen dripping with rain in the barnyard. I remembered the Old Country saying: "Every mile is two in winter." In my mind I added: "And every mile is ten in winter mud." I walked slowly, moved mechanically. My feet now dragged as well as slipped. I counted my steps as I walked: "One, two, three, four, five," and then began again, distracting my mind from my predicament. I imagined myself coming back down this muddy road in a liberated car. I imagined how good it would feel to be back on the hard-topped highway again. I imagined what it would be like to be taking a hot shower and eating a hot supper. How far away they seemed!

I was about halfway to my destination when I heard the sound of an automobile. Where, I could not tell. It is curious how, in our day, the noise of a machine is the familiar indication of human life. When hunters are lost in the Maine woods, chain saws are now set going to guide them out of the forest. The sound of the car grew louder. A green Plymouth station wagon lifted into view over the crest of the rise ahead. A young farmer in a heavy jacket, rubber boots and a leather hunting cap sat at the wheel. At my uplifted hand, he slowed to a stop.

"I'm mired down in a farmer's yard," I told him. "Do you know anybody with a tractor to pull me out? I was looking for Henry Mullins, the man who caught the big beaver."

"*I'm* Henry Mullins," was his reply. "*I* caught the beaver."

It developed that he lived with his father, Joe Mullins, next door to his grandfather. He had come home early from cutting posts, intending to go to town by a back road. If he had done so, he would have missed me entirely. At home, his young sister had told him a man had called and was stuck somewhere in a car. Thinking it was a customer interested in buying his posts and that the car probably had skidded into a ditch, he had started off down the road.

So luck was with me after all. I climbed into the green car. We turned around at the crossroads and headed back.

"That tractor," he volunteered, "is tricky. Sometimes it starts. Sometimes it doesn't. I don't know what it will do in this rain."

Then came the most encouraging words I had heard all day.

"If it doesn't start, we can always hitch up the horses."

Rocking and splashing up the muddy lane, we came to a stop beside the weathered International Harvester "Farmall" tractor. As soon as we climbed out, we were surrounded by more than a dozen hunting dogs. They had been in the woods with Mullins. Mainly they were coon dogs and foxhounds.

Starting the balky tractor proved to be much like cranking a giant old-fashioned outboard motor. Mullins wound a hay rope around the belt wheel used in sawing wood. Then, with the end of the rope in our hands, he, his eleven-year-old brother and I pulled, as though in a tug-o'-war, running through the mud, spinning the wheel, turning over the big engine.

Once we ran. Twice we ran. Three times we ran. Over and over, panting, we splashed through the rain and mud without eliciting a cough from the engine. I began to look to see if I could catch sight of the horses. Then we tried once more. With the first sound it made, the engine took hold, thundered, never halted, never sputtered, never ceased its clattering uproar. I have rarely heard a more welcome sound that its ragged thunder. Mullins flattened out a cardboard carton and put it as a dry cushion on the metal bucket seat where a pool of water had collected. His brother climbed on the framework beside him and I climbed up on the other side. So we started off down the field of dripping weeds which I had climbed hours before.

One small front tire was almost flat. But the great mud tires on the rear wheels drove us, bucking and slewing, amid the hummocks and ruts and mudholes along the way. Behind us trailed the hounds. I looked back. Strung out in a long pack, they padded along, lifting their heads to the sky. Their mouths were open. They were baying on our trail. So, with the tractor lurching and the mournful voices of the hounds rising and falling behind us, I interviewed Mullins on his capture of the giant beaver.

He was twenty-eight, rather gaunt and Lincolnesque, friendly, deliberate of movement and speech. It was on the second day of his second trapping season that he caught the ninety-pound fur bearer on the

Maine River, about four miles from his home. Corn land bordered the stream. For several years the beaver had been growing fat, feeding in the fields at night, clipping off the cornstalks and carrying them back to the water like succulent saplings. In one cornfield it had cut away an extensive open area like a clearing in a forest. A beaver in a cornfield, Mullins declared, will do more damage than a dozen raccoons. On the morning he caught the giant animal, he had two other beavers in his traps. They weighed about thirty pounds apiece. The largest other beaver he ever caught weighed forty-nine pounds.

The pelt of the big beaver was rather coarse. It brought only about twelve dollars. What happened to its skull is still a mystery. One of the Conservation Department men called a week or so after the capture to see if he could get the skull for the collection at the capital. For hours he and Mullins hunted everywhere without turning it up. After he had skinned the beaver, Mullins had thrown the carcass to the dogs. They had gnawed on it, worried it, dragged it "every which way," crunched up or buried the bones. All remains of the skeleton had disappeared.

While we had shouted back and forth, question and answer, lifting our voices above the clatter of the tractor and the long-drawn baying of the hounds, Mullins had steered a winding course down the slope, avoiding the worst stretches. Now, in the barnyard, he wheeled into position, hooked on a chain and slowly dragged my car to higher ground. Eventually I was turned around, headed out, hauled to the entrance of the lane and pointed down the hard slope toward the road. When, in saying good-bye, I paid him for dragging me from the mud, Mullins mildly remonstrated:

"I never took anything for helping people out!"

Going back down the muddy road where I had walked with so much labor, back to the highway, free at last, I switched on the heater in a white car now plastered and mottled with dark Missouri mud. The rain slackened in the late afternoon as I drove east in my wet clothes through fifty miles of hills mantled in mist. I realized how lucky I was. I might still be mired down, still seeking help, with night falling on my moonscape of mud. I felt like a small boy determined never to run away again. But, even then, I remembered the fairyland beauty of feathery grasses spangled with droplets of water, which I had stopped in the rain to enjoy. For still another time, as I rode home from my adventure, my mind flashed back to Alice. Hers had been a kindred emotion when, in the midst of the complications of Wonderland life, she had declared:

"I almost wish I hadn't gone down the rabbit hole—and yet—and yet—"

The White Squirrels

FOLLOW the sun. Follow the moon.

This we had done when we rode west across the continent to meet the fourth season at the Silver Strand, beside the Pacific.

Follow the roll of the earth.

This we were doing as we zigzagged east with the winter. Almost a hundred times, during our journey, the globe would revolve in this direction, each time carrying us toward an earlier sunrise. A minute a day, the hours of light were lengthening.

But, during the days we traced a wandering path across lower Illinois, closed-in skies hid the sun, delayed the dawn and hastened the dusk. We rode in gray light across a drenched, muddy, misty world, across the flat black land of the winter cornfields. Where lowland meadows were cut by little streams, cattle stood knee-deep in ground mist. In this time of February thaws, ditches brimmed and puddles everywhere mirrored in a dull sheen the somber light of the clouded sky.

It was in this section of the trip that Nellie began concentrating on the "fieldmarks" of automobiles. It was a mystery to me, I had pointed out, how anyone able to note slight plumage differences in sparrows and warblers and shore birds had difficulty telling a Ford from a Rambler or a Chrysler from a Buick. Her explanation, not without logic, had been:

"The trouble is, automobiles keep changing their plumages."

When we neared Mt. Carmel on the Wabash River, a flurry of fine snow was sweeping across the empty cornfields. Like the ditches, the Wabash was brimming. It flowed past Mt. Carmel, wide and muddy, its waters flooding the lowlands to the east. A century before, all this stretch of river and swamp had been part of the life of a remarkable boy whose name later became famous in American ornithology.

The son of a pioneer druggist, the first of ten children, Robert Ridgway was born at Mt. Carmel two days before the Fourth of July in 1850. When he was only four years old he made his first drawing of a bird. By the time he was ten, he had assembled a private museum of nests and eggs and was producing accurately colored paintings of the native birds. In his effort to record the exact hues of the feathers, he ground pigments and combined them with gum water of his own manufacture in a back room of his father's drugstore. Many years later, this early interest in colors was to reach its culmination in his famous *Color Standards and Color Nomenclature*, which contained examples of 1,115 named hues, each produced by hand-mixed pigments. The process of creating them consumed a full three years. This work is recognized as one of the great milestones in the standardization of colors and their names.

One summer, when the water of the Wabash was abnormally low, the cargo of a sunken river steamer, the *Kate Sarchet*, was salvaged near Mt. Carmel. It included a rusty rifle. To provide the young ornithologist with a collecting gun of his own, Ridgway's father had the barrel bored out and the weapon transformed into a percussion-cap, muzzle-loading shotgun. By following a formula found in an old book, Ridgway mixed together chlorate of potash, yellow prussiate of potash and white sugar to manufacture his own gunpowder.

Knowing nothing of taxidermy or of preparing bird skins, he had no way of preserving the specimens he collected except by painting pictures of them. When he was fourteen, bright-colored songbirds, such as he had never seen before, appeared in numbers one winter around Mt. Carmel. He named them the "roseate grosbeaks." Their identity remained a mystery for months. A neighbor suggested he send his painting to the Commissioner of Patents in Washington. The Commissioner, who knew nothing about birds, turned the drawing over to Spencer Fullerton Baird, then beginning his brilliant career at the Smithsonian Institution. Baird identified the bird as a purple finch. He suggested that young Ridgway send him drawings of any other birds that puzzled him. So began the most important correspondence of Ridgway's life.

Less than three years later, when he was still not quite seventeen, he returned home one March day, after climbing to the nest of a red-tailed hawk, and found a letter from Washington awaiting him. Baird offered him the position of zoologist on a U.S. expedition being sent to explore the fortieth parallel from the eastern slope of the Sierra Nevada, in California, to the eastern slope of the Rockies, in Colorado. Thus, about the middle of April 1867, Ridgway broke home ties. Driving with his parents to Olney, some fifty miles to the north, he boarded the first train he had ever ridden on, his destination the nation's capital.

Later he remembered that, at frequent intervals, in stretches of still primitive forest, the wood-burning engine stopped to load on fuel stacked beside the rails. The Fortieth Parallel Expedition, led by the noted government geologist Clarence King, embarked from New York in a side-wheel steamer bound for Panama. A similar craft carried the party up the Pacific Coast to San Francisco. There the group headed inland for two years of scientific exploration.

When this adventure ended, Ridgway returned to Washington to illustrate and prepare scientific descriptions for the monumental five-volume treatise on North American birds being written by Baird and Dr. Thomas M. Brewer of Boston. At the age of twenty-four, he was appointed Curator of Birds at the Smithsonian Institution. Only two other museums in America at that time had salaried officials in charge of a department of birds. For several years young Ridgway lived in one of the red-brick towers of the Smithsonian building and during more than half a century, until his death in 1929, he remained a member of the scientific staff of this world-famous institution.

Quiet and unassuming, he turned out a vast body of valuable work. He published more than 13,000 pages of material on birds. Two genera, twenty-three species and ten subspecies of birds were named for him. He was one of the founders of the American Ornithologists' Union. Between 1901 and 1919, eight volumes of his *Birds of North and Middle America* appeared under the imprint of the Smithsonian Institution. This was his magnum opus. It was hailed as one of the greatest works on systematic ornithology ever written. For it Ridgway received the Brewster Medal of the A.O.U. and the Daniel Giroud Elliott Medal of the National Academy of Sciences.

During all the years that Robert Ridgway worked in Washington, far from the Illinois country of his boyhood, he said he felt he was in prison. The sensitive, living man inside the shell of his reputation was, he once confessed, "homesick for forty-five years." In 1913, he could stand it no longer. He returned to Olney, where he had boarded the train that originally carried him away. There, with his wife, he settled down at Larchmound, a pleasant, elm-shaded home on the south side of town. Arrangements had been made for him to continue his Smithsonian work in these congenial surroundings.

The road that carried Nellie and me into Olney next morning follows the line of an ancient buffalo trace. Olney, thirty miles west of the Wabash, has a unique distinction. It is The City of the White Squirrels. No other community in the world contains so many albino gray squirrels. Hundreds climb among the trees or race across the yards. The insignia of a white squirrel adorns the shoulder patches of Olney policemen. It appears on the sides of Olney fire engines. It is part of the highway signs that welcome visitors to the city.

In Olney we found Lee and Ida Cantwell, two friends my books had brought me. Laden with facts about the white squirrels and Ridgway's Larchmound, they had driven down from their home in Mattoon, Illinois, to spend the day with us in the midst of our final journey with a season. We joined forces on a white-squirrel safari.

How did the Olney albino colony originate? Various answers to that question have been advanced. The volume on *Illinois* in the American Guide Series even suggests that the white squirrels may have been introduced by Robert Ridgway. However, the correct story seems to be the one published in the *Olney Daily Mail* and inserted in *The Congressional Record* for Tuesday, July 14, 1959, by Congressman George E. Shipley. It gives credit to Thomas Tippit, of Olney.

When we all called on Tippit, later that afternoon, I found him to be a small, erect, spry man in his seventies. He recalled the arrival of the first white squirrels, about 1902, when he was fifteen. A farmer brought a pair of albinos to town and, for nearly a year, they occupied a cage in a window of Jap Banks' saloon on Main Street. When they were no longer wanted as an attraction, Tippit's father—a newspaper editor and one-time mayor of Olney—told him and his brother to hitch up the cart, get the animals, and turn them loose in the wooded stretch beside their house.

In Tippit's woods, the white squirrels multiplied. They spread out into the parks and backyards of the city and into the surrounding country. An informal census has placed their present number at between 600 and 700. Although they may interbreed with ordinary gray squirrels, for some unexplained reason the strain of albinism is dominant. Since 1925 a city ordinance has prohibited trapping, killing or shipping away any of the white squirrels. In 1943 the Illinois state legislature passed a law protecting the famed Olney squirrels. In this community, as *The Congressional Record* summarizes it: "The children love them, the people feed them, the Chamber of Commerce advertises them, and the law protects them."

Before the 1925 city ordinance was enacted, white squirrels were shipped to a number of other communities. Yet, in no other place did they obtain a foothold. Only in the region of Olney have they been able to thrive. Why so high a percentage of the offspring here should be white is still a riddle. But all over town, as we drove about, we encountered the albino squirrels. Even in the dull light of the overcast day, they were strikingly beautiful as they raced up the trunks or leaped among the branches of the bare winter trees.

The tree in which we saw the greatest number of squirrels was a lofty elm that overhangs the eastern side of the house at Larchmound. Five of the white animals climbed among its branches. As many as a dozen have been observed at the same time in this one tree. Ridgway used to sit at the bay window that overlooks the base of the elm and watch the squirrels and the birds that came to feeders he had fastened to the trunk. We looked out through that same window on a similar scene.

And later, when the Cantwells guided us to Bird Haven, the wooded tract a few miles north of Olney which Ridgway maintained as a sanctuary, we followed the same winding trails he had followed among the trees. The eighteen acres of Bird Haven held a central place in the affections of the ornithologist. On its rolling land grow more than seventy species and varieties of trees. As a boy, Ridgway had seen hundreds of swallow-tailed kites performing their incomparably graceful evolutions over the open prairie. In the summer of 1910, he observed the last of this species he ever saw in Illinois, a single pair passing over Bird Haven.

It is at Bird Haven that Ridgway is buried. In the fading light of that winter afternoon we walked along a trail through the woods, across a rustic bridge and up a hill. At the top, in the land that was dearest to him, Ridgway's grave is marked by a granite boulder. The bronze tablet on its side bears the simple inscription: "Robert Ridgway. 1850–1929."

Big Bone Lick

BETWEEN Beaverlick and Rabbit Hash, during a lull in the subsequent days of rain, we dipped on a muddy road into a small valley among the Kentucky hills. We were less than two miles from the Ohio River and twenty-three miles southwest of Cincinnati. Down the length of this valley extended the deep-cut serpentine of a creek. Joined by Dark Hollow Branch and Gum Branch and Beaver Branch, Big Bone Creek was nearing the end of its flow and its juncture with the Ohio. Held within a loop of this stream, a stretch of boggy ground contains a spring where bubbles, rising through murky, chemical-filled water, continually break on the surface of a pool eight or ten feet across. As we stood beside it, amid the dead winter vegetation of the low ground, a faint sulphurous smell filled the air.

Each time Nellie and I have looked forward to one of our extended seasonal trips, we have listed all the things we have long wanted to do, all the sites we have long wanted to visit within the portion of the country we would traverse. High on our winter list of places we especially wanted to see with our own eyes was this Kentucky hollow. For, years before the first white settlers came to "the dark and bloody ground," this out-of-the-way valley was known in the capitals of Europe. It appeared on maps of the New World as early as 1744. In that year Jacques Nicholas Bellin, the French cartographer, exhibited in Paris his pioneer map of Louisiana. On it the site of this salt spring was noted as "the place where they found the elephant bones in 1739." To Benjamin Franklin the valley was "The Great Licking Place." To pioneers it was "The Jelly Ground." To the Indians it was "The Place of the Big Bones." To paleontologists it is "The Graveyard of the Mammoths." To geographers it is "Big Bone Lick."

The world first heard of this remote valley more than two and a quarter centuries ago. Twenty-five years before the beginning of the French and Indian War, during the reign of Louis XV, Captain Charles Lemoyne de Longueil, commander at Fort Niagara and later governor of Montreal, set out through the wilderness to explore the valley of the Ohio River. As his birchbark canoe drifted downstream between the Licking and the Kentucky rivers, his Indian guides told him of a small swampy stretch up a side stream where the ground was strewn with immense bones. According to a legend of the red men, they were the remains of a fabulous race of giant white buffaloes that, long ago, died from drinking the salt water of the springs.

When De Longueil reached the valley, that summer day in 1739, he found a quaking bog impregnated with salt. All across it and around its edge, bleached white by the sun, projected tusks and leg bones and skulls of mammoths and mastodons. These Ice Age elephants had been extinct for thousands of years. Some of the Big Bone tusks measured eleven feet in length. Some of the teeth weighed ten pounds. Some of the leg bones were big enough to use for tent poles. Men sat on vertebrae as on small stumps. What De Longueil saw in this wilderness valley—as Dr. Willard Rouse Jillson, formerly State Geologist of Kentucky, puts it in his book, *Big Bone Lick*—was "the greatest natural depository of the bones of the great Pleistocene mammals that man's eye has ever beheld in any part of the world."

For ages the bog had formed a baited trap. The huge beasts, coming for salt, had mired down in the gluelike ooze and, dying, had left their skeletons in the little valley. The bones of more than 100 mammoths and mastodons are said to have been taken from this one spot. They form prized accessions to the paleontological exhibits of leading museums of the world, in London and Paris and New York and Washington. The great French scientists Cuvier and Buffon studied these prehistoric bones when they reached Europe from the wilds of America. Thomas Jefferson, when he was President, reserved a special room at the White House for the 300 items of his private collection of fossils from Big Bone Lick.

We looked about us with intense interest when we reached this graveyard of prehistoric monsters. The valley itself is only a few hundred acres in extent. Wooded hills of uneven height rise around it. On a slope to the north a few houses and a white church mark the site of the village of Big Bone (pop. 20). In the days of the pioneers, the "jelly ground" of the quaking bog extended over several acres. Today the swampy area around the salt spring covers perhaps an acre or less. With us as we stood there were William Fitzgerald of Florence, and his wife, Anne. Fitzgerald, the only authentic Kentucky colonel of my acquaintance, had been one of the prime movers in setting aside the spring and the surrounding area—so rich in its historic and scientific associations—as the Big Bone Lick State Park. At the time of our visit the initial grading and construction already had begun.

A week or two before, a sudden melting of the snow on the surrounding hills had sent a torrent rushing down the twisting bed of the Creek. Bushes on both banks tilted downstream. Winding in and out among these bushes, each with its burden of flood deposit, we gazed down into the greenish water of the creek and examined the steep banks as we advanced.

For in such a millrace of water, scouring and cutting into the blue clay of the lower banks, prehistoric bones may be brought to light. During summer, when the water is low, Fitzgerald sometimes walks barefoot in the mud of the stream bed in search of fossils. One of the best finds he ever made, a huge vertebra that once formed part of the backbone of an Ice Age mammal, was uncovered in this way. When he kicked what he thought was merely a soft ball of mud, he discovered there was a fossil inside. After lying for thousands of years in the ground, these recovered bones are always dark, almost chocolate in color. For some reason one bend in the creek, where elm trees overhang the water, has proved an especially rich hunting ground for fossils. It was here, in 1960, that Ellis Crawford, Director of the William Behringer Memorial Museum of Covington, discovered the jawbone of a mastodon. In a cornfield just north of the stream—where we saw a flock of twenty robins flying, calling, hunting for food in the wet ground—a farmer turns up fragments of bones with each spring plowing.

The fossil lode at Big Bone Lick is far from exhausted. During the summer following our visit, the first large-scale scientific excavations ever attempted in the valley began under the direction of Dr. C. Bertrand Schultz, paleontologist and director of the University of Nebraska State Museum. Working at a leased five-acre tract just north of the creek, the team of scientists removed more than 60,000 cubic feet of surface soil and recovered approximately 2,000 bones during the first season of a five-year project. Eventually they may descend as deep as twenty feet into the fossil-bearing blue clay beneath. All the uncovered bones are being taken back to the Nebraska laboratories and subjected to scientific tests to determine their age.

As we looked around us for a final time before leaving—at the valley, the winding creek, the surrounding hills—I considered all that long parade of visitors that had come to this place of ancient bones before us—Indian hunters, English traders, French *coureurs de bois*, scouts and trappers, settlers pushing west into the wild "Kentuckie Country," frontier scientists, ladies and gentlemen of fashion. Here in the 1750's Mrs. Mary Ingles, known as the first white woman in Kentucky, had escaped from her Shawnee captors and had begun her wilderness odyssey of hardship that eventually carried her home to Virginia. Here the Father of American Ornithology, Alexander Wilson, had delighted in the flashing colors of innumerable Carolina paroquets—a bird now extinct. Here in 1841 that eccentric naturalist of the frontier, Constantine Samuel Rafinesque, had arrived in search of prehistoric bones. Here, the eyes that had been the Rockies and the faraway reaches of the Columbia River, the eyes of Captain Clark, had searched the ground for fossils. Here Gen. George Rogers Clark and his leather-stockinged Indian fighters had replenished their provisions. And here, at the height of his fame, Sir Charles Lyell, the English geologist, had arrived on a pilgrimage to this remote bit of land so closely linked with prehistoric times. They all had been part of the long and varied pageant that—like ourselves—had been drawn to this one small and still secluded valley.

High Water

THE month of February—"February the short, the woorst of al" as an old English writer described it—had almost reached its end. Off the Silver Strand, gray whales were plowing northward again. And here in Kentucky, melted snow and days of rain had raised the water level of all the creeks and branches.

As we moved eastward along our wandering course, the rhythm of night and day had subtly altered. At first imperceptibly, then noticeably, the nights had grown shorter, the days longer. The tide of light was flowing in. The tide of warmth would follow.

South of the Ohio, in the latitude of Kentucky, the earliest signs of the midwestern spring were already apparent. We passed a woman, with a brown paper bag in one hand, digging dandelions beside the road. Between the showers, children were flying kites. And one night when we slept in Hardin County, the birthplace of Abraham Lincoln, the frog chorus from the flooded lowlands reached *fortissimo*. The frogs call. The lambs arrive. The birds return. This is the way the spring comes back.

In such a pre-spring spring—but well aware of how swiftly the late-winter weather could change—we turned south to Mammoth Cave and Bowling Green and Goodletsville, across the Tennessee line on the old Natchez Trace. It was there that Alexander Wilson first saw the birds he named the Nashville and the Tennessee warblers.

In falling rain we stopped at Transylvania College at Lexington, Kentucky, once the home of that ill-starred genius Rafinesque. In rain we splashed along the buffalo trace that leads to Blue Lick and, in rain, we rode across the fertile Bluegrass region, that land of racehorses, white-fenced pastures and country mansions. The rain still fell—the late-winter rain, the father of floods—when we mounted the long bridge over the Ohio at Maysville. Flotsam, gleaned from lowlands down hundreds of miles of riverbank, spotted and streaked with lines and swirls the brown water sweeping past below us.

Toward the close of that day, the downpour ended. Openings, ragged and temporary, were torn in the western clouds and the glare of a smoky winter sunset tinted the lonely bluff top along which we walked. We had come some twenty miles north of the river. We were in the hill country of southern Ohio. Below the sheer drop of the cliff that formed the western edge of the bluff lay the curving arm of a creek. Looking over the edge, we followed downward with our eyes the trunks of great sycamores rooted on the stream banks. Behind us, paralleling the lip of the cliff, extended the folds of an immense earthen serpent. Nearly a quarter of a mile long, this work of unknown hands, of a forgotten race of men, is one of the most celebrated of all the relics of the ancient Mound Builders.

From the Great Lakes to the Gulf of Mexico and from the Atlantic to the Rockies, explorers and pioneers encountered the varied earthworks of these Stone Age Americans. Some are round or square or rectangular hillocks. Others take the form of birds or serpents or beasts. Among the latter the most famous is this serpent mound near the community of Peebles, in Adams County, Ohio. Running down the 1,348 feet of its winding length is a central core, or backbone, of stones. Over the stones are ranged layers of different soils, first gray clay, then yellow clay mixed with stones, then dark soil supporting the dense sod that forms the green skin of the serpent. The average width of the body is about twenty feet, its height from four to five feet. Recent evidence indicates that the mound dates back to about the beginning of the Christian era. For nearly 2,000 years, this titanic reptile of earth has appeared to be dragging its length up and down over this rolling bluff top. Still debated is its original purpose, whether it represented a symbol of religious significance or a showpiece to wonder at, a kind of Eiffel Tower of primitive times.

When pioneers settled in the Ohio Valley, forest trees had engulfed the narrow ridge and the effigy mound along its top. Later, when the forest had been cut and second-growth trees had sprung up again, a tornado swept directly over the bluff, leveling the woods at its top. The present state of preservation of The Serpent Mound is largely due to the work of one man, Frederic Ward Putnam, of Harvard's Peabody Museum of American Archaeology and Ethnology. Through his efforts, in 1886 about $6,000 was raised for the purchase of the site. During the three succeeding summers Putnam and his assistants, living in tents on the bluff top, cleared and restored the area. In 1900, Harvard University deeded the site to the Ohio Historical Society. It is now maintained as a state memorial.

In the stillness of the winter sunset, after the days of rain, we wandered down the length of the winding mound. We heard the monosyllabic "check" of a passing redwing, the "peter-peter-peter" of a tufted titmouse and, faraway, the excited barking of a dog chasing a cottomtail. Then there was silence again. The sounds, the silence, the sky flaming a darker red, the chill at the end of the February day—all these were parts of a timeless world, features of other ages as well as of our own. We could imagine ourselves in that remote period, beyond the threshold of written history, when this earthwork was raw and new, when an unknown race of men completed their task and left their mark on the earth to tell other races of men, unknown to them, that they once had lived.

How many years went by before its completion? How many men and women contributed their days of strength to the labor? Their names are unknown. Their history is forgotten. But this work of their hands remains, more permanent than the victories of Napoleon. What in the lives of modern man will endure so long?

Among those mounds of the Old World, the barrows on the heaths of England, W. H. Hudson—as told in *Hampshire Days*—and Richard Jefferies—as recalled in *The Story of My Heart*—spent hours contemplating, in imagination, the existence of the primitive men whose hands had raised those tumuli. To both came the emotion of being very close to the builders who had known the earth in another, long-ago time. So, in the stillness of the winter sunset on this ridgetop in Ohio, I felt very close to those ancient men who had chosen a spot so beautiful for their master labors. Remotely distant, infinitely far removed from life today, they too, perhaps, had been stirred by sunsets, by all the beauty of the scene outspread below this eminence.

As we advanced down the writhing length of the earth-serpent, we saw how the inside of each curve imprisoned a half-moon of collected water. A pool had formed where the open jaws grasp a mass of rocks, supposed to represent an egg. Below the vertical western face of the ridge, water spread out over the lowland from the creek, catching the light of the sky, glowing with tintings of red between the branches of the sycamores. Everywhere the ground was soggy and streams were overflowing. All across the countryside around us, each twisting rivulet and creek was hurrying its water toward the same destination, the brown expanse of the Ohio.

Next day we turned south and east toward this same destination. Our general plan was to follow for 150 miles upstream the wanderings of the northern river bank, from Portsmouth to Ironton and Gallipolis and Parkersburg. It had been days since we had last seen a paper and we rarely listened to the radio. We had never experienced an Ohio River flood. So we drove lightheartedly on.

Our first surprise came when we reached U.S. 23, which follows the Scioto River south from Chillicothe to Portsmouth. Beyond the highway as far as we could see stretched a tan-colored lake of muddy water. The rising Ohio had backed up this tributary, and miles of lowland were already flooded. Not long afterwards, a highway truck blocked the road ahead. Beyond it, the concrete dipped downward and disappeared entirely under water. We shunted off onto a detour that eventually brought us out on U.S. 52, the main highway along the Ohio. We came to Portsmouth over a bridge only a few feet above the rising flood.

Down side streets, as we rode through town, we glimpsed the great concrete flood wall that rose high above the lower windows of the factory buildings. Beyond Portsmouth, roadmen were flagging down cars and turning them off onto a rough, muddy, pothole-riddled detour that was to carry us "a little way around a hill." The little way extended itself interminably. And the hill seemed to us a mountain.

After bumping along for almost ten miles, going around the hill, we found ourselves back on U.S. 52 not far from Hanging Rock. At Ironton we crossed back to the Kentucky side and, in the early twilight, in falling rain, came to Ashland. There we got the last motel room in town and settled down to read the alarming headlines and flood news in the local paper.

More rain was predicted. The crest of the flood was expected to reach sixty feet. Telephone service had been knocked out. Communities were cut off. Floodgates were going in at all the river towns.

Pumping stations had been turned on in Ashland and across the river at Ironton. This was our first taste of a real flood. Would we be cut off? Would our trip be delayed? We pored over maps that evening. Early in the morning, we decided, we would return to Ironton, double back and try to go inland away from the floodwaters of the river valley. Then, across higher land, we could head east for the upstream bridge to Parkersburg. Before we went to bed, we looked out. It was still raining. We went to sleep wondering what the morrow would bring.

The first thing it brought was more rain. We were up at five and away, after a hasty breakfast, at six. The sky, heavy, hanging low, trailed the slate-colored vapor of its clouds across the tops of the higher buildings. Morning papers were filled with flood and disaster. Crossing the Ohio, we noticed even greater accumulations of debris drifting by on the rising water. On the outskirts of Ironton, I pulled into a Sohio filling station. The owner, in a slicker and rubber boots, filled my tank.

"Can I get north on 23 this morning?" I asked.

"No. It's under water."

"How about 52 west of Portsmouth?"

"It's out. The bridge is flooded."

"Is there any way of going north?"

"No. There's only one road open out of Ironton. That's the one you came in on—52 going east."

Already backwater covered the open fields on either side and pressed close to the filling station. Creeping up the side of a nearby telephone pole, it had edged an inch or two higher since the station opened. This was not the flood as I had imagined it. There was no rushing torrent. There was no menacing sound. There was only the slow, still, steady rise of the tan-hued water. But soon the filling station would be surrounded. The water was creeping closer even while my tank was being filled. I was the last customer. The owner was locking up as we left.

We swung around and sped upstream, where the ever-widening river was leaving its banks. We passed the bridge to Ashland and got as far as Chesapeake, twenty miles beyond, before we met a barricade set up by highway workers. Ahead the road was flooded and impassable. But here a bridge carried us across to Huntington and the West Virginia side. Perhaps, if we could not go inland in Ohio, we could go inland in West Virginia and so escape from the river at last.

How about the road to Charleston? We might have trouble, we were told, but we should be able to get through. It had been open an hour ago. We started out. The trouble was that, in this hilly country, all the roads followed the valleys of tributary streams and they, too, were in flood. Waterfalls poured down the rock faces of the highway cuts. Time and again we slowed down to ford sheets of brown water fanning out across the roadway. At Barboursville, a bridge was under water and we negotiated another rutted and devious detour. Twice rock slides narrowed the road.

When we came to Milton, we found water from Mud River backing up into the town. A long row of houses, lower than the highway, ran like a chain of islands, each surrounded by water that rose as high as the porches. The red brick building of a consolidated school was set as though in the midst of a lake. Near it a jet trainer, a surplus warplane mounted on a concrete pedestal, barely cleared the flood. People were taking pictures, and schoolboys, giddy with freedom from classes, were calling:

"No pictures! Restricted area!"

On the far side of Milton the highway dipped and disappeared under water. Once more we detoured, zigzagging among back streets until we were released on the open highway again. A few miles outside of town we overtook a trailer truck loaded with new automobiles. The sight encouraged us greatly. Such a valuable cargo, we reasoned, would be transported with care. The driver apparently knew that the road ahead was open. Dark clouds still hung low but the rain had stopped. Three times in half an hour we encountered mud slides. Once, a good-sized embankment, rocks and soil, had come down, bringing a pine tree with it. But we were gaining altitude, going inland. The real threat of the flood had receded behind us.

Somewhere along our route we went through a Deerwalk and a Wolf Summit. Side roads stretched away, rutted and miry. Under the lowering sky, we turned east, winding among bare winter mountains, threading narrow valleys, coming out on great vistas of tumbled and rolling land. Sometime that afternoon we passed a side road leading to a community that had originally been called Molehill but that had changed its name to Mountain. By now, a parade of telephone trucks was passing us, hurrying toward the stricken areas.

The air grew colder as we followed mountain highroads toward Clarksburg and Grafton. At the top of one turn we found ourselves surrounded once more by trees encased in glittering ice. Not long after four o'clock that afternoon, we stopped for the night at Grafton. The uncertainty of the flood hours was past. High water was behind us. Roads ahead were clear. We slept soundly, free from worry, that last night in February. When we awoke, we were in the first day of the last month of the season. We tore the second sheet from the calendar of the year. Only three weeks remained of all our winter days.

Snowflake Country

WE stopped at the top of the hill. Outspread below us extended the wide lower valley of Lake Champlain. Beyond rose the Green Mountains, now white, lifting in a line of rounded summits like shining clouds low along the horizon. Our descent carried us into a land rich in history. Riding among apple orchards that ran up and over the lower hills, we passed Crown Point and Fort Ticonderoga. At the far end of Chimney Point Bridge, we entered Vermont, our first New England state. Now all the winter of the Pacific shore, the western deserts and mountains, the Gulf Coast, the Mississippi and Ohio valleys, the Appalachian highland and the Adirondacks lay behind us. Ahead remained the final days of the season drawing to its close in this northeastern corner of the land.

Among the drifts of the open fields, Vermont farmers were already spreading manure from their stables. Horned larks, and once a flock of more than a hundred redpolls, flew wildly down the road before us. Osier clumps, vividly red against the snow, rose above the ice of swampy tracts. The red of osier, the green of pine, the pale tan of winter leaves on sapling beeches, the blue of late afternoon shadows on the snow and the play of sunrise and sunset tintings across the mantled fields—such are the colors of a New England winter.

When, about noon, we reached the ice-locked marshes of the Dead Creek Waterfowl Sanctuary, I swung into a turnout beside the road. We sat in the winter sunshine eating our lunch. After a time, something white among the silvered branches of a distant dead tree caught Nellie's eye. We turned our glasses in that direction. The creature we saw magnified in the round windows of our binoculars had first tried its wings over the tundra of the Great Barrens of the far north. It was that large and striking bird of prey, a snowy owl.

The dead tree and the white owl had been left a dozen miles behind when we halted to look up a long lane toward a yellow frame house just north of Ferrisburg. Here had lived and worked Rowland Evans Robinson, one of New England's famed nature and regional writers of the last half of the nineteenth century. Born in the village of Ferrisburg in

1833 and dying there in 1900, he achieved most of the work on which his reputation depends after he had become blind. We looked around at the magnificent scene that extended away in the March sunshine—the lake stretching its unbroken plain of white toward the west and the Adirondacks rising beyond. To lose the sense of sight in such surroundings, in a land so beautiful, seemed an even greater tragedy, as when a vibrant bird is blinded. How much more was lost by becoming blind *here!*

In the best of his nature books, such as *In New England Fields and Woods*, Robinson reflected the evolution from hunter to naturalist. At first he was "the sportsman-farmer." His gun and the game he killed played prominent roles in his nature sketches. But with the passing of time the appreciator became ascendant. We find him writing "A Plea for the Unprotected" and "A Century of Extermination" and entitling one of his last books *Hunting Without a Gun*.

"Back and forth across the land, in swift and sudden alternation," Robinson noted in one of his essays, "the March winds toss days of bitter cold and days of genial warmth . . ." As he had known it long ago, we were now experiencing the winter of northern Vermont. This was March, the month of continual change. The sunshine spread its brilliance across the white fields as we drove north from Ferrisburg. But before nightfall the wind had veered. The smell of snow was in the air. I remarked this fact to the waitress who served us in a restaurant at Essex Junction.

"Snow!" she exclaimed. *"Who wants it?"*

Well, children do. Skiers do. Artists do. Plants do. Many kinds of wildlife do. And on a farm less than fifteen miles away, beyond Jericho, under the shadow of Mt. Mansfield, a man had lived who took such passionate delight in it that he devoted virtually his entire life to snowflakes.

When we turned in that direction the following morning, our wheels rolled through a two-inch blanket of white that had descended in the night. The road twisted among hills, then, with the highest of the Green Mountains lifting its white-topped bulk above us, it straightened out and cut across level land. About a mile farther on, I turned into a drive leading to a farmhouse set among shade trees. We saw a design painted in white on a dark triangle under the eaves. We had reached "the house with the snowflake on it."

I think that among the men who have lived in my time the one I most regret never having met is Wilson Alwyn Bentley, the farm boy who became world famous as the Snowflake Man of Jericho. The writer of the Book of Job asks the question: "Hast thou entered into the treasures of the snow?" No one has ever entered more fully into these treasures than the man who had lived under this roof in this remote section of Vermont. Although Bentley's education stopped at grade school, he was commissioned by the *Encyclopaedia Britannica* to write its section on snow and frost. Although his camera equipment was restricted to the barest necessities, and his money was always limited, his immense collection of snowflake photographs remains unsurpassed.

One winter day, eleven years after he was born on February 9, 1865, his mother let him peer through a cheap microscope at the fragile beauty of a snowflake. That was the beginning of his lifelong delight in these frail crystalline creations of winter, so delicate that a breath will cause them to dissolve and disappear forever. In 1885, when he was twenty, his mother persuaded his farmer father to buy him a compound microscope and a heavy studio camera. They cost about $100. As long as he lived, his father looked back on this outlay as an unnecessary extravagance. But for almost half a century afterwards, as each winter arrived, this same cumbersome outfit was set up in an unheated shed to record on large glass plates the magnified images of snowflakes. Every storm, for Bentley, filled the whole sky with falling jewels. Make haste as he would, he could catch and photograph but a minute proportion of the infinite number of separate and distinct designs. He congratulated himself all his life on having been born in northern Vermont where the snows are frequent and the types of flakes particularly varied. Vermont winters are long, but they were never too long for Bentley.

Everyone I talked to who had known the Snowflake Man described him as a quiet, gentle man, kindly by nature. His neighbors thought him a little queer, "chasing snowflakes in every storm." He was slight of build, only five feet, four inches tall, with a prominent New England nose. He never married. His was a poet's emotional response to the beauty of the snow. Long years afterwards he spoke with regret of one particular flake, one of the most beautiful he had ever seen, that broke before he could record its image. "But beauty vanishes, beauty passes, however rare, rare it be" and the snowflake is beauty in its most fleeting form. Its fragile ice shatters or melts away and no one will ever see its like again. Its design is lost forever.

Few flakes reach the ground in perfect condition. Often they bump or cling together in the air. Each descends according to its shape. Some spin, some drift, some slip sidewise. It was Bentley's habit, when a winter storm began, to stand at the door of the unheated shed, holding out a smooth board about a foot square and painted black. To prevent transmission of any heat from his mittened hands to the wood, he held the board by wire handles. Inside the shed, he examined the accumulated snow crystals through a magnifying glass, holding his breath as he did so. Damaged flakes were brushed away with a feather from a bird's wing. Perfect ones were transferred with extreme care to microscope slides. With the camera pointing toward a window, each picture was taken through the microscope with the light passing through the snowflake. A combination of wheels and ropes, formed from odds and ends, enabled Bentley to focus his unwieldly apparatus while watching the ground glass at the rear. There the images of the flakes appeared magnified from sixty-four to 3,600 times. Exposures were long, ranging between ten and 100 seconds. In this manner flake after flake was photographed during a storm.

Some of his finest photomicrographs were taken, three years after he had obtained his camera, during the famous blizzard of 1888. But of all the storms that he enjoyed, the one that brought him the greatest yield occurred forty years later, in February 1928. The snow began falling on February 9, his sixty-third birthday. Before it stopped he had added to his collection a hundred photographs of new snow crystals. He used to refer to them as a "birthday gift from kind winter." All of his glass plates, as soon as they were taken from the fixing bath, were washed in the ice-cold running water that flowed from a spring in his backyard.

Through his lifework, Bentley preserved in his photomicrographs the forms of nearly 6,000 snow crystals. Nowhere else is the immense prodigality of nature's innovation more vividly demonstrated than in the production of these creations of ice. In his nearly fifty years of searching, Bentley never found two of them alike. It was his belief that each snowflake is unique, that nowhere else on earth would another be found that would be identical. Yet it has been calculated that in a ten-hour storm a million billion flakes may fall on a single acre of land.

The pictures Bentley recorded at this remote farmhouse among these winter hills have been used in college textbooks. They have appeared in illustrated periodicals in many parts of the world. They have been employed in teaching science and art. They have been included in encyclopedias. Artists turn to them for inspiration. Fifth Avenue jewelers base designs on them. They are found in leading museums in many lands. To Bentley they brought such honors as membership in the American Association for the Advancement of Science and a fellowship in the American Meteorological Society. His magnum opus, *Snow Crystals*, prepared in collaboration with Dr. W. J. Humphreys, of the U.S. Weather Bureau, contains more than 2,000 of his finest snowflake pictures. It appeared in 1931, in time for Bentley to see and enjoy this climax of his half-century-long labors. He died three weeks later, on December 23, 1931.

Night in the Sugarbush

THE path we followed in the frosty night ascended a slope of moon-lit snow, vanished in the black shadows of a clump of evergreens, reappeared crossing the white glitter of another snowfield, and ended at the door of a long, low structure crouching beneath billowing clouds of steam that rose luminous in the moonlight. Five miles away Rudyard Kipling had written *The Jungle Book*. Two miles away John Kathan, the earliest settler in this part of the Connecticut River Valley, had encircled his cabin with a log stockade to ward off Indians. Half a mile away Murder Hollow Brook followed its deep gulch to join the river. Around us, in dark and immense columns, rose the trunks of ancient sugar maples. We were at Pine Grove Farm, south of Putney, in the oldest sugarbush in Vermont.

When we pushed open the door of the weathered building, warm, moist air swirled around us. We heard the roaring of a wood fire and another sound like the spatter of falling rain where maple sap bubbled in shallow pans. Two gasoline lanterns spread a diffused, watery light through the steam-filled interior. The humid air we breathed was sweet with the perfume of the boiling sap. For the first time in our lives we were in the midst of that fragrant annual rite that heralds the close of the New England winter and the coming of the New England spring— sugaring time, when maple sap is boiled down into the exquisitely flavored syrup that pioneers knew as "Indian molasses." Night in the sugarbush is a never-to-be-forgotten memory of winter in Vermont.

As we came in and closed the door behind us, a wiry man wearing a plaid cap and with his hands encased in thick leather gloves straightened up in the glare of the open firebox door. He was George Ranney, the owner of Pine Grove Farm. In quick succession he fed half a dozen four-foot lengths of wood into the flames. As a rule, he told us, it takes about five cords of wood to boil down 100 gallons of syrup. The most prized fuel for boiling sap is quick-burning slabs from a sawmill. But this year highway construction had provided free odds-and-ends wood that filled a large shed opening into the sugar house. The last stick to go in was an unusually crooked section of a tree limb. Ranney worked it inside among the flames and slammed the door.

"That," he remarked, "will straighten it out."

We had met him that afternoon when—to watch the gathering of the sap—we had driven down from Windmill Hill, west of Putney, with Edward H. Dodd, Jr. Ever since *Grassroot Jungles* days, more than a quarter of a century ago, "Tommy" Dodd and I have worked on books together. No other friend has opened so many doors going in the direction I wanted to go. As editor and later president of the century-and-a-quarter-old publishing house of Dodd, Mead & Company, he has played an all-important part in almost every manuscript I have produced. Where else, as in *Of Nature, Time and Teale*, has a publisher written a book about an author? On retiring early, when many kinds of life were open to him, he and his wife, Camille, had chosen the simple existence of the country year. Except for trips to the South Seas for a long-continuing study of Polynesian art and history they make their home in the Vermont hills, at the end of a country road, in a house built in 1776. Over the years, in many ways, he has become one of the most admired of all my friends. Together we had planned the four American Seasons volumes and now, in the fourth and final journey, together we were riding on one of its adventures.

Up the slope of a ridge and over the top ran the great maples of the sugarbush. In the sunshine of the afternoon, we followed sled roads plowed through the snow and winding among the trees. We had arrived, on this bright March day, during the excitement of a sap run. The clear, shining liquid, the "sweet water" of the Indians, was falling drop by drop into more than 1,900 metal buckets hanging from metal spiles driven into shallow holes bored in the tree trunks. Ranney told us each bucket holds about sixteen quarts. When full, it weighs more than thirty pounds.

Several times I lifted one of the hinged metal lids that keep out rain, snow, animals and falling bark and watched a quick succession of drops form at the tip of the spile. When I timed them, I found they were forming and falling at the rate of more than one a second. During the heaviest runs, they follow one another so rapidly that 150—even, for short periods, 300—have dropped into the buckets in a minute's time. A tree a foot in diameter may contribute thirty quarts of sap in twenty-four hours, and there are records of as much as eighty gallons of sap flowing from one taphole in a season. While the average seasonal yield of a mature sugar maple is about twelve gallons, the sap yield of exceptional individual trees has gone as high as 250 or 300 gallons. Where is the best place to tap a tree? That is a question endlessly debated in sugarbush country. On the south, or sunny, side; above the "instep" of a main root; on the lower side of a leaning tree; on the side where most branches grow and the bark is thickest—all these beliefs have staunch adherents.

Nellie and I caught some of the falling drops on our forefingers and licked them off. The sap was cold and refreshing, faintly but deliciously flavored. Draughts of this fluid allay the thirst of many a worker following his rounds among the trees. It may even, at times, provide a drink for weary horses. In pioneer times, when uncovered wooden buckets were used, it was a rule to hang them four feet above the ground. This kept deer and cows from drinking from them. When writing his classic *Sylva of North America*, François André Michaux noted: "Wild and domestic animals are inordinately fond of maple juice, and break through their enclosures to sate themselves; and when taken by them in large quantities it has an exhilarating effect upon their spirits."

From time to time we stepped aside to let a sturdy horse-drawn sled go by. On it rode a 1,000-gallon tank in which the sap is collected from the buckets and transported to a storage tank on the slope above the sugar house. On this same March day, all across New England and in New York and Pennsylvania and Michigan and north across the line in Canada, similar activity was in progress. As many as 20,000,000 sugar maples are tapped annually in this $50,000,000 winter's-end industry.

All maples have some sugar in their sap. But it is from the hard or rock maple, the true sugar maple, *Acer saccharum*, that the yield is sweetest and the flavor best. On the average, I was told, the sap of this tree contains about 3 per cent sugar. However individual trees run as low as one per cent or go as high as 12 per cent. For some unexplained reason, New Hampshire's famous sugar maple, "Sweet Sue," produces sap with three times the sugar content of that of similar trees that grow around it.

Not only from tree to tree and from grove to grove, but from run to run and year to year the richness of the sap varies widely. In a sugar-bush of a hundred trees, John Burroughs once wrote, there is as wide a difference in the quantity and quality of the sap produced as among that number of cows in regard to the milk they yield. Sometimes thirty gallons of sap will produce a gallon of syrup; at other times fifty gallons of sap will be required.

"How sweet is the run today?" I asked Ranney.

He did a little calculating and found that, although the flow was copious, the sugar content was rather low. He was having to boil away forty-four drops of water to obtain one drop of syrup.

The sugar that contributes its sweetness to maple syrup is synthesized by the leaves in summer and stored in the root systems of the trees in winter. About the beginning of the present century, studies carried on in Vermont showed that the total yield of sugar by a tree is likely to be roughly proportional to the area of its summer leaves. One characteristic of the trunk of a sugar maple is an abnormal abundance of sapwood. The cross section of one of these trees a foot in diameter is likely to show a central column of heartwood hardly thicker than a man's thumb. It is this feature of the trunk that speeds up the flow of sap and aids the tree in carrying nutrients rapidly to its buds as spring approaches. Yet the precise manner in which that sap moves upward is still imperfectly understood.

But to New Englanders the rising of the maple sap each year is like a rising barometer. Their spirits lift with it. "Sap's running" and "sugarin' time" are words of good cheer. They usher in a harvest time, a time of sugar parties in the snow, a kind of festival of winter's end.

"How often do runs occur?" I wanted to know.

They may occur, Ranney told me, from the middle of February to the first of May. The richest and heaviest flows come when the temperature seesaws violently, when frosty nights are succeeded by brilliant days, when the weather seems to leap from spring back to winter, then to spring again. "Sap weather" is a series of freezing nights and sunny days with the temperature standing, roughly, at twenty degrees at night and rising to forty-five degrees at midday. The sap ceases running if the thermometer falls below thirty degrees or rises to about fifty degrees F. Usually the strongest flows are brief, lasting from two or three hours to a day at most. During a season there may be one run or a dozen runs or only "drizzles." The weather, not the date on the calendar, is important in stimulating a run of sap. Everything depends on the weather—and that, in New England, is proverbially unpredictable.

Yet it is because of this changeable climate, as well as its latitude and altitude, that New England and especially Vermont and New Hampshire provide the right conditions for strong runs of sap. When sugar maples were introduced from America into Europe, where the climate is more uniform, the changes less sudden and excessive, sap runs of importance failed to materialize. The sweet and deliciously flavored syrup of the sugar maple is a product of North America alone. The great sap runs that characterize the end of the New England winter are peculiar to the New World.

Some sugarbushes now employ a maze of plastic tubing, letting gravity transport the sap directly from the trees to the sugar house. In a few places, on steep slopes where collection is difficult, Ranney has installed such tubes. But they have their drawbacks. Squirrels and porcupines sometimes bite into them, as they do into maple twigs, to get to the sweet fluid flowing within.

America, as we had seen in our travels through the four seasons, is the land of beautiful trees. And one of the most handsome of all is the sugar maple. With the flame of its foliage it ushers in the winter, and with the sweetness of its sap it draws the winter to a close. Near the far edge of the sugarbush we came to two immense maples growing side by side. They were encircled by twin necklaces of buckets. I counted fifteen catching the sap of these two trees alone. The larger the tree, the more buckets it will support; the more open its surroundings and the more sunshine its foliage receives, the richer the sap is likely to be. For years, Ranney told me, he has been cutting hickory and butternut trees and weeding out the poorer maples to open up his sugarbush. The same taphole is never used a second time. The opening is filled in by the tree in four or five years.

Not far from the twin giants, we came upon the remnant of another immense maple. It lifted its massive, shattered bulk, a gnarled and lichen-covered stub, to a height of perhaps forty feet. Its top had been carried away. Only the four lower branches remained. Great scars, made by the axes of pioneers in the crude early methods of tapping, extended as high as my head. Before the Revolution, this tree was producing a harvest of sweet sap. It is the last survivor of Vermont's first sugarbush.

The Indians, who had used such primitive means of obtaining sap as breaking off the end of a branch, had taught the men of the Massachusetts Bay Colony how to produce maple syrup. It is one of the oldest of America's agricultural products. In 1764, John Kathan's son Alexander—who built a cabin in a clearing on what is now Pine Grove Farm and lived there to the age of ninety-five—tapped trees of the virgin forest and boiled down the sap in an iron kettle over an open fire in the first recorded instance of the making of maple syrup in the state.

It was Kathan's habit to make small notations after dates in his almanacs. In March 1803 he wrote: "What a sight of pigeons did fly all the 13th"; on March 5, 1804: "Sea two robins"; in February 1811: "Killed 110 rats in the corn house in one day"; on July 22, 1811: "Had new tatoes"; on April 5, 1781: "A man and a horse crossed the river on the ice." How such simple entries bring the long-ago past to life! Earlier, in his historic note set down on March 19, 1764, Kathan recorded: "Tapped trees. Made 21 pounds of molasses."

A century and a decade later, in 1874, twenty-three of the original trees of this pre-Revolutionary sugarbush still were standing. By 1924 only four were alive. Now only this single venerable stub of a tree remained. Its four branches still put forth leaves in spring. It still tenaciously clung to life. But we were seeing it in the last days of its long, long span of years.

But other trees, descendants of those ancient maples of the virgin forest, still supplied an abundant harvest of sap. We saw it boiling and bubbling in Ranney's sugar house when we returned that evening. We watched the clear liquid flowing by gravity from the storage tank higher up the slope into the first of a series of four shallow, slightly tilted and interconnected boiling pans. It came in as colorless fluid and was finally drained away as amber syrup.

Ranney called our attention to the corrugations that run the length of the pans to increase their heating efficiency. At the elevation of the sugar house, the sap boils at about 220 degrees F. As it boils, it is moved slowly by gravity from one to another of the interconnecting pans. We noticed how the bubbles forming across the surface of the boiling liquid were first white, then more and more yellow or amber-tinted as the gradual flow advanced from pan to pan. Ranney's rig will boil about six barrels of sap into syrup in an hour.

In the first unit, where the fluid is thinnest, the boiling is most violent. As we peered into it, the sound of the bubbling suddenly rose in volume. The seething contents of the pan mounted toward the rim. We stepped hastily backward. Ranney said:

"I'll take care of that."

He reached calmly for a small container of cream and poured in no more than a drop or two. Almost magically the rushing sound subsided into a steady murmur. The small addition of fat had broken the surface tension. A little white of egg or a piece of salt pork dipped into the boiling sap will produce the same result. In all, as it becomes thicker and darker, the sap travels thirty or forty feet, boiling its way from pan to pan, before it is drawn off as syrup. To produce maple sugar, the thickening fluid is stirred or beaten while the boiling continues.

At intervals Ranney drank milk from a vacuum bottle, and his son Robert refreshed himself with water from a canteen. Sometimes during the long days in the sugar house, they boil eggs in the sap. For the duration of sugaring time each year, workers around the boiling sap lose all desire for sweets.

"I notice," Ranney remarked, "that I always crave sour food, pickles and dishes with vinegar in them."

Apparently, sufficient sugar is obtained from the inhaled steam. In fact, at the end of a long day during the boiling of a sap run, workers often observe that their eyebrows and eyelashes have become sticky.

Hour after hour in the night, the crackle and roar of the fire, the drowsy sound of the bubbling sap continued. Often either Ranney or his son added wood to the fire. Occasionally a great gust struck the sugar house and drove down swirling clouds of steam through the long, rectangular openings where two hinged sections of the roof had been folded back on either side of the ridgepole. When heavy rain falls, boiling is suspended and these sections are closed. Otherwise, too much rainwater would reach the pans. Just before a storm, when the atmospheric pressure is lowered, Ranney has observed that the sap boils noticeably faster.

Helen and Scott Nearing, in *The Maple Sugar Book*, tell of a Vermont farmer who wore a pedometer during a busy day in his sugar house. At the end of seven hours he found he had taken 29,090 steps. Ranney and his son seemed always occupied. They kept constant track of the boiling sap. They fed the fire. There was rarely a lull in their activity. The final pan received the most frequent attention. There the syrup was checked with a hydrometer to determine if it had attained the desired density. A time-honored, rule-of-thumb test is to pour some of the syrup from a ladle; if it tends to thicken and form an "apron" along the edge, it is ready to remove from the pan.

We watched Ranney, before he packed the hot syrup into waiting containers, strain it through felt-and-flannel cones to remove the gritty residue, largely lime deposits, called sugar sand or niter. We watched him hold up a sample of the syrup and compare it with the tinted liquid in a series of glass vials, grading it according to color: Fancy, A, B or C. Then he poured the batch of syrup, still hot, into the sterilized containers in which it is sold. Packing it while hot insures against fermentation. Also, in cooling, the contents contract slightly, leaving a vacuum which permits the syrup to expand in hot weather during storage. The filled cans formed rows, and the rows lengthened. Held within each container was the rich sweetness, the delicate flavor that had been extracted amid these clouds of fragrant steam.

Returning home from a visit to the New World in the eighteenth century, an English traveler reported that farmers in Connecticut made it a rule to leave one sugar maple at the edge of every field so that "in the heat of midsummer the weary reaper could tap the trunk and obtain a cool and refreshing drink." Such arboreal soft-drink stands, of course, represent a humorous misconception. Usable sap no longer flows when the maples are in leaf. As soon as the buds begin to unfold, the fluid loses its sweetness and becomes viscid. If collected too late in the season, the sap produces syrup with an unpleasant, rather bitter "taste of buds." Especially prized by connoisseurs is syrup made from first-run sap. It has a delicate bouquet and flavor unequaled during the later runs.

It was late at night when Ranney banked the fire and ended the long day's work at the sugar house. The next morning he would have to rise at 2:30 A.M. to supervise the machines that milked his 120 cows. Then by nine he would commence boiling sap again. The harvest of the sugar maples has to be gathered when it comes or, as Ranney put it:

"When the sap runs, we boil sap. It's work that can't be spread out to a more convenient time."

As we descended the moonlit slope, with Ranney's collie Cinderella Boots racing about in the snow before us, I saw a few far-scattered lights—perhaps marking the location of other sugar houses—glimmering faintly among the dark New Hampshire hills across the river. I turned for a last look at the low building crouching under its thinning clouds of steam, under its tall smokestack where a swarm of small sparks, like red fireflies, still whirled away to expire on the air or come down harmlessly on the snow.

Driving back to Windmill Hill along wooded roads, with a can of new-made syrup beside me, I noticed how my headlights picked out small, tan fluttering moths among the trees. According to an adage of the region, when "moth millers" become numerous, sugaring is almost over. In spite of the lateness of the hour when I went to bed, I lay awake a long time remembering all that I had seen. Never again would news that sap is running in New England be a mere item in a paper. Always now it would evoke memories of our experience, inerasable memories of the sights and sounds and smells of day and night in the sugarbush. Like the remembrance of the honking of wild geese flying north, they would form nostalgic links with the near approach of winter's end.

The Deer Yard

LATE in the afternoon, down a long last descent through the snow-filled forest, we came to Jackman and Moose River, in northern Maine. The Canadian border cut through the wilderness hardly a dozen miles to the north. We looked at the winter world of forest and frozen pond and evergreen-clad mountainside about us. Somewhere out there lay the deer yard we would visit. We wondered where. In the morning we would know.

THE WEASEL SQUATTED at the edge of the forest, its two tons of metal resting on wide caterpillar treads. We walked around it, the snow squeaking under our feet in the near-zero weather. Eight solid wheels, revolving in line, turned each endless tread. The rectangular, steel-walled box of the body, ten feet long and five wide, extended over the treads and rose almost as high as my chest. Above it a metal framework supported a roof and side curtains of thick brown canvas. Everything about this awkward-appearing vehicle was heavy, ponderous, rugged. It had been designed for use by the U.S. Army in the far north, in Greenland and Iceland and Alaska. But it could roll over mud and shifting sand as well as over snow. Weasels had lumbered across the soft volcanic dust on Iwo Jima. We looked at the vehicle before us, its faded red paint scuffed and scratched, and wondered what service it had seen.

After the war, Henry Duquette, owner of a Jackman restaurant, had purchased the Weasel as army surplus for winter travel in the forest. No matter how deep the snow, it rolls over the top, packing it down with its treads, making its own road as it advances. Such a road would carry us into the snow-filled forest to a deer yard that Tilford McAllister, game warden in the Jackman region, had been observing that winter. West of Moose River, beyond Gander Brook, near Burnt Jacket Mountain, it occupied a cedar—or arborvitae—swamp extending along the shore of a forest-rimmed lake about five miles away.

Duquette, a mild-mannered, soft-spoken man, took his place behind the steering levers and gearshifts of the driver's seat. He looked ahead

through the heavy glass of the windshield. At his right, a panel of in-
struments ran along the metal housing that enclosed the engine, a
ninety-five-horsepower Studebaker Champion. Bearpaw snowshoes,
ready for walking out of the woods in an emergency, occupied a rack
overhead. He switched on the ignition and stepped on the starter. The
motor ground, volleyed, settled into a steady roar as it warmed up.
Nellie and McAllister and I clambered into the rear where three bucket
seats were ranged side by side across the metal body of the Weasel.

With a metallic clatter of treads, we backed, swung about almost in
the length of the machine, and charged a six-foot wall of ice and snow
beside the road. The Weasel reared upward, then leveled off and
headed away across an open stretch of snow that funneled into the
winding white ribbon of an old logging road. We crossed Gander
Brook, locked in ice. All around us stretched an uninhabited winter
wilderness.

Ahead of us to the west, hardly six miles away now, the Canadian
boundary dipped down through the forest. To our left lay Little Big
Wood Pond and to our right, less than three miles off as the raven flies,
Crocker Pond with its cluster of quiet log cabins where we had spent
our vacations after each of the seasonal books was finished. This was
the country of Sandy Stream and Slidedown Moutain. We knew it
well, but only in summer dress.

All day, all night, the week before our Weasel ride to the deer yard,
snow had fallen. Fourteen inches piled up on the drifts already covering the forest floor. Everywhere we went, our treads unrolled the first
man-made tracks on this virgin snow. No human being had been this
way before us. No snowshoes had left their telltale marks on the new
drifts. Only the tracks of wild creatures of the forest were imprinted on
its surface.

As we advanced travel grew rougher. The Weasel reared and
plunged, yawing, slewing suddenly sidewise as we rode over large ob-
stacles in the way. But this machine was made to travel over rocks if
need be. We had been riding for about an hour when we came to a
forest hunting cabin, half buried in snow. Ahead rose a stand of cedars.
We had reached the edge of the deer yard. Duquette swung the Weasel
around in a pivoting turn, heading back the way we had come. Beside

the cabin he cut off the ignition. The sound of the motor, the clatter of the treads ceased. Instantly the great silence of the forest rushed in upon us.

"Haven't we sacred everything within miles?" I asked McAllister as we unloaded the snowshoes.

"No. That's a curious thing. Deer have become so used to power saws and logging trucks that they are less frightened by mechanical sounds than by the sight of a single man walking silently in the woods. In fact, where lumbering is going on, the sound of the power saws seems to attract them. They come to feed at night on lichen in the tops of the feeled trees."

For nearly a mile the cedar swamp followed the shore of the lake. It extended back into the forest about half a mile. It was here the deer had yarded. Each year, as soon as the snow begins to pile up in the north woods, these animals gather into bands—usually from six to thirty—and, choosing some area protected from the cold winds and provided with such food as twigs, bark, tree lichens and evergreen boughs, settle down for the winter. Most frequently cedar swamps are selected. In soft snow, the small feet of the deer provide little support. Individual animals flounder, almost helpless, in deep drifts. By banding together, trampling down the snow to a solid footing, they are able to get about, escape their enemies and reach food until spring releases them. Then the groups disband and scatter through the forest. How long they remain in their winter quarters depends upon the severity of the season. During mild winters, the deer may be confined to their yards for only a few weeks; during severe ones, they may remain there for three or four months.

Since that March day I have asked many friends what they thought a Maine deer yard is like. Most have described—what I had assumed and several books in my library imply—a large area trampled down as cattle pack down the snow in a barnyard. But wherever we went among the cedar trees, nowhere did we come upon such a scene. Instead we found ourselves in the midst of a maze of narrow, winding, interconnecting trails. Each was merely a rut in the snow only a few inches wide and perhaps a foot and a half deep. Traveling single file along such trails, the animals walked on solid footing. Sometimes large

concentrations of deer do trample down half an acre of snow and produce paths "as wide as Main Street." But most often a deer yard is
comprised entirely of such a network of narrow trails. Even when a
band is starving, the animals rarely make any effort to reach additional
food by breaking new paths through the surrounding drifts.

Although Nellie had never been on snowshoes before, she got along
amazingly well. McAllister broke trail and we started off. Both McAllister's and my webbed shoes had been made by Charles Holway, the
famous snowshoe-maker of Solon, Maine. Taking our time—sometimes
with Nellie along, sometimes, on the more rugged slopes, McAllister
and I alone—we followed the trails of the deer yard. They led us beside the pond, over rolling hills, along a nameless forest brook. One
path ended where this stream fell over rocks in a tumbling rapids. Here
deer had come to drink. At another point along the course of the brook,
the animals had used their sharp forehoofs to break a hole through relatively thin ice. Like birds, deer can also obtain water by eating snow.
Along each path twigs were nipped off as far as the animals could
reach. Even after the snow is gone in spring, the interconnecting trails
of such a yard must be clearly evident, blazed by the browsing of the
deer. Sometimes in summer, while paddling across a forest pond bordered by a cedar swamp, McAllister has noticed how deer in previous
winters have browsed as far as they could reach while standing on their
hind legs. The result has been an almost ruler-straight line running
along the lower branches of the trees.

As our snowshoes carried us over the drifts, around fallen trees, beside stumps crowned with high peaks of snow like inverted ice-cream
cones, past outstretched branches that seemed as hard as iron, we noticed in several places where the deer had walked beneath tilted tree
trunks that stretched no more than two or two and a half feet above
their trails. Sunk in these narrow ruts, with their chests level with or
below the surface of the snow, they passed with ease under such ob-
structions. Four or five times beside the trails we discovered round or
oval depressions in the snow. They were about a foot deep and roughly
the size of a dishpan. Here deer had slept. The animals seem to have
no special places for resting and sleeping in a deer yard. They lie down
wherever fancy dictates. The same place apparently is not used a sec-

ond time. The heat of the animal's body melts the snow in contact with it and leaves the bowllike depression lined with ice, making it unsuitable for later use.

When we returned to the cabin about noon, Duquette had a fire going in the potbellied stove. Lunch was ready. And we were ready for lunch. By then our 6 A.M. breakfast of pancakes and maple syrup seemed an event of the remote past. As we ate roast beef sandwiches and doughnuts and drank hot coffee, Duquette reported that while we were away he had measured the depth of the snow. On the level it was four feet deep. The greatest depth either he or McAllister could recall was seven feet.

We were buckling on our snowshoes again when the ringing sound of chopping, as though some lone woodsman were wielding an axe, came from the deer yard. A few minutes later, as we came over a rise, there was a flash of red and black and white and a bird as big as a crow disappeared among the trees. This was the woodchopper—a pileated woodpecker. We came to the stump where it had been excavating a deep rectangular hole in a search for carpenter ants. Spreading in a wide apron around its base lay a bushel or more of yellow chips.

Wherever we went along the meandering trails we were alert for the sight of a deer. Once, as I rested beside a fallen tree at the top of a slope, listening intently, I heard a snorting in the woods beyond. But whichever way we turned, the deer melted away before us, moving off down their interconnecting trails. They were warned of our approach by whispers of sound caught by their great, uplifted ears, by faint scents detected by their sensitive nostrils, by subtle changes in the tempo of forest life.

In the afternoon, the still air that had hung over the forest all morning began to move. The breeze freshened, became a wind. The trees around us were filled with long creaking and sudden rushing sounds. As we were heading back toward the cabin and neared the edge of the swamp where it meets the pond, we felt the strength of the wind increase. Rushing through the trees, the long gusts came in quick succession. They drowned out all sounds of our approach as we drew near the shore. Our scent was whirled away behind us. It was thus, without giving warning, that we came upon the deer.

They were sunning themselves at the edge of the trees, a doe and a buck. Bucks may, or may not, yard with the does during winter; in this instance they had. The two deer stood side by side. Their coats shone in the sun, their heads were held high. The winter had been relatively mild, and the animals had come through it in excellent condition. When we first caught sight of them, they were looking intently out across the pond. Their graceful forms, their uplifted ears, stood out against the immaculate whiteness of the level snow beyond. For perhaps two minutes they remained motionless. Then the buck swung his head in our direction. Some slight movement may have caught his eye, for with a great bound he whirled toward the trees. The doe followed. In three or four leaps, made with the grace characteristic of the deer family, they gained the woods and disappeared. On a previous visit, at this same spot, McAllister had watched a single-file parade of five deer following the edge of the pond.

Ahead of us, as the Weasel clattered its way back along the trail and out of the woods, every clearing was swept by luminous sheets of windblown snow. Already the deep tracks we had made coming in were disappearing. At the edge of the forest where we had started, we tilted down the snowbank, flattened out and came to a stop. We had seen the winter deer yard. And we had seen more. We had seen the beauty of the Maine forest in its season of snow. Bidding our companions good-bye, Nellie and I turned south toward the rocky headlands of the coast.

Coast of the High Tides

WHERE the Maine coast meets the winter sea in a boundary line of rock and ice, the shore is pierced by innumerable coves and inlets. It abounds in points and promontories. It is fringed with chains of rocky islets. So convoluted and broken is it that although the air-line distance, from Kittery on the south to Calais on the north, is only 225 miles, the length of the coastline is more than ten times that distance, 2,379 miles. This is almost twice the length of the shore line of California.

This was the coast we followed north in the final days of the final season. Nosing out onto promontories and curving around arms of the sea, we progressed along a shore armored with rock. Both geographically and scenically we were at the opposite extreme from the flat, sandy, sunny beach of the Silver Strand. There we had looked out on the silky swells of the early-winter sea. Here, where great tides rose and fell and where combers exploded and shattered in foam against the cliffs, it was the late-winter sea we observed in action. The four-foot snows of Moose River had been left far behind. In the milder climate and the saltier air of the coast, the white blanket covering the open fields was at most a few inches thick.

Somewhere in his writings, Maurice Maeterlinck maintains that: "The best part of traveling is the before and the after, the least pleasant is the traveling itself." But not for us on these journeys with the seasons. From beginning to end, it was the present moment, the present scene, the present beauty, the present interest that absorbed us. We experienced and enjoyed the hours as they came.

And never had the gift of the days seemed sweeter than in these closing hours of our long adventure. At times we resembled a child with an ice cream cone that is almost gone. We appeared trying to save every minute as we followed this winter coast that is known to millions of visitors only in summer months.

Everywhere the sea dominated the land. Its influence was reflected in such place-names as Head Tide and Starboard. Near its mouth, we crossed the Penobscot, a river born in the north woods near Sandy

Stream. We passed snowmen melting in village yards, redpolls seed-hunting among the alders, logging trucks bouncing along, mud-spattered and decorated with necklaces of tire chains draped over their front bumpers. On our right, toward the sea, we saw the snow-covered bulk of Mt. Cadillac, rising to a height of 1,532 feet in the Acadia National Park, the highest point on the Atlantic coast north of Brazil.

All this we saw in the light of lengthening days. The sunset that had brought to a close that short December afternoon along the Silver Strand had ended a period of sunshine only nine hours and forty-eight minutes long. At White Sands, sunrise and sunset were ten hours and ten minutes apart. By the time we reached the Vermont sugar bush, the period had extended to eleven hours and thirty-nine minutes. Here along the Maine coast we were nearing the time when day and night would be equal and then, as spring advanced, when the days would be longer than the nights.

One old New England custom I had read about as a boy was having mince pie for breakfast. We decided that for once in our lives, when we came to Maine, we would do as the New Englanders do. But we found the New Englanders no longer do it. Pie for breakfast seemed unheard-of. So we contented ourselves with what no doubt was a better diet, an old-fashioned lobster supper at a restaurant beside a cove. While we ate, a woman at another table observed to her companion:

"She never seems to realize that as you get older your circle keeps getting smaller."

We ate on and as we dipped bits of lobster into melted butter we ran over in retrospect varied things we had overheard in restaurants along the way, fragments of conversations, not infrequently compressed expressions of human attitudes and experience.

In a California town: "Christmas is the worst time in all the year when you are poor."

Among the foothills of the Rockies: "The view *is* beautiful but my wife keeps telling me: 'You can't eat the view.' "

On the Texas coast: "I know people hate him. But one time he explained it all to me. He said: 'This is what I was faced with: Would I have a lot of friends or half a million dollars?' "

Near Cherryfield, while crossing the Narraguagus River, we looked to the north and saw a large bird with stiffly outspread wings soaring in wide circles over the woods and open fields. Even without our glasses we perceived its head and tail were white. It was a mature bald eagle, a bird we had last seen 1,200 miles away, where the Illinois River joins the Mississippi. Later, from a restaurant overlooking the bay on the main street of Machias, we sighted a second eagle—or, possibly, this same bird—descending in a long curving glide to the top of a distant tree. I pointed it out to the waitress. Her immediate reaction was:

"Is that a sign of spring?"

All along this northern coast, thoughts of the new season were uppermost in everyone's mind. Its arrival was now hardly more than forty-eight hours away. When tomorrow had become yesterday, winter would be gone. Everywhere we went, as we advanced up the coast, we saw news of spring published by pussy willows shining above the snow, by later sunsets, by children playing ball and skipping rope in school-yards. The owner of a filling station remarked, as a sign of the season, that there appeared to be more cars on the road—or, as he put it, "more cahs on the rudd."

This same highway that we followed, in the spring of 1833 had carried John James Audubon by carriage and mail coach to Eastport and the beginning of his voyage to Labrador. Along this route, in another season of the year, more than a century and a quarter later, we passed the turnoff to a community with the picturesque name of Med-dybemps. Better a thousand times, to my way of thinking, a Med-dybemps or a Cat Mousam Road than all the stereotyped "News" of the New World, than all those innumerable New Viennas and New Berlins and New Lisbons that are so familiar to our maps.

Near the top of the coast, on our way to Eastport, we dipped into the valley of the Dennys River. Under ancient elms on the farther slope, a large yellow house caught our eye. Under its roof had lived Thomas Lincoln, the adventurous young man who had accompanied Audubon to Labrador. Ten thousand miles and more away—as we had traveled—beside the Sonoita River, on the Mexican border at Patagonia, we had seen the handsome little Lincoln's sparrow that had been named in his honor.

As we had progressed north along the Atlantic coast, we had seen the range of the tides increase. At Baltimore, Maryland, on Chesapeake Bay, the average range between high and low water had been only one foot, one inch. At New York City, it was four feet, five inches; at Portland, Maine, eight feet, eleven inches. When we circled Carry-ingplace Cove and came to Eastport, on Passamaquoddy Bay—only half a dozen miles from the easternmost point of land in the United States, West Quoddy Head—we found ourselves in the presence of one of the great tides of the world. Here, at its ebb, the water had dropped more than eighteen feet from the level of its flood. At Calais, Maine, less than twenty miles to the north, the range is even greater, as much as twenty-three feet, and to the east, at the head of the Bay of Fundy between Nova Scotia and New Brunswick, a combination of certain as-tronomical conditions may produce tides in the Minas Basin with the record range of fifty-three and a half feet, a rise and fall equivalent to the height of a four-story building.

From this coast of the high tides, on June 6, 1833, the 106-ton schoo-ner, *Ripley*, sailed north with Audubon and his party. One of the birds Audubon observed at Eastport before his departure was "the Bonapar-tian gull." On this March day, we watched this smallest of American gulls sweep in buoyant flight above the incoming tide. Black-headed in mature breeding plumage, it was now, in winter, white of head, with a single round spot of black behind its eye. A few bufflehead and black duck and surf scoters rode the waves among great rocks shaggy with seaweed. Eiders fed farther out, among the offshore islands. In dark contrast to the white of the gulls, a small band of crows hunted along the tide line. Here, too, were a few ravens. When winter comes, each year, there is a noticeable movement of these larger birds from the interior to the coast.

Across the rise and fall of the great tides, hardy water birds easily survive the cold. But when winter gales come raging in from the sea, particularly those from the southeast, they often carry pelagic birds from the open ocean far inland. All along the upper coast of Maine, after such a storm, the bodies of dovekies are sometimes found scat-tered across the snowcovered fields and even in the woods. A year or two before, when the weather cleared after an onshore gale, a horned grebe was encountered walking down the main street of Dennysville.

I talked to one veteran outdoorsman of the region about these winter birds. He proved to be a cautious Down-Easter given to qualifying his statements. He would say: "fully one-half—well, let's say one-fourth" or "as many as 1,000 eiders—well, let's say 800 eiders" or "ten years ago—well, let's say seven years ago." But he knew well the many islands of the bay and his mind was stocked with observations. He remembered winters when gyrfalcons came down from the north, sometimes snatching up waterfowl before the eyes of hunters who had just shot them. He recalled Bohemian waxwing years. He remembered snowy owl invasions when he had seen as many as twelve of the large, white, round-headed birds scattered like snowmen across a single field. In former times, he recalled, bald eagles wintered all along this northern shore.

A few weeks hence, above the tides of this coast another tide, a living tide of returning birds, would flow in from the sea and up from the south. The immense concentrations of breeding birds on the shore and cliffs and islands of this region amazed the early explorers. More than three and a half centuries ago, James Rosier, in his *A True Relation of the Most Prosperous Voyage Made this Present Yeere 1605 by Captaine George Waymouth*, refers to the Maine coast with its "many birds of sundry colors, many other fowles, in flocks, unknown." Soon, now, the returning waterfowl would be scattered across the bay and the returning seabirds would be nesting on the islands. Once more, so many years later, Rosier's quaint description would be apt for "much fowle of divers kinds breed upon the shore and rocks."

Between Eastport and Calais there are two small rocky islets known as The Wolves. They have the distinction of lying almost exactly on the forty-fifth parallel. Once again, as we drove north, we reached and crossed this halfway point between the equator and the pole. That night we stayed at Calais and the next morning, in the last dawn of winter, with the hills of New Brunswick on our right, we commenced the 147-mile run to Caribou. Our ascent to Jackman had been at one side, our ascent to Caribou was at the other side of Maine's more than 16,000,000 acres of forest.

The day was mild and melting. Beyond the higher ground of Topsfield, in a lowland stretch where frost heaves had broken the hardtop, puddles caught and held the color of the sky. For a mile or more we advanced along a road bounded by white snow and dark-green spruce and decorated throughout its length with hundreds of small pools of shining blue.

Beyond Dark Cove and Peekaboo Mountain, north of Danforth, we observed the looming white shape of Mt. Katahdin lift higher into the sky to our left. To our right, beyond the St. John River, in New Brunswick, we could visualize a unique one-tree orchard we had visited years before. In a lifelong hobby, the owner had grafted onto the branches of this single tree all the species of apples growing in the province. Spruce boughs, the natural winter insulation of the north-country, were banked high around each isolated house we passed along the way. Once, as we went by a cabin in a forest clearing, we caught sight of a pair of bright red snowshoes thrust upright into a drift beside the door.

After Mars Hill the forest fell back. The country opened out. Immense fields extended across undulating land. Beside the road huge storage sheds were banked with earth to their eaves. We were in Aroostook County, in the famed potato empire of northern Maine. Instead of the blustery, windy weather of the usual March, the weather we had expected, on this day that brought the winter to a close we experienced calm, mild air and sunny skies. Across a rolling, brightly lighted land we drove the final miles to Caribou.

North of Caribou

MORE than a hundred times, since we had left home, the land around us had rolled downward into darkness and upward again into the light. At the close of this twentieth day of March, on the final downward ride of the season, we saw all the drift-covered fields tinted under the swirling flames of sunset. Near a barnyard we watched a cream-white cat walking on pink snow. Then, almost suddenly, the ball of the sun dropped behind the black pointed trees of the remote horizon. The still winter night closed around us. The moon, one day short of full, lifted into a clear sky above the dark New Brunswick hills.

We drove north on U.S. 1 over Caribou Stream and Otter Brook, Hardwood Brook and Halfway Brook. We left behind the lines and chains of tiny twinkling lights that, like some greater constellation, outlined the huge Loring Air Force Base. We rode alone on a lonely road. The twin beams of our headlights on the curves of the winding highway swept from side to side. Birches leaped out in shining lines of white. Red osiers stood spotlighted above the snow. Once, where the moon-shadows of poplars barred the roadside drifts, an owl in swift, low and silent flight slipped in and out of the headlights' glare. The snow grew deeper as we went north. We glimpsed one farmhouse in the moonlight buried to its eaves, and where a side road dipped to join the highway it cut through a drift ten feet deep.

It was after nine and we were on a height of land somewhere north of Caribou when we turned back again. The town was a mere pinhead of neon colors on the horizon. Orion glittered far to the west. Its position marked the old age of the season. At the same hour of the night during the months of our diagonal course through the winter we had seen this constellation shining a little higher in the sky. Now in the west it appeared and disappeared, was brilliant one second, obscured the next, the light of its stars winking on and off among the black spires of the roadside spruces. Out in the open, between wooded stretches, it raced along above the dark horizon line. It seemed keeping pace with us, accompanying us as it had accompanied us through all the wanderings of our winter journey.

In that journey, so short a time ago, 10,000 miles of the fourth season lay before us. Only yesterday, it seemed, 1,000 miles still remained. Now on this deserted road amid the snows of this far northeastern corner of Maine, in this still moonlit night, our wheels rolled down the last of those winter miles. The months and weeks and days, once untouched, were now reduced to minutes, then to seconds.

Far away from the hush of this moonlit northern night, over the ocean, off the mouth of the Amazon, the rays of the sun shone directly down on the equator. The vernal equinox, that dramatic milestone of the year, the end of winter and the beginning of spring, arrived and was gone. Spenser's "ever-whirling wheele of change, the which all mortall things doth sway" continued its unwearied turning. And everywhere in the northern hemisphere, in city and country, in lands of many tongues, in igloo and ranch home and penthouse as well as here behind the tiny rectangles of the lighted windows of the far-scattered farmhouses rising pale in the moonlight, human beings would be profoundly affected by the changes that would follow.

For us, so long on winter's traces, this moment had even greater significance. It marked not only the end of our wanderings through the fourth season but the end of our wanderings through all the divisions of the year. We had rounded the great circle. We had come to the beginning again. The shift of an apostrophe told the story. What on previous trips had been the season's end was now the seasons' end.

Back in our room at the Red Brick Motel, on the southern edge of Caribou, I opened once more the small, scuffed, brown-leather copy of James Thomson's *The Seasons*. It had traveled with us through all the sequence of spring and summer and autumn and winter. It had ridden with us in four successive cars. It had accompanied us through the Everglades, in Death Valley, amid the rain forests of the Olympic Peninsula, where the Never-Summer Mountains rise in Colorado. I paused at the words I had read at Imperial Beach, below the Silver Strand: "See, Winter comes to rule the varied year." Now, at Caribou, at the season's end, I read again the final lines: "The storms of Wintery Time will quickly pass, and one unbounded Spring encircle all." On the blank page at the end of the book, I set down the date and place and the words: "The end of winter. The end of the four seasons."

The next morning Nellie and I turned south. We headed toward the far-off, oncoming tide of spring. Here amid the miles of drifts in northern Maine the chief sign of the season was highway workers rolling up the snow fences. Yet even here, in this calendar-spring, this winter-spring, we could visualize that tide as we had followed it north in our first adventure with a season. We could see it again, invincible, gathering its forces in the Everglades, sweeping north over the Kissimmee Prairie, on through the Okefenokee Swamp, across the low barrier islands of the Carolinas, ascending the tilted coastal plains and racing up the valleys of the Great Smokies. With color and life and action it was on its way. At the average rate of fifteen miles a day, it was moving up the map, a tide of green, a tide of violets and dogwood and azaleas, a tide of bird song and sunshine and breezes soft and perfumed. The year was beginning again.

Throughout this long flow of the season, life in an infinite variety of forms, life dormant in bur and bud, in burrow and pupa-case, life biding its time, would respond to the increasing warmth. As we rode south through a land of the later spring, we knew that under the ice crystals of the drifts, beneath fields of white and rivers of ice and in the hard and frozen ground, life was waiting, confident, undespairing. Its activity was merely suspended. The stillness, the seeming death of winter, is but an illusion. The apparent conquest of the season is only temporary. Like the moon's waxing and waning, like the tide's ebb and flow, life retreats and is triumphant again. This, as Richard Jefferies noted long ago, is the allegory of winter.

When Nellie and I had come home from that initial journey with the spring, we had wandered for nearly 100 miles after we crossed the Whitestone Bridge onto Long Island. We had turned aside and made delays, loath to have that first adventure end. Now, again, at the conclusion of this last of all our travels with a season, we stretched out our days of freedom. We moved south by loops and zigzags. We followed a laggard's path.

As we lingered on this homeward trail, at Echo Lake where the mayflies danced in the spring dusk, at the white cabin beside the Pemigewasset where, in starlight, the first season had come to its end, by Mt. Chocorua and along Bearcamp River, our minds were filled with memories of other moments, other times in the quartet of seasons that "fill the measure of the year." We talked, as we rode along, of all that we had seen, of the hundred miles of warblers and the night of the falling stars, of painted forests and timberline tundras in bloom, of our million-duck days at Bear River and that magic twilight song of the unseen bird at Sutter's Mill.

Ours had been an adventure unique and we were profoundly thankful. No two other persons in history had ever known the experience we had shared. We had observed firsthand the infinite diversity of the American seasons. We had crisscrossed, from sea to sea, this land unsurpassed for the variety and magnificence of its scenery, for the interest of its wild inhabitants. And, it seemed to us, we had seen it in the nick of time. For during the period of our protracted travels, during the more than twenty years that had elapsed between the inception and completion of our design, the country was steadily changing, becoming less wild, more settled. We had seen its Clear Creeks and Pleasant Valleys when, in the main, its streams were clear and its valleys pleasant.

This we learned from our experience with the four seasons: We want them all. We want the rounded year. We crave no unending Golden Age, no perpetual spring of old mythology. We cherish the variety, the whole sequence of the seasons. In truth, as William Browne wrote in the seventeenth century: "There is no season such delight can bring as summer, autumn, winter and the spring."

And so we came home at last. We came home rich in memories. We drove down the long lane at Trail Wood to our 160-year-old white cottage under the hickory trees. We unlocked the door in spring that we had locked in autumn. We found calendars of another year hanging on the wall. That evening, with logs blazing in the great fireplace, we watched the darkness fall beyond our windowpanes. It seemed the final curtain descending at the end of the completed whole of the eternal drama of the year.

Another spring is coming in as these words are written. The white magic of another winter is gone. Another night is falling over our woods and fields and pond. I switch on the lamp above my study desk. Its soft light falls on typed sheets of field notes, on marked maps, on odds and ends, mementos of our winter travels. I am nearly at the end of that self-imposed task that for more than two decades has been my work and my relaxation, my livelihood and my diversion. While I have been wandering across the country and writing of what I have seen—a kind of Plutarch of the seasons—two new states, Alaska and Hawaii, have been added to the Union, the population of the United States has grown by 50,000,000 and the earth has traveled through space 10,000,000,000 miles.

I set down these final words in the dusk of an early spring day. You are reading them when, where, under what conditions? Now the light—my light here, your light wherever you are—falls on the last page of the last book of the last season. We have traveled far together. We have watched the successive seasons flow and merge and intermingle. We have seen the beauty of the land through the whole cycle of the year. To those of you who have journeyed so long, who have traversed the four seasons in our company, to all farewell.

For here ends the story of our travels
through the spring and summer
and autumn and winter of
The American Year.

INDEX

INDEX

INDEX

BOOK DESIGN BY

AVERY FISHER

THE TEXT OF THIS BOOK has been set in JANSON, a recutting made directly from matrices that have survived in the possession of D. Stempel, A.G. of Frankfurt-am-Main. Research has indicated that the punches may be the work of Nicholas Kis (1650–1702) rather than Anton Janson, a Leipzig type founder from 1668 to 1687. However, there has been no revision of the endorsement of the cutting, by typographic experts, as an archetype of the Dutch style that influenced the designs of William Caslon, the English engraver of gun stocks who turned to the art of type founding in 1720.

ALTHOUGH THE CHOICE of a suitable text type (for legibility, weight, and 'color' of the printed page) is of paramount importance, the hallmark of book design is the display type selected for the binding, introductory and title pages, and section and chapter headings. TRAJANUS was chosen because of its consummate beauty and lightness, even in the largest sizes. It is a calligraphic roman type face in the style of the *scrittura umanistica* of the late fourteenth and early fifteenth centuries. It echoes the first true Roman type faces as well as the last great Roman written forms.

TRAJANUS was designed in 1938 by Warren Chappell, an American draftsman designer and typographer, who worked in punch cutting with Rudolf Koch at the Offenbacher Werkstatt and the Schriftgiesserei Gebrüder Klingspor. It was cut for hand composition and for Linotype by Stempel, the type founders responsible for the JANSON described above. The TRAJANUS in this volume was set entirely by hand.